W9-BDI-713

# ELMTOWN'S YOUTH

# ELMTOWN'S YOUTH

## The Impact of Social Classes on Adolescents

**AUGUST B. HOLLINGSHEAD**
ASSOCIATE PROFESSOR OF SOCIOLOGY
YALE UNIVERSITY

**SCIENCE EDITIONS**®

**John Wiley & Sons, Inc.,** New York

First Science Editions printing 1961

Science Editions Trademark Reg. U.S. Pat. Off.

© 1949 by John Wiley & Sons, Inc.

SEVENTH PRINTING, AUGUST, 1965

PRINTED IN THE UNITED STATES OF AMERICA

This volume is dedicated to my wife

CAROL E. HOLLINGSHEAD

and our daughters

ANNE and ELLEN

# PREFACE

THIS VOLUME IS AN ANALYSIS of the way the social system of a Middle Western Corn Belt community (Elmtown, Home State, U.S.A.) organizes and controls the social behavior of high-school-aged adolescents reared in it. It describes the relationships existing between the behavior patterns of the 735 adolescent boys and girls in the study and the positions occupied by their families in the community's class structure. Seven major areas of social behavior are covered—the school, the job, the church, recreation, cliques, dates, and sex.

The presentation of the material is divided into five parts. Part I discusses the problem on which the research was focused and discusses in some detail when, where, and how the data were obtained. Part II gives the communal, family, and social setting of the study. Part III tells the story of the 390 boys and girls who were in high school. Part IV traces the impact of the class system on the 345 young people who had left school prematurely. Part V is a brief summary and conclusion. It asks the question: What can we do to mitigate the problem this study poses?

Although the book is basically a scientific report, the writing is directed to the intelligent general reader rather than the specialist in sociology, anthropology, psychology, education, social work, vocational and child guidance. I hope these specialists will find this volume useful. But, if it is to have some measure of value in making parents aware of the kind of society in which they are rearing their children, it will have to reach a larger audience. Therefore, I hope it will find its way into American homes and will be read by parents who desire to see what a segment of contemporary American society has done to the boys and girls reared in it.

I have relied upon two types of data to tell the story of the boys and girls, fathers and mothers, and other local people who make up the subject matter of this book: statistics and Elmtowners' own stories. The statistics may be viewed as the skeleton on which the muscles and skin of narrative are spread. The poignant remarks of Elmtowners tell a story the statistics cannot. On the other hand, the statistics present a comprehensive picture of a specific phase of behavior for the whole group. The two have been blended in the text so that each supplements the other to give force and meaning to the report.

This study is one of a series made under the auspices of The Committee on Human Development of The University of Chicago in Middle Western communities.* It had its origin in a post-doctoral research training fellowship awarded to me in April, 1941, by the Social Science Research Council.† The field work was done between May, 1941, and December, 1942, while I was on leave from the faculty of the Department of Sociology, Indiana University. The drafting of the report was interrupted completely from January, 1943, to December, 1945, by my service in the United States Army Air Forces. The preliminary analysis of the data was completed at Indiana University and the first draft of the manuscript finished before I joined the faculty of Yale University in July, 1947. The data were rechecked and the manuscript was rewritten at Yale.

The modest history of this project cannot be completed without some mention of the obligations I owe to the many persons

---

* *Adolescent Character and Personality*, by Robert J. Havighurst and Hilda Taba, New York, John Wiley & Sons, Inc., 1949, is the first to appear. It may be viewed as a companion volume to this one, since it is focused in part on the same adolescents, although it is concerned with a different problem.

† Grateful acknowledgment is hereby made to the Social Science Research Council of New York City for the fellowship which supported the field phase of the research, and for a grant-in-aid for the year 1947–1948 which enabled me to complete the analysis of the data and to finish the manuscript; similar acknowledgment and thanks are also due the Graduate School, Indiana University, which generously supported the project from September, 1942, to January, 1943, and from January, 1946, to August, 1947; to The Committee on Human Development of the University of Chicago for the use of recording machinery, typing of interviews, and the use of their offices in Elmtown and Chicago; and to the Committee on Bursary Appointments, Yale University, for clerical assistance on the final manuscript.

who have contributed their experience, interest, time, and energy to it. First and foremost, I must name two noted sociologists with whom I was associated in earlier years, the late professors Robert E. Park and E. B. Reuter. Reuter first interested me in the sociology of adolescence, and Park encouraged me to apply for the fellowship and aided me in its prosecution. Both men were in touch with the planning and field phases of the project and gave their time and abundant knowledge to it. Dean Robert Redfield, my fellowship advisor, did far more than I can mention here; he was always a friend, counselor, and inspiration. Professor W. Lloyd Warner, with whom I worked, gave sage advice and arranged for the recording of interview materials. Professor Robert J. Havighurst, of The Committee on Human Development, also has been in close touch with the study and has contributed in many ways from the beginning to the reading of the final manuscript. I am especially indebted to Professors Redfield and Havighurst. A number of other members of The University of Chicago faculty made contributions from time to time. This group includes Professors E. W. Burgess, William F. Ogburn, Everett C. Hughes, Herbert Blumer, Louis Wirth, Albert J. Reiss, Jr., Mandel Sherman, Samuel Stouffer, now of Harvard University, and Guy E. Swanson, now of the University of Michigan. I feel particularly obligated to the field staff with whom I worked in Elmtown: Bernice Neugarten, Marchia Meeker, Mr. and Mrs. Gordon Beebe, and Mr. and Mrs. Arch Cooper. Mr. and Mrs. Cooper and Mr. and Mrs. Beebe lived in the community when I did and shared the problems and the responsibilities of field work.

Several of my former colleagues at Indiana University contributed in many ways to the research. Among them were: Professor Edwin H. Sutherland, who helped with the analysis of the social structure; Professor John H. Mueller, who gave unstintingly of his time and knowledge in working out statistical problems; Professor Alfred C. Kinsey, who gave help in the formulation of questions on sex; finally, Dean Fernandus Payne, who aided in the procurement of funds to complete the field work and the statistical analysis. My assistants, Richard Morris, Roy Richards, Richard Lambert, Jean de Rameriz, Vir-

ginia Dixon, and Francis Krauskopf, of Indiana University, and
Robert Fieldhouse and James Carroll, of Yale University, performed faithfully and well the detailed tasks of typing, card
punching, sorting, and machine calculation on which they
worked.

My colleagues at Yale University have contributed their time
and talents to the final preparation of the manuscript. Maurice
R. Davie read and edited the entire manuscript; Leo W. Sim-
mons also read all of it and made constructive suggestions.
Raymond W. Kennedy read and edited parts of it; Stephen W.
Reed, John Ellsworth, Edmund Volkart, and John Sirjamaki also
read and criticized particular chapters. Harold F. Kaufman, of
Mississippi State College, read and criticized Chapter 2; he was
helpful particularly with the clarification of the statements on the
procedures used in the stratification of the adolescents' families.

Finally, I owe the greatest debt to the people of Elmtown
for the interest they showed in the work done there. Without
their cooperation, the study could not have been made. In the
drafting of the report every effort has been made to present
the facts of social life in Elmtown and at the same time protect
the individual who supplied the data. In order to do this, I
have had to change identifying details, add some details, blend
facts from several sources into a single composite, and drop out
other facts from the total situation. The one objective in this
necessary phase of the work has been the preservation of the
privacy of the personality. The names used are wholly fictitious.
If an Elmtowner or anyone else has a name similar to any used
in this book it is pure coincidence. In spite of the need to
protect Elmtowners' identities, I have striven to maintain the
integrity of the data in their social setting.

A. B. H.

*Yale University, New Haven*
*February, 1949*

# CONTENTS

xi

# PROBLEMS AND PROCEDURES

CHAPTERS 1 AND 2 TELL THE STORY of the way the study began; the problem it deals with; how Elmtown was selected as the site of the research; how the data were collected to test the hypothesis that the social behavior of adolescents is functionally related to the position their families occupy in the community's social structure; how we learned that Elmtown had a class system; and, finally, how each of the 535 families studied was located in this class system.

Readers who are not interested in these necessary details of scientific procedure may wish to omit Part I and begin with Chapter 3. The story of Elmtown and Elmtowners begins there and runs on through the remainder of the book. If a reader chooses this course, he may later desire to return to the description of methodological procedures in Chapters 1 and 2 to learn our methods of collecting data and our reasons for organizing and analyzing them as we did.

# 1

# THE RESEARCH PROBLEM

THIS BOOK DESCRIBES certain significant relationships found to exist between the social behavior of adolescents and social stratification in a Middle Western community immediately before the effects of World War II were apparent locally. The study on which it is based developed out of a post-doctoral research training fellowship awarded to me in April, 1941. Although the fellowship was granted to study field research methods, the materials presented in subsequent pages are not focused upon an exposition of research techniques. Only enough space is devoted to a discussion of procedures to enable the reader to understand how and perhaps why certain things were done. My purpose is to relate what the methods followed revealed when they were applied to the problem studied.

The planning phase of the project began in May, 1941, when I went to the University of Chicago for a conference with my fellowship advisor, Dean Robert Redfield. Later, together with Professors Lloyd Warner, Ernest W. Burgess, Robert J. Havighurst, and Mandel Sherman, we discussed the plans of The Committee on Human Development of the University of Chicago to start a long-range, cooperative, interdisciplinary field study of a number of problems germane to the social sciences in a "typical Middle Western community" selected by the Committee. After some discussion, a visit to the proposed community, and another conference, The Committee on Human Development invited me to cooperate with it.

The next three months were spent in preparation for the field work. These preparations included several trips to the community—which I have called Elmtown—to become acquainted with the main outline of its history, population, and economic

3

base; to "feel out" some of the local people on a proposed study of "character development" of boys and girls; to establish contacts with civic leaders; and to locate a place in which to live during the ten months my wife and I planned to reside in Elmtown.  On these sorties we stopped at filling stations, stores, and roadside shops, playing the role of curious tourists interested in the country, or of outsiders looking for some local person.  We asked casual questions about industries, soil, climate, weather, crops, landmarks, buildings, the road to some place.  Friendly operators or bystanders gave us the information and often traced out, on our map, where so-and-so lived.  When we talked with Elmtowners who knew about the proposed study, however, our connection with The Committee on Human Development and its stated interest in "character development" were kept in the foreground at the time of our initial contact.  Their reactions to the proposal appeared to be either favorable or neutral—at least on the surface.  No one was overtly hostile; most gave the impression, "Well, we shall wait to see what happens!"

The housing question was the most serious immediate problem; its solution added color to our stay in the community.  After several weeks of fruitless hunting, hinting, waiting, and advertising, a suitable furnished house was procured.  It had been the scene of a sensational murder, with many facets, a generation earlier.  This house had become the center of various stories and much mystery.  Sensational history or not, a furnished house three blocks from the high school was ours when we moved to Elmtown in August, 1941, with our two small daughters.

Another phase of the preparation was a survey of the literature on adolescence, to learn what had been done in the way of research and development of theory.  We learned that physiologists had done extensive work on physical maturation; psychologists had developed a psychology of adolescence; educators had made many studies of the growing child, particularly from the viewpoint of the school; and sociologists, with few exceptions, had ignored the subject.  One sociological contribution was made by the Research Planning Committee of the American Sociological Society in a conference of eminent sociologists, psychologists, anthropologists, educators, and psychiatrists interested in adolescents and adolescence which met at Yale University in April,

1934. Out of its deliberations and discussions came an outline of the type of research believed fruitful for an understanding of adolescent behavior from a socio-cultural viewpoint.[1] Two other distinctive theoretical statements on the sociological aspects of adolescence were made a few years later by the late Professor E. B. Reuter, who had been a member of the conference mentioned above. Little interest in actual research into adolescent behavior from the viewpoint of the sociologist grew out of this conference or Reuter's speculative writings [2] other than the work of Reuter's associate, Jessie R. Runner.[3]

As study after study passed through our hands, we saw that in the past half-century physiologists, psychologists, educators, clergymen, social workers, and moralists have turned their attention to the physical and psychological phenomena connected with adolescence, and that of the millions of words written on the subject most have had a worried tone. This interest in the adolescent, with its emphasis on the "problems" of adolescence, can be traced to the monumental work of G. Stanley Hall.[4] Hall blended evolutionary theory, the facts of physical growth (as they were then known), instinct psychology, and a liberal sprinkling of ethnographic facts taken out of their cultural context with a set of strong moral judgments. He assumed that the individual in the course of his life recapitulates the evolutionary development of the human species.[5]

Hall conceived of adolescence as the period in the life cycle of the individual from age 14 to 24, when the inexorably unfolding nature of the organism produces a "rebirth of the soul" which brings the child inevitably into a conflict with society. This was believed to be a period of "storm and stress," of "revolution,"

[1] "Sociological Research in Adolescence," *American Journal of Sociology,* Vol. 42 (1936), pp. 81–94.

[2] E. B. Reuter, "The Sociology of Adolescence," *American Journal of Sociology,* Vol. 43 (1937), pp. 414–427; and "The Education of the Adolescent," *Journal of Educational Sociology,* Vol. 14 (1940–1941), pp. 67–78.

[3] Jessie R. Runner, "Social Distance in Adolescent Relationships," *American Journal of Sociology,* Vol. 43 (1937), pp. 428–439.

[4] G. Stanley Hall, *Adolescence, Its Psychology and Its Relations to Physiology, Anthropology, Sociology, Sex, Crime, Religion, and Education,* D. Appleton and Company, New York, 1904, two volumes.

[5] *Ibid.,* Vol. I, p. viii.

in the individual. In the "new birth" the "social instincts under-go sudden unfoldment." [6] Hall also asserted that "the adolescent stage of life" is marked by a struggle between the needs of the organism and the desires of society, which is "biologically antagonistic to genesis." [7] "All this is hard on youth . . ." [8] This psychology of adolescence included in its scope physiology, anthropology, sociology, sex, crime, religion, and education. Needless to say, this is a broad area which only a system maker who ignored facts as they exist in society could cover in a single sweep.

Hall's prestige as a psychologist, educator, and university president was so great and his influence over students so dominant that his theories were accepted widely by psychologists and educators. Gradually, however, the weight of empirical information indicated that these views were largely doctrinal. But, even now, the idea that adolescence is a period of "storm and stress," of conflict between individual and society, is held by many people, in spite of the fact that this has never been demonstrated to be true. On the contrary, common-sense observation will cast grave doubts upon its validity. Nevertheless, a recent summary of the field of adolescent psychology insisted upon the "causal" connection between the physical manifestations of adolescence and social behavior. [9]

Eventually, the conclusion was reached that, from the viewpoint of the sociologist, adolescence is distinctly different from psychologists', physiologists', and educators' concept of it. *Sociologically, adolescence is the period in the life of a person when the society in which he functions ceases to regard him (male or female) as a child and does not accord to him full adult status, roles, and functions.* In terms of behavior, it is defined by the

---

[6] *Ibid.*, p. xv.

[7] *Ibid.*, p. xvi.

[8] *Ibid.*, p. xviii.

[9] Wayne Dennis, "The Adolescent," in *Manual of Child Psychology*, edited by Leonard Carmichael, John Wiley and Sons, Inc., New York, 1946, pp. 633–666. We would agree with Dennis if he or any other psychologist demonstrated any "causal" connection between the physical phenomenon of puberty and the social behavior of young people during the adolescent period, irrespective of cultural milieu.

roles the person is expected to play, is allowed to play, is forced to play, or prohibited from playing by virtue of his status in society. It is not marked by a specific point in time such as puberty, since its form, content, duration, and period in the life cycle are differently determined by various cultures and societies. Sociologically, the important thing about the adolescent years is the way people regard the maturing individual. The menarche, development of the breasts, and other secondary manifestations of physical adolescence in the female, and the less obvious physical changes in the male connected with sex maturation, such as rapid growth, voice changes, the appearance of labial, axial, and pubic hair, derive their significance for the sociologist from the way they are regarded by the society in which the adolescent lives.

The phrase "adolescent behavior," as we shall use it, refers to the social action patterns of young people. We believe that adolescent behavior is a type of transitional behavior which is dependent upon the society, and more particularly upon the position the individual occupies in the social structure, rather than upon the bio-psychological phenomena connected with this age, such as puberty, or the assumed psycho-organic conditions variously referred to as "drives," "urges," and "tensions" in psychological, educational, and lay usage. This is not to assert that anatomical, physiological, and psychological facts connected with this phase of the life cycle have no bearing on behavior during the adolescent years. They undoubtedly do, but their functional importance for the maturing individual is defined by the culture.

Since we are concerned with adolescent behavior rather than adolescence, we have placed little emphasis upon physical and psychological phenomena. No efforts have been made to connect the data which we collected with the physiological phases of the pubertal cycle which each boy or girl might have been passing through while the field work was in progress. This type of study remains to be made; when it is, it may combine many of the techniques we used with those used by physiologists and psychologists, to determine whether there are significant relationships between the physical, psychological, and sociological aspects of adolescence. Such a study ought to be a cooperative venture that would include specialists from these fields as well as from anthropology and psychiatry.[10]

## The problem

Our attention was not focused fully upon the problem we studied until some two months after we settled in Elmtown. The problem finally formulated grew out of a compromise between promises The Committee on Human Development had made to leading Elmtowners, our interest in social control, and information we acquired after we moved to Elmtown. Representatives of The Committee on Human Development, in their original conferences with prominent Elmtowners, told them that the Committee intended to study the community from many viewpoints, but that its primary interest was the development of character in boys and girls. This proposal was accepted without too much explanation or elaboration. However, the association of "character" with "goodness" in the thoughts of these people created an impression that set some limits on what we did. We knew about this emphasis and planned accordingly. By the middle of August, 1941, a tentative project was drafted. We believed then that a study of the behavior of high school pupils would throw some light on the larger question: Is the social behavior of an adolescent a function of physiological changes in the maturing individual or of his experiences in society?

When we talked with Elmtowners, during the first weeks of our residence there, about the behavior of high school pupils, person after person said, in effect, "You have to know this town or you cannot understand these high school kids." This persistent emphasis on the relationship between the community's institutions, family, wealth, "politics," history, and "the way these kids act" was backed by specific details in instance after instance. In addition, we learned that a considerable number of boys and

[10] The National Society for the Study of Education had a committee of experts on various phases of adolescence prepare a comprehensive series of papers on the subject from the physical, physiological, somatic, psychological, and sociological viewpoints which was published in 1944, but none of the contributors attacked the subject with the synthetic approach suggested here. See *The Forty-Third Year Book of the National Society for the Study of Education*, Chicago, 1944, pp. ii–358.

girls who should have been in school (if the school law had been enforced strictly) were not there. This meant that if we confined our study to high school pupils a portion of Elmtown's adolescents would be excluded, but we did not know how large this segment was until some weeks later. The casual information we had acquired concerning these out-of-school adolescents indicated that they came from "unfortunate families" or "the relief class." Gradually the conclusion was reached that the tentative problem we had formulated did not encompass what appeared to be the really important factors that motivated and controlled the social behavior of high-school-age boys and girls, namely, family background, the community's social structure, and the place the family occupied in it. We believed that these should be included; and this conviction led to the restatement of our original ideas of what we intended to do. On October 3, the following entry was made in the diary I kept: "I will study the social behavior of all high-school-aged boys and girls, whether they are in school or not, to see if their activities are related to their family backgrounds." On October 15, the working hypothesis we have since been concerned with was written into the diary in these words: *"The social behavior of adolescents appears to be related functionally to the positions their families occupy in the social structure of the community."*

This statement grew out of a synthesis of the things we observed during those first few weeks, what Elmtowners told us about "the way things work around here," and the principal assumption we made relative to the social behavior of adolescents, namely, that it is an adaptive, complex adjustment to their status in society. The phrasing of the working hypothesis marked a major step in the process of bringing the field work into focus, but this was only one step in a long series, each of which was a test of our assumptions. It centered attention chiefly upon four things: adolescents, their family backgrounds, their behavior, and Elmtown's social structure.

Thus defined, the problem became a task in observation of the many ways adolescents spent their time; the collection of data relative to the community institutions they were connected with and the ways they participated in them; who their friends were; what they talked about; and eventually the measurement of these data against their families' position in the social structure. The pursuit of such information carried us along the main streams of adolescent and adult activity: the school, the job, the church, property ownership, politics, recreation and pleasure, cliques, dates, and courtship. It often led us into back alleys Elmtowners preferred to ignore: gambling, sex play, drinking, theft, misuse of authority.

To sum up: This study was focused on the study of the social behavior of high-school-aged adolescents in Elmtown, Home State, Middle Western U.S.A., during the school year 1941–1942, to determine whether the observed behavior of the adolescents was related to the position their families occupied in the community's social structure. The data we gathered to test this hypothesis were collected gradually with as little disturbance as possible to the customary ways in which Elmtowners thought and acted as they pursued their daily activities. No aspect of the field work was experimental, since we were interested in observing and gathering information about what the study group did under the conditions then prevailing in the community and under the conditions they themselves created by their activities, rather than in seeing how they would react to controlled situations presented to them, perforce, in an artificial manner.

# 2

# FIELD PROCEDURES

THE TECHNICAL PROCEDURES used to accumulate the data necessary to test the hypothesis are described in this chapter. All data were assembled in Elmtown from personal, documentary, and observational sources either by me or by my wife, in many instances by both, between June, 1941, and December, 1942. This nineteen-month interval was divided into four periods of varying length. The first lasted about three months, from late May to the latter part of August, 1941, during which six two- and three-day trips were made to Elmtown from Bloomington, Indiana, to locate a place to live and gather general information about the community. The second or field phase opened with our removal to Elmtown. The first two or three months of our stay there were devoted simultaneously to building a role for ourselves and getting Elmtowners interested in the project. These months may be called the early field phase. The third or mature field phase began in November, when we started systematic interviews with adolescents and adults; it lasted until the close of the school year in June, 1942; shortly after this time we moved back to Bloomington. The fourth or post-field phase lasted six months, from July through December, 1942, when eleven automobile trips were made to Elmtown from Bloomington, Indiana. On these occasions we spent from two to five days there filling in gaps in the schedules, visiting friends, and rechecking data, particularly with respect to dating and sex practices in the out-of-school group.

A tentative time table, made in August, 1941, scheduled the familiarization phase first, then the phases of observation of and initial interviews with the adolescents. It was assumed that, by this time, we would be known and trusted and the project would

11

be accepted. The third development was to have been the accumulation of data from the families of the adolescents. This time table was followed roughly, but the changes in the research problem, which called for the inclusion of all high-school-aged boys and girls in the study and the placement of their families in the social structure, injected new factors into the field work. Therefore, the visits to the homes of the adolescents did not begin until after Christmas, 1941. Most of them were completed by the end of April, but a few rural families whose children were in the out-of-school group were not visited until August, 1942.

### The study group

The solution of the problem set by the hypothesis required the systematic accumulation of synchronous data from several areas of community life simultaneously. The first move toward its solution was the formulation of a rule to determine which boys and girls should be included in or excluded from the study. After considerable investigation, the decision was reached to include adolescents who were in these categories: (1) those enrolled in Elmtown High School in 1941–1942, and (2) those who had been graduated, or should have been graduated, from an elementary school between 1938 and 1941 and who resided in the community during the school year 1941–1942, but who were not in school. This excluded high school graduates and their scholastic peers who had left school. It included all boys and girls who either were or belonged in high school, irrespective of age, by virtue of their membership in a class that finished the eighth grade between 1938 and 1941—one high school "generation."

The class lists of children enrolled in the fifth, sixth, seventh, and eighth grades of the Elmtown Central School and the community's 32 rural schools for 1938–1941 were obtained. A simple check of the high school enrollment cards indicated whether or not a person was in high school in 1941–1942. If he was not, careful inquiry was made to determine whether or not he resided in the community. If he was still a resident his name was retained, but the names of those who had moved away were eliminated. Detailed inquiry revealed the settlement of new families. If their children were in school, they were included; if they were not, but met our criteria, they too were included.

In this way, 752 boys and girls who belonged to the then current high school "generation" were located. Seventeen were eliminated for two reasons: 12 girls were attending a religious academy whose officials refused to cooperate; and 5 boys were dropped because adequate data relative to their family's position in the social structure were not available. Thus, 369 boys and 366 girls became the objects of detailed study.

These 735 adolescents belonged to 535 different families. Obviously some families had more than one child in the study group. However, most families, 71 per cent, were represented by one child, 23 per cent by two, 4 per cent by three, and 2 per cent by four or more.[1] The inclusion of two or more children from the same family created a situation in the statistical treatment of the data which necessitated a choice between the isolation of all families with more than one child in the study from those with only one child, or the treatment of each adolescent's family as a separate case, even though two or more children came from the same family. The latter device was used to simplify procedures and keep the analysis uniform from case to case.

SEX AND AGE. The sexes were divided almost equally in each age group. The wide difference in the number of adolescents at ages 13, 18, and 19 (Table I) resulted from the way the study group was selected. Although the elementary school classifies students largely on the basis of age, and the modal age when a child finishes the eighth grade is 14, some children finish when they are 13. Conversely, retarded pupils do not complete it until they are older than normal. Thus, there were 24 thirteen-year-old youngsters who were ahead of their age level, and 94 eighteen- and nineteen-year-olds who had been retarded in school. This accumulation of eighteen- and nineteen-year-olds was produced largely by failure in the elementary grades rather than in high school. These young people belonged scholastically with the high school "generation" and were included, whereas their age mates who had been successful in high school were eliminated. Only 10 of the eighteen-year-olds and 5 of the nine-

---

[1] All percentage figures will be to the nearest whole number unless greater precision appears to be called for by the particular calculation.

TABLE I

AGE AND SEX COMPOSITION OF ADOLESCENTS

| Age * | Males | Females | Total |
|-------|-------|---------|-------|
| 13 | 11 | 13 | 24 |
| 14 | 77 | 75 | 152 |
| 15 | 73 | 80 | 153 |
| 16 | 78 | 74 | 152 |
| 17 | 80 | 80 | 160 |
| 18 | 44 | 39 | 83 |
| 19 | 6 | 5 | 11 |
| Total | 369 | 366 | 735 |

* Age given is age attained by January 1, 1942.

teen-year-olds were in school in 1941–1942. The remainder had withdrawn, but by our standards of selection they belonged in the study.

NATIVITY. Elmtown was "home" to parents and children; it had been home to 81 per cent of the young people and 62 per cent of their parents since birth. One-third of the adolescents belonged to families that had resided in the community since the Civil War; another third dated their family's settlement to the decades between 1860 and 1900; the remainder settled there during this century. All the adolescents were native-born whites, and 96 per cent had been born in the Middle West. Their parents were also predominantly Middle Westerners: 83 per cent had been born and reared in this region. The 4 per cent of adolescents and 17 per cent of parents who were not natives of the Middle West came from all parts of the United States. From the viewpoint of national origins, exactly 50 per cent identified themselves as "American." The other half reported that their families came originally from one of the European countries— Germany, Ireland, Norway, Poland—with which Elmtown's "foreign elements" were identified.[2]

Three adolescents out of 4 (76 per cent) lived in town; the fourth resided in the country. About 3 out of 5 country dwellers were farmers' children; the remainder, 39 per cent, came from rural non-farm families.

[2] See Tables I and II of the Appendix.

These demographic characteristics indicate that the study group was well balanced as to sex and age (in the middle ranges, 14 through 17) and were mostly products of Elmtown, Home State, and the Middle West. All the national-origin groups in the community's population were represented in large enough numbers to give us representation from potentially diverse smaller sub-groups in these divisions of the population.

In passing, we must point out that we assumed that the adolescent's position in the social structure was the same as that of his parental family. That a high-school-aged boy or girl had the family's position ascribed to him was clear at the time we formulated the hypothesis. At this age the youngster had not established, in most cases, a position of his own in the social structure.

### The researcher's role

Although chemical and agricultural research is familiar to many Elmtowners, social research is unknown and generally not appreciated except by a few civic-minded, college-trained leaders. Consequently, the role we were to play had to be built up by us, since no prototype existed. I had lived in the Middle West for a decade, and my wife was a native of the region. Thus, we knew some things about its culture, history, and people. We believed that a satisfactory role could be built up in the community if we were favorably known, primarily by people in leadership positions and secondarily by some persons throughout the social structure. Our efforts to make Elmtowners like us were premised on two assumptions. If they liked us as persons, they would, in the first place, forget that they were the subjects of study, and would, secondly, be more likely to respect the work we were doing. We believed that the role the field worker shapes for himself has a definite bearing upon whom he has access to, and from whom he is excluded, as well as upon what he is or is not told about persons and activities.

The general role we tried to create for ourselves was influenced by several extraneous factors which had no connection with the project, except as Elmtowners believed they did. The most important of these were the international crisis and the location of two war plants in an adjacent county. Our entrance on the scene a few months later led some Elmtowners to think that we had been sent there to collect information either for "our government"—these people had no idea what phase of "government" was involved or how the data were to be used; it was just "the government"—or as foreign spies. Many others were suspicious of the project, if not of us personally, because it was unusual and, to them, a "strange" thing. This was natural, since nothing like this had ever happened to the community before and few persons knew about community studies, or their purpose or worth. Although these factors entered into the formation of our role when the field work began, they receded into the background as we lived and worked with the people. Gradually we were accepted in our own right as plain, ordinary people like themselves. The mystery of our work was no longer a mystery, or, if it was, most people forgot their original anxieties.

ELMTOWN HEARS ABOUT THE STUDY. The Committee on Human Development sent several representatives to Elmtown for one-day familiarization trips in the spring and summer of 1941. A full-time paid social anthropologist and his family moved there in August, 1941; so the community had some idea about the project in general when we began our work. The anthropologist worked independently of us, but there was frequent contact between us, and with the Committee in Chicago. So far as this study is concerned, however, the following procedures were used to publicize our work. The President of the Board of Education was interviewed first, then several members of the Board. The project was discussed in general terms with each person, and the cooperation of each was asked. The Superintendent of Schools and the high school principal were given a careful explanation of what we intended to do; they were told that we had talked with the several members of the Board of Education and had their approval; finally, we asked them to cooperate with us. We visited the ministers and the publisher of *The Elmtown Bugle*, outlining the project to each. The presidents of the two women's clubs were told about the study. Other community leaders also were visited—labor, fraternal, patriotic, political, industrial, legal, medical, and farm. Known critics were paid a friendly visit to secure their acceptance of the project and to gain their good will. A "piece" was written for the paper which explained the project in general from the viewpoint of The Committee on Human Development. The publisher of *The Bugle* promised to publish it as it was written. When it appeared it was changed substantially, but we had the advantage of front-page publicity. Talks were arranged before the women's clubs, the two men's service clubs, the American Legion, the high school students, and union and church groups. These talks stressed popular beliefs concerning the importance of the church, the school, and youth associations, such as the Boy Scouts and Girl Scouts, in the life of the child; and stated that this study was being made to learn something about the "character development" of high school boys and girls. We minimized any interest in the study of the community as a community.

During this deliberate "sales" phase, the same explanatory story was told to everyone, except that minor variations were made in response to the way different persons reacted, their apparent understanding of what we were trying to do, and their degree of warmth or hostility toward the study. Each person interviewed was stimulated to talk about the community, its young people, his idea of the project, or any subject he desired. When the person started to talk, we remained silent and allowed him to talk himself out. No notes were taken before him in these original interviews; they were recorded either on the typewriter or electrically as soon as the interview was over. Another rule we followed rigidly was not to give names when we repeated anything another person said. If we used information previously acquired from an Elmtowner about the community to set up rapport with a second person, it was always presented anonymously.

A friendly smile and "Hi" to an adolescent, or "Good morning," "How do you do?" "Good evening" to an older man or woman was well received, even by strangers, and were a necessity with acquaintances. Elmtowners like easy familiarity, and our appearing like themselves opened many doors. Sometimes we were stopped on the street by curious strangers who knew who we were. They usually wanted to know "what this thing [the study] is all about, anyway." We tried to tell them and then get them to talk. Storekeepers, workmen, clerks, anyone was grist for the mill, especially during the early phases of the field work.

My wife and I, as individuals and as a couple, participated in any and all community activities as time and circumstances allowed. We refused no private invitation unless a prior engagement precluded attendance. My wife was invited into the Women's Club and into several women's sewing and bridge circles. I was invited into the Rotary Club and attended all meetings until I left Elmtown. I taught the men's and women's Bible Class in the Federated Sunday School for several months, but my wife and I attended all churches more or less in rotation. Upon the outbreak of war, the County Defense Council asked me to serve on the Tire Rationing Board. I accepted, and my fellow board members elected me chairman. A few weeks later the Defense Council made me County Rationing Director. We willingly accepted speaking engagements, for they gave us additional contacts with people and enabled us to view the community from an additional facet. We believe that this widespread participation aided the central focus of the research, for it enabled us to meet many parents in non-interview situations.

At the very beginning, we approached the high school students informally through our dachshund. For several days we took him for a walk around the school building during the lunch hour, and many students became interested in him and his antics. In this way we established rapport with a number of them in a non-school atmosphere. Late in the second week we started going to the places where the boys loafed, ate, and played games in the late afternoon. By going from one place to another on different days, we broadened our acquaintance. Some boys were friendly from the first, but most were reserved and diffident. However, after a few days we could talk to them without attracting undue attention. After we became known to a number of students, and after the project had been explained to the high school teachers and pupils in an assembly, we began to talk with the girls. However, I was not able to "loaf" so openly in the drugstores and soda fountains where the girls tended to congregate, for the local mores would not tolerate this type of behavior from a strange young man with a family. Our early contacts with the girls were generally made in their homes or at school and by my wife.

## Sources of the data

The data used to test our hypothesis were derived principally from participant observation, schedules, interviews, official records, tests, autobiographies, *The Elmtown Bugle,* historical pamphlets, and visits with the adolescents, their parents, and other local people. Schedules were completed on 549 families and 752 adolescents. Some 1,600 persons were interviewed in connection with the schedules or in non-schedule interviews. Pertinent facts were abstracted from such official records as relief cases, tax assessment sheets, court cases, and police arrests. Access was gained to elementary and high school records, and apt items were abstracted. Tests such as the Ross Mooney *Problem Check List,* the Alex Bavelas *Ideas on Moral Values,* a *Guess Who,* and *Interest Index* were given to the high school students. Then, too, freshmen and seniors wrote autobiographies in May, 1942, with the cooperation of two English teachers.

The research problem required that the data be collected from three different sets of Elmtowners: the adolescents, their parents, and persons outside the family group. The accumulation of information about the adolescent was the first objective, if we were to understand his behavior and assess its significance against the backgrounds of family and community. To achieve this goal, the family had to be called on and observed, schedules had to be filled out on it, and interview materials obtained. The third parties to the process, the outsiders so to speak, were the source of data about the way families fitted into the social structure and about various matters relative to the adolescents. They were teachers, employers, operators of businesses, clergymen, youth leaders, police—in short, institutional functionaries of all kinds—and just plain Elmtowners.

The adolescents were the principal source of information about their activities, thoughts, attitudes, social relations, and participation in communal life. We came in contact with them from morning until night, day after day, as they moved from one activity to another. Most of our time was spent around the high school before school, at noon, and in the late afternoon and

early evening, observing, talking, questioning, and visiting, looking to the establishment of rapport and to the acquisition of personal and group data about these young people. Most school
activities, many church affairs, Boy Scout and Girl Scout meetings, dances, and parties were attended. We skated and bowled
with them, shot pool, and lost small change in poker games to
boys who had already acquired a culture trait so prevalent among
their fathers. We "ganged" and "clowned" with the adolescents
in their "night spots" and favorite "hangouts," after the game,
dance, or show. Our policy was to be with them whenever and
wherever possible. As they learned that we did not "carry tales"
to their parents, teachers, preachers, police, or other adult control agents who might disapprove of some of their activities, and
that we did not give "moral advice" or try to steer them in "the
right path," they gradually accepted our presence as normal in
many activities. Their early attitude of carefully keeping us at
"arm's length" arose, we learned later, from the emphasis we
had placed on "character development" in the explanation of the
project. Because the adolescents, like their elders, equated
"character" with "goodness," many of them thought we were
trying to "spy on," "get something on," or "reform" them. The
observational technique of being with them as often as possible
and not criticizing their activities, carrying tales, or "interfering"
overcame the original suspicion in a few weeks.

As soon as we became acquainted with an adolescent and were
able to recognize him, we watched him to learn who his associates
were. After the youngster was seen in a given situation, we
interviewed him to discover who his associates were; how often
he "ran around" with these boys or girls; were they his "regular
pals"; which one was his "best friend"; and which ones he "palled
with." Gradually we came to know well all the high school
students and their pals who were not in school. Not all the withdrawees were known so intimately, but about 200 came to be
known very well. However, considerably more data were
gathered about the students than about the non-students, since
the latter were scattered widely in the community and tended
to participate in communal life as young adults rather than as
students.

Through being with them constantly, we learned who associated with whom, how often, under what circumstances, and in general what a group did. Practically all types of activity were observable, except those associated with the violation of the more stringent taboos, sex and liquor in particular. Direct observation of private, personal amorous activity in cars parked in favorite nooks, where "the view is lovely" but not seen in the dark of late evening, was taboo by mutual consent. We knew where these parking spots were and, from gossip, kidding, and bragging, who frequented them and usually how often. Eventually considerable information was gathered on what happened there, when, and with whom.

Some intelligent Elmtowners realized the close connection between a child's family experience and his behavior, and some openly criticized us because apparently we were not studying the families as well as the adolescents. Most of this criticism never reached us, although some did indirectly, and a few persons "spoke to us" in the early months of the field work about our failure to find out about these youngsters' families. When this happened, we asked them naively for their advice, explaining that we were in the community to learn and anything the critic could contribute would be gratefully received. In this way a critic, in most instances, was changed into a friendly helper. These critics usually, when asked to help, made an effort to justify their position with illustrative material about certain youths whose behavior could be explained only, as they saw it, on the basis of experiences in the family.

This point was emphasized with lengthy illustrations on many occasions. For instance, one critic believed that an intimate knowledge of the internal organization of a family and a working understanding of the notions of the parents on child rearing would lead to an understanding of the behavior of young people. To illustrate her point, she went into detail about the transference by a neighbor's daughter of behavior she had learned in the family into non-family situations.

Jackie acts the same way with her teachers as she does with her mother and the girls she goes with. One minute she is all smiles and the next she won't speak to them or even go around with them. She has had a lot of trouble with the high school teachers, the principal, and the Superintendent. She will criticize a teacher in class, stand right up to her and argue belligerently. Her attitudes in school have come to open rebellion several times. This is where Henry's (the father) warped ideas come in; when Jackie gets in a fight with her mother, a teacher, or the students, it's always their fault. Jackie has had some big fights with several people, but it's always the other person's fault, according to Jackie. I can be unbiased; I know it's not always the other fellow's fault. When Jackie gets in a fight with the teachers, Henry is ready to fire the teacher. Henry has fought all his business associates, and he has tried to start impeachment proceedings against several public officials. In every fight, he is always right. Jackie is just like him. The whole thing goes back into the family, but you couldn't breathe it to them or the family would be on you.

Although some persons like the woman just mentioned believed that the family should have been studied rather than the children's activities, they also warned us to be careful lest we find ourselves in serious difficulty. We realized, as these Elmtowners did, that our approach had to be fitted into what the community expected or we would not be able to attain our objective. This dilemma called for adroit use of methodological procedures which would enable us to collect the data we deemed necessary to test our hypothesis without arousing so many tensions that we would have to withdraw under fire from an aroused, hostile public opinion.

RECORDING THE DATA. Verbal and observational information collected from the many persons and sources mentioned in the preceding section was recorded as it was given or as soon after as circumstances permitted. Originally, one family and two adolescent schedules had been drawn up, but before the study was over four additional ones had to be made and filled out for each adolescent in high school, and an extra one for each out-of-school adolescent. All schedules were filled out question by question by us in personal interviews. The *family schedule* was filled out during home visits in the presence of the person giving the information. In most cases, this was the mother of the adolescent, but in some cases an older brother, sister, or the father. All homes were visited once, 84 two or three times, and 67 four or more times. The number of visits was determined in part by the interest the family had in the work and their willingness to talk about the community, its institutions, people and what they did, and in part by its position in the social structure. We were careful to see that the homes we visited more than once were scattered throughout the social structure both in town and in the country.

The adolescent schedules were completed in many different places. The original high school schedule was filled out in semiprivate interviews in one corner of the high school principal's office. The students were called in one at a time from the study hall and interviewed for about twenty minutes. This was not a wholly satisfactory place to interview students, but it was the best available at that time. The later schedules were filled out at home, in school, in student hangouts, in our car, or wherever we could see the boy or girl privately. Schedules for the out-of-school group were filled out whenever and wherever we were able to locate the subject—at home, in a hangout, on the job, on the street. Interviewing under these circumstances was difficult and uneven at best; it was, however, the only way it could be done, and on the whole we believe that it is typical of a field study which attempts to reach every case in a universe defined as this one was.

Materials gathered from Elmtowners who were neither adolescents nor members of a family studied were accumulated at odd times and places from June, 1941, through December, 1942. Teachers, clergymen, law enforcement officers, operators of recreational establishments, interested citizens, and the raters discussed in a subsequent section were interviewed systematically time after time by the use of undirected closed interviews, openended interviews, and some by schedules. How they were interviewed depended upon the types of data they were able and willing to furnish and the way we desired to use the data they provided.

Because it had originally been planned to record observations and interviews in a "Research Journal," elaborate notes were made on each conversation during the first few weeks. Observations about the arrangement of furniture in a home or an office, the way a person spoke or sat, his reaction to our proposal, and our estimation of him were recorded on the typewriter, and the sheet was placed in the "Journal." This record was made immediately after the visit with a person, before someone else was interviewed in order to keep impressions and reactions to situations and persons gained from one experience separate from those which came from another. Notes on a conversation were written as soon as possible in order to preserve as much of the original wording and flavor before counter-stimuli confused or obliterated them.

The task of typing conversations and details of an experience consumed many hours. Fortunately, arrangements were soon made to record interview material electrically. After we started recording interviews electrically the "Journal" became a "Daily Diary." Each evening the names of persons visited that day, where we went, and what we did were recorded in it. From then on, interviews were recorded as nearly verbatim as memory allowed.

These interviews may be divided into two broad groups: the more or less aimless conversation which is sometimes called an undirected or concealed interview; and the directed, open-ended interview. The particular type used depended upon the person, the circumstances under which the interview occurred, and the type of data we desired at the moment. Both types were used on a single person at different times, often in the same interview. When the concealed interview technique was followed, we sketched and recorded it immediately after we left the person who gave the information. In the recording of these materials, we attempted to recall the questions asked and the answers of the interviewee in the exact sequence of the conversation. Key phrases and words were written on a blank sheet; often whole sentences were recalled. We were almost always alone during the sketching and recording of an interview; so no one interfered with the recall process. As soon as an interview had been sketched, it was recorded. Interviews held late at night were sketched immediately, but they were not usually recorded until the next morning.

The process whereby material gained in an interview, especially a closed interview, is transposed from the interview situation to a record is crucial in this type of research. In the process, some data are inevitably lost, others are telescoped, and some may be overemphasized. Moreover, the exact word order of each person's conversation cannot be reproduced. The interviewer may in the recording phase place emphasis where the original speaker did not intend it. The field worker may be scrupulously honest and sincerely attempt to reproduce what was said and how it was said, but his unconscious "biases" may "load" the interview. Then, too, the field worker's interest in his problem may be so intense that he "sees things" in the data that are not "so clear" to local people. In some cases, he may make them "too clear."

These biases or sources of error were known, and attempts were made to neutralize their influence by the use of a notebook whenever possible. Closed interviews and visits were relied on during the first few weeks, but, as we became acquainted and the local people developed an interest in the study, an open notebook was used in most interviews because people expected us to take notes on what they said. When a person did not want us to record his remarks, he would say, "Don't put this down; just let me tell you about it." When this occurred, we put our pen down, closed the notebook, and let him tell his story. These stories were recorded later because of their value for the study. Usually the material given in these interludes furnished insight into a personality, some type of social action, or an obscure point in the prestige structure. This technique enabled us to record most interview data as they were given without creating tensions in the speaker.

### Stratification procedures

Stratification of the adolescents' families had to be done in the field simultaneously with the other phases of data collection. This was a major activity throughout the year, and during April and May, 1942, it consumed most of our time. Since this was a crucial operation in the test of the hypothesis, we shall discuss in detail how it was done. However, before we outline the techniques used, we shall call attention to the fact that numerous studies of American communities have found the social structure to be stratified into classes, castes, or a combination of classes and castes.[3] Yet no commonly accepted methodological tool has been developed for the stratification of a community's population. This is strange, because every investigator who has studied the community from the viewpoint of class or caste has had to face the problem of stratification of the population. Therefore, each one has worked out his own system in his own way, without regard to what others have done, and with little attention being given, at least from the viewpoint of the reader, to how it was done. Consequently, there is no agreement regarding the method of stratifying a community. Methodological techniques which enable a field worker to place persons in the social structure rapidly, accurately, consistently, and objectively are still *desiderata*.

The question we faced was: How could the families be placed in the social structure? Three possibilities were open to us. First, a single factor index, such as occupation, income, education, or area of residence, might have been used. This was rejected, because interview materials indicated that a family's "station in life" or "class," to use local terms, was derived from the possession of a number of socio-cultural characteristics rather than one—family background, occupation, education, wealth, personal behavior, religion, their origin, to mention only the more obvious ones. The second alternative was reliance on a composite index such as that of the Chapin scale.[4] Considerable thought and experimentation were given to Chapin's and

[3] Robert S. Lynd and Helen Merrill Lynd, *Middletown*, Harcourt, Brace and Company, New York, 1929; and *Middletown in Transition*, Harcourt, Brace and Company, New York, 1937; John Dollard, *Class and Caste in a Southern Town*, Yale University Press, New Haven, 1937; Hortense Powdermaker, *After Freedom*, Viking Press, New York, 1939; Arthur Hosking Jones, *Cheltenham Township*, University of Pennsylvania Press, Philadelphia, 1940; W. Lloyd Warner and Paul S. Lunt, *The Social Life of a Modern Community*, Yale University Press, New Haven, 1941, and subsequent volumes in the Yankee City Series; Allison Davis, Burleigh B. Gardner, and Mary S. Gardner, *Deep South*, University of Chicago Press, Chicago, 1941; Allison Davis and John Dollard, *Children of Bondage*, American Council on Education, Washington, D. C., 1940; James West, *Plainville, U.S.A.*, Columbia University Press, New York, 1945.

[4] F. Stuart Chapin, *The Measurement of Social Status by the Use of the Social Status Scale*, University of Minnesota Press, Minneapolis, 1933, pp. 2–16.

Sewell's [5] scales, but both were abandoned because Chapin's had been standardized on city families and Sewell's on Oklahoma farm families. If the Chapin scale had been used for town families and the Sewell scale for farm families, there would have been no common measure of socio-economic status between the two.

The third possibility appeared to be the development of a procedure which would apply a common measure to all families. Therefore, a rating procedure was developed which, we believe, met the objections to a single criterion and previously developed scales. Like most ideas, it grew out of the work others had done. In the 1930's, a number of sociologists, in their research for a methodological tool which would enable them to place persons and families functionally in the social structure, experimented with the use of local people long resident in a community as raters or judges of their fellows' prestige, status, or class positions.[6]

This idea seemed to be sound in view of the size of Elmtown, the stability of the population, the knowledge one person had about another, and the way the people referred to one another, to social groups, organizations, and institutions. Then, too, the use of local people as judges to place the families of the adolescents in the social structure would utilize local values to define

[5] William H. Sewell, "The Construction and Standardization of a Scale for the Measurement of the Socio-Economic Status of Oklahoma Farm Families," *Oklahoma Agricultural Experiment Station, Technical Bulletin 9,* Stillwater, Oklahoma, 1940.

[6] See: Wilson Gee, "A Qualitative Study of Rural Depopulation in a Single Township: 1900–1930," *American Journal of Sociology,* Vol. 33 (1933), pp. 210–221; Carl Frederick Reuss, "A Qualitative Study of Depopulation in a Remote Rural District: 1900–1930," *Rural Sociology,* Vol. 2 (1937), pp. 66–75; George A. Lundberg, "The Measurement of Socio-Economic Status," *American Sociological Review,* Vol. 5 (1940), pp. 29–39; Edgar A. Schuler, "Social and Economic Status in a Louisiana Hills Community," *Rural Sociology,* Vol. 5 (1940), pp. 69–87.

While this study was in progress, Harold Kaufman utilized the same general idea in a New York community. See: Harold F. Kaufman, "Prestige Classes in a New York Rural Community," *Cornell University Agricultural Experiment Station, Memoir 260,* Ithaca, New York, 1944, pp. 3–46; Harold F. Kaufman, "Members of Rural Community as Judges of Prestige Rank," *Sociometry,* Vol. 9 (1946), pp. 71–85.

position, standing, or class in a more functional way than an arbitrarily imposed factor such as a single criterion index could have done.

DEVELOPMENT OF THE TEST INSTRUMENT. Within three months after the field work was started, evidence accumulated which indicated that Elmtowners divided the social structure into several strata. They spoke of each other as members of "the aristocracy," "the 400," "the society class," "our community leaders," "the class below the society class," "the little business people," "the hard-working people who pay their bills but never get any place," "the reliefers," "the ne'er-do-wells," "the canal squatters," "the river rats," "the criminal class." When Elmtowners made such remarks, they almost invariably identified persons who, in their opinion, occupied these positions. Moreover, they justified their identification of persons and families with these positions by statements about their wealth, occupation, education, their way of living, the location of their homes, their behavior, and their participation or non-participation in organized community activities.

It became apparent, after a short time, that different people identified the same families with particular prestige groups when they discussed position in the social structure. For instance, some half-dozen family names were used as examples of people who belonged to "the upper class" or "the aristocracy." Other families appeared to be notorious for their "criminal records," "dependence upon relief," and generally low prestige. A different group of names was used, more or less consistently, with reference to various positions which did not imply either high or low stations. Gradually, the tentative conclusion was reached that families who were repeatedly cited as occupants of a given prestige position functioned as reference points for many people when they thought about the way persons and families were distributed in the social structure.

The identification of the same families with the same social positions by a number of different people provided the idea that family name could be used as an index of position in the social structure. It was reasoned thus: If there is consensus that "the Sweitzers are tops here" ("real aristocrats," "silk stockings"), that "the Soper tribe is on the bottom," and "Joe Emerson is plain middle class," then Elmtowners know "who is where" and "why." As one prominent Elmtowner put it, "I can hang just about everyone here on the peg he belongs on and tell you why." If this was true, a list of families might be compiled from those frequently mentioned by different people and used as an instrument to stratify the families of the adolescents. Furthermore, if this could be done, a number of carefully selected, well-informed Elmtowners could compare the families of the adolescents they knew well with those on the list. Thus, the families would be stratified by the use of the same complex of socio-cultural values the people followed in everyday life. By relying on the judgment of a number of people, personal biases would be minimized.

The first step in the development of this idea was the analysis of interview materials to learn the names that recurred with the greatest regularity, who used them, how they were used, and if those who used them appeared to rely on more or less common criteria to place the people they referred to in the social structure. Fifty interviews were analyzed and information about 30 families abstracted. Great care was taken to see that several families were selected from each station in the social structure. At this point interest was centered on learning "why" each family was placed the way it was by the person who supplied the information.

This analysis revealed that these 30 families had been placed in similar, if not identical, positions by different interviewees, and, equally important, that they used a more or less common set of criteria to explain why different families were in the same station or position. More than 100 items were mentioned in the interviews. They were grouped under five general headings: (1) the way a family lived—this included place of residence, type of dwelling, and furnishings; (2) income and material possessions; (3) participation in community affairs, politics, religion—"civic minded," "radical," "conservative," "good community man," "don't give a damn about education"; (4) family background, including ancestry, kin, and national origin; (5) reputation or prestige.

The next step was a trial run of the idea. The full name and address of the husband and wife were typed on 3″ by 5″ cards. These 30 cards were taken to 25 people previously interviewed who were asked to do two things: (1) to tell how representative they believed these families were of the different positions ("station," "pegs people belonged on," "classes"—in local usage) in the community; and (2) to place each family where they believed it belonged in terms of its "station," "peg," or "standing." No more specific instructions or criteria for placing the 30 families were given to these raters. Nineteen divided the cards into five groups; 3 into three groups; 2 into four groups; and 1 into two groups. In each case, the person was asked if he believed that there were more or less "groups" than these, or if the number he gave represented the principal "stations," "pegs," "classes," "prestige groups." After the sample families had been placed in their respective groups, the interviewees were asked to justify their judgments.

This test study showed three things: (1) 76 per cent (19 of the 25 persons interviewed) believed that there were five strata in Elmtown; (2) there was a high order of agreement on which families belonged in each group with certain definite exceptions; and (3) the raters justified their judgments, on the whole, by the use of the same types of symbolic referents that appeared in the interviews. A detailed study of the 747 different evaluations brought out two points: first, the 25 raters agreed with one another on 77 per cent of their ratings; and, second, 91 per cent of this agreement was concentrated on 21 families. Consistent disagreement occurred on 9 families and some on a tenth one. These ten names were dropped after a restudy of the interviews and the remarks of the 25 raters indicated that either these families were unstable in their positions or there was considerable disparity between the prestige assigned to adult members—that is, the wife might be given one station and the husband another.

It was believed that this study gave a preliminary affirmative answer to two hypothetical questions: (1) Could a list of families be compiled whose positions were so well known that a number of carefully selected Elmtowners would agree on the place each family occupied in the social structure? (2) Would the families on the list be representative of the principal strata of the social structure?

The 20 families on the *control list,* as it will be called hereafter, were as representative of the five classes or strata in the social structure and the sub-groups within it—town, farm, ethnic, religious, economic, educational, moral, and so on—as we were able to make them. By class position the 20 names were distributed as follows:

| Class Position | Number of Families |
|:---:|:---:|
| I | 2 |
| II | 3 |
| III | 4 |
| IV | 6 |
| V | 5 |
|  | — |
| Total | 20 |

After the control list was made, the question was: Would a group of representative raters agree among themselves that the families on it represented the *five* different strata that appeared to characterize Elmtown?

Twelve adults, all long-time residents who had cooperated on other phases of the study and appeared to be representative of the five strata, but had not rated the names originally, were asked to classify the 20 names on the control list, judging each on the following points:

(*a*) The way the family lived.
(*b*) Income and possessions.
(*c*) Participation in community affairs.
(*d*) Prestige or standing in the community.

Ten of these 12 raters divided the 20 families into five groups, 1 into four, and 1 into three. The ratings obtained from the 10 raters who divided the families into five strata were correlated with the ratings of 10 of the original 19 raters who had divided the original families into five groups and had rated, therefore, each family on the revised list.

The coefficients for each of the five correlations ranged from a high of $r = +0.97$ for the highest position (class I) to a low of $r = +0.84$ for the fourth position (class IV). The composite coefficient was $r = +0.88$.[7] These coefficients were high enough to satisfy us that the 20 names on the control list were diagnostic of the five major classes or strata in the Elmtown social structure as it was conceived by 29 out of 35 raters, or 83 per cent. They also indicated the reliability of the rating procedure as it applied to these 20 families. It is admitted that the ratings of the deviant 17 per cent were ignored. This was necessary for technical reasons inherent in the correlation process. If they could have been included, the correlation coefficients would have been lower, but we do not believe that they would have been so low that the procedure would not have been justified.

The next question was: Would raters be able to equate the families in the study with those on the control list? To answer this question a third test was made. Every tenth name on the list of adolescents' family names was selected from the alphabetized file. The name and address of the parents were typed on 3″ by 5″ cards. These were taken to 8 of the first group of 25 raters. In this series of interviews, the rater was given a typed list of the 20 families from the control list. He was asked to equate each of 53 families named on the cards which he knew personally with the family on the control list which he believed it most closely approximated with respect to the way the family lived, income and possessions, participation or non-participation in community affairs, and general standing or prestige. The successful use of the control list as a stratifying device was dependent upon the rater's knowing in a rather intimate way, or thinking he did, both the family on the control list and the family in the study with which he equated it. Twenty-nine of the 53 families were rated by all 8 judges. The ratings on these 29 families were then split into two series by random sorting of the eight different ratings we had for each one. The ratings of one group were then correlated with those of the other by strata. The five coefficients thus obtained ranged from $r = +0.75$ to $r = +0.87$ with a composite of $r = +0.82$. These coefficients were high enough to indicate that the rating device was reliable. The important point was to have enough raters to assure several

[7] Standard errors have been omitted here in accordance with our policy of keeping detail to a minimum. They are available upon request.

ratings for each family. For this reason we used only the 29 families for which we had 8 judgments. This gave us two groups of 29 families with four ratings on each family in each group for each stratum.

SELECTION OF THE RATERS. The next step was the selection of the raters to be used in the rating of the 535 families. Persons selected as raters had given freely of their time and knowledge about Elmtown's culture and people. Some were in key positions in the institutional structure; others performed functions which brought them into contact with many types of people; and a few were "plain" citizens. All knew the community through years of living in it, and they were willing to discuss many aspects of community affairs.

Four criteria were used in the selection of prospective raters: (1) persons who had a child or close relative in the study were eliminated; (2) those who had been used in the preliminary tests were excluded; (3) only adults who had resided in the community 20 years or more were considered; and (4) raters had to appear to be stable in their station. We believed that mature persons possessed a better understanding of the prestige structure, its components, and its method of operation than did young people. Then, too, we wanted the families rated by their peers. Care was taken to select persons from every ethnic and religious group and from every stratum, so that the raters would be representative of all sections of the population.

Persons who met these standards were approached privately and the nature of the proposed rating scheme discussed. We explained that we were interested in an appraisal of each family which the prospective rater knew personally, or knew about in a personal way. We were not interested in gossip or "backbiting," but in facts and factual information that would help us understand the family and, in turn, the children. Each person was assured that what he said would be kept confidential and that the success of the project depended upon this condition. Its importance was stressed, as well as the time it would take. After the prospective rater had some grasp of the problem, he was asked if he would be willing to help.

Thirty-five persons were invited to act as raters, and 31 agreed to aid us. As the interviews progressed, the list was supplemented by six husbands (or wives) who were incorporated into the rating procedure. Since these persons only sat in on the conference and did not rate families independently, we did not treat them as additional raters.[8] The persons who consented to act as raters were class-typed by the same techniques they used on the families they typed, supplemented by comparative material accumulated from the raters themselves and from other persons. They were not asked to rate themselves or each other.

THE RATING PROCEDURE. The raters evaluated the families in private conferences held in various places. A box of 5″ by 8″ cards, showing the name of each family and its address, and the control list were taken to these conferences. We generally sat at a table or a desk while the rater sat opposite. The rater was given a typewritten copy of the control list. The names and addresses of the families on the control list were arranged alphabetically, so that the rater would have no cue to our opinion of their position in the social structure. The rater was told that we were desirous of having him tell us as many things as he wished about each family he knew—things which would enable us to understand the children and the family situation in general. He was told that each family had been interviewed at least once, and the children twice or more, so that we had some knowledge of the family; but that we were desirous of getting insight into its way of life and its relationship to the community from people who knew the family well, knew its background and its strengths and weaknesses, and were willing to impart this information, as well as to rate it in relation to the families on the control list by the use of the four criteria used in the test runs.

The story given to the different raters about what we desired varied in its details in accordance with our judgment of their comprehension of the study, and their personalities, education, and reaction to the problem before them. They were assured and reassured that all information would be regarded as strictly confidential. Some families not in the study, who were known to both the rater and to us, were ranked by both parties before the first families in the study were ranked, so that the rater would understand how we wanted him to use the control list. This

[8] However, their presence is indicated in Table III of the Appendix.

preliminary discussion gave the rater some idea of what was expected. It also served to focus his attention on the families he knew and to stimulate him to impart information about them.

The data given by the rater on each family were recorded on the card either verbatim or as notes. Any information he gave but did not want placed on the card was recorded later. Such information usually involved dishonesty, sex delinquency, crime, or other reprehensible behavior by some member of the family he was rating. These descriptive data were given freely, and no effort was made to interrupt the speaker. After the rater had finished his general remarks about a family and the notes were completed, he was asked to name the family on the control list he believed it most closely approximated. The name of the family selected from the control list was written on the bottom of the note card. The rater was free to choose the families he gave information on, the information he supplied, and the families on the control list with whom they were equated. During conferences, the raters often spoke of a family as being a member of a given class, such as "the working class" or "little business people." When this occurred, we accepted the rater's terminology and used it without placing emphasis upon the fact that this was what we were seeking to define. When a rater was this explicit, he frequently said, "The Jacksons are a class above the Sweets," or a "class below," or "they are in the same class."

Although it was possible for a family to be rated by every rater, no family was. The number of ratings received by a particular family ranged from 22 for 7 class V families to 7 for 10 class V families. No rater claimed that he knew as many as half of the families personally. However, 6, who had spent their lives in the community and occupied public or semi-public offices, knew the people so well that they were able to rate 200 or more families; one class III woman rated 261. In contrast to these persons, a class V woman gave judgments on 33 families. The average informant believed that he knew about 75 families well enough to place them in the community's social structure in relation to the control families.

Rural families were class-typed by the same raters in the same manner as the town dwellers. No appreciable difference was noted in either the criteria or the way the raters placed rural or town families. In Elmtown, the interrelations between farm people and town people were too close for a wide divergence of interests to develop. Practically every town family had its roots in the soil in some way or other. All class I families owned large tracts of land, and the majority of class II families owned a farm or two. Many class III's had interest in farms through either purchase or inheritance. The class IV's were split more definitely between rural and town dwellers, but the family usually had relatives living on farms, or its members had lived there part of their lives and knew a number of farm people. The social ties of the class V raters were limited almost exclusively to the town, as they were not landowners and very few came directly from farms. However, many had worked on farms and knew farm families.

STRATIFICATION OF THE RATED FAMILIES. After the field conferences had been completed, the ratings for each family were taken off the field cards and placed on a special *rating schedule,* which revealed how each rater had equated each family with relation to the families on the control list. The next step was the translation of these ratings into numerical values. This was done by weighting the families on the control list in the following manner: class I was given a weight of 1; class II, 2; class III, 3; class IV, 4; and class V, 5. Each rating received by a family was then weighted according to this scheme and the data placed on Hollerith cards. As the reader can see, the raters and the families of adolescents in the study were class-typed operationally by the use of research instruments and procedures. Therefore, we always use Roman numerals to refer to the class position of Elmtowners that we established instrumentally: class I, class II, class III, class IV, class V.

The total rated score awarded by the several raters was computed for each family; this score was divided by the number of raters and *the mean score assigned to the family as its class score.* Mean scores were used rather than raw scores, since the total score a family received was produced by the number of raters and the way they rated it relative to the families on the control list. The mean scores received by individual families ranged from 1.00 to 5.00, with the average deviations on individual families ranging from 0.00 to 1.12 in a prestige class.

The most conspicuous agreement between the raters was found at the extreme ends of the prestige hierarchy. The high order of agreement among the raters on these families indicated the salient position they occupied in the social structure. They, as the ratings reveal, were prominent representatives of the highest and lowest strata in the community. The histories, reputations, property holdings, places of residence, and power of the class I families were bywords among the population. Seven families were awarded the distinction of possessing the lowest prestige by 22 raters who equated them with class V families on the control list. This gave them a mean score of 5.00 and an average deviation of 0.00. The remaining 524 families occupied prestige positions in this range. The mean prestige rating for each class and the average deviation are given in Table II.

### TABLE II

MEAN SCORES AND AVERAGE DEVIATION OF EACH CLASS, NUMBER OF
FAMILIES IN EACH CLASS, AND NUMBER OF PERSONS RATING THEM

| Class | Weighted Interval | Number of Families | Number of Adolescents | Number of Raters | Mean Number of Raters per Family | Mean Rating | Average Deviation * |
|-------|-------------------|--------------------|-----------------------|------------------|----------------------------------|-------------|---------------------|
| I | 0.51 1.50 | 4 | 4 | 21 | 21.0 | 1.04 | 0.04 |
| II | 1.51 2.50 | 29 | 31 | 23 | 14.3 | 1.93 | 0.16 |
| III | 2.51 3.50 | 129 | 158 | 20 | 13.4 | 2.91 | 0.25 |
| IV | 3.51 4.50 | 235 | 312 | 26 | 12.1 | 4.17 | 0.47 |
| V | 4.51 5.50 | 138 | 230 | 22 | 10.5 | 4.71 | 0.39 |

* Calculated from the mean.

The mean scores received by the several prestige classes indicated that the raters equated the families very closely with the corresponding families on the control list. The low average deviations showed the high order of agreement between the raters for all the prestige classes, but particularly for classes I and II. The mean scores also showed the generally high regard the raters accorded the families in these classes. The mean scores for classes II and III were slightly higher than the mid-point of the interval; on the contrary, the scores for class IV were below it. These departures from the theoretical midpoint were indicative of the raters' biases toward persons of higher and lower prestige. Thus, families in classes II and III were given slightly higher scores than we might expect theoretically, whereas those in class IV were placed lower on the scale than might be expected.

The difference of 1.26 class intervals between the mean scores for classes III and IV was indicative of the prestige gulf that exists between the two largest socio-economic groupings in Elm-town, namely, the "business and professional classes" and the "working class." This difference appeared in various forms so persistently that we are convinced that it is symbolic of a funda-mental prestige differential between these broad groups.[9] This is not to say that the differences between the several prestige classes as determined here were not significant; they were, as we shall demonstrate, but it should be made clear that there was a greater prestige difference between the 30 per cent of the families in classes I to III, inclusive, and the 70 per cent of the families in classes IV and V than between discrete classes within each group.

Seventy-five per cent of the total disagreement between the raters as to the position of particular families in the social struc-ture involved 74 families. Case study of these families indicated that either the families as units or some of their members were moving from one stratum to another. Slightly over 85 per cent of these families were upwardly mobile; the remainder were on the road down. When a family member or the family as a whole was mobile, people were uncertain about its position. The raters recognized this and were confused by it. Several raters com-pared a husband with one family on the control list and a wife with another one. When such cases occurred, both ratings were

[9] Robert S. and Helen M. Lynd, *Middletown*, New York, 1929, and *Mid-dletown in Transition*, Harcourt, Brace and Company, New York, 1937, found this cleavage so pervasive that they organized their data in terms of it; that is, "working class" and "business class."

recorded and we later used "clinical judgment" in assigning a rating to the family in lieu of the rater's uniform judgment.

The distribution of these doubtful cases was: class II, 2; class III, 7; class IV, 16; class V, 14. The 2 class II families we helped to rate were moving in opposite directions. One was moving from a very strong class III station to a weak class II one. The husband had already successfully adjusted to class II activities such as membership in the Rotary Club and leadership in his church, but his wife was finding difficult the transition to female associations and behavior connected with class II. The other family was losing its position through economic failure and erratic behavior of some of its members. The same type of situation prevailed in the other cases, whether they were class III's or class IV's. In these cases, we weighed the judgments of the raters who were uncertain against our knowledge of the family and our own judgment of the situation and then rated the family in accordance with the indications of the evidence. We directly influenced 39 out of a total of 6,521 ratings, or 0.6 per cent, by the use of "clinical judgment."

The greatest amount of disagreement between raters occurred among families near the bottom of the social structure, but not on the bottom. Twenty-one per cent of the families whose ratings placed them in class V were regarded as either class IV's or class V's by different raters. Four class III and 8 class IV raters helped to rate these families. They tended to equate them with class IV. No class III rater placed any of these families above this position, and a number were placed below it. The class IV raters equated 21 of the 29 families in question with class V families on the control list, and they were uncertain as to whether or not the remaining 8 were class IV's or class V's. Four class V raters agreed, on the whole, with the judgment of the class IV raters. However, one family that had been equated with one class V family or another on the control list by all raters from the higher classes, because of its notorious history, was regarded as a class IV by 3 of the 4 class V raters and as a class III by 1.

Generally speaking, placement of families tended to be uniform from rater to rater when the rater and the rated belonged to the same class, were well known to each other, and when the family being rated was stable in its position. Differential placement was encountered when the rater and the rated came from different classes, especially when the rater was uncertain about the position of a mobile family. When raters belonged to a class below the family rated, there was more uncertainty over a family's position than when raters and rated were in the same class. When the rater was two classes below the family rated, there was greater disagreement than in the case of a single class difference. When three or more classes intervened between the rater and the rated, greater agreement was experienced in the ratings than when there were only two intervals between them. This apparently anomalous situation might be accounted for by a general tendency for persons of low prestige to accord high prestige to persons who are markedly different from themselves; also extreme cases are always clearer as to type than intervening ones.

A TEST OF THE STRATIFICATION PROCEDURE.  The repetition of an experiment or a set of observations by an independent investigator on the same or essentially similar data is an ideal in scientific research which is seldom possible in the social sciences. But the cooperative nature of this research, combined with its relative independence, made such a check possible.

In 1943, The Committee on Human Development independently class-typed the sixteen-year-old boys and girls living in Elmtown for another study. The stratifying instrument in this case was an *index of evaluated participation* which the Committee had developed under the direction of W. Lloyd Warner; it utilized other criteria than the judgments of individuals about their fellows.[10]  There was an overlap of 134 families between the two studies. Therefore, a test of the two procedures was possible on 25 per cent of the families which we stratified by the use of the control list and the 31 raters. It is believed that this is a large enough sample to give some real indication of the validity as well as the reliability of the two stratifying procedures.

[10] A description of the *index of evaluated participation* is given in W. Lloyd Warner, Marchia Meeker, and Kenneth Eells, *The Measurement of Social Status,* Science Research Associates, Chicago, Part I (in press).

The 134 cases included in the two studies were certainly a cross section of this study, since they constituted a complete enumeration of one age grade then living in Elmtown.

The placement of families in the two higher classes was practically identical by the two methods, as Table III reveals. There

TABLE III

FAMILIES OF SIXTEEN-YEAR-OLD ADOLESCENTS STRATIFIED BY INDEX OF
EVALUATED PARTICIPATION AND THE RATING TECHNIQUE

| Class | I.E.P.,* Number of Cases | Stratified by Rating Technique, Number of Cases | Percentage of Agreement |
|-------|------|------|------|
| I | 2 | 2 | 100 |
| II | 8 | 9 | 89 |
| III | 44 | 44 | 83 |
| IV | 61 | 55 | 72 |
| V | 19 | 24 | 77 |
| Total | 134 | 134 | |

* Index of evaluated participation, Warner method.

was some disagreement between the two methods in class III. Most disagreement appeared between the two methods in classes IV and V. On the basis of our experience this was where disagreement could be expected. Then, too, there might have been some mobility in the interval between the two studies to account for the observed differences. Finally, the two techniques might have stressed different factors in these low status groups. At any rate the agreement between the two studies was so high that it should be clear that the two stratification techniques as used by independent investigators produced a valid and reliable index of stratification in the samples studied.

## Analysis of the data

Throughout the planning, field work, analysis, and writing phases of this study we were faced by the dilemma inherent in the use of *interviews* and *schedules*. The *interviews* furnished detailed data on the way in which social processes worked as they were seen, rationalized, and discussed by Elmtowners of all ages and conditions. They provided insight into and some understanding of limited segments of community life strained through the emotional biases of the participant—highly personalized at times, and colored by the stake the teller's ego had in the events, processes, or situations he related. By their poignancy and specificity they provided explicit materials on the inner workings of social processes in the unfolding of events not witnessed by us. They also furnished interpretations of the interrelations between persons and their interests and the social system.

The interview is a research tool without parallel, but an unstructured interview has at least one weakness. It does not enable the researcher to quantify the data obtained. We do not wish to imply that data must be quantified, but we do believe that it is desirable to know how often a given event, condition, or process occurs in a society. In order to learn this, data must be quantified in some manner. The structured interview or *schedule* was used for this purpose. The schedules furnished specific answers to the questions on which we believed we needed to have data in order to test our hypothesis in whole or in part. Data accumulated by the use of schedules and interviews complement, as well as supplement, one another. One provides insight into processes operative in many facets of communal life; the other enables the researcher to calculate the incidence of the process and often to determine the conditions under which it operates. The statistical data provided by the schedules were the basis for the inclusive tables and charts presented in the different chapters and in the Appendix. The interviews were drawn upon to illustrate specific incidents, to give focus to a general process, and to allow Elmtowners to speak for themselves under selected conditions with respect to some point in the social system.

The assumption that the behavior of the adolescents is conditioned in significant ways by the position of their families in the social structure implies that family position is the *independent variable* and the adolescent's behavior the *dependent variable*. If this implication is valid, and the fact of the prior existence of the family in the society indicates that it is, the independent variable should be isolated out of its social and cultural matrix and held constant. The discrete data relative to various segments of adolescent behavior should then be measured against this fixed variable. This technique has been followed in the analytical portions of the report.

In the analysis of the data, we have relied upon statistical procedures to give us the answer to the question on which this research was focused: Is there a significant relationship between an adolescent's behavior and the class to which his family belongs?

Chi square ($X^2$) was selected as the tool to test the significance of the relationship between class position and the behavior of the adolescent for two reasons: first, this technique enables the investigator to apply mathematical procedures to categories that are not strictly quantitative in all their aspects; and, second, it weights every case in the distribution proportionately to every other case. In our use of $X^2$, the 1 per cent level of probability was adopted as the criterion of significance. This is written at the bottom of the tables immediately after the chi square figure ($X^2 = 98.3748$ for example) as $P < 0.01$; or $P > 0.01$. This means that the distribution of a specific behavior trait, when measured against the class index, resulted in a $X^2$ that was significant at the 1 per cent level of probability when $P < 0.01$ was written in this manner. It means that distributions such as the ones presented in this study might be attributed to the chances of sampling error 1 time out of 100. Since practically every $X^2$ calculated for the different behavioral configurations as measured against class was larger than that required by the test, the chances were less than 1 in 100 that the observed behavior of the adolescents was attributable to chance. Therefore, we were able to assume with confidence that there was a real, rather than a chance, relationship between the behavior of the adolescents and the class their families occupied in the social structure. For this reason we shall limit our use of the term significant to its statistical connotation. Thus, when we say that an adolescent's behavior is significantly related to class position we mean that the chances are at least 100 to 1 that it is a product of class conditioning rather than of the chances of sampling.

After we had determined that there was a significant association between class position and a behavioral trait we measured the degree of relationship between them, in most instances, with the coefficient of contingency. The nearer the coefficient of contingency came to 1, after it had been corrected for the broad groups used, the closer the relationship between class and the item or trait measured.[11] The coefficient of contingency is given at the bottom of each table to the right of the probability figure (for example, $C = 0.59$); the corrected coefficient of contingency is written, for example, $\bar{C} = 0.73$ to the right of the uncorrected $C$. Such a corrected coefficient of contingency as the example given means that there was a high order of relationship between the factor of class position and the behavioral configuration measured against it.

One final point about procedure may be in order before we turn to the analysis of the data. In a town of 6,000 people, everything that is done, or not done, and then talked about tends to be personalized. One person does something at some time; other persons know about it, find out about it, and, above all, gossip about it, and then pass judgment on it. Acting, talking, and judging take place against a background of interpersonal relations, social interests, and cultural values. No matter how impersonal the investigator wishes to be in this type of research, the personalization process enters into his data and his analysis. He must quote what one person said about another person or persons as well as interpret the thoughts and actions. To get the data in the first place he has to interact with persons, observe their acts, listen to them talk about themselves and others, and hear them justify, explain, praise, and condemn. Actions and talk about actions are the raw material of behavior and of this study. To tell meaningfully of actions and the talk about them, the researcher must retain the flavor of the social setting. This is often best done through paraphrase and direct quotation, even though it may lay the writer open to the charge of dealing in personalities and personal things. We shall run this risk, because we believe that the individual acting in relation to other persons in a social and cultural setting keeps society functioning, and until the sociologist develops technical media of communica-

[11] The coefficient of contingency was corrected in accordance with the formula and table given in Thomas C. McCormick, *Elementary Social Statistics*, McGraw-Hill Book Company, New York, 1941, pp. 206–207.

tion more meaningful to other sociologists and the lay public than the language of the people, he had better let the actors in the social process speak for themselves. We have done this whenever it appeared to be justified, but in each quotation all names have been changed and identifying details deleted in order to protect the actor and his roles in Elmtown. The basic picture, however, has been retained.

# THE SOCIAL SCENE

THE SOCIAL SETTING IN WHICH the 735 adolescents lived is described in the next five chapters. They are focused upon the description of the community, the social structure, the class system, the schools, and the place of the adolescent in the community.

# 3

---

# THE COMMUNITY SETTING

## Geographic background

A STRANGER APPROACHING ELMTOWN from any direction will be impressed by two dominant features of the landscape—its flatness and the great river which meanders across the extensive glaciated plain. The land beyond two low morainal ridges, parallel to the river, is "as level as a plank floor." Through the thousands of years which elapsed between the last glaciation and the entrance of the pioneer settlers on the local scene slightly more than a century ago, the prairie grasses, chiefly big blue stem, built upon the glacial till a deep black, humus-rich soil which ranges from two to five feet in depth. Between the moraines and the river, glacial boulders, cobbles, and water-washed stones the size of a man's fist are intermixed with gravel and streaks of clay. Here the soil is thinner, lighter, and less fertile. One tongue of the last glaciation left a small terminal moraine that runs across the center of the communal area at right angles to the river. East of this low ridge, the moving, grinding ice gouged a depression which eventually became a shallow lake covering thousands of acres. In this area, the glacier's excavations left a thin layer of clay, boulders, and gravel over a coal sheet which extends under the entire region. In the last twenty years, the lake has been drained, and giant shovels now strip the coal from its shallow beds.

The river valley and low-lying sections along the tributary streams originally supported a luxuriant hardwood forest of oak, maple, walnut, hickory, and ash, with now and then a beech and cedar thicket. Bison, deer, elk, wolves, bears, panthers, lynx, wild cats, badgers, skunks, raccoon, and smaller animals flour-

ished here before the white man claimed the area for his own.
Thousands of migratory waterfowl flying through the Mississippi
Valley rested on and around the old glacial lake as they moved
north and south.

The climate is humid continental, long-summer phase. Two-
thirds of the annual precipitation of 31 inches falls from April
through September, averaging 3.2 inches in these months, with
little variation from month to month except in July, which is
considerably drier. Vast oceans of cold arctic air sweeping eastward across the northern half of the continent bring killing frosts
from early October to late April and often into the first week of
May. Chill rain, sleet, snow, and occasionally a howling blizzard
sweep out of the northwest as the winter cyclones move south
and east. This cold, dry arctic air is countered by the warm,
moisture-laden currents that push northward from the Gulf of
Mexico. These currents, in ceaseless conflict as one or the other
sweeps across the region, produce the climate.

In winter, the thermometer may drop as low as 20° below zero
for several nights in a row, usually in January, the coldest month,
when the temperature averages 24°. Summer temperatures may
on occasion reach from 100° to 105° in the shade; July, the hottest
month, averages 75°. The periodic rains of summer combined
with the heat produce high humidity. Even in the severe
droughts of the middle 1930's, the prairies around Elmtown produced good crops. Soil and climate have been combined into an
agricultural complex that has given the region its name: the
Corn Belt.

## Transportation and communication

The old glacial sluiceway, now known as Indian River, has
served as a transportation artery from prehistoric times to the
present. The Indians who dwelt along its banks—Illini, Sac and
Fox, Shawnee, Pottawattomie, Kickapoo, Mascouti, and Miami—
used it as a highway or a boundary. In the seventeenth and
eighteenth centuries French traders, explorers, and missionaries
moved up and down it in their travels from the Great Lakes to
the Gulf of Mexico. Although a few pioneer settlers pushed into
the Indian River country overland from farther east in the 1820's,
the Indians still held the region. But, by the early 1830's, their

hold was breaking, for probably as many as twelve or fifteen white families had staked their claims near the river in what is now Home County. By the close of the 1830's, immigration had begun in earnest, and the river came into its own as a highway. As the country began to "settle up" and produce crops, log rafts and flatboats were used to float them to market. In addition to crops, enterprising settlers floated maple, walnut, and oak logs down river to a sawmill on the river's bank.

The increase of settlers in the late 1830's coincided with the canal-building period in the Middle West. In this "ambitious, empire-building age," canals were projected throughout the plains, lakes, and hills in such a way that the Atlantic Ocean would be connected with the Gulf of Mexico. An essential link in this grandiose dream was to run parallel to Indian River. The legislative act of 1840 which authorized the organization of Home County stipulated that the county seat must be located on canal land and upon, or adjacent to, the canal. This limitation meant that the county seat would have to be on the north side of Indian River, although most of the county lay south of it. The following spring, Elmtown was located near the east-west center of the county at a point where the canal came within about a quarter of a mile of the river.

The canal was completed in 1848, and packet boats drawn by mules or horses began to move mail, produce, freight, livestock, and passengers through the county. It was eclipsed three years later by the arrival of the railroad, but it continued to move some freight for a quarter of a century. Since the railroad ran its tracks to a point about three-quarters of a mile north of the canal, where the proud little county seat village was growing into a town, and on to the west, Elmtown was situated between the canal and the railroad tracks. Physically, it was boxed in on three sides. The river lay beyond the canal to the south; eastward the canal swung north in a wide arc; to the west a creek and swamp more or less limited future growth. The flat prairie to the north was the one area of easy access. (See the map on page 52.)

The original town was plotted in checkerboard fashion with all streets except Canal Street following the cardinal points of the compass. Before the railroad came, the main business houses

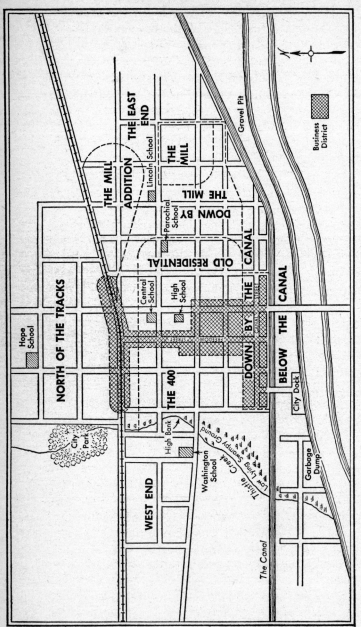

Social Base Map of Elmtown

The names on the map represent residential areas in Elmtown. In the order of prestige value they rank, from high to low: The 400, Old Residential, The West End, Down by the Mill, The Mill Addition, The East End, Down by the Canal, North of the Tracks, Below the Canal.

were built along Canal Street, which ran east and west in an arc on the north side of the canal. The railroad built a depot on the south side of the tracks on the corner of Iron Horse Road and Freedom Street, which ran north and south between the canal and the railway. This development changed the growth pattern of the business section from an east-west axis to a north-south one. The fact that most of the trade area of the community until about 1880 lay south of the river tended to keep the business section close to the canal and along Canal Street until the end of the nineteenth century.

An important element in the original location of the town was the intersection of a north-south road with the river near Canal Street. A ferry linked the north and south sides of the river from early pioneer days until 1855, when a group of enterprising businessmen erected a toll bridge. The toll bridge was a boon to the Elmtown merchants on Canal Street, for it kept the trade from the south of the river in that part of town. But in 1900 the toll bridge was replaced by a free steel structure. In the meantime, the trade area had begun to move on to Freedom Street toward the railroad.

The river played a passive role in communication from the pioneer era until the late 1920's. During the era of "Coolidge prosperity" and agricultural depression, farmers, businessmen, and politicians—with millions of bushels of corn and small grains produced in the region on hand—were searching for cheaper transportation between farm and market than the railroad provided. United by their need, they sought development of a waterway through federal action. Today, a federal-state waterway links the Great Lakes and the Gulf of Mexico, and chains of barges move up and down the river daily carrying the corn, oats, and coal produced locally to distant markets. Elmtown boasts of being a "port," for several times each week barges tie up at the municipal wharf to take on or discharge cargo.

"The automobile lifted us out of the mud" is literally, but not wholly, correct. Five paved state and federal highways run through the community. In addition, several black-topped, farm-to-market roads fan out into the hinterland. These main roads are connected with a grid of graded, all-weather gravel roads that surround almost every section except certain wooded portions near the river. The road grid is so highly improved that 93 per cent of the farms are on graded, all-weather roads. Thus within half an hour's time a person can go by automobile from the most remote farm on the periphery of the communal area to Elmtown in any type of weather. This development has come since the first automobiles chugged and rattled over the mud tracks of town and country about 1910. By 1920, the people were turning to automobiles in ever-increasing numbers, and it was during the middle 1920's that the public roads were graded, paved, and graveled. There are still some mud roads that lead from the farmer's yard to the country road or state highway, but most farmers have graded and graveled their own roads. In town, the outlying streets and roads are neither graded, paved, nor graveled, and the people who live in these poorer sections are not "out of the mud."

The telephone reached Elmtown shortly after 1900, electricity came shortly after the telephone, and the radio about 1921. Today practically every town family, except those south of the canal, has electricity in the home. In 1940, 70 per cent of the farm homes had electricity furnished either by the public service company or by a rural electric cooperative. Almost all town families, and 9 out of 10 farm families, own a radio. Fifty-six per cent of the farm homes had telephones in 1940.

Two sleek, streamlined, high-speed passenger trains pick up and discharge passengers, mail, and express daily. In addition, two steam passenger trains also serve the community. By private automobile or bus, Chicago, Peoria, or Indianapolis can be reached in a few hours over paved highways, for a concrete north-south highway passes near the center of town and an east-west transcontinental one skirts the city limits.

The flat terrain, the absence of any nearby large towns, and the excellent road grid have caused Elmtown to become the center of a highly integrated community. There are no competing towns in the county or on its borders; so the community is roughly rectangular in shape. (See the map on page 55.) The two main concrete highways cut across the area at right angles and transect the border of town. The secondary roads lead either to these highways or into town. Only two hamlets, String-town and Sandburr Village—located on the north-south highway

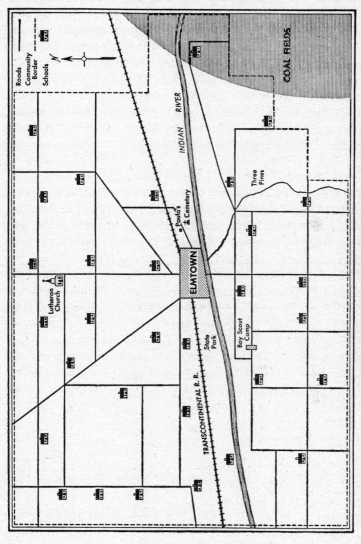

Roads
Community Border
Schools

COAL FIELDS

INDIAN RIVER

Three Pines

Paula's
Cemetery

ELMTOWN

Lutheran Church

Boy Scout Camp

State Park

TRANSCONTINENTAL R. R.

Social Base Map of the Elmtown Community Area

immediately south of Indian River, where 15 to 20 mill workers' families live in small homes surrounded by an acre or two of land—feebly vie with Elmtown for the people's trade, loyalty, and interest. A combination service station and store, a garage, and lunchroom are the only services at these centers. The communal area outside Elmtown is divided into 37 different neighborhoods, but these are little more than names for a rural school district or an area that is associated with some family, landmark, or historic place. Rural people look to Elmtown for their services, feel they are part of it, and are united with it by function, sentiment, and experience.

### Economic base

Elmtown is supported by a combination of agriculture and diversified industries, which range from coal mining to the manufacture of fine leather gloves. In 1940, 37 per cent of the employed male workers were engaged in agriculture; 24 per cent were in manufacturing and mining; and the remaining 39 per cent were scattered throughout the professions, trade, maintenance, and service industries. Every industry group used by the United States Census, except forestry and fishery, was found in Elmtown or Home County in 1940.

Between the two World Wars, three small mass-production industries developed in Elmtown: a paper mill, a foundry, and a metal factory. These establishments will be called hereafter the Mill, the Foundry, and the Factory. Almost all employees in these industries are people born and reared in the community. In 1941–1942, the Mill employed some 700 persons, the Factory 150, and the Foundry 65. In addition, about twenty small manufacturers, employing 5 to 20 persons, operated plants which were largely processors of food and food products, such as milk, cream, and cereals.

The rich coal vein which underlies the region has been mined since the pioneer era by conventional shaft and slope mines. The output of these mines had never been more than 100,000 tons per year. Late in the 1920's, stripping operations were begun on the eastern edge of the communal area in the old glacial depression where the overburden was thin. By 1941, when close to a million tons were produced, strip mining had raised the coal industry to the big-business level.

The Mill, the Foundry, and the largest strip mine are owned, in part, by outsiders; the Factory, the smaller strip mine, and all the smaller factories are owned by local people. Three or four Elmtown families also have extensive interests in the Mill, the Foundry, and the big strip mine, but these are controlled by outside capital. The top local managerial officials in these industries were sent into the community by the owners a quarter of a century earlier. When the study was made, they owned their homes and were considered members of the community. Their children were reared there, had married into local families, and the boys were working into executive positions in the Mill and the Foundry.

The county agricultural agent estimated that corn has been planted on 60 per cent of the crop land year after year for at least half a century. In the past fifteen years, the farmers have changed almost completely from natural to hybrid seed. Along with better methods of tillage, this change has resulted in much higher yields. For instance, in 1924 the average yield was 33 bushels per acre; in 1939 it was 50 bushels. Oats are the chief secondary crop, used in rotation with corn and beans. About 20 per cent of the crop land is planted annually in oats and 10 per cent in soybeans. The remainder is planted in wheat, sorghums, alfalfa, and lesser grasses.

Soybeans are sold a few weeks after threshing and shipped to Chicago or other processing centers. About four-fifths of the oats are marketed and processed elsewhere. The annual corn crop, approximately 5,000,000 bushels,[1] is either marketed directly or "fed out." Extensive cattle-feeding operations are carried on by many farmers throughout the winter months. In late October or early November, Western Poors are bought on the Chicago market and trucked to the farm. There they are fattened on locally grown corn, then hauled to market in the spring and summer. About a score of wealthy farmers have developed pureblood Hereford and Angus herds; there are also a few Shorthorn

---

[1] This figure is for Home County; one-half of this amount is grown around Elmtown.

enthusiasts in the community. Hundreds of farmers raise and fatten from 50 to 200 hogs each year. Corn, cattle, hogs, and chickens have been woven into a highly successful agricultural complex on the rich prairie land.

Except for one garden area of about 60 acres, there are no commercial truck crops. Nearly every farm home and many town ones, however, have a garden where potatoes, root crops, cabbage, lettuce, tomatoes, squash, peppers, eggplant, rhubarb, and berries are grown for family use. Some have a "family orchard" where a few apples, peaches, sour cherries, plums, and pears produce indifferent crops because the trees are not properly pruned or sprayed.

The Elmtown farmer of the present generation has turned from the horse to the gasoline engine as a source of power to pull his plows, cultivators, disks, harrows, harvesters, corn pickers, ensilage cutters, grinders, and elevators. Between 1925 and 1940, the percentage of farms with tractors increased from 34 to 83 per cent, while the number of horses in the county declined 60 per cent. In the same period the farmer has turned from steel-tired to rubber-tired vehicles. More than 92 per cent of the farms had one automobile in 1940, and one-fifth had two.

Home County land has a much higher value per acre than the state average. In 1940, the average value of farm land per acre in the state was almost $82.00; for Home County it was $110.50.[2] Home County also has a much higher tenancy rate than the state; for the state it was 43 per cent; in Home County, 73 per cent. The average size of farms in Home County was also larger than the average for the state. The figures in 1940 were: average size of Home County farms, 164 acres; for the state, 145 acres. The tenant-operated farms averaged 187 acres, and the combined part-owner, part-tenant ones, 250 acres. The foregoing figures are indicative of three things: (1) Home County land is far more valuable than the average land in the state; (2) Home County has a tenancy rate almost twice that of the state; and (3) the size of the farms is related to tenancy. The social implications of these facts will become evident when the school system is

---

[2] These figures were rounded to the nearest quarter-dollar from the figures given in the United States Census for 1940.

discussed in Chapter 6. Before leaving this subject, the reader might be interested to learn that the rich farm land surrounding Elmtown is owned, with few exceptions, by families who now live, or in the past lived, in the community. About 25 families whose ancestors settled here in the pioneer era have accumulated more than 60 per cent of it. Their lands are farmed by tenants under the supervision of the owners, who live in town. The remainder is held largely by small owners who farm it themselves.

## Population

Elmtown is the only community in Home County with a population of more than 2,500. In 1941, it had approximately 6,200 inhabitants, and 3,800 additional persons lived on farms and in non-farm dwellings scattered over 160 square miles of rural communal territory. The town grew steadily, decade by decade, from its founding in 1842 to 1900; for the next twenty years, its population remained stationary at the 1900 figure of 4,500. After 1920, it started to grow again; between 1920 and 1930 the largest net gain since the Civil War era, 1,063 individuals, brought the population to slightly more than 5,550 persons. This growth was related to the mechanization of farms and the development of Elmtown's mills. Between 1930 and 1940, there was another net gain of 577 persons. The rural population grew rapidly from 1850 to 1890, but in the last half-century it has decreased 30 per cent.

The population has been almost exclusively white since the area was settled a century ago; in 1940, 93 per cent was native-born. In 1941, only one Negro family lived in town, and there were only a few Orientals and Mexicans. For the past half-century, the age and sex structure has been typical of the mature portion of the population of the United States; children predominate, and the sexes are evenly balanced.

The early settlers drifted here from states farther east—Ohio, Pennsylvania, New York, Massachusetts, Connecticut, and a few from Virginia and Kentucky—between 1825 and 1850. Their descendants—as well as many later settlers whose ancestral lineage can be traced through four or five generations in the United States, often across several frontiers—like to refer to themselves as the "native stock," the "real Americans," the "old American stock."

The pioneers pre-empted the land at $1.25 per acre from the Federal Government or bought state lands from the canal company. They settled along Indian River and its tributaries, generally in timbered areas; "land that can't grow a tree can't grow a crop—or a man" was a frontier belief. Then, too, the problem of water was real; the springs were close to the streams, and as yet the technique of deep wells and windmills had not been developed. Moreover, the moldboard plow, the plow that broke the prairie, was unknown. These early settlers cleared the land, and built their homes, schools, churches, and roads. They founded little towns around grist mills, sawmills, hotels, saloons, stores, and blacksmith shops. Their leaders formed the first county government, and a few who became financially interested in the canal made fortunes which were turned into land, the investment commodity of the frontier. Socially and culturally, these pioneers set the standards for those who came later.

Four waves of European immigrants have reached the community since the "Americans" drove off the Indians and "brought the blessings of civilization to this beautiful valley." The first European immigrants were Irish laborers brought in by the canal company to dig the canal. These "canal diggers" were a "hard-working, hard-drinking, hell-raising lot." The local people expected the Irish to dig the canal and move on. Many did, but others became permanent settlers and formed the nucleus of an "Irish element." From the beginning the Irish had a different status from the "Americans." They came directly from Ireland, and they were laborers and Catholics, qualities which set them off from the early settlers. Before many years, Irish women and girls came, farms were purchased, businesses founded. The church sent in a priest who built a church and parochial school. Today the Irish are an important element in the population. In point of numbers, they rank next to the Norwegians among the groups who trace their ancestry directly to some European country rather than to the frontiers of colonial America.

The second wave of immigration began in the early 1850's when four or five well-to-do German families, fleeing from the Revolution of 1848, reached Elmtown. These families established a tannery, a brewery, and a foundry and imported German tanners, brewers, molders, and allied workmen to man the shops; a few others started stores, markets, saloons, and industries which flourished for more than a half-century but have now perished. The abandoned factories remain as specters of the role they once played in community life. Today most of the descendants of these Germans are scattered throughout the town, but a few have moved to farms.

The third immigration is identified with the post-Civil War railroad-building era. It was composed of Norwegians who first came in considerable numbers between 1865 and 1870; however, a few families settled in one township in Home County in the late 1840's. The Norwegians bought land from local capitalists who had originally pre-empted entire townships in the northwestern portion of the county and in adjacent counties as a speculative enterprise in the canal era. This land had been held a generation or more without being settled; when the Norwegians came, it was a vast prairie several hundred square miles in extent dotted by shallow lakes in summer and ice fields in winter. The Norwegians bought most of this supposedly worthless land at prices that ranged from $8 to $20 an acre. They tiled, ditched, and drained it, and thereby demonstrated its great fertility—to the astonishment of the "Americans."

The Norwegians began as farmers, but they are now about equally divided between town and country. The townward migration was brought about largely by the size of the families reared by the first two generations, coupled with the fixed supply of land. Technological changes that resulted in each farmer's cultivating more land, on the average, than his father's generation did was also an important factor in this process. The only solution open to a large part of a family was to move off the farm. Currently they are the largest "non-American" element in the population.

A Polish group comprised the last immigration. In 1905, the then existent foundry was closed for several months by a strike; and, in 1906, the employees of the tannery struck, partly in sympathy with the molders and partly for their own ends. In retaliation, a few months later the owners of the tannery and the foundry imported Polish laborers as strikebreakers. The Poles successfully broke the strike and were kept in the employ of these concerns until operations ceased in the early 1920's. In the intervening years, Polish families developed, and a new population element was added to the four pre-existing ones. By 1941, there were some 85 Polish families; all lived in Elmtown, and most made their living in the Factory, the Foundry, or the Mill.

Strictly speaking, this "Polish" element is composed of a polyglot collection of eastern European immigrants, their children, and grandchildren; locally, however, they are all labeled Poles. Many families are mixtures of two or three nationalities. For instance, a father may be Hungarian and a mother Ukrainian. Their children may have married young Poles, Slovenians, and Italians, but there have been few marriages outside this eastern European melange. The Poles arouse strong feelings, apparently for two reasons: they came to the town as strikebreakers, and they happened to be the last immigration. Since they came most recently, they have not been assimilated to the same extent as have the Irish, Germans, and Norwegians. Then, too, their names and features make them more noticeable than the earlier immigrants; thus, it is easier to identify them and to point the finger of scorn.

An extensive lore of fact, legend, and myth is connected with each segment of the population. The Irish are supposed to be Catholics, Democrats, "hell raisers," fighters, "boozers," cheap politicians, troublemakers, and philanderers. The Germans are good, thrifty people, hard workers, money makers, a good element, some of the finest people. The Norwegians are characterized as clannish, cold sexually (but "a lot of the girls go wrong"), disinterested in education, religious ("religious as hell"), a good thrifty sort, hard workers, good citizens. The Poles are believed to be scabs, filthy, ignorant, law breakers, "damn fond of their women and whiskey," "dumb," unable to learn American ways, pretty good citizens, a problem in the school. Needless to say, these descriptions are stereotypes. Therefore, they are not expressed by all the people, perhaps not by a majority, but they were encountered frequently enough to show that they represent the prevailing belief of each segment of the population to which the particular set of beliefs does not happen to apply.

The epithets applied to the Poles, for instance, were voiced by persons of Norwegian or Irish extraction. Poles, in turn, made derogatory remarks about the Irish or Norwegians. Concepts associated with each group probably originated in the "old American stock" and were diffused to the others.

These stereotypes are used as symbolic devices to express social distance between the speaker and the group mentioned. As such, they are conventional mechanisms which Elmtowners have developed to help place people in the social structure on the basis of ethnic origin rather than individual merit. Stereotypes are applied indiscriminately to the group, but individuals may modify the way the stereotype is applied to them by other Elmtowners. This process allows individual variation to take place; it also enables the ambitious individual, who is desirous of achieving a higher place in the social structure than his original group occupies, to climb the social ladder, even if only a rung or two. When he does, the deviation is explained on personal grounds. Conversely, persons who resent the rise of such an individual may call up the stereotype and rely upon it to disparage the upwardly mobile person.

The "Irish invasion" of Cog Wheel, the elite men's club, is an illustration of this resentment. Before the middle 1930's, persons who were identified with the Irish element, for some reason or other, had not been elected to membership; yet the club was one of the oldest of its kind in the Middle West. This fact eventually became the subject of gossip, and an issue was made of it by an Irish clergyman who was stationed in Elmtown but who was not himself an Elmtowner. He related how he maneuvered himself into a position where he was asked to become a member. He then worked to have some Irish leaders invited to become members. In the course of a few years, three men who had Irish ancestry, but who were third- and fourth-generation residents, were invited to join the club. Shortly after the clergyman had gained his objective, he resigned. Then certain anti-Irish members began to drop pointed remarks that were designed to eliminate the Irish element. By the spring of 1942, the campaign had succeeded, and the Irish members originally elected to membership had dropped out and no additional ones had been elected. Needless to point out, no Pole had ever been considered for membership, but there were a few persons of German and Norwegian descent in the club.

In 1941, Elmtowners thought of themselves as Americans and Middle Westerners. They were, but, when specific issues arose in some phase of community life, ethnic heritage often entered the discussion in some way. When an Elmtowner wanted to explain why some action had occurred, he was very likely to bring in the ethnic background of a person, family, or group. To illustrate: At the time of our first visit, the community was preparing to celebrate its centennial. On this occasion, our impression was that this was a community project and that all elements in the population would take part. After we moved to the community, we heard stories of one kind or another about those who had participated in this glorified pageant of the past. As motion pictures of the parade and other festivities were shown, scenes explained, and persons identified with different roles, we began to realize that in general only prominent families, and a few others not quite so prominent, had been included. Further questioning brought out the fact that the names mentioned had, in most instances, a very definite Anglo-Saxon sound. When we casually commented upon this fact, we were told that the centennial was a pioneer pageant and that only "Americans" had been in Elmtown at that time (a century ago).

The question was asked: Were the people who helped build the community since the pioneer era included? The answer was invariably the same, "No." Eventually, it became clear that the backers of the centennial were primarily interested in glorifying their own ancestry; therefore they limited participation in the pageant, in the main, to families who traced their ancestry *in the community* to that era. This action was symptomatic of the way the social system operated, as well as an indication of how pride of ancestry was used by those in control to limit participation in community activities.

### A "typical" community

Elmtown's institutions are typical of a Middle Western countyseat town which politically, religiously, educationally, professionally, economically, and socially dominates its tributary area. All types of basic businesses and services common to a town of

6,000 people in the Corn Belt are found here. In addition, it is proud of its locally owned and published daily newspaper and its hospital. Two banks serve the financial needs of the farms, industries, and stores, and a small-loan business caters to the "little people." Several national insurance companies have local agents here. Chain stores compete with those owned by merchants whose families have been in business for two or three generations. A dozen doctors, 5 dentists, 20 lawyers, 15 nurses, and several other independent professionals live and practice in Elmtown. Organized churches in Elmtown itself consist of one Catholic as well as nine Protestant, including one Norwegian Lutheran; there is another Norwegian Lutheran church in the country. There are no state institutions either in the community or in Home County; neither are there any colleges, health resorts, or other establishments which might give it a distinctive character.

In the twelve states comprising the Middle West, there were 215 towns in 1940 that ranged between 5,000 and 10,000 in population. One hundred and eight of the 215 were the largest towns in their counties; they were also county-seat towns. Moreover, they were classed as agricultural-industrial; that is, between 25 and 50 per cent of their male workers were employed in agriculture, and more than 20 per cent were engaged in industry. Elmtown was one of these towns. In terms of its location, size, economic base, population, and institutions, Elmtown may be characterized as a typical Middle Western town. If the communal area is included, the "typical town" can be called a "typical community." In this study, town and country were treated as a unit. Therefore, Elmtown and its dependent institutional area may be said to be a "typical Middle Western community" functionally, structurally, culturally, and historically. Moreover, it may be assumed with some confidence that the knowledge gained about its social structure could be duplicated in any similar community in the Middle West with only minor changes in detail.

# 4

---

# THE PRESTIGE STRUCTURE

AN ELABORATE SOCIAL STRUCTURE, integrated mainly around institutional relationships—family, job, church, property, law, government, health, recreation—and prestige, organizes Elmtowners' daily activities. Age and sex are minor but important dimensions of it. There were indications that this structure would have been complicated further if there had been a larger representation of Negroes and Mexicans in the population.[1]

The outlines of this structure became clear within the first two months of the field work, but details were not fitted into their proper places until much later, because an understanding of the social structure as a system of interpersonal relationships was dependent upon the accumulation of knowledge about the people, the way they regarded one another, the way they acted, and their explanations of their behavior. To comprehend completely the minor bypaths, alleys, and blind corners in this social system, a person would have to live a lifetime in Elmtown. Even then it is doubtful that he would understand the whole in all its subtle meanings, for this could come only by personal participation over long periods in every phase of organized social life, combined with intimate knowledge of the people, their backgrounds, activities, interests, obligations, and aspirations.

## Values and the social structure

The main aspects of the social structure are linked together by the evaluation system which characterizes the culture. "Who is who" and "what is what" are determined by the way Elm-

[1] One Negro and six Mexican families resided near the railroad tracks in 1941. They had no children in the study, so their presence is ignored.

towners evaluate persons, ideas, things, functions, and each other's actions. The community is a whispering gallery of gossip and narrative about what so-and-so did on such-and-such an occasion. A large part of the talk that goes on between one Elmtowner and another involves other Elmtowners; quite frequently all the persons are well known to one another. An essential element in this talk is judgment, good or bad, about what the person talked about has done, is alleged to have done, intends to do, or the gossipers think he is going to do. Elmtowners have a vast store of valuable personal, often intimate, information about other Elmtowners which they have accumulated through years of living together, for the families of two-thirds of the people have been living in the community for two generations and about one-third for four. This knowledge is shared by dozens of other persons, often many more in the case of the prominent, the notorious, or the victims of unfortunate circumstances. Private lives are not private because other Elmtowners are aware of what other Elmtowners do from day to day.

In such a situation, John Jones is not merely male, adult, human. He is John Jones, a resident of Elmtown, Home State, citizen, farmer, owner or tenant, a good farmer or a poor farmer, an honest farmer or one noted for sharp practices. John Jones is more than a farmer; he is a member of a family; possibly he is connected with several other discrete family units by kinship ties. He may be son, husband, father, nephew, or uncle. Whatever his position, the different functions he performs in his relations with the many facets of the social structure and the role he plays in each are *evaluated by* Elmtowners who know him.

The John Jones family is identified by its ethnic background—"American," Norwegian, Irish, English, Polish, or German. It derives its livelihood from some economic pursuits; its income is scaled from a few hundred to many thousands of dollars a year. It owns real property in varying amounts, or none. It lives somewhere in some kind of abode. It may or may not have a connection with one of the local churches; if it does, its members play certain roles which are evaluated by other Elmtowners. The family has some identifying political label: Republican, Democrat, Independent, or "damn radical." The children above six years of age, and practically all adults, have or have had some contact with the educational system, and the educational level attained by each member is known generally by several persons.

Institutions and associations, as well as persons and families, are an integral part of the value system. The Mill is a good place, the fertilizer factory a "lousy" place to work; the Mill employs the "better element"; the fertilizer factory hires "anyone." Each grocery, hardware, dry goods, ten-cent, furniture, and drug store is evaluated in comparison with other stores that sell the same type of merchandise. Quality of goods, prices, treatment of the customer, ownership, type of employee, trade catered to, reputation of owner and employees—all enter into the evaluational process. Restaurants and taverns are rated from clean to "dirty holes" or "dives." The theaters are ranked in a series from top to bottom. The churches too are placed in a prestige hierarchy, with the Federated (the "society" church) at the top and the Faithful Holiness Tabernacle, located in a loft facing the canal, at the bottom. Even the men's service clubs are evaluated differently; one is "top drawer," the other is made up of the "little fellows" along Freedom Street. The high-ranking one holds its meetings in the dining room of the Country Club; the other meets in a room connected with a tavern. Fraternal organizations are assigned graduated ratings. One women's club is very exclusive; consequently it rates highest. Its members, as one member said, "come from the older, more exclusive, well-established families. The other club selects its members from newcomers here, but they are all nice ladies, nevertheless." Dozens of private associations—bridge clubs, bowling teams, and fishing, hunting, and boating clubs—are given some type of rating. The Country Club enjoys a unique prestige position; it is the only one of its kind in the county.

## The class system

That the prestige structure is stratified into classes in the thoughts as well as the actions of Elmtowners is apparent in their remarks about the community and in the questions they ask. Various forms of this query were often put to us: "I suppose you have discovered that there are several social strata (social classes or different kinds of crowds) in this town?" Another form was: "Do you know how this town is organized?"

The following illustrations are representative of the great amount of evidence on the class consciousness of Elmtowners:

1. These comments were made by a professional woman with wide contacts in the community (she was later placed in class III):

> There are definite classes here. The top group is made up of people with money and family connections. You can rate, though, if you have enough money and little or no family. This is a tragedy because people with real family background, breeding, and education do not rate unless they have money. I am disturbed at how these people look down on others in town.
>
> Below this level is one composed of the prominent business and professional families who have family but not much money. Family is important here, but it is not so important as leadership. The small businessmen, foremen at the mills, teachers, machinists, service station operators, and people like that are in a lower, but middle, group.
>
> The ordinary workman in the foundry, the Mill, the mines, and the clerks in the stores are mostly ranked as lower class around here, but they are not so low as the older Poles, the canal squatters, and the people back of the old tannery.

This woman explicitly stated that there were classes in Elmtown. Moreover, she identified five strata, and gave her reasons for placing people in each level, but she did not indicate how she believed the classes were distributed in the total population.

2. Henry Dotson, a lifetime resident prominent in business circles, was interested in the study and convinced that an understanding of the class system was essential if we were to understand the activities of the high school students. Therefore he volunteered to tell us his opinions about the class system, its manner of working, and the position of individuals in it. Fortunately, he was not averse to having his statements recorded. Mr. Dotson spent the hours from eight o'clock one evening until one the next morning dictating his impressions. The following material was selected from the transcription of the interview:

> I know what the system is, and I'll try to tell you how it operates. I won't be able to tell you all of it, but I'll tell you the main class groups and the main sections in some of these classes, and I'll give you illustrations. We will start out with the top and work down.

The top class is what we call the four hundred or society class. A lot of these people are three-ninety-eights, but they think they're Four Hundred. The society class has a lot of families on the fringe, families who have had money and lost it. This whole business is based on two or three things. First, I'd say money is the most important. In fact, nobody's in this class if he doesn't have money; but it just isn't money alone. You've got to have the right family connections, and you've got to behave yourself, or you get popped out. And if you lose your money, you're dropped. If you don't have money, you're just out. There's no use talking about people being in a certain class or a certain portion of a class unless they are accepted by the people in that group as equals. If they're not accepted, they just don't belong in that group. So, acceptance is what I am going to use along with family connections and money. [Many illustrations of the "society class" were given here.]

The next class starts with the fringe and takes in certain other elements. This is what you'd better call the upper middle class. This level is made up mainly of the women who dominate the Country Club, along with some other groups, especially the top and the fringe. The society class dominates the Country Club, but not actively. They really control things from behind the scenes. The women in this class are very active in the social life of the Country Club; they split a gut to do things right. It's amusing the way the women in this crowd work and scheme for a little social favor with the society class. These women work hard to keep the activities going out there, but I'm pretty sure they don't have so much say-so in the Country Club as they think they do. Now here are some illustrations of the type of people you find in this class: [the interviewee used names, but we have substituted the occupations or positions some of the persons named held] the president of the First National Bank; the manager of the Public Service Company; the personnel manager at the Mill; most of the lawyers; several doctors; owners of large, family-operated farms who are interested in social affairs; owners of insurance agencies; the Superintendent of Schools [and persons of this nature]. All the active leaders in the large churches in town are in this class, but most of them do not belong to the Country Club. They are just segments of the same class.

The next class down doesn't have any social connections of consequence. I call this the lower middle class. You won't find this class with any social connections outside of the churches and the lodges. Lots of these people have good jobs with good incomes, and many have good businesses, but they don't have any social life at all. Their activities are wrapped up in the church, the Legion, the lodges, and the little clubs around town. Take Harry Glick, the foreman of the forming room at the Mill. Harry's a pretty good friend of mine; so I can tell you about his social life. It consists entirely, absolutely, and completely in going around to Catholic dinners. He really enjoys that. I guess it's all right if you enjoy that sort of thing, but I don't. There are a lot of people in this class who like that sort of thing. You go over to the Lutheran, the Methodist, or the Baptist Church and you will see them at every church dinner. These people go for church dinners in a big way.

A number of substantial farmers are in this class. They run their farms, pay their debts, send their kids to school, own good cars and machinery, and run their farms in a creditable manner. For instance, take Bill and Frank Emerson, who run the Emerson Implement Company. They're in this class. They have a good sound farm background. They went away to school a couple of years; later their father bought them that business. They started in a small way, but now they are coming along nicely and doing pretty well.

The working class is made up of good solid people who live right but never get any place. They work at the Mill, over in the Factory, and in the mines. They work as clerks in the stores, own little businesses like neighborhood groceries, a few trucks—that type of thing.

There is a really low class here that is a lulu. It is made up of families who are not worth a . . . damn, and they don't give a damn. They're not immoral; they're not unmoral; they're plain amoral. They simply don't have any morals. They have animal urges and they respond to them. They're like a bunch of rats or rabbits. Have you ever heard of the Sopers? They don't have any common decency. They're a tribe like the Jukes and the Kallikaks. They shell out kids like rabbits, and they never go any place in school. They're always getting in jams. The kids have been problems for years. The poor little kids are half-starved and ragged all the time. There are dozens of families like the Sopers in this town. They squat along the canal, and in back of the old tannery and up north of the tracks by the old abandoned coal chutes. A few are scattered in shacks along the river and out in the strip-mine area.

3. The following materials were given to us by a member of one of the most highly respected families in the community, under circumstances similar to those reported for Mr. Dotson. One afternoon, when we had been discussing the study in general, he remarked, "To understand that high school, you have to

understand this town." When we asked him what he meant, he
explained:

We have an aristocracy of wealth in this town, and a hell of a
lot of poor people. The kids in the high school know this. Those
kids are wise; we don't fool them. I knew what this town was like
when I was in high school and these kids do too. They know who
the silk stockings are, and the pegs most people belong on. There
are only three or four silk stockings in high school now who come
from the families of the top aristocrats.

Jack Woodson and Gordon Schweitzer belong to the real, old
aristocracy. Their families have had money for four generations.
Both are great-grandsons of early families here. Jack Woodson has
the blood of the five original great families in his veins. He has a
second cousin in the high school, but they don't have anything to
do with one another. The families have drifted apart completely.
One of Jack's grandfather's sisters married into the canal Irish
against the family's will. Her father gave her her share of the estate,
but her husband was a typical Mick and they ran through it. That
family has been looked down upon by the silk stockings ever since
I can remember because they're poor. If you lose your money, the
aristocrats push you out. It's an aristocracy of wealth, nothing else.
That's the way it goes through the generations. It makes me laugh
sometimes.

The inner circle of top aristocrats is made up of people who have
a close community of interest; they all have property and a good
income. They run around in pretty closely knit groups, and it's
mighty hard for a stranger to break into one. Mother says it took
her ten years to be invited into a whist club that was made up of
the silk stockings of her day. Mother thinks that was her greatest
social triumph. Most of the husbands are dead now, but the women
still play whist and 500. That's the most powerful group in town.
I call them the first generation of matriarchs because they're so
powerful. There used to be twelve couples in the old Whist Club,
and they were known as the Big Twelve. There are only eleven
left; so they are often called the Big Eleven. This is the group that
can really put the pressure on. They own a lot of interests, land,
town property, the banks and other things, and they have great
prestige and power. When they want something done, they bear
down on their children, in-laws, relatives, and grandchildren. If
voting's involved, they let their tenants and employees know how
they feel. When an issue comes up, I can see this crowd pull together. I've seen them take sides on so many issues I can just

about tell ahead of time how they'll line up. When something comes up, the matriarchs run to the telephone and those lines buzz. Then they visit each other and talk it over. This is the crowd around here you'll have to be careful with; they can freeze an outsider so quick it's not worth talking about.

When I want something, I always go to this group. I usually work it this way. I first sell Mother on the idea and she does the rest. If she puts it over with old Mrs. Easton, that's Jack Woodson's maternal grandmother, it's as good as done. I think old Mrs. Easton is the most powerful person in town. If I can convince Mother, and if Mother can convince her, she rounds the matriarchs up behind it. If I can't get them on my side, I know I'm licked; so I drop the idea.

Those top aristocrats are all on the same level, but there are several groups. There's the old matriarchs I just told you about. Then there's the Big Eight. It's made up of four couples who have a very close community of interest: horses, good liquor, sports, travel, and gambling. Mother still calls this the younger group, but there are three groups younger than this one. The youngest one is in high school.

We ran around in a pretty closely knit crowd before the Deweys came to town. I knew Mrs. Dewey in school; in fact, I went out with her a few times. So when they came to town, we kind of took them in and then the old group seemed to break up. We have reformed with the Deweys in and the Jensens out. Since we reformed, people like Helen Jensen, who is very jealous of Mary Dewey, call us the "no longer young club." The Jensens now move in a group we consider a class below us.

There's a lot of jealousy among the women in these two groups, especially toward Mary Dewey. I think all the women and most of the men in that group would like to get into our group. I get a big kick out of some of the things these women say and how they pick at each other. Mary Dewey and Helen Jensen get clawed more than anyone else. Boy, Mary Dewey's a climber but she's made the grade; that's what counts. The way she manages things has burned up a lot of women in this town. I have to keep still though, because my wife takes it pretty seriously.

Bill Jensen and I used to be very close friends, but we're gradually drifting apart. We seem to be going in different social groups. We used to hunt and golf together, but I haven't been out with him for three years. We're still friendly but we don't go out as we used to. Since we've reorganized, we're gradually becoming part of the Big Eight. As we grow older, we're running with that crowd more and more. There's a close community of interest between us. We like to eat, gamble, drink, travel, play golf, ride horseback, and we're all active in the Country Club.

Well, this whole town's like this. It's made up of tight little circles of people who have the same community of interest, about the same amount of money and act the same. They're all on different levels just like a stairway. You go out there in town and talk to people and you'll find little circles and crowds picking and clawing at each other just like the women in our crowd do with the crowd Helen Jensen's in now. If you know this town, you can hang just about everyone on the peg he belongs on.

Take that Soper tribe. They're absolutely on the bottom. Old Jake Soper has been sent to the State Farm seven or eight times in the last ten years, and four of the boys have been in jail for one thing or another. Three of the girls have illegitimate children. Old Jake is supposed to be the father of two of them. That outfit has been on relief for the last six or seven years. The kids don't go to school and you can't make them. Pearl Soper was in school with me. The fellows used to hit her like a punching bag when she was in the eighth grade. She didn't even finish. Just quit and hung around the tannery flats taking on anyone at two bits a throw. No one in that tribe has ever amounted to a damn.

Now do you see why I say you can't understand that high school until you know this town?

These Elmtowners told us several things about the community's prestige structure which may be summarized briefly as follows:

1. They asserted the existence of classes and gave them names.
2. They assigned differential prestige to the several strata.
3. They identified particular persons as members of specific classes.
4. They mentioned some criteria for placing persons in each class.
5. They thought of themselves as members of classes.
6. Finally, and this is important from our viewpoint, they associated behavior with class.

## Stratification of the prestige structure

As similar material was accumulated, it became evident that Elmtowners think of themselves as members of classes and that they act in part toward one another on the basis of their judgments about each other's class position. Persons who possess a cluster of similar values tend to be grouped into more or less common prestige positions. Persons with other values and correlated traits are assigned other levels or "pegs."

The way this process works was brought to our attention shortly after we moved to Elmtown. An attorney asked in a friendly way if we were getting acquainted. He was told we were. Then he went on to tell us how he and his wife were evaluated when they came to Elmtown a quarter of a century earlier.

I discovered the first two months I was here that this town is class-conscious. When I first came here I went around to a few affairs and I met some people. I don't remember where it was I met Homer McDermott of the four hundred crowd. One evening I was walking down the street and I saw him coming the other way. He held out his hand and said, "Good evening, Mr. Jennings." I saw he was disposed to visit; then he began to ask me questions something like this: "Mr. Jennings, I understand you are a new attorney in town."

I said, "Yes, I hope to practice law here."

"My family has been here for a long time." Then, as we strolled along the street, he asked, "Mr. Jennings, did you learn your law in a law office?"

"No, I did not."

"Did you go to law school?"

"Yes."

"Well, Mr. Jennings, where did you attend law school?"

"I attended the University of Michigan Law School and finished last year."

"Oh, you did! Well, that's the very finest law school, they say." He was fumbling around for another question, and I just let him fumble. Then he said, "Mr. Jennings, did you belong to a legal fraternity?"

"Yes, I belonged to a legal fraternity."

"Mr. Jennings, what legal fraternity did you join?" I told him. "Oh, Mr. Jennings, that is the very finest legal fraternity; all the 'Betas' at Home State University join that fraternity. That is a very fine thing." He went on like that for a little while and then asked, "Did you go to college or did you go directly to law school?"

"Mr. McDermott, I have a kind and indulgent father. He made a little money and he wanted me to have an education; so he sent me away to college."

McDermott went on, "Ah, Mr. Jennings, I see. Very good. And where did you attend college?"

"Oh, I went to a Presbyterian college in southern Ohio."

"Oh, I see; religious colleges are very fine institutions!" Then he got around to the point and asked, "Did you belong to a fraternity in college?"

I said, "Yes, college education with all the trimmings."

Then he asked, "What fraternity did you belong to?" When I told him I belonged to Phi Gamma Delta, he said, "Oh, that is a very good fraternity. My fraternity, the 'Betas' at Home State, were always close friends with the 'Phi Gams.'"

*About that time, I saw what he was up to: he was trying to place me socially.* His next shot was, "Did you participate in social activities in college, Mr. Jennings?"

"Oh, yes, we had two literary societies; I belonged to one of them. I debated and things like that." That seemed to satisfy him and so we went our ways. About two weeks later, Mrs. Jennings was put through the same kind of a grilling by old Mrs. Sweitzer. When new people come to this town, the local people want to know who they are and where they come from.

Such a "grilling" is part of the Elmtown ritual of becoming acquainted. Mr. Jennings was not merely a lawyer; he was a fraternity man, a college debater, a Michigan Law School graduate—symbols that were valued highly in Elmtown. Mrs. Jennings also met the test when it was applied to her by Mrs. Sweitzer. Since the conclusion reached was that the Jennings' were pleasant, educated persons with family background, the McDermotts, Sweitzers, Binghams, and other established families in the four hundred soon assigned them a position in the prestige structure equivalent to their own, on the basis of the prestige-giving values and symbols the Jennings family possessed.

Persons and families with a cluster of traits appropriate to the "upper class," such as those of the Jennings', McDermotts, and Schweitzers, were identified with this stratum by other persons in it, as well as by persons in other strata. For example, Luke Jenkins, trucker in the Factory, illustrated this tendency, as well as some of the important factors in the evaluation process, when we remarked, while visiting in his home, that Elmtown was a nice place:

Yes, Elmtown is a very nice city. We like it, but it has its draw-
backs like any other place. It's a town of very few rich people. I
doubt if there's a person in town with a million dollars in cash, except Johnson, the circus king. Several other people around here
have that much but they are all landed people. They're land poor.
They're like the Hewitts. Young Hewitt and his mother are looked
upon as the wealthiest people in the county. They own more
land than any other person here in town, but they never earned a
dime of it. Old Lady Hewitt inherited three or four sections and
she married about five or six. Old Hewitt, before he died, accumulated four or five more sections by sharp deals. Now young Hewitt
will get all that. His wife will inherit three or four farms and several houses here in town.

There are lots of poor people here, too, a hell of a lot. All this
end of town is full of poor people. [When Mr. Jenkins said this, he
waved his arm toward the Mill.] There are a lot of poor people
above the railroad tracks, too. The real poor people live below the
Mill and east of the highway above the tracks. They call that Polish
Town around here, but really they're not Poles. There are a few
Polish up there, a few Austrians, some Bohemians and a lot of English. I'm English myself, but not that kind of English. The English
who live up among those foreigners are what we call "Bunglish."
They used to work in the shaft mines up in there.

We're poor too, but we're not so poor as a lot of people. Since I
got on down at the Factory, we're doing all right. Before that,
things were pretty tough. For two years we were on relief.

Luke used a number of different values to categorize the town:
wealth or lack of it, family background, ethnic origin, and
morals. He implied that there are two kinds of rich people:
those with liquid wealth (Johnson the circus king) and those with
landed wealth (the Hewitts and others like them). He also indicated that there are two kinds of poor people: the respectable
poor like himself, and the poor who live among the "Poles" and
behind the Mill. He also gave us some idea of his own evaluation of himself: he identified himself with the working group
who are poor, but not so poor as many families.

### Analysis of class evidence

The analysis of interview materials revealed four salient points
about the class system. First, institutional functions are evalu-

ated differentially; second, values are ascribed to persons who perform the function; third, social relations are channelized along class lines; and fourth, behavior is associated with class position. We shall now turn to a brief explanation of each of these points.

That institutional functions are differentially evaluated was unmistakable from the remarks and actions of Elmtowners. Some are viewed as very desirable, others are not so desirable, still others are avoided because of the low value they carry. Thus, banking and the practice of law and medicine are evaluated highly, whereas picking papers, bottles, and junk out of the town's trash dump possessed a very low value. The specific value assigned to a function belongs to the function rather than to the person who performs it. For instance, ownership of land is evaluated highly. If the owner does not fit the role associated with the function, he is disparaged, not ownership as such. Township relief is opprobrious; therefore, relief occupies a very low position in the scale of values irrespective of the individual on relief.

Evaluation of functions has three principal facets: pecuniary, power, and moral. The pecuniary is symbolized by the number of dollars a person receives for performing the function. The power facet is characterized by a series of conventional rights, duties, and privileges associated with the function. The moral aspect is symbolized by the degree of approbation or derogation the society attaches to the function. These three facets are integral with one another, and they result in the assignment of prestige to the function. Although values assigned to functions are not equated in the pecuniary, power, and moral areas, they commonly form a more or less coherent pattern. The association of values with functions applies to hundreds of different institutional offices which vary from formal continuous ones, such as president of the Home County Bank, to periodic ones, such as the placement of wreaths on veterans' graves in Everest Cemetery on Memorial Day.

The ascription of the value assigned to an institutional function to the person performing it eventually results in the transfer of values from institutional offices to persons. In this process the functionary becomes identified with his function, and the position the function occupies in the hierarchy of values becomes associated with the person. This transfer process carries over from husband to wife to dependent children, and from ancestors to descendants with certain modifications we shall not discuss here. As a consequence, a person tends to have high prestige if he functions in an institution which is evaluated highly by the culture, as for instance banking and medicine. On the contrary, a person is assigned low prestige if he functions in an institution that is discredited in the moral aspects of the value system. This generalization may be given point by reference to Polish Paula, the "madame" of the Elmtown brothel, who has an income of more than $10,000 a year. She also has power, as measured by the enforcement of law—her "house" has not been raided for over a quarter of a century. Yet she occupies a very low prestige position, even though she has "helped build, remodel, or pay off the mortgage on every church in town." On the other hand, the chairman of the Board of Directors of the Home County Land Bank is much sought after by every committee that stands for decency and good government because of his moral record. Yet he is known in religious circles as a "tightwad" and a "skinflint."

Another example is the differences in evaluation between garbage collectors and insurance salesmen. From a strictly utilitarian viewpoint, the collection of garbage in a town of 6,000 is more important to health and welfare, both collectively and individually, than the sale of insurance as a hedge against individual disaster. But the culture places distinctly different values on these two functions; collecting garbage is very menial, selling insurance is dignified. Therefore, high prestige is assigned to the insurance salesman, and the garbage collector is placed very low in the hierarchy.

Literally thousands of different values are shared and used daily by Elmtowners to assign to one another positions in the prestige structure. *The important ones are associated primarily with the economic functions from which the family derives its livelihood, and secondarily with its connections in the familial, property, ethnic, religious, political, educational, recreational, and welfare systems.* Personal and family history, reputation, behavior, and character are also of considerable significance; age, sex, and physical appearance are taken into consideration, but they are of minor importance in the determination of prestige positions in the class structure.

The third characteristic of the class system, the channelization of intimate associations between persons along class lines, is evident in the repeated references to cliques. The interviews cited above either explicitly state or imply that each stratum is composed of persons and families who have formed closely knit social groups or cliques [2] whose members are recognized to have approximately equal standing in the community.

The clique is integrated around two types of factors: first, a commonly shared set of likes and dislikes which tie the members together and which separate them from other groups; and, second, standing in the community or class. Although members of different cliques may be enemies in a social sense, they commonly work together when an issue involving class interests is at stake. As John Bingham remarked with reference to the "top aristocrats," "When an issue comes up, I can see this crowd pull together." On all levels, the clique is the social group within which persons work out most of their intimate, personal relationships during periods of leisure and recreation.

Mrs. Daniel, a housewife and mother of a high school boy, was talking about the experiences she had had in the ten years the family had lived in Elmtown when she said:

> The first two or three years we were here, we were out of things. We were strangers, and it was a little hard to get acquainted, but we have become gradually a part of a definite group here in town. We meet around at one another's houses, play bridge, and have nice dinners. All the women pride themselves on being good cooks. None of the women in this group smoke and none of them drink. We just meet, play bridge, eat, talk, and have a good time. *There are other upper middle class groups, but we do not associate with them. In some of them, the women smoke and drink and gamble. Our group doesn't believe in these things; so we never mix socially.*

[2] A clique is an informal group composed of a minimum of two to about twenty persons. It tends to be age- and sex-graded within a relatively narrow range of prestige positions. Adult cliques usually do not include more than two classes, most frequently one, in their membership. Cliques are the smallest organized units within a class, but there are many cliques of different ages within the class.

There are several upper class groups who are above us socially and economically. The Joseph Stones are in one of these. The Stones live in back of us. I hardly know Mr. Stone, but I know Mrs. Stone as a neighbor. She is real nice; she has invited me to two of her bridge parties. I have had her over here twice. We talk back and forth as neighbors in the yard, but Mr. Daniel and I have never been invited to any of their parties and we never invite them here. They belong to a group that is spoken of as the Little Eight. There is also a Big Eight group of upper class people. Then there is an older upper class group that is sometimes referred to as the Older Federated group. I hear them spoken of that way but I don't think they go very regularly. I am sure they do not take their religious obligations too seriously.

Then there is a younger upper class group. It is often spoken of as the Social Register. The Scott Hewitts across the street are in this group. They are very exclusive, especially Mrs. Hewitt. I would not say she is a snob, but she certainly hasn't been at all friendly or neighborly. We have been neighbors for seven years, but she has never asked me to one of her parties, and she has them all the time. Mrs. Hewitt is a sister of Howard Worthington; he's in the Little Eight. Their father died recently and left the entire Scott and Worthington fortunes to them. The Frederick Deweys are also in that group. They came here about the time we did. Mr. Dewey is said to be a brilliant engineer, and Mrs. Dewey comes from a very wealthy banking family in Peoria. They are reputed to own a large part of the mines and mills at Diamond City. I don't know Mrs. Dewey at all well, but I have been told by everyone who knows her that she is a very kind, warmhearted, considerate woman. I have had a couple of women clean for me who have worked for Mrs. Dewey, and they have never said an unkind word about her. She seems to be a very forthright person. The Deweys are the only new family in that group.

Mrs. Daniel was clear on a number of points relevant to the present discussion; first, she and Mr. Daniel belonged to a small, closely knit social group or clique whose members met frequently on an equal basis; second, within the group, she implied that association was intimate, free, and voluntary; and, third, membership in the group was centered around mutual likes and dislikes. And so far as the Daniels were concerned, membership in this clique was earned only after they had lived in Elmtown for several years. Another point of importance is Mrs. Daniel's reference to cliques and classes and the place her group occupied in the class order: "upper middle class." She also told us that there are "upper class" groups, and other "upper middle class" groups similar in position to the one to which the Daniels belonged. A few persons were identified as members of the different groups, and some criteria of membership in each were laid down: age, sex, family connections, wealth, period when a family came to the community, group likes and dislikes, and connection with a particular church.

Many Elmtowners made these points as they tried to tell us "how things work around here." Some were more articulate than others, *but almost every person who talked about the way the community was organized made the point that social relations were organized around cliques and classes.*

The association between class position and behavior made so consistently by Elmtowners will become clear in the next chapter where the socio-cultural complex which characterizes each of Elmtown's five classes is described in detail. At this time we state only that this association was made in one way or another by practically every adolescent and adult. Some put it on a class basis; others used the clique to illustrate their point.

# 5

## CULTURAL CHARACTERISTICS OF THE FIVE CLASSES

ELMTOWNERS IN GENERAL are inconsistent in the way they talk and act with reference to the idea of classes. If they are asked bluntly, "Do you believe there are 'classes' in the community?" they are very likely to say, "No." Yet, they will tell you the Binghams are "a leading family here," or the "Sweitzers are like the Binghams, Woodsons, McDermotts, and Jennings'. These families are different from the rest of us; they are very exclusive. I guess you'd call them our aristocracy." During the course of the conversation, the same speaker will say that there are several different "types of families" in the community and, justifying his judgment by describing the "way they live," place them in different categories. The democratic tradition that there are no classes in American society is the reason for this type of behavior. Therefore, Elmtowners deny the existence of class directly but act as if classes exist. However, many Elmtowners openly say that there are three classes in the community, "upper," "middle," and "lower," but when they are requested to name persons in, let us say, the "lower class" they generally divide the class into the "good" lower class people and the "worthless, ne'er-do-wells." The same kind of break appears in the "middle class." Separation of the "middle class" into "upper middle" and "lower middle" is quite conventional.

Even though Elmtowners are inconsistent in their designations of a particular class, the systematic analysis of selected cultural traits associated with each of the five classes, based upon data collected from the 535 families of the adolescents, supplemented by interviews and observations, reveal that the pos-

session of a constellation of differentially evaluated social symbols—functional, pecuniary, religious, educational, reputational,
power, lineage, proper associates, memberships in associations—
are relied upon by Elmtowners to "hang people on the peg they
belong on," to determine "their place in the community" or "their
standing in life."

### Class I [1]

Wealth and lineage are combined through the economic, legal,
and family systems in such a manner that membership in class I
is more or less stabilized from one generation to another. Consequently the members of class I tend to have their position
ascribed through inheritance. In view of this, very few of its
members have achieved their positions in the prestige structure
through their own efforts. Because the station of the family is
transferred to the children and because few persons achieve
class I positions through their own efforts, only a very few persons are able to enter its ranks in any one generation. Although
wealth is the prime requisite for achieving positions associated
with class I, once such positions have been attained, they do not
need to be reinforced by further pecuniary accumulation. In
fact, there can be a decline in the amount of wealth possessed
by a family through two or more generations without the loss
of its class identification, providing it conforms to the approved
social code. If some members show an inclination to do so, the
family may recoup its fortunes through "brilliant marriages" or by
the help of other families. It is generally assumed, both within
and outside the class, that persons in this stratum have the
"ability" to provide the material things customarily associated
with a class I family. Class I persons strongly emphasize the inheritance of abilities and characteristics; they consider acquired
traits the outward expressions of "hereditary qualities." This
belief is expressed in the doctrine of "good blood" and "bad
blood." It is assumed that class I families have "good blood"
and that the lower ranking classes have "bad blood" in increasing potency as descent of the social scale occurs.

[1] Although only 4 adolescents belonged to class I families the characteristics of this class are described here because of its importance in the control
of Elmtown's institutions.

Marriage between social equals is desired but achieved only in about four cases out of five. Marriage with a family from a lower stratum is strongly disapproved—even the threat of one brings the force of gossip and personal pressures into play to "break the affair off" before "something happens." On the other hand, a potential marriage between equals is approved, and subtle pressures are brought to bear by relatives and friends to see it consummated, for a "successful" marriage will bring two estates together and assure the family of its station for another generation. Divorce is condemned in the strongest terms, since it not only breaks a family but also brings disgrace upon the relatives. Moreover, it often results in the division of a family heritage, an undesirable consideration in this competitive economy. Children are desired, but only one or two and, at most, three; too many children break estates into too many pieces.

When children are born, they are delivered in a large city hospital, usually in Chicago, by a specialist recommended to the family by a local doctor to take the case during the lying-in period. Children are carefully attended and given every consideration due future scions of a proud "old family" whose reputation in future years will rest on their shoulders after the present generation has been borne to rest beneath the green sod of "Everest" in the shadow of majestic tombstones that signify prestige of a bygone era, or rolled into the marble crypts of the mausoleum to face eternity by the side of relatives and friends of this "exclusive 2 per cent" of the community's families to which Elmtowners refer as "the society class."

Accumulated wealth provided these families with the highest incomes in the community. The two banks, the large industries,[2] practically all the business buildings in town, as well as extensive farm lands, were owned by class I families. Although all but three or four families enjoyed an income estimated a number of times to be "at least $5,000," a few incomes "from $25,000 to $35,000 a year"[3] were reported. The men were almost exclusively engaged in large business or farming enter-

[2] Except the Mill and the largest strip mine, which were owned in part by four or five local families, though the majority of the stock was owned by outsiders.

[3] Income figures given here and in succeeding sections are for 1941.

prises, but there were a few independent professionals who had either been born into this stratum or married into it; in two or three cases they had moved into it by personal effort.

Large tax bills accompany extensive ownership; consequently these families have a direct interest in keeping assessments and tax rates low. They accomplish this effectively, within the community and the county, through the control of the two major political party organizations on the township and county levels. The candidates for public office, except the district attorney and the judge, are generally not members of class I, but this does not mean they are free from controls exerted by class I interests. Money, legal talent, and political office are instruments used to translate interests into effective power. They are relied upon to implement decisions in contests which involve raising tax bills through public improvements, such as new public buildings, schools, roads, or welfare programs. This behind-the-scenes control results in the formulation of conservative policies and the election of officials who act in the capacity of agents for class I interests.

Although class I families have the highest standard of living, their level of consumption does not exhaust their incomes; so a sizable proportion is saved. All homes are owned; many have been inherited. They are located in two residential areas, but concentrated mostly in one (the 400 area of the map on page 52). Practically every family owns two or three cars. The "family car" is generally a Packard, Cadillac, or Buick, less than two years old. The "business car" may range from a Cadillac to a Ford; in age, it may be the latest model or an old "jalopy." Some of the older men have been running these "business cars" for twenty years without undue cost or trouble; their sentimental attachments to the car have replaced their earlier feelings about their saddle horses. The "young folks" usually have a late model light-weight coupé or roadster as a personal car.

Leisure, not labor, is dignified; consequently as little time as possible is devoted to making a living. Wealth invested in lands, securities, and businesses assures the family a secure income with a minimum of effort. The wealthier families have managers who supervise their holdings, and only nominal supervision of these agents is necessary.  The men may spend a few hours a day in the office, but most of the work is done by "the office girl."  The remainder of the day may be spent in going out to the farm or farms, "to see how things are going."  A walk over the farms is always in order in good weather.  There are fine, blooded cattle, either Angus or Herefords, to be admired, hogs to be inspected, and instructions to be given to the tenant or farm manager.  Almost all families keep one full-time maid who does the daily chores of cooking, cleaning, washing, ironing, and keeping the house in order, and a considerable minority hires an additional woman part-time to do the heavy cleaning.  Yard men do the gardening in the summer months and fire the furnace in the winter.  This hired help frees both the men and the women several hours each day from the confining requirements of making a living and keeping the household in order.  The leisure time thus gained is consumed in many ways by different persons.  In fall and early winter, the men spend several mornings each week in the duck blinds at the Hunt Club, owned and maintained by a select group of upper class families.  In spring and summer there is the thrill of fishing in local lakes or in the "game fish" lakes a hundred miles to the north.  Practically all families belong to the Country Club, where they while away many pleasant hours during the summer months either on the golf course or lounging and visiting on the veranda over a coke, a beer, or a long highball.  The women belong to the "Friday Morning Club"; they meet and listen to speakers or just visit and gossip.

Travel is an avidly followed leisure time pursuit.  Most families own or rent cottages near the northern lakes, and the women and children move to "the lake" for the summer.  The head of the family makes trips there over a week end that lasts from Friday afternoon to Monday evening.  A trip to Florida, the Gulf Coast, or California during January or February is the order of the season.

In their leisure hours they associate almost exclusively with other class I persons who belong to the same clique.  Sometimes cliques are composed of older women who play whist, 500, or bridge; middle-aged female cliques tend to confine their social activities to contract bridge and gossip.  There are two or three younger women's cliques; these groups play bridge between discussions on child care and baby rearing. Several are made up of couples of about the same age who have like interests (the Big Eight). It is difficult to generalize about what these mixed cliques do, as there is considerable variation from one to another.

Education is not highly regarded, either as a tool for a professional career or for knowledge in the traditional sense. Less than one-half of the men and women above 60 years of age attended college or university, and a very few were graduated. Practically all middle-aged persons were graduated from a public high school, and most attended either a good small college or a large Middle Western university. A few of the women were graduated, but most dropped out, after a year or two, either to stay home or to get married; some of the men were graduated, but only a few continued their education on a professional level. The younger people finish high school, and the majority attend good colleges or universities, but only about half of the men and a third of the women graduate. A considerable proportion of those who finish college do not return to the community to live their adult lives.

All class I families belong to a church; almost all are in the Federated, but they do not attend services with any marked frequency or regularity. However, they contribute freely to the church budget. Ten families from class I guaranteed and paid 71 per cent of the Federated Church budget in 1941. The year before one family spent more than $1,600 on the church parlors, but only one member came to services three or four times during the year. Some elderly persons and children from about 5 to 12 years of age are the only regular participants in religious affairs.

The ritual entailed in the social code is meticulously observed by the women; the men more or less ignore it or consider it "funny." Essential elements in the social ritual are clothes, stationary, good breeding, and self-assurance. Feminine apparel must be in accordance with the prevailing exclusive mode. It must be tailored by either an acceptable local dressmaker or by the lady herself in some cases, or it must come from an exclusive shop in a distant city. Its quality has to be excellent, exclusive in style, chic and smart, but not "popular" lest it lose its symbolic

value.  Absolute conformity in the use of note paper, personal
cards, and invitations is stressed in the formal relations between
the generations and between the new and the old families.[4]  The
women of a clique simply ignore the niceties of this convention
in their informal relations with each other; however, the ritual
is called upon when the occasion demands its use.  Good breeding is observed at all times in the relations between men and
women and those of different ages.  Curiosity in any form by an
outsider is considered to be the height of bad breeding and a
violation of the social code.  However, the women have no
hesitation about inquiring into the affairs of people who rank
lower than themselves in the prestige structure.  An air of complete self-confidence and easy assurance may be observed among
both men and women in their relations with equals.  An occasional flash of hauteur is considered good form among the women
"who have arrived" and a requisite to maintaining social distance in their relations with persons "who have not arrived."  This
pose—the velvet glove on the steel fist—sometimes is believed
to be the only effective way to put "social climbers" in their place.
Personal publicity in the local paper is avoided, because they
believe notices in the social column advertise a person's "social
weakness."

For the class I's, violation of the social code appears to be a
vastly greater sin than violation of the Ten Commandments.
High personal morals are prevalent, especially among older men
and women, but middle-aged and younger men and women drink
and gamble among themselves in a none too genteel manner.
Some of them may not observe the laws of the community with
care, yet there are no arrests.  The prestige position a family

[4] Two subdivisions are discernible in class I. The largest is composed of
"old families" who have lived in Elmtown for generations and have been
in the "society class" for at least two. The second section is made up of
the "new rich," who have made "fortunes" through manufacturing and
business enterprise. These families are not too well established in their positions, and the "old families" are rather dubious about their breeding and
manners and are not on very intimate terms with them. The women in
these families tend to wear dramatic clothes designed for stagy effects.
Their charity and benefit activities, like their clothes, are means to one end
—higher prestige.

enjoys appears to determine the light in which an act is interpreted by law enforcement agencies.

### Class II

Almost one-half of the families in class II have achieved their
positions through their own efforts; the remainder have inherited
them, but a further rise is virtually impossible, as their origins
are too well known and not enough time has elapsed between the
start of their ascent and the present to allow them to be accepted
in the exclusive circles of class I.  The typical class II family is
aware of the social distance between itself and class I; nevertheless, it attempts to identify itself in every possible way with
class I rather than with a lower class.  Both the men and the
women minimize the social distance between themselves and
class I even though they realize that there is a sharp line of
demarcation between the two classes.

The class II man focuses his attention upon the aggressive
manipulation of economic and political processes; consequently,
he is likely to be hyperactive in civic leadership through memberships in the power-wielding associations, such as the Chamber
of Commerce, the Rotary Club, the Masonic Lodge, veterans'
organizations, the Country Club, and the major political parties.
Within their own sphere, the women are as active as the men
in civic matters.  They occupy the offices and committee chair-
manships in the Women's Club, which is essentially a class II
and class III organization; however, the "Friday Morning Club"
is for class I women principally, but the leading women in class
II are invited to join it.  The Daughters of the American Revolution, the Country Club, the Home and Garden Club, the
Women's Christian Temperance Union, and the Federated, Methodist, and Baptist women's societies are led by these women, as
are intercommunity improvement committees of one kind or another.  Class II women do not play an active role in the auxiliaries of the lodges and the veterans' organizations; by tacit
agreement these offices belong to class III women.  In 1941, 77
per cent of the leadership positions in civic organizations were
concentrated in class II; class I held 6 per cent; class III, 12 per
cent; and class IV, 5 per cent.

Class II's prestige appears to depend as much upon civic leadership as upon economic success. A considerable proportion of the working day of many business and professional men is donated to community affairs, and the donor neither receives nor expects any compensation for his efforts other than the pleasure derived from the manipulation of human relationships in a controversial situation. A sense of personal assurance, self-mastery, and keen awareness of the way in which power is exercised is found among these men and women. As the outwardly prominent prestige bearers of community leadership, they are generally respected by the bulk of the population who look to them for "community betterment." Few people realize that these leaders may be controlled from behind the scenes, and often are, by powerful class I families who desire to have a particular person in a given office to act as their agent. Extreme personal rivalry for coveted offices often leads to personal feuds between near and would-be titans who form with other leaders alliances and power blocks pledged to back their efforts to gain control of a given office or community situation.

Approximately four out of five families in class II trace their ancestry to pioneer "American" stock, the remainder tracing their origins directly to Norwegian, German, and Irish elements who have lived in the area for two or three generations; no Poles are represented here. One-half of the class II town families live in the "best residential" section. Ninety per cent own their own nicely furnished, well-kept homes which they have either built themselves or bought.[5] Greater prestige is attached to a house with a genealogy than to a recently built one, even though the new home is more comfortable, more convenient, and better built. Elmtown reveres the homes of its "old families," and the halo of past glory is somehow transferred from the old to the new owner.

The family's income is earned largely by the male head through active daily participation in the practice of a large independent profession (law, medicine, engineering, dentistry); in the opera-

[5] This and subsequent figures on specific items and traits apply to the 29 families in class II with children in the study. It probably is representative of other families in this class.

tion of a family-owned business; as a salaried executive in an enterprise owned by class I families (the president of the Home County Bank); or as a salaried professional in a public office (the Superintendent of Schools). It may be supplemented by income from a farm or two that the family has inherited or bought; some securities; perhaps a small rental house or two. Insurance is considered a protection against the hazards of disaster and old age. Annual family incomes ranged between $3,000 and $10,000 in 1941, with the mode near $4,500. Most, but seldom all, of the family income is spent on daily living; however, the fraction left over for investment is not so large as it is in class I. Prudence in spending is exercised widely, for the family saves to educate its children; to buy durable quality goods, such as nice homes, furniture, automobiles; and for investment in insurance policies, a few stocks and bonds, a farm, a rental house, possibly a small business building. Security rather than wealth appears to be the economic goal. This is not to imply these people would not like to become wealthy—they would; but since they realize that they cannot achieve wealth in the normal course of events, they content themselves with striving for security. They were successful enough in the depression years to avoid all types of direct public assistance. There may have been some indirect forms, such as mortgage relief, but data were not collected on this point. All families have commercial accounts in the local banks, and all but three have savings accounts. In a crisis, bank credit is available and used when necessary. Another important point is that lawyers are used extensively as agents and for counsel in normal business activities rather than in a crisis only.

Wives as homemakers, mothers, and social secretaries [6] run the home with the help of one general servant, usually part-time, or the hourly services of a scrub woman. The laundry is done at home, generally by the "help." Their homes, well-managed and run with a minimum of menial labor by the housewife, are a source of feminine pride, but an ambitious wife should not allow her home to outweigh "community interests," for both

[6] One mother from class II was gainfully occupied. She had been trained professionally and was a federal civil service employee when she married a widower with two children.

husband and wife must work as a team in the promotion of "community interests" if the family is to enjoy maximum prestige. Women's "community activities" generally are arranged to take place in the afternoons; the wife is seldom expected to be "out in the evening." Community demands on the husband's evenings, however, are so numerous that he is home only a few nights a week. Almost every Saturday night there are "get-togethers" in private homes; cliques of husbands and wives eat, drink, play cards, talk, and relax from the strains of daily life with obvious enjoyment.

A family car is a necessity. Prestige factors decree that it shall be a new one, under four years old, preferably large but not necessarily so, and well kept. Only a half-dozen families own two cars; in each case one car is used by the father in his business. Typically, the car is shared by the family.

Marriage, which occurs in the middle twenties, is for life and not until divorce breaks it. In our sample, all adolescents were living with at least one parent, and 85 per cent with both. Children are expected, and in most cases "parentage is planned"; thus, families are small in size. The mean number of children is 2.3 per family. Parents jointly accept the duty of rearing children correctly so the family will not be "disgraced" by their "misbehavior." Parents sacrifice time, energy, and their own desires "to rear the children properly" and "to give them advantages" they may not have had themselves. Education is believed to be the prime requisite to success. Thus, an education is indispensable in the family's plan for the children's future. In passing it may be well to point out that class II adults are the most highly educated group in Elmtown. Four out of five parents have completed high school and one-half have attended a college or university from one to four years. All have graduated from the eighth grade. The college-educated fathers are concentrated in the large professions; a few are in business. The non-college fathers are in business enterprises of one kind or another. Those who have achieved success without a college education admit the lack of it, often in an indirect way, and indicate, none too subtly, their belief that they could have gone much further in business if they had had better educations.  Both college and non-college fathers and mothers emphasize the need for a college education to their children.  The children expect their parents to assist them materially in reaching and consolidating a desirable future.  The boys are headed for business or a profession.  The girls are steered toward a desirable marriage after an education has been secured; for they must be trained for the kind of life that is expected of them.  Girls are respected, well treated, and are not married off for the purpose of getting rid of them.

Almost every family is affiliated with and active in one way or another in church work.  Ministers rely upon them for lay leadership in money-raising drives, Sunday School work, dinners, and other forms of the church program.[7]  Class II is predominantly Protestant (91 per cent) with a very heavy concentration in the Federated Church (60 per cent); the Methodists are a poor second (20 per cent).  The remainder are split equally between the Catholic and all other Protestant churches.  Approximately one-half of the adults attend church regularly and as a couple, if married.  The men who do not come give as an excuse that Sunday is the only morning in the week they can sleep or that they need to work or to go out of town.  They seldom admit that they have no interest in religious services, at least not enough to make the effort to go.  They have, however, no objection to their wives going to or supporting the church in a financial way.[8]

Since class II families have neither the time nor the money to travel extensively they usually make a few trips each year to a neighboring city to attend the theater or an intercollegiate football game.  Their vacations are spent most often in automobile trips to various parts of the country or in a rented cabin at one of the northern lakes.  Only limited use is made of public recreational facilities such as parks and playgrounds, as they have access to the Country Club.  Eighty-five per cent of the class II families belong to the Country Club.  Golf and gossip are the

[7] Of the families represented in the adolescent study, 40 per cent of the fathers and 67 per cent of the mothers were leaders in their respective churches.

[8] Only three mothers did not attend church more than a few times a year, but two-fifths of the fathers were in this category.

chief activities in this "social" center, but each member normally has two or three large private parties each year to pay "social debts."

### Class III

The pivotal position of class III, lying as it does between the two extremes of the prestige structure, was demonstrated by the attitudes its members revealed toward themselves, as well as toward the other classes. As a rule, class III's exhibited strong class feelings. Above them they saw the class I's, who, they realized, were superior to themselves because of their wealth, leisure, lineage, and way of life. They also knew that the class II's occupied a position superior to their own, but a position that rested on different bases: dignified occupations, income, higher education, leadership and social activity—traits that they too possess, but not in such generous amounts.

The cavalier treatment they receive from class II's in community activities, coupled with the fact that class II's identify themselves psychologically with class I's and many times act as its agents, builds resentment among class III's toward the class II's rather than the class I's. Class III's look down upon class IV's as the "common man," but they do not condemn or scorn them, as too many of the class III's trace their immediate background to this class, possibly a generation, perhaps only a few years ago. The class III's believe that they have lifted themselves above "the ruck," "the masses," "the common man," by their own efforts, but they are close enough to respect those who are working valiantly to meet the demands of a commercial society where material things must be purchased by one's own efforts in a market economy. However, they often express doubts that "the workers have what it takes"—that is, the personal qualities they have. The social system is not blamed for a man's failure to rise; on the contrary, the failure is attributed to hereditary personal qualities. Curiously enough, class III's attribute their failure to rise further to behavior of the class I's or class II's who "keep us down." The inconsistency of this rationale does not occur to them.[9]

[9] Each stratum has developed a complex of categorizing attitudes as a rationale which it applies to its own members and the members of other

Family income is earned largely by the male head, but no disgrace is attached to a family whose income is supplemented by the earnings of the wife. Family incomes range from $2,000 to $4,000, with the mode at $2,800 to $2,899. Forty-two per cent of the 129 families in class III own small businesses, farms, or are independent professionals. The other 58 per cent derive their livelihood from wages and salaries. This employed group is scattered in the mines, mills, offices, banks, and in the public service.[10] Owners of businesses and farms and the professional workers enjoy some independence of action and leisure in the daily work routine. The employee group has little freedom of choice as to how they spend their time on the job.

One-sixth of the mothers are gainfully employed outside the home, largely as school teachers, nurses, music teachers, stenographers, bookkeepers, secretaries, seamstresses, and beauticians. These women received their training prior to marriage, were working usually when they were married, and three-fourths continued intermittently to supplement the family income rather than to support the family. A few operate small businesses, such as corner groceries, tobacco and dress shops. About one-fourth of these working mothers have had to make the family living after their husband's death.

Class III families have sufficient income for the conveniences and comforts of life, but they have little surplus to invest in productive, wealth-producing enterprises. The family income is spent on consumer goods—automobiles,[11] clothes, electric appliances, radios, telephones, furniture, club dues, commercial

strata to explain how each has come to be what it is in the social structure. These categorizing attitudes take the form of beliefs about the nature of the people who occupy stations associated with each of the several classes. See Vilfredo Pareto, *The Mind and Society*, Vol. 2 (1935), pp. 621–623.

[10] Their distribution by socio-economic group is given in Tables IV and V of the Appendix.

[11] Seven families out of 8 own an automobile. Their cars are predominantly new models and small in size: 49 per cent are less than two years old, and 70 per cent are under four years of age. Fifty-two per cent are small-sized popular makes—Fords, Chevrolets, and Plymouths; 34 per cent are medium-sized, and 14 per cent are large-sized cars. Only a few of the large- and medium-sized cars are under two years of age.

amusements, popular magazine subscriptions, some domestic help, and a two-week vacation. They live under more or less standard conditions in their homes where quantity of furniture and convenience are stressed rather than quality. Home furnishings tend to be standard in design, similar in price, and uniform in the kind of article in a room; one can almost predict the arrangement of furniture. These families most nearly fit the typical American stereotype represented in popular magazines.

Practically all families maintain commercial bank accounts, and three out of four have savings accounts. Those with savings accounts, insurance policies, and real property generally have bank credit available to them in a crisis. One-fifth of the families, however, do not have bank credit, and these resort to the local small-loan broker for loans that range from $50 to $300 to tide them over a crisis; salesmen, clerks, and mill foremen, unless they own real property, are not considered good credit risks by the banks.[12]  Class III families tend to invest their savings in either real estate, insurance, or speculative enterprises, only to lose much of it to financial sharpers. Lawyers are not consulted to guide business activities before action is taken, but afterwards when difficulty arises.

Class III's strive to live in the better residential areas, and they have succeeded to a large extent. Twenty-five per cent have managed to locate in the best residential area, not on the best streets, but within the district (the 400 area of the map on page 52). Some 53 per cent live in the second best or "old residential" area. Thus, almost eight out of ten families live in desirable areas. The remainder are scattered throughout the other districts, except that none live below the canal. Their homes are largely bungalows of five, six, or seven rooms. A few families live in commodious apartments in remodeled upper class mansions of an earlier era in the older residential area. Two-thirds of the homes are owned by the occupants. Home ownership is general among the families who own small businesses and the

[12] The small-loan broker, however, is a "good risk," for he obtains 85 per cent of the money he loans from banks at 6 per cent per annum and loans it to his "clients" at from 3.5 per cent to 4.5 per cent per month.

professional people. However, less than one-half of the foremen at the mill, salesmen, and service workers own their homes.

Approximately two families out of three trace their ancestry to a European country rather than to the "American" stock group.[13] Ethnic background is connected directly with religious affiliations in many families. Thus, the Catholic and Lutheran churches claim large blocks of class III people. Among the Protestant group, class III prefers the Federated and Methodist churches, but a few are Baptists. The low prestige assigned to the Free Methodist, Pentecostal, and Church of God groups repels class III persons.[14]

Church guilds, study groups, missionary societies, and welfare organizations are kept alive, in large measure, by class III women. The women are twice as likely to be avid church workers as the men, but there is a significantly higher average attendance at church services among both men and women than in any other class.[15] Regular church attendance appears to confer a kind of moral respectability peculiar to this stratum. To resign from church membership is widely condemned; to do so flaunts a class value and possibly implies the personal rejection of religious and ethical values, or so it is interpreted. The Sunday Schools are staffed almost completely by men and women from class III. Church committees are made up in four cases out of five from it. These people, along with the class II's, run the high-prestige churches.

Class III mothers marry, on the average, a year earlier in life than the class II mothers and give birth to their first child 18

[13] Thirty per cent are of Norwegian descent, 20 per cent Irish, and 10 per cent German. No Poles, however, have achieved a class III station.

[14] Church affiliation by prestige class is recorded in Table VI of the Appendix.

[15] Each minister rated the church activity of each family in his church from September, 1941, through April, 1942. These ratings were analyzed by $X^2$ for significance of difference and association. For fathers, church activity with a 20-cell table and 12 degrees of freedom, $X^2 = 239$; the coefficient of contingency for the raw scores was 0.49; when corrected for broad groupings it was 0.55. The contingency table for the mothers' activity had 20 cells and 12 degrees of freedom, $X^2 = 350$; the coefficient of contingency, uncorrected, was 0.57, corrected 0.66. Specific figures are given in Table VIII of the Appendix.

months earlier in life than the class II's. The class III women also have more children than the class II women. The mean number of children is 3.6. Another difference is the birth practices in the two classes; among the class III's, practically all babies are delivered in the local hospital, whereas the class II mother goes to a city hospital. The families are equally stable in classes II and III. For instance, 82 per cent of the class III children live with their own parents, whereas the figure was 85 per cent for families in classes I and II. Strict sexual fidelity is required of the wives, but the husbands are known, on occasion, "to play around with other women." The wives do not "run around with other men" to any appreciable extent, and they bitterly condemn a woman who does. The children are the mutual concern of both parents and are reared without the aid of servants or domestic help. They are taught early in life that the family will help them as much as it can, but their future success will depend upon their own efforts rather than on their family or inherited wealth. Family decisions are made generally between husband and wife, but the wife exerts far more influence than her husband on things that pertain to the home, the garden, and the children. She makes decisions, usually independently, that affect the family "socially." The father generally plays the dominant role in an "economic" question, but with the advice, often the agreement, of his wife.

Class III is not so well educated as the higher classes; moreover, there is a distinct difference in the amount of education received by the men and women. Eighty-six per cent of the fathers have completed the eight grammar grades, 23 per cent have completed high school, and 7 per cent have taken some type of advanced training, but only one has graduated from college, and none holds an advanced collegiate degree. Ninety-nine per cent of the mothers have completed eight grades; 63 per cent have completed high school; and 46 per cent have received some type of specialized training beyond high school. Twenty-six per cent have completed a course in technical training, and 10 per cent have graduated from a recognized college or university. It is interesting to note that approximately one-half of the fathers have no formal school training beyond the eighth grade, but 97 per cent of the mothers have at least one or more years of high school.[16]

Leisure tends to be utilized in some type of organized group activity segregated on a sex basis and, to a considerable extent, an age basis. Both men and women are ardent joiners of lodges with auxiliaries, social clubs, church groups, patriotic societies, civic betterment groups, political party organizations, and the ubiquitous clique. It has often been observed that Americans are joiners; this is particularly true in class III, where membership in many associations, implemented by active participation, confers high prestige within the class. To be elected to office or to be on a committee adds a few additional cubits to one's stature. The most coveted memberships are in the Country Club and Rotary. An estimated 15 per cent of the Country Club's membership and 10 per cent of Rotary's comes from class III, the rest from classes I and II. However, an estimated 85 per cent of the Lion's Club membership is drawn from this stratum.[17] The picture is similar for the exclusive women's organizations. Although class III's cannot "make the grade" to these relatively exclusive organizations in appreciable numbers, a few do, thus preserving the traditional belief that "one can go anywhere if he only has the stuff in him." The majority belongs to clubs with lesser prestige, but clubs dominated by class III; clubs where they will not be snubbed by people who consider themselves better than these above-average people who aspire "to climb the social ladder" but do not quite have the symbols which would lift them into more selective organizations with higher prestige. These people, like the typical member of each class, want to associate with people similar to themselves. Here they feel comfortable, for they are "among my kind of people." This appeared to be an important principle in the organization of the leisure time activities of each class.

[16] See Table VIII in the Appendix. These figures indicate indirectly that a girl with training beyond high school was faced with the dilemma, when she was ready to marry, of marrying a man with considerably less education than she possessed or of not marrying.

[17] These estimates were derived from the judgments expressed in interviews, combined with the explicit ratings of fathers in the study who also belonged to these clubs.

Although class III persons are more actively engaged in politics than the other classes,[18] evidence gained from interviews and direct experience in Elmtown politics did not lead to the conclusion that class III is politically powerful. On the contrary, it looks to classes I and II for leadership, direction, and policy making. As a consequence, many politically active class III's resent their impotence in the light of the work they do, but their control is limited because all policy-making offices are in the hands of the higher classes. Then, too, a very potent factor in this situation is the local paper. *The Elmtown Bugle* is owned and published by a class I family whose chief concern outside the paper is the political control of the county. By common consent, this family has been singularly successful since the early 1890's; even during the depression of the 1930's, it held the county solidly Republican and on the side of "*The Bugle*'s candidates."

Class III advertises its activities in the society column of *The Bugle*. When Mrs. John P. Doe gives a party, she is expected to write a "piece" for the paper which tells when and where the party occurred, who was there, the kind of entertainment offered, the refreshments served, and a detailed description of the decorations. If she does not, her friends are likely to inquire why she did not have a "piece" in the paper. Afternoon affairs are advertised in this manner and, in most cases, mixed evening parties. These evening affairs are generally known as "pot-luck suppers" where each couple brings some dish. However, they are referred to in the society column as "a covered-dish dinner." Entertainment at the afternoon parties may be card games, sewing, or gossip. Bridge, both auction and contract, is played, but bunco, pinochle, and bingo are more popular.

Evening parties are held almost exclusively on Saturday night and attended by the couples in a clique. Cocktails and highballs usually flow freely, but few persons become intoxicated. Business, scandal, personal gossip about a fellow townsman, and earthy stories monopolize the conversation before and during dinner. After dinner, bridge, hearts, rummy, or poker is the

[18] From two-thirds to three-fourths of the county offices are staffed by personnel either elected or appointed from this class. The less important appointive offices in the wards and townships go to the faithful workers in class IV.

game of the evening. If the group plays bridge, the item in the paper early the following week will so state. However, if poker or one of the other games is played, this statement is made: "Cards were played, and, in the course of the evening, Mr. Blank and Mrs. Blanket were the winners." Trips out of town for almost any reason are mentioned in *The Bugle*. Class III's might be said to be seekers after respectable personal publicity of any kind—social, economic, political, religious, educational. Class I persons, on the other hand, avoid personal publicity; class II's as a rule try to keep from being mentioned too frequently in the local press.

This obvious search for publicity may be a symbol of the strain inherent in this class's pivotal position between the two conspicuous layers of the social structure. The class III's attempt to buy prestige by conspicuous activity—the purchase of home furnishings, memberships, cars, and clothes. To reinforce their position, they attend church and work in charitable organizations and avoid scandal as they would a plague. Outwardly they are very "moral" and conservative, but some evidence indicated a wider departure from professed moral standards among the class III's than among the class II's. They are extremely jealous of their good name and religious values. They are honest and generally pay their debts, but, for some, the strain of "keeping up a front" is greater than their ability. These people go into debt and soon gain a bad name for their lack of prudence and, consequently, suffer a loss of prestige.

The public record of criminal charges and convictions contains a few names of persons in class III, but none from classes I and II. This indicates either that class III persons are more likely than the higher classes to commit criminal offenses, or they lack the power to avoid charges after an offense has been committed.[19]

### Class IV

Class IV persons, on the whole, are aware of the inferior prestige position they occupy in comparison with the higher classes; furthermore, they resent the attitudes most persons in

[19] Between 1934 and 1941, 10 criminal offenses had been charged against class III fathers, and there had been 7 convictions.

these classes exhibit toward them. However, they take pride in the fact that they are not so badly off as the people in class V. They discriminate sharply between "people like us" and the socially ambitious higher classes and the improvident "reliefers," "loafers," and "the criminal class" whom they despise. They believe that class III's put on airs they do not rightfully deserve. Conversely, a self-respecting class IV avoids contact with class V's whenever possible. They conceive themselves to be "the backbone of the community."

The higher classes characterize class IV's as poor but honest, hard workers, who pay their taxes, raise their children properly, but never seem to get ahead financially. From the viewpoint of the class I's and class II's they add little to the community beyond providing the labor that keeps the factories going, and customers in the stores. Their function is to work, to behave themselves, and to keep things going. They are respected generally for what they are—hard workers who make their own way in life—and not for intellectual, political, economic, or social achievement. These are the prerogatives of the higher classes.

Class IV works for a living day after day on the farms, in the mines, the mills, and the shops of Elmtown; its members are wage earners.[20] The economic folkways prescribe that the father should support his family, but 30 per cent of the mothers are gainfully employed outside the home either as supplementary or chief breadwinner in occupations that carry little prestige, and low hourly or weekly wages.[21] Annual family income for the class IV's range from $800 to $2,700, with the mode at $1,500 to $1,600. Their income is large enough to provide the necessities of life and a few comforts, but few if any luxuries. Family income is spent as it is earned; little is left over for a "rainy day." As a rule, the family buys wherever it can get the most for its money. Its groceries come from the local chain outlets when the family has cash; when it is short of money, purchases are often made at a locally owned grocery that will extend credit. Credit

[20] The chances were 12.5 to 1 against a class IV father's owning a business. When he did, it was a very small one, as defined by Dun and Bradstreet's *Registry* for "Elmtown," May, 1941. A very small business is defined therein as one with a value between $500 and $2,000.

[21] See Table V of the Appendix.

grocers know that these families buy from the chains most of the time and they resent it, but there is little they can do to stop the practice. Many durable consumer goods are purchased on credit from either local stores or mail-order houses. Mail-order purchases in Elmtown are limited almost exclusively to class IV, particularly among town families.[22] Radios, refrigerators, washing machines and tools with a mail-order brand name on them are not seen in class III town homes, except on very rare occasions, but they are encountered regularly in class IV homes, as no stigma appears to be attached to purchases made either in a chain store or from a mail-order house. These people are proud of their possessions, and they exhibit little hesitancy about telling where they bought an item, or what it cost, particularly if they believe they struck a bargain. A good bargain appears to generate ego satisfaction, and it is good form to brag, at least a little, over a "good deal."

The meager savings of a lifetime are generally invested in a small home, bought on contract or mortgaged to a local bank, lumber yard, or a national insurance company; furniture for the house; and a family car. However, 25 per cent of the families do not own an automobile,[23] and only 35 per cent either own or are buying a home.[24]

Home ownership is concentrated in certain occupational groups. Four out of five owners of small businesses, two out of three clerks, one-half of the craftsmen, but only one laborer out of ten owns a home. Ninety per cent of the rural non-farm families own their homes or are buying them. Class IV farmers, on the other hand, are almost exclusively tenants; only two families own farms. This low figure results from the identification of land ownership with prestige among farm people. Farm owners are classed as III's in most cases by the raters, whereas tenants are said to be class IV's. Irrespective of the differences

[22] A few class III families buy in this way, but in order to achieve favorable status one must buy from stores approved by one's associates, and the mail-order houses are *not* approved in class III circles.

[23] When a class IV family buys a new car, it is a small one; when it buys a large one, the car comes off a used-car lot.

[24] These families are in the prime of life; the mean age of the father is 45.5 years and of the mother 42.1 years. They have been established 15 years or more.

in the percentage of home ownership for farm tenants and the rural non-farm families, it should be noted that for the class as a whole the chances are two to one against home ownership.

Cash reserves at best are not more than a few hundred dollars. Thirty-five per cent have small commercial bank accounts, and 17 per cent have savings accounts. The commercial bank accounts are limited largely to the farmers, little businessmen, and the craft and skilled workers; only 11 per cent of the laborers and service workers have commercial accounts. Bank credit is available to approximately two families out of five. Farmers, very small businessmen, and craftsmen may procure loans if they have security for a chattel mortgage. For families who do not have bank credit the local small loans broker acts as the credit agency. He does an extensive and lucrative business in class IV; 28 per cent of the families maintain an account with him (19 per cent had loans they were paying on in the spring of 1942). These families are considered to be excellent risks by the broker, for they have borrowed sums ranging from $50 to $300 repeatedly and his losses have been less than 1 per cent.[25]

Many families were on state and federal relief during the worst years of the depression in the early and middle 1930's; however, data were not compiled, since no state or federal records were available in the county and it was not considered advisable to ask the families directly about this point. Figures on relief furnished by the Township Supervisor were available from January 1, 1937, through December, 1941. Eight per cent of the class IV families had been on township relief from one month to three years in this period; none involved total relief. Township relief was given in a niggardly spirit, in the smallest possible amounts, to families where there was illness, accident, disease, death, desertion, or "plain hard luck" beyond the recipient's control. When disaster struck families in the higher classes, they had enough resources to meet it without resort to public aid.

All ethnic elements are found in class IV in about the same proportion in which they are found in the general population. In Elmtown proper, class IV families are excluded largely from

[25] From 1935 to 1942, inclusive, the average borrowing family had opened 16 loans and two had opened 44.

the best residential area by economic factors, and they in turn avoid the area below the canal.[26]

The family pattern is sharply different from class III. Family stability so characteristic of the higher classes begins to give way to instability; exactly one-third of the families have been broken by separation, divorce, or death. This is a strong contrast to class III, where only 18 per cent have been broken by these same factors. Males marry when they are in their early twenties, females in their late teens. Children normally are born from 10 to 18 months later. In our families, 55 per cent of the class IV mothers gave birth to their first child before they were 20 years of age, whereas only 19 per cent of the class III mothers gave birth to their first child before their twentieth birthday. Class IV women also have more children. The mean number per family is 4.3.

The roles of the wife and mother are encompassed by her domestic duties—cleaning, washing, ironing, mending, preparation of the family's meals, cutting out and making the children's clothes, particularly little girls'. There is no part-time help except in an emergency such as childbirth or illness; even then, it is dispensed with as soon as possible. Class IV housewives are discriminated against if they have ambitions to join the Women's Club or other "social" organizations. "Their place" is "in the home" or "on the job." They are judged by the way they keep their houses, dress their children, and manage the family budget. Emphasis is placed on wifely virtues—good housekeeper, good cook, good mother, good sewer, careful of her children's welfare. The husbands are judged as providers and by their moral actions. Neither the men nor the women are expected to do more than work hard, pay their bills, raise their family in the manner expected of this class, vote "right" in elections, and, above all, eschew any radical or "bolshevik" ideas.

Formal educational experience is limited almost exclusively to the public elementary and high schools. One-third of the fathers and a fifth of the mothers have not graduated from the eighth grade; one-sixth of the fathers and one-fourth of the mothers

[26] Detailed figures on families by residential area and class are given in Tables I and X of the Appendix.

have attended high school, but only slightly more than one father out of twenty and one mother out of eleven have graduated from high school. The present generation is receiving more education than its parents did, but the average is not more than two years of high school. Most class IV children aspire to a high school diploma, but the parents often are not convinced of its value, and they have few, if any, scruples about letting a child quit school or actually taking him out to work without a good reason.

Categorization of the religious situation within class IV is complicated by several factors. In the first place, ethnic sub-groups, such as the Irish, Norwegians, and Poles, are more closely tied to the churches than the "American" stock. Then, there is the problem of claimed religious affiliation versus actual participation in church activities. A third complicating factor is the avoidance of religious participation in some churches by class IV persons, whereas people from the same stratum are active participants in others. Thus, denominational, ethnic, and role factors operate in this class.

As a rule, religion is either shunned or embraced with enthusiasm. Many families claim that they have neither time nor money to support the churches, and one-third indicate hostility toward religion for one reason or another. Some persons are outspoken in their criticism of the churches as institutions maintained for the rich people or for people who "think they are somebody." Fourteen per cent of the families have no affiliation with a local church, and, of those who do, two-thirds of the fathers and one-half of the mothers do not attend. These people claim to be church members, but, by the practical test of participation in church activities, they are not. Twenty-four per cent of the fathers and 19 per cent of the mothers are not known by ministers of the churches with which they claim affiliation. Although men and women who claim church affiliations, but for practical purposes are members in spirit only, are scattered throughout the churches, proportionately more are found in the Federated and Methodist churches than in the lower-ranking Protestant churches, such as the Baptist, Free Methodist, Assembly of God, and Pentecostal. There are no differences between the reality of membership and claims of membership between the Lutheran and Catholic groups. The conclusion reached is that either these claimants' ancestors were Presbyterians, Congregationalists, or Methodists and they have "inherited" their religious sentiments, or they attempt to acquire status by claiming a religious affiliation with a church that carries high status.

Class IV persons more or less active in religious affairs are concentrated in the Lutheran, Catholic, and low-ranking Protestant churches. The Catholic and Lutheran churches are attended very well each Sunday, but the class IV's stay away in significantly larger proportions than the higher classes. The low-ranking Protestant churches are all small except the Baptist, which is sometimes referred to as "the society church of the mill workers."

Proportionately, class IV's are not so active in the churches as the higher classes. Only 5 per cent of the fathers are reported by the ministers to be "church workers," whereas 40 per cent of the class II fathers are in this category. The mothers are more active than the fathers, but even here only 18 per cent are church workers. Among the class II mothers, the figure is 67 per cent. Obviously this class does not manifest its spirituality by work on church boards, committees, and societies. In the Methodist Church the chances are 20 to 1 that an active class IV woman will be found in the kitchen at a church dinner rather than on the planning committee for the affair. Several active class IV Methodist women are known as "kitchen Methodists."

Civic and community organizations are largely outside the experience of these people. Exclusive organizations, such as the Country Club, the Friday Morning Club, Rotary, and Lions, are closed to them, and only a few women belong to the supposedly "community-wide" Women's Club. Even the Farm Bureau and rural women's clubs are not joined in appreciable numbers. A few men belong to the Masonic Lodge, the Knights of Columbus, the Knights of Pythias, and the Odd Fellows. Their wives join the appropriate feminine complements to these organizations, but the preponderant majority of the members in these organizations come from the three higher classes. On the other hand, the Eagles, Redmen, Woodmen, and their auxiliaries are composed in large part of class IV persons who not only belong but take an active part in fraternal affairs. The local labor organizations are run almost exclusively by class IV men.

Practically all leisure time, outside the daily, weekly, and yearly work routines, is spent within the community either at home or in activities offered to the public. Approximately three leisure hours out of four are spent at home listening to the radio, looking over the local paper, "working around the place," "fixing things up," and, for the men especially, cleaning and repairing the car. There is very little reading of magazines, books, or newspapers that originate outside of Elmtown. The motion picture theater, the most popular recreational spot, is visited by the average family once a week. Visiting friends and relatives is also a very popular pastime. On a warm Saturday evening, Freedom Street swarms with town and rural people from the two lower classes. They sit in their cars, on running boards, lean against fenders, walk in droves along the sidewalks. As friends and acquaintances come by, the latest gossip, scandal, news, and jokes are told and retold. During the summer months, the softball leagues are manned largely by the young men and women in class IV, who exhibit their skills in evening play before their friends, relatives, and social equals. The city park and an adjacent state park are popular picnic and family reunion spots. The family does not travel for travel's sake. Even though an extended trip may be made for a definite purpose, such as visiting a relative, these trips are not viewed as pleasures in themselves, but as a means to renew family ties. There is very little travel to the lakes or to resorts, and few extensive summer tours; these luxuries are beyond the reach of the family budget.

Intimate associations in cliques are limited to intraclass relationships, as class III's avoid clique ties with class IV's, and class IV's, in turn, avoid class V's. Clique activities are highly informal and consist generally of visits back and forth between couples in the evening, on Sundays and holidays rather than of planned parties and dinners with drinks, games, and polite conversation as their central focus. Adult cliques tend to be organized around age and sex, with more leisure time being spent with one's own sex than in the higher classes. In the evening, the men may meet at the fire station, the police station, the city hall, a tavern, the labor temple, or the lodge parlors where they talk, play poker, cribbage, pinochle, dominoes, checkers, or argue. They may wander downtown to "see what's going on."

There appears to be a definite attempt on the part of the factory workers to "get away from the wife" for a few hours at least once or twice a week. While the men are away, the women may call on a neighbor, putter about the house, or just relax from the labor, noise, and excitement of the daily grind of preparing meals, putting up lunches, cleaning the house, washing and ironing clothes, going to market, and caring for the children. The man's escape from home may be an adjustment to a tired, irritable, and frustrated wife who has a task that is too difficult for her to do "with what she has to do it with." The higher classes know little about the leisure activities of the class IV's, and they care less. This class is taken for granted, and the existence of its members is largely ignored except in so far as they perform economic and political functions.

Periodically, the attention of the community is focused very briefly on some person who has committed a crime. This occurs more frequently in class IV than in class III, for 14 per cent of class IV fathers were convicted in local courts of offense between 1934 and 1941, but only 4 per cent of class III fathers.

### Class V

Class V occupies the lowest-ranking stations in the prestige structure. It is looked upon as the scum of the city by the higher classes. It is believed generally that nothing beyond charity can be done for these people, and only a minimum of that is justified since they show little or no inclination to help themselves. It is the opinion of the upper classes that:

> They have no respect for the law, or themselves.
> They enjoy their shacks and huts along the river or across the tracks and love their dirty, smoky, low-class dives and taverns.
> Whole families—children, in-laws, mistresses, and all—live in one shack.
> This is the crime class that produces the delinquency and sexual promiscuity that fills the paper.
> Their interests lie in sex and its perversion. The girls are always pregnant; the families are huge; incestual relations occur frequently.

They are not inspired by education, and only a few are able to make any attainments along this line.

They are loud in their speech, vulgar in their actions, sloppy in their dress, and indifferent toward their plight. Their vocabulary develops as profanity is learned.

If they work, they work at very menial jobs.

Their life experiences are purely physical, and even these are on a low plane.

They have no interest in health and medical care.

The men are too lazy to work or do odd jobs around town.

They support the Democratic party because of the relief obtained during the depression.

This group lives for a Saturday of drinking or fighting. They are of low character and breed and have a criminal record for a pedigree.

Class V persons, passive and fatalistic, realize that they are "on the bottom" and believe that they can do nothing to improve their position. They desire money, possessions, education, and favorable prestige, but they do not know how these are achieved. When a class V person attempts to improve his position, he is discriminated against by the higher classes, and by many members of his own class who think he is trying to "put on airs." One woman with considerable insight into her class position summarized it thus:

> Survival for us depends on staying on good terms with the rich people and the law. Whenever I think about myself and the kids, I am reminded what my father used to say, "We are the ones who are told what to do, when and how" around here. This town takes us for granted. Most people think the people down here [the tannery flats] are too ignorant to do anything and don't care; I guess they're right.

To generalize a little more, class V persons give the impression of being resigned to a life of frustration and defeat in a community that despises them for their disregard of morals, lack of "success" goals, and dire poverty.

Family support comes from many sources. The father is the chief breadwinner in three families out of five, but his earnings are meager. Ninety-two per cent are unskilled and semi-skilled laborers or machine operators. Not one is a farm owner, and only 8 are farm tenants; 2 are notions salesmen; and 8 operate very small businesses, such as hauling coal from local mines, ash and trash hauling, repair and sales of old cars. Fifty-five per cent of the mothers "work out" part or full time as waitresses, dishwashers, cooks, washwomen, janitresses, cleaning women, and unskilled domestic workers. Many younger women and girls work on the production line of a local manufacturer who is reputed to give them preference in his shops because they can be hired for lower wages than class IV workers.

Income from wages provides them with enough money to obtain the most meager necessities of life; however, in many cases it is inadequate even for this, and they rely upon private charity and public relief. Annual family income ranges from about $500 to a high of $1,500. The modal income fell in the $800 to $899 bracket. Income varies from year to year, depending upon work conditions and wages. Between 1937 and 1941, the private earnings of 53 per cent of these families were supplemented by township relief during at least one-fourth of each year. This figure does not take into consideration federal subsidies, such as W.P.A., and N.Y.A., which prevailed in that period; neither does it include private charity in the form of "outfitting the children" with clothes.

Gifts of partially worn-out clothing, linens, bedding, old furniture, dishes, and food are a regular part of the private relief and indirect wage system supported by the two highest classes and to some extent by class III. They are given informally to persons who perform domestic service for the donors. Begging by class V's is frowned upon strongly; consequently, needy families do not solicit things in an overt manner, but any class V person knows how to make his wants known to an employer in a humble, discreet manner that generally brings the desired results. Semipublic charity is dispensed through sewing circles, guilds, and clubs that make clothing for infants. The ever-popular rummage sale, one of which is held almost every Saturday by some "middleclass" organization, may be viewed as another form of charity to the two lower classes. Many class V women regularly buy their family's best clothes from these sales. As one class II woman said, "This year, Mrs. Gordon Sweitzer [class I] will have a striking dress, next year you will see it on Mrs. Luke Jenkins [class IV] in the Baptist choir, and three years from now Pearl Soper [class V] will be trying to catch some loafer's eye with it."

Bank credit is non-existent, and even the small-loan broker has learned through experience to be careful with class V:

> Before I loan one of them a cent, I investigate carefully and make sure they own what they put up for security. There is not a person in that class who has not been in here at one time or another for a loan. If they have a job and can give me good evidence they can pay back a loan, I will let them have from $10 to $25 at first. If they pay it back, just as they agreed to, I will let them have a little more next time. Eighty per cent of the loans I have written off were made to the class represented by the names you have there. [A group of class V's we were checking for loans.]

Exactly one-half of the class V families studied have procured small personal loans, none over $50; this is the limit the broker will loan to persons he does not believe to be "good risks." Repeated loans to class V's are discouraged; the mean is eight loans per family for those who manage to obtain them. On the other hand, the broker encourages class IV's to borrow time after time, since he considers them "good risks."

The uncertain nature of their employment results in long periods of idleness; also illness, real or imagined, may result in a voluntary layoff for a few days that, to persons in the higher classes, appears to be laziness. Whatever the conditioning factors, these people are far more irregular in their employment than the class IV's. They will leave a job casually, often without notice, and for flimsy reasons. Employers do not like to hire them unless labor is scarce or they can be induced to work for low wages. Even then they are placed in the simplest and most menial jobs. The work history of a father or mother is generally known to employers, and he acts in the light of it when a son or daughter of one of these families asks him for employment.

All population elements are represented, but three families out of five (58 per cent) trace their ancestry to "American stock" that came to Elmtown before the Civil War. In spite of popular belief, "the Irish element" has contributed less than 9 per cent to the ranks of class V. The Poles are found here twice as frequently, and the Germans and Norwegians only one-third as frequently as we may expect if chance factors alone are operating.[27] The concentration of "American stock" is overlooked by Elmtowners who commonly use a European ancestral background as a symbolic label. This is understandable in the case of the Poles; they were imported as strikebreakers, and they have not outlived this experience or their ethnic background. Many of these "American" families have lived in Elmtown as long as its "leading families"; however, length of residence is their only similarity to leading families, for through the generations they have achieved notorious histories. Unfortunately, the unsavory reputation of an ancestor is remembered and often used as an explanation for present delinquency. It is interesting to note that the doctrine of "blood" which explains the rise to eminence of class I is used in the same way to justify the derogation of class V. And, significantly, present behavior of class V gives the people who hold such beliefs a basis for their conviction. Sociologically, such an explanation is unwarranted, but Elmtowners are not sociologists! Often such remarks as the following are made about these families or some member of them, "Blood will out"; "You can't expect anything else from such people"; "His great-grandfather was hanged for killing a neighbor in cold blood!"

Class V families are excluded from the two leading residential areas.[28] They are found in the others, with large concentrations north of the tracks and below the canal. Below the canal and the Mill Addition are populated mainly by "Americans." Down by the Mill is "Irish heaven," whereas the section north of the tracks is divided into the Norwegian and Polish areas. A low, flat, swamp-like sub-area within this section, Frog Hollow, is almost exclusively Polish. The higher ground north of the tracks, populated mainly by Norwegians with a slight intermingling of Irish and Germans, is known as "Ixnay." Below the canal is referred to by many names, all symbolic of its undesirability: down by the garbage dump; where the river rats live; behind the tannery; the bush apes' home; squatters' paradise; where you'll find

[27] These probabilities are derived from $X^2$ analysis. The figures on class and national origins are given in Table II of the Appendix.

[28] See Table IX of the Appendix.

the God-damned yellow hammers; the tannery flats; and along the tow-path.

The dilapidated, box-like homes contain crude pieces of badly abused furniture, usually acquired secondhand. A combination wood and coal stove, or kerosene burner, is used for both cooking and heating. An unpainted table and a few chairs held together with baling wire, together with an ancient sideboard—with shelves above to hold the assorted dishes and drawers below for pots, pans, and groceries—furnish the combined kitchen and dining room. There may be some well-worn linoleum or strips of roofing on the floor. The "front room" generally serves a dual purpose, living room by day and bedroom by night. Here too the floor is often covered with linoleum or roofing strips, seldom with a woven rug. Two or three overly used chairs in various stages of disrepair share the room with a sagging sofa that leads a double life as the routine of day alternates with that of night. If an additional bed is needed, an iron one may stand in a corner or along one wall. A simple mirror that shows signs of age, perhaps abuse, shares the wall with a few cheap prints or pictures cut from magazines that show how undressed a woman may be without being nude. Now and again a colored print of a saint and a motion picture star will be pasted or nailed beside a siren. An improvised wardrobe made by driving a row of nails in the wall generally occupies one corner. A table, radio, and some means of lighting the room complete its furnishings. Old iron beds that sag in the middle, made with blankets and comforts in the absence of sheets, a chest of drawers, a chair or two, and a mirror that looks out on the stringy curtains and the bare floor complete the furnishings of the tiny bedrooms. Musical instruments, magazines, and newspapers other than *The Bugle* seldom find their way into these homes. Less than 1 per cent have telephones.

Privacy in the home is almost non-existent; parents, children, "in-laws" and their children, and parts of a broken family may live in two or three rooms. There is little differentiation in the use of rooms—kitchen, dining room, living room, and bedroom functions may be combined from necessity into a single use area. Bath and toilet facilities are found in approximately one home in seven. City water is piped near or into 77 per cent of the homes within the city limits, except those below the canal. Water for these homes is either carried from the town pump, also located in this area, or from the river. Outside the town, wells, springs, and creeks are used for a water supply. Some 4 per cent of the homes were equipped with furnace heat; the rest were heated with wood- or coal-burning stoves.

The family residence is rented in four cases out of five (81 per cent). The few that are owned have either been inherited or built along the canal and in the tannery flats by their present owners. A few Poles have bought homes in Frogtown from the English and Scotch who formerly inhabited this area. Although it is popularly believed that these people buy cars rather than homes, only 57 per cent own cars, the great majority (83 per cent) being more than 7 years old.

The family pattern is unique. The husband-wife relationship is more or less an unstable one, even though the marriage is sanctioned either by law or understandings between the partners. Disagreements leading to quarrels and vicious fights, followed by desertion by either the man or the woman, possibly divorce, is not unusual. The evidence indicates that few compulsive factors, such as neighborhood solidarity, religious teachings, or ethical considerations, operate to maintain a stable marital relationship. On the contrary, the class culture has established a family pattern where serial monogamy is the rule. Legal marriages are restricted within narrow limits to class equals. However, exploitive sex liaisons between males from the higher classes frequently occur with teen-age girls, but they rarely result in marriage. Marriage occurs in the middle teens for the girls and the late teens or early twenties for the boys. Doctors, nurses, and public officials who know these families best estimate that from one-fifth to one-fourth of all births are illegitimate. Irrespective of the degree of error in this estimate, 78 per cent of the mothers gave birth to their first child before they were 20 years of age. Another trait that marks the family complex is the large number of children. The mean is 5.6 per mother, the range, 1 to 13. There is little pre-natal or post-natal care of either mother or child. The child is generally delivered at home, usually by a local doctor, the county nurse, or a midwife, but in the late 1930's some expectant mothers entered the local hospital.

Hospital deliveries, however, are a recent innovation and not widely diffused. Death, desertion, separation, or divorce has broken more than half the families (56 per cent). The burden of child care, as well as support, falls on the mother more often than on the father when the family is broken. The mother-child relation is the strongest and most enduring family tie.

Formal educational experience is limited in large part to the elementary school. Two parents out of three (67 per cent) quit school before the eighth grade was reached; the third completed it. Seven fathers and six mothers out of 230 have completed a year or more of high school; only one father and four mothers have graduated. None has attended any type of school after leaving the public school system.

Religious ties are either very tenuous or non-existent. Only 71 per cent of the families claim any religious connections; many of these are merely "in spirit." More than 9 families out of 10 have no active connection with a church, and active hostility toward churches, ministers, and pious people is encountered more frequently than real or professed church work. One woman epitomized the situation when she said bitterly, "The 'Everyone Welcome' signs in front of the churches should add 'except people like us'—we're not wanted." She was right—they are not wanted by the congregations and several of the ministers. Ministers in the high-prestige churches (Federated, Methodist, and Lutheran) indicate they have no objections to class V persons coming to service and participating in church activities, but they know that members of the congregation resent the presence of these people; so they do not encourage their attendance. Ministers in the low-ranking churches do not believe that their people resent the presence of class V's in church activities.

Three ministers related stories about unpleasant experiences they had with certain of these families before they learned that it is wise to "follow the line of least resistance" and let them alone. Four frankly stated that these people are beyond help, as far as the ministers are concerned, and they do not try to reach them in any way. Seven reported that they officiate at funerals, weddings, and baptisms if they are asked; two refuse to perform these rites on religious grounds.

The church schedules reveal that attendance at religious services and participation in auxiliary church activities are limited, with few exceptions, to the higher-ranking classes. Ninety-eight per cent of the class V fathers are either completely unknown to the ministers or do not attend church if they are known. Five attend church services rarely or irregularly; not one is categorized as a "church worker." The participation figures for the mothers are little different: 90 per cent either are unknown or do not attend church; 7 per cent attend services either rarely or irregularly; 3 per cent are reported to be church workers. These church workers are in the Pentecostal, Pilgrim Holiness, and Church of God congregations that meet in abandoned stores, lofts, and private homes. Even the Free Methodists, who are largely class IV's, apparently do not welcome too intimate contact with these women in their strivings for salvation through good work. One minister cynically said with reference to them, "You will find in the churches these women who shout the longest and loudest about sin—hours on end—while their husbands are out lying with some harlot."

Their extensive leisure time is spent in the community or in nearby ones, since they have little money to spend in travel; neither are their automobiles in good enough repair to stand the rigor of long trips. The men and boys are more mobile than the women and girls; when they leave the community, it is usually in search of work, adventure, often to avoid the sheriff. When the family goes away, it generally carries its belongings with it in a search for economic betterment. In these periodic moves, it usually encounters the same kind of conditions, so it comes back after a few months or years. Possibly as many as one-fourth of the families drift in and out of the community. These floating families have a more or less fixed routine which they follow in the course of the years. They may go to Michigan in the summer to pick and pack fruit, on to Wisconsin for the cranberry season, then back to Elmtown for the winter and early spring. The younger children may enroll in school, the older boys try to find work in the bowling alley or on barges that ply the river; the girls and women find work as maids, cleaning women, or dishwashers until the family decides to move again.

Class V persons are almost totally isolated from organized community activities. A few men claim membership in veterans' organizations, but they neither pay dues nor attend meetings. Workers in the Mill belong to the union, since this is a closed shop; the others follow lines of work not organized by the unions. Time has little value in the daily routine. Even getting to work on time and staying on the job are not too highly regarded. Employers complained bitterly about their loose work habits. They claim that these people come to work at irregular times, leave when they feel like it, and lay off on the least excuse. Since they do not participate in organized community affairs, hours off the job and during the periods of unemployment or layoff are spent the way the person chooses without too much interference from neighbors. Leisure is expended in loafing around the neighborhood, in the downtown district, along the river, and at home. Their social life consists of informal visits between neighbors, gossip, petty gambling, visits to the cheaper theaters, going to town, drinking in the home or public taverns, with now and again a fist fight. The family is so loosely organized that the members usually go their own way in search of amusement or pleasure. The cliques are severely age- and sex-graded; men associate with men and women with women, except in their ubiquitous sex play.

Organized dinners and parties where guests are invited to the home on a Saturday night are unknown. Festive gatherings take place on Sunday when many branches of the family unite for a brief spell of merrymaking. The low-ranking taverns are filled on Saturday nights with class V's of all ages who gather there for their big social night. Small children are kept up until after midnight in the hot, smoke-filled, poorly lighted, noisy "poor man's night club." Young couples wander in and out; often preliminary "passes" are made in preparation for a later seduction. Almost every Saturday night the police are called to some low-ranking tavern to break up a fight between half-drunk customers.

The police, sheriff, prosecuting attorney, and judge know these families from frequent contact through the years, whereas the ministers and school officials may be only slightly acquainted with them. Between 1934 and 1941, 8 per cent of the mothers and 46 per cent of the fathers had been convicted once or more in the local courts.   Public drinking, disorderly conduct, family neglect, and sex offenses were the charges against the women; they averaged 1.5 convictions each.   The men were more or less chronic offenders who were convicted of habitual public drunkenness, 49 per cent; miscellaneous offenses, 30 per cent; offenses against property, 12 per cent; sex and family neglect, 9 per cent. They averaged 4.1 convictions each in the eight years covered by reliable court records.   Their misdeeds are prominently written up in *The Bugle*.   If they do not reach the paper, they are known by some persons in the higher classes who delight in telling about them to their acquaintances.

# 6

# THE SCHOOL SYSTEM

THE SCHOOL IS the only tax-supported institution devoted exclusively to the training of young Elmtowners in knowledge, skills, and values cherished by the culture. Practically all children between 6 and 13 years of age spend from six to seven hours a day, five days a week, from early September until the following June in and around a public elementary school located within walking distance of their homes. After age 14 most children are connected with the high school for at least a brief period, but as they grow older an increasing percentage leaves school for the work world, so that approximately only one-third graduate from high school.

The Elmtown schools are operated by a combination of local laymen and professionally trained educators under the authority of state law. State law decrees that a school district must provide a common school education[1] at public expense; however, the school is essentially a local responsibility, particularly with respect to policy. State educational officials have little control over the Elmtown system beyond their power to withdraw state aid funds in extreme cases for violations of law or administrative rulings.

The territory encompassed by the Elmtown communal area is organized into 33 school districts. Thirty-two are rural districts that support one-room schools where grades 1 through 8 are taught. Each of these schools is administered by three trustees elected by the citizens of the district. They are supported largely by real estate taxes levied by the school board on its taxing district, which coincides with the area of the school

[1] The courts of Home State have ruled that a common school education includes four years of high school.

121

district, supplemented by some state aid funds. These rural schools have no connection with the schools in Elmtown.

The Elmtown schools are organized into one district which includes the town and a few sections in Elm Township adjacent to one side of the incorporated area. There are three two-room ward schools, a central elementary school, and a high school in the system. Grades 1 to 4 are taught in the ward schools, 1 through 8 in Central School, and 9 through 12 in the high school. Since we are concerned primarily with high-school-aged young people, and since the high school is a center of conflict, our discussion will be confined largely to Elmtown High School.

Even though school districts are not required to maintain a high school—and none of the 32 rural districts within the communal area has done so—the state law, however, has made it obligatory upon an elementary school district to pay the tuition on a per capita basis of its pupils who wish to attend an available high school.[2] A statute passed in 1917 provides that, for the purpose of levying a tax to pay the tuition of eighth-grade graduates in high schools established in other districts or towns, the territory in each county not included in a high school district is a non-high school district. In accordance with this statute, all land in Home County not in a high school district is organized into a non-high school district and a tax levied to pay for the tuition of pupils who attend high schools in other districts. Inasmuch as the only high school in the community is located in Elmtown, pupils from the non-high school district covered by the rural portion of the communal area come to Elmtown High School. Thus, the rural territory is covered by two districts, the common school district and the non-high school district. This means the levying of two taxes, one to support the local elementary school and the other to pay high school tuition on a per capita basis for students from the non-high school area who attend high school. The tax rate levied to support the elementary school varies from one district to another, whereas the rate is uniform on all non-high school land in the county. Real estate

[2] The courts have ruled that it is impracticable to maintain a high school in every district, but it is not impossible to give every child the benefit of a high school education by sending him to a convenient district where a high school is maintained.

within the Elmtown School System, however, is taxed only once, since this is a single administrative unit that includes all the schools under one Board of Education. The significance of this point will become clear when the relationship between the policies of the Elmtown Board of Education and land ownership is discussed.

### The Board of Education

Responsibility for the operation of the Elmtown school system rests in the hands of a seven-man Board of Education. The President of the Board is elected annually at the school election held in April. Two members are elected also at the annual election for three-year terms. Theoretically, any adult citizen in the district may be a candidate for the school board, and, if he receives enough votes, elected. In practice, the members of the Board of Education come mainly from the two upper classes and have to qualify under informal ground rules. Even to be considered for the Board a person has to be male, Protestant, Republican, a property owner, preferably a Rotarian, or at least approved by the Rotarians. (Rotarians are proud of the way they have controlled the selection of the Board for more than twenty-five years.)

When a vacancy is to occur, the selection of a man for the Board of Education is left to the President of the Board. He discusses possible candidates with his friends on the Board and in the Rotary Club. Generally he invites a fellow Rotarian with whom he believes he can work to become a candidate. The President then files this man's name with the election clerk; nothing is said publicly about the impending vacancy or the forthcoming election until after the last date for filing has passed. Then *The Bugle* runs a news item stating that the date for filing names for the school election has passed, that such-and-such men have filed as candidates for the Board of Education, and that Mr. X has filed again for President of the Board. Little additional publicity is given to the election until *The Bugle* carries the necessary legal notices of the polling places and names of candidates. On election day, only a handful of voters go to the polls to elect the hand-picked candidates. In 1940, 132 votes were cast; in 1941, 114; and in 1942, 84. This carefully con-

trolled system for the selection of Board members has resulted
in the election of conservative men who have represented through
the years the political, economic, social, and educational interests
of classes I and II rather than the other four-fifths to seven-
eighths of the population.

The man who was President at the time of the study was
elected to this office in April, 1939, after serving several years
as an ordinary member of the Board. He was a self-made man
who had come to Elmtown as a young man to open a law office.
Through the years, he had developed a stable law practice, and
he was recognized as an able, courageous, and forthright community leader.

The six regular Board members in 1941–1942 represented
diverse property and business interests. One was the third-
ranking executive in the Mill; he was believed popularly to be
"the Mill's representative" on the Board. Another was the owner
and president of the Factory and the chairman of the board of
directors of the First National Bank. The third, a physician, was
the most prominent lay member of the Lutheran Church, who,
according to the minister, "represented the Norwegians, but the
Board does not pay much attention to him." The fourth was
the secretary of the Farm Loan Association and allegedly spokes-
man for the farm owners and the Farm Bureau. The fifth was
the owner of a retail store. The sixth member was a "leading
businessman" with "influential family ties"; his wife belonged
to one of the prominent land-owning families in the county.

The President was the key officer on the Board. As its head
and chief executive, he made day-to-day decisions in collaboration with the Superintendent on all questions which involved the
school's relation to the community. Since the President was
closer to the administration of the system than the other members of the Board, he played a more influential role than the
others in the formulation of policy. The Board as a whole was
responsible for salary schedules, maintenance of the school plant,
appointment of personnel, and general policy.

Evidence derived from personal interviews showed that the
members of the Board of Education for more than a generation
have been concerned primarily with two phases: operating the
schools as economically as possible, and seeing that teachers

conform, in the classroom and in their personal lives, to the most conservative economic, political, religious, and moral doctrines prevailing in the local culture. Past and current Board members believed that the school should reflect in its administration and teaching all that is traditionally good and wholesome in Middle Western American small-town life—if it did not cost too much.

From interviews and attendance at Board meetings it became clear that the question of cost was uppermost in their thoughts whenever any innovation was suggested. The problem of cost versus educational values was particularly acute whenever the high school was involved, for high school education was far more expensive than elementary training. The members of the Board were of the opinion that not everyone had the ability to justify a high school education. They believed that many boys and girls who were in high school would have been better off on the farm or at the Mill. They were interested, however, in seeing that everyone who could profit by a high school education was provided with the necessary facilities, but they were not clear in their conception of who could profit by such an education. In general, they meant sons and daughters of the three higher classes, and of class IV, if they behaved properly. Adolescents in class V were not considered to have enough ability to profit from a high school education. No Board member was found who at any time believed that it was the responsibility of the community to provide educational facilities for *all* high-school-aged adolescents. When it was suggested that the traditional type of high school education might not be the type needed for the lower classes, the suggestion was countered usually with the argument that vocational education cost too much per student to be put into effect on a broad scale; besides, the boy or girl could learn the same type of skill "from life."

We concluded from the information given to us by Elmtowners, and by what we saw in the high school, that the members of the Board had a highly developed sense of responsibility for the preservation of the economic power and prestige interests of classes I and II. Their sense of responsibility to the remainder of the community was interpreted in terms of these interests. Thus, the policies they followed and the actions they took with respect to the school reflected the interests of classes I and II, and to a less extent those of the little business and professional people in class III. The relationship between the well-being of the community as a whole and the education of approximately four-fifths of the children was not comprehended by the classes the Board members represented. This inference will be supported by ample evidence in later sections of this chapter and in subsequent ones.

### Financing the schools

Inadequate financial support has hampered the school system for at least half a century. This condition was aggravated by the economic depression of the 1930's. In 1931, the Taxpayer's League forced a revaluation that cut the assessed valuation of farm and town property by 25 per cent. The tax rate on the remaining valuation was not revised upward; consequently the amount raised by taxes to support the schools was reduced automatically. Teachers' salaries were cut from one-fourth to one-half, and all other expenditures were reduced to a minimum. The Board of Education might have raised more money for the schools by the reorganization of the system, but this would have meant an increase in taxes.

After the cut in assessed values, real estate in the community was evaluated at $8,000,000. Some $3,000,000 was in town and $5,000,000 in the rural area; but 62 per cent of the population lived in town and 38 per cent in the country. As a result many people believed the owners of farm lands were not paying their share of the cost of maintaining the school system. This issue centered in the high school because it was more expensive to maintain and because the graduates from the 32 country school districts came to high school in Elmtown.

Three different tax rates were levied on rural and town real estate to support the schools. In Elmtown, property owners were paying a $2.00 rate on each $100 of assessed valuation. The non-high school district levied a rate of 44 cents on each $100 of assessed valuation in the county. In addition, each of the 32 elementary districts levied its own rate, which varied from district to district; in no case did it exceed $1.20 per $100 of assessed valuation.

The state law allowed a school district to levy as much as $1.38 per $100 of assessed valuation without a special election. By special election, the people of a district could tax themselves more, as the people of Elmtown had done, but in the county no elementary district approached this maximum, and landowners feared that any change in the organization of the Elmtown school system would increase their taxes. The fear that the rate on the non-high school land might be raised to the $1.38 limit, or higher, was the resistance point around which the landowners rallied to block attempts to reorganize the Elmtown school system on an adequate financial basis.

Although all the schools were involved in this argument in one way or another, it was centered in the high school because of the service Elmtown High School performed for pupils from the rural area. To illustrate: In 1941–1942, one-fourth of the high school students came from the rural area and three-fourths from the town. The non-high school district paid the Elmtown Board of Education $10,150 tuition for these rural pupils. This represented one-fourth of the $42,470 high school budget. Some landowners argued that the rural pupils were paying their way. On the surface, this argument appeared to be sound, but members of the Board of Education argued that the tuition paid by the non-high school district was figured on current educational costs—instruction, plant operation, and fixed charges for insurance and depreciation. It did not attempt to include either the original cost of the high school plant or the cost of a new one. Operation of the high school represented 55 per cent of a $77,000 school budget, but it included only 36 per cent of the pupils serviced by the system.

Opposition to changes in the schools from 1920 to 1941 came from families in class I who resided in Elmtown. These families were able to block all efforts to reorganize the school system through control of the Board of Education. It might appear paradoxical that a group of townspeople rather than the farmers opposed improvements in the schools. On the contrary, it is a logical product of the property and class systems. In 1940, 73 per cent of all farm land in Home County was operated by tenants, and the county agent estimated that 75 per cent of the land in the Elmtown area was tenant-operated. Six class I families combined owned more than 30,000 acres. Several others owned individually from 1,000 to 2,000 acres. One man, who was never described as a big landholder, casually remarked, "I have a real interest in this high school business. My wife and I own ten farms in this county, and I have a first mortgage on eighteen more." One large landowner said, "The people in this town are interested in keeping their taxes down and nothing else."

The general consensus of class I was that the school was adequate and nothing needed to be done. They were convinced also that the only way the schools could be changed would be through the united action of "the laboring class." As an astute class I behind-the-scenes political figure put it, "The laboring class are the people who always vote for that sort of thing anyway, but all the property owners in the group would be against it. I doubt whether the laboring people could swing it."

### Personnel

Salaried personnel hired by the Board executed its policies and made the school system function. Forty-one of the 45 persons employed by the Board were professionally trained. Forty were teachers licensed by the state. The school nurse, the clerk of the Board, and the custodians were Elmtowners. The Board followed two policies in the employment of teachers and administrators: local girls were hired whenever possible in the elementary schools; outsiders were appointed to administrative positions and in the high school.

These policies combined with the administrative organization of the system and its shortage of funds produced a series of intraschool conflicts which kept practically every employee on edge. The clerk of the Board functioned as the Superintendent's secretary. She was hired by the President of the Board and reported directly to him. Her family had been politically active in Elmtown for three generations. The Superintendent did not trust her, and she did not approve his educational policies. The chief custodian was a strict Lutheran who reported "things going on at the high school" to the Lutheran minister and to the Lutheran member of the Board. His first assistant was a Norwegian and a Lutheran. Neither one approved of the high school dances, parties, and carnivals held in the school. The custodians were hired by the Board and administratively directly under it, but for practical purposes they took their orders from the Superintendent and principals. As local people, they believed in the rightness of the values prevailing in the Board and the community in so far as they pertained to the training of boys and girls in the public schools.

Elementary teachers were split into two distinct groups, outsiders and local girls. Three-fourths of these teachers had been born, reared, and educated in Elmtown. After they had completed Elmtown High School, they had gone away to teachers' colleges or state universities for their professional training; then they had received appointments in the local system. These women generally came from class III families, with a few from class II. Local girls hired into the system followed one of two paths. They either taught for a few years, then married and raised a family, or stayed on year after year as "maiden ladies." Those who married had to leave the system immediately, as local sentiment would not tolerate a married teacher between 1930 and 1941, when so many persons were out of work. The "pedagogical veterans" who made teaching their career were often highly respected by families in the three higher classes. As a class I woman phrased it, "They are such fine teachers. They know the background of each child and teach accordingly." Class IV parents with some frequency accused them of "giving good grades to the children of Board members and the aristocrats." The local teachers usually lived at home with their parents, or in the family home if the parents were dead; so their living expenses were generally lower than those of the outside teachers, and they were better able to get along on the salaries they received than the outsiders.

All outside teachers were dissatisfied, for one reason or another, with either the school or the town. Their frustration was veiled carefully from the local teachers and the townspeople for fear of being considered "disloyal" or "unprofessional." Even among themselves they "guarded their tongues" for fear that their remarks would be carried to the town's gossips, the Superintendent, or the Board. As a group, they were frustrated by the controls imposed on them by the community and the low salaries they received.  Their private lives were circumscribed by taboos, customs, expectancies, and obligations that ranged all the way from where they had to live to where they could buy necessities and to how they might utilize their leisure time without creating a chain of gossip that would reflect adversely upon the teacher, the system, and the profession.

Teachers were required to live in town, and it was suggested that they locate within the three better residential areas, but not in the 400 area.  Unmarried teachers were restricted to a relatively few homes and apartments.  One man said that when he came to town he was told that since the houses and apartments owned by the members of the Board and "a former County Superintendent of Roads" were all rented, he could rent from whomsoever he desired, but not near the canal, north of the railroad, or more than three blocks east of Freedom Street.  "We were told that, if we got over on the east side close to the Mill and down by the canal, we would be talked about and looked down upon."  Yet this teacher severely criticized the elementary school principal when he bought a house outside the approved area.  The president of the bank believed that the elementary school principal was presumptuous in buying a house.  His comments were, "He doesn't need to think that because he bought a house the Board is under any obligation to keep him.  I don't think a person with a school teacher's salary shows very good judgment when he buys a house and puts a $4,000 mortgage on it."

Strong hints were made by businessmen, especially through the Superintendent, to the effect that teachers should purchase their coal, clothes, groceries, cosmetics, and other accessories from locally owned stores.  One teacher was criticized for buying her cosmetics from a drug store owned by a small chain with headquarters in another community.  In this case, the wife of a local druggist called the Superintendent's wife's attention to what the teacher had done, and he in turn enlightened the teacher.  Teachers were forced to contribute to community enterprises, such as Girl Scouts and Boy Scouts, tuberculosis and cancer drives, and the milk fund for underprivileged children.

The community's interest in their religious life was not neglected.  They were obliged to attend church, teach Sunday

School classes, sing in the choir, act as youth leaders, and make annual pledges.

The outside teachers were largely isolated from the community's social life. The Superintendent and the high school principal belonged to Rotary; the elementary school principal was in the Lions Club; but the other men did not belong to any civic or fraternal groups. The women teachers were invited into the Women's Club but, as one teacher said, "As complimentary members only—we don't actually belong." The Superintendent related his feeling of isolation in these words:

> We have been here for two years now and I am convinced we are completely and absolutely outsiders. Actually, we have no friends. We don't have a single family in this town that we could call up and tell we were coming over to spend the evening. This is the worst town I have ever seen in that way. The people will be fine to you on the street or in church and treat you nice on public occasions. Everybody will shake hands and make pleasant remarks, but it doesn't go farther than that.

Teachers were not expected to hold parties or dinners and thereby attempt to further their interests by inviting townspeople to them. If they did, the local people criticized them for putting on airs. The Superintendent warned his teachers on orders from the Board not to smoke in public or to be seen in a tavern or at a public dance. The difference between what a teacher could not do and what a Board member could do is illustrated by this wishful statement of one teacher:

> I would really like to see what they have in the Five Stars. I have been told they have good meals in there and a fine bar, a roulette wheel, a crap table, and other games. I have on occasion passed there and seen members of the Board get out of their cars and go in there for an evening. I know some parents patronize it, but, if a teacher were seen in there, the Board would ask for his resignation right now.

Demands on outside teachers and the low salaries produced a very high rate of turnover in the high school, where all the professional personnel were outsiders. All outsiders from the Superintendent to the least inexperienced girl believe that they were inadequately paid. The Superintendent received $3,500; [3] he was looking for "something nearer $5,000" where the schools were adequately supported. The $2,415 salary of the high school principal was considerably higher than the salaries of his teachers. They ranged from $1,300 to $2,050 with a mean of $1,525. The most common high school salary was $1,300. This figure was the "going" wage for new teachers. Some of these new teachers had had ten years' experience and held masters' degrees. The majority, however, were inexperienced college graduates who came to Elmtown for seasoning before they moved on to a better position. The agricultural teacher received $2,050 to cover twelve months' work and the use of his car. Actually he was paid less than the $1,300 teacher who had a nine-month appointment, without the need to use a car. The elementary school principal's salary was $1,575. His teachers were paid from a low of $917 to a high of $1,391, with a mean of $1,000. The $1,391 teachers were local girls; all had been in the system for fifteen or more years, two 23 and 25 years respectively.

In the two years he had been in the system, the Superintendent had lived through hectic experiences. Eight out of 15 high school teachers were new in the fall of 1941; five had been hired the week school started to replace teachers who had resigned at the last minute to accept positions elsewhere. Three had been in the school a year or less, and four from two to three years; only one had been in the system over four years. The principal had been there four years, but he was desperately anxious to leave. He did resign at the end of the year under pressure from the Board and the Superintendent. Three of the four high school teachers who had taught in Elmtown more than two years were married men with families. They desired to leave, but their family obligations made them hesitate even though they received salaries that were lower than the average semi-skilled mill worker.

### "Trouble" in the schools

The policies pursued by the Board of Education through two generations were forced into the open in the spring of 1941. One

[3] All salary figures are for 1941–1942.

evening *The Elmtown Bugle* made some aspects of the dramatic story public in a front-page article.

> Elmtown high school has been dropped from the list of schools accredited by the North Central Association, the highest accrediting agency in the country and whose approval is recognized by every college and university in the land, it was announced today from the office of [the] Superintendent of Elmtown public schools.

> The reasons given by the North Central Association for its action were: Very inadequate building facilities and insufficient income to carry on a modern program of education and retain experienced teachers in Elmtown High School.

> Members of the Elmtown Board of Education and other school officials were at a loss which way to turn to remedy the conditions . . .

This action was the culmination of twenty years of criticism of Elmtown High School by the State Superintendent of Public Instruction, educational examiners from the State University, and the North Central Association of Schools and Colleges. The Elmtown Superintendent of Schools stated in October, 1941:

> This situation has been building up for a long time. In the summer of 1921, the University examiners told the Board it had to raise more funds to operate the high school and either the building had to be enlarged or a new one built, because the building was overcrowded to the point where it was dangerous. There were then 216 students and we have 406 enrolled now. Through the years the State University, the State Superintendent, and the North Central Association have written letter after letter to the President of the Board and to the different superintendents warning them the town had to do something about the high school or it would be cut off the certification list. As I have looked over these letters, I have seen they were getting tougher year by year. The situation has come to a head now and, unless the Board and the community do something, the University will drop us from the accredited list too.

The Superintendent believed the action of the North Central Association was the mildest effective warning that could be given to the community. Its objective appeared to be directed toward bringing the issue into the open so that a responsible community movement would develop into some appreciable improvement in the high school. Earlier warnings received from the North Central Association, the State Superintendent of Public Instruction, and the Board of State University Examiners had been discussed in Board meetings, buried away in the clerk's file, and nothing effective had been done to meet their criticism.

The action of the North Central Association hurt the community's pride, but it did no material good to the financial support of the high school. If the State University disaccredited the high school—and this was what worried the Board of Education and served as a goad to action—the school would be ineligible to claim state aid funds. This would have meant the loss of more than $8,000 a year, one-fifth of the high school budget. Another more practical consideration to some parents and many students was the fact that, if it were disaccredited by the state, its graduates would have to take entrance examinations before they could enter any college or university.

The North Central Association had adequate justification for the removal of the high school from its accredited list on the basis of the high school building's condition, without taking other factors into consideration. The building had been built in the late 1890's on *one-fourth* of a block between the business and residential sections. The original brick building was two stories in height, with a basement half below and half above ground. Furnace, toilet, cloak, recreation, and storerooms were in the basement. The first floor contained the Superintendent's and principal's offices and two classrooms; the second was divided into three rooms. A wide wooden stairway connected the center hall with two narrow halls, between *four and four and one-half feet in width,* which led to the classrooms.

This building had been adequate for the 75 to 80 students in the late 1890's and early 1900's; however, it had proved to be inadequate by 1912. Four years of agitation for a new high school followed, but, in 1916 and 1917, two wings containing four rooms each were built on the old building, and the first floor was remodeled into a study and assembly hall that seated approximately 175 students when the seats were placed in double rows with the aisle on the outside. The wings crowded the building against the sidewalk on one end and the alley on the other. No provision was made for gymnasium, athletic fields, laboratories, demonstration rooms, or library.

By the fall of 1941, this building was in very poor repair, and the physical facilities were inadequate for 400 students. For instance, the boys' toilet had one urinal, two stools, one lavatory, one electric light, and no mirror. The cloak rooms, adjacent to the Commons Room, consisted of rows of hooks screwed into two-by-four timbers placed on scaffolding. There were no lockers for books, clothes, or personal items. Everything had to be left in these open rooms—one for the girls, the other for the boys. Upstairs a single drinking fountain of the bubble type at each end of the narrow hall furnished water.

The Commons Room was cut off from the furnace room by chicken wire nailed on two-by-four studs. Flattened toilet-paper cartons fastened to the wire prevented students in the Commons Room from seeing into this makeshift supply room and janitor's headquarters. The furnace, an antiquated, hand-fired, coal-burning one, was adjacent to this area. It was some three feet below the surrounding floor in a sump provided with an electrical pump to expel ground water that seeped into it. The steam boiler had an auxiliary hot air blower attached that appeared to be a fire hazard since it was installed under the central stairs and immediately adjacent to a wooden wall. There was no insulation between the hot pipes and the dried timbers and boards.

The high school had become so overcrowded in the late 1930's that the Board of Education had adapted part of Central School to high school uses. This building, located two and one-half blocks away on one-half block of land, was the only modern structure in the school system. It had been built in the early 1920's after a terrific struggle between the "better families" and the "laboring class." Then the elementary school situation was the most pressing question before the community, and it had been solved by a new two-story brick building for the upper elementary grades. The bonds for this building had been voted at a second election. The first time they were defeated; subsequently the mill workers complained so bitterly that the chief executive, according to local folklore, told his workers they were entitled to a good school and to go vote the bonds. It is still believed by conservative elements that the issue was carried by "the Mill vote" at the second election.

The first floor of Central School was used by both high and elementary school classes. Woodworking, domestic science, agriculture, band, orchestra, and physical training were carried on here. The equipment was generally new and in good repair, but the facilities were insufficient to care for the needs of both the elementary and the high schools. The result was severe overcrowding in all areas.

The band room, for example, was a revamped storage space located under the bleachers at the back end of the combination basketball court, gymnasium, assembly hall, and auditorium. The floor area was about twelve by twenty-five feet, but only part of it could be utilized fully as the ceiling sloped down to the floor under the receding bleachers. All band equipment, instruments, and uniforms were stored around the walls. A very small cleared space in the center was the instruction and practice area. About 10 or 12 pupils could be seated here comfortably, but many more than this actually used it at one time. The band teacher's desk was located against the wall at one end. The room was ventilated by a single small window high under the bleachers. In this room five days a week the band and orchestra teacher, for the elementary grades and the high school, instructed from 180 to 200 boys and girls. When this room was in use, the din was terrific, as there were no sound-absorbent materials on the walls or ceiling.

These conditions were known generally, but no one was sufficiently interested to attempt to do anything about them. Although parents were urged by the Superintendent and teachers to visit the school, they ignored the invitation.

Members of the Board of Education had not visited the high school to see for themselves the overcrowded conditions, the vast amount of traffic in the narrow halls, or the physical condition of the plant. This became evident in October, 1941, when I was appointed to a special Evaluating Committee to rate the high school in accordance with instructions from the State University. This committee was composed of ten local people and two research workers. Although all members accepted their appointments and although a day and hour were arranged for a visit to the high school, when the time came only three local people appeared. Two were members of the Board of Education, the third was a prominent official who had graduated from the local high school some twenty-five years before and acted as citizen-at-large.

In the course of the inspection made by the citizen-at-large, the two Board members, the Superintendent of Schools, and myself, the following facts became apparent:

(1) The two Board members had not visited the school heretofore while it was in session. That the halls were so narrow surprised them. (The committee had to walk down them single file.) One Board member said, "I want to see how you regulate traffic when classes pass." The other remarked, "Yes, that is something I have to see. I have often heard the children talk about the student traffic cops."

The committee arranged to be in the building when the classes changed. It observed how the students on the second floor walked in single file to the ends of the building, then down the stairs to the first floor, while those on the first floor walked toward the center stairs and then up them. Those who had classes in Central School left the building by the side exit. The scheme worked as long as there was no disturbance. To prevent disturbances, a senior boy acting as a traffic policeman was stationed at each entrance to the hall to regulate traffic.

(2) One Board member noted that there were only four lights in the study hall ceiling. They were placed so far apart that the center of the room was in deep shadow, and the students sitting in this area had difficulty reading. He was very surprised and said, "Now, we've got to correct that right away no matter what the cost."

(3) The building's poor repair was noted by the citizen-at-large as he looked around at the cracked and discolored plaster on the walls and ceiling. He noted, "It hasn't changed a bit since I was here twenty-five years ago. In fact, I don't think the old building has changed any, except that it is a lot older and in much worse condition." As we looked into one room, we noted a patch of semi-dry plaster about four feet wide and six feet long on the ceiling. One member of the Board said with obvious excitement, "What's that?" The Superintendent replied, "That's

where the plaster fell off last week. It hit two children on the head when it fell, but fortunately it did not hurt them seriously, as it broke into small pieces before it hit." The Board member's response was, "Oh, God! This is serious." Both Board members had children who had classes in this room each day.

(4) While we were looking around the science room on the second floor, one Board member looked out the window and asked the Superintendent, "Where is the fire escape?" He replied, "There isn't any fire escape." The citizen-at-large stated, "There has never been a fire escape on the second floor as long as I can remember." The Superintendent went on, "This is probably the only school building in the state which you will find like this." The Board member replied, "That's terrible. That's absolutely incomprehensible! I think it's criminal. If a fire should ever get started in here, the chances are there'd be a heavy loss of life. That's bad. I just can't see why the state fire marshal hasn't done something about this building." Again he repeated, "I don't see why the state fire marshal hasn't condemned the building."

This Board member vigorously pushed the issue of the poor lighting in the study hall and the lack of fire escapes at the next meeting of the Board, and these defects were corrected by the installation of more lights and fire ladders on the outside of the building.

The committee members, who made the inspection, met later in a downtown office to discuss how they should rate the school on a ten-point rating schedule the committee was required to submit to the State University. The men were very frank in their appraisal of the extremely poor physical conditions under which the school was operating, but they dodged placing responsibility. No one implied that the real reasons for the impasse were traceable to the policies of the Board of Education for more than a generation, and to the latent but controlling factor—the way in which the community's power system was related to the school system. When the final rating was made, the committee agreed that the building, light, heat, ventilation, sanitation, safety factor, location, and financial support of the school were *very poor*.

At the same time, it decided that the "policies of the Board of Education" were *excellent* and the administration of the school was *superior*. The remaining eight points of evaluation were concerned with teaching, records, and general housekeeping functions of a routine nature handled by the teachers. They were rated as "average for cities of this size."

This incident indicates the extent to which the community relied upon the members of the Board of Education and the school authorities to manage the school efficiently and to give the pupils a good education. They were lulled into complacency by the educational policies of the Board of Education, working in cooperation with the school authorities, who believed in publicizing the school's good points and ignoring or suppressing events and conditions they considered "bad publicity."

The question may be raised: Who was responsible for such conditions? This is a difficult question to answer, for some persons might place blame upon the Superintendent of Schools, and many Elmtowners did. The Board of Education was believed by many persons to be responsible. Still others accused the "big landowners" and "propertied interests."

\*    \*    \*    \*    \*

The reader may be interested to learn that Elmtowners gave the most effective answer to this question when they rejected the plans of a majority of the Board of Education to build a new high school at a special election in the spring of 1947. By a vote of $2\frac{1}{2}$ to 1, Elmtowners defeated the Board's proposal to float a special bond issue to erect a new building. Five members of the Board and the President resigned after their program was defeated. The one member who did not resign was a member of an "old family" which owned large tracts of land in the community. In his precinct, not a single vote was cast in favor of the proposed bond issue for a new high school. The man selected to head the new Board of Education was one of the wealthiest men in the county. Elmtowners were agreed in the summer of 1948 that he was a leader of the opposition to the proposal for a new building. Elmtowners with whom we talked in 1948 also believed that it was the organized opposition of "the money" and the "big landowners" which defeated the Board of Education in its efforts to provide the community with an adequate school plant.          *     *     *     *     *

The professional educators could certainly not be accused of being the seat of the trouble; however, they were by many Elmtowners who sought a scapegoat they could whip with impunity. The Superintendent of Schools was the key to the school situation from the viewpoint of Elmtowners who did not want to do anything about the schools as well as of those who wanted to improve them. What neither group appeared to realize was that the educational policies were formulated by the Board and that the Superintendent was merely a hired administrator. His contract with the community was professional and contractual, since he was hired by the Board on an annual basis. The Superintendent as a hired administrator was brought into a pre-existing communal situation. He had to adjust to and become a part of a social, political, and educational situation he did not create. If he was to succeed he had to organize his thoughts and activities in accordance with local beliefs, prejudices, and ground rules of what to do and not to do. Otherwise he would be released by the Board as a failure.

The Superintendent's first responsibility was to the Board that hired him; he must answer to it for his actions as well as for the actions of his teachers and pupils. He acted as liaison between the principals, teachers, and pupils on the one hand and the Board and the school's patrons on the other. The Superintendent was subject to many types of pressures from the community as they related to him as a person (from the school system, from the Board, and from students and teachers). He knew that what the teachers did in the classroom and in the community, especially what they were alleged to do, reflected on his "standing with the Board."

The Superintendent was haunted by the fear of being discharged since he was caught between the Board of Education and the school. He had his professional values to live with as well as the controls exerted by the community. He believed that, if he were dismissed, he would have difficulty in finding another place: "Such things follow a man." His immediate policy was to please everybody by doing nothing in the school crisis. He rightfully believed that it was the responsibility of the Board of Education to solve the difficulty of the school system. He was aware of a mounting tide of gossip to the effect that "there must be something wrong with this man. We have had a lot of teacher trouble since he came. Now the school's lost its rating. The Board better look into things in the high school pretty carefully." The Superintendent conceived of himself as a trouble-shooter who had to keep a badly overburdened and worn-out machine going. He was convinced that the school fight would eventually "backfire" on him; the best policy for him was to keep things going smoothly from day to day, then get out as soon as possible. He summarized his position in these words:

> On the surface it's all very nice here, but underneath there are deep animosities. The situation in town is not what we would like to have; so many things could happen. The fact of the matter is I'm going to get out of this school as fast as I can. I have made moves already to find another position, but a man has to be careful about that or it will not do him any good professionally. But just between you and me, I'm going to get out.

His anxieties were justified by the experiences he had had in the three years he had been in the system, as well as those of his predecessor, who had been the central figure in a recent intra-school intrigue which resulted in the dismissal of the elementary principal, nine teachers, and the Superintendent after a school strike by the high school pupils.

The new Superintendent moved slowly the first year. By quiet investigation, he tried to trace gossip, rumor, and innuendo to their source. He made every effort to placate the teachers and place the school system on a plane where it would be above reproach locally. In spite of his efforts, one-third of the outside teachers resigned. The second year, he directed his efforts toward the reorganization of the school records, a new grading system, and the establishment of student government in the high school. It was generally agreed by teachers, pupils, and townspeople that he accomplished his objectives in a laudable manner.

With several of the high school teachers, I believe that the widespread dismissal of teachers in the spring of 1939 served as an emotional release to the members of the Board of Education and Elmtowners in general.  By firing the Superintendent, the elementary principal, and eight outside teachers, the Board made the outside professional educators the scapegoats in the situation.  They thereby transferred their collective guilt and that of the group responsible for Board policies from themselves to the teachers they dismissed.  By projecting their frustration upon the professional educators they felt relieved of responsibility for the conditions in the schools.  However, they used as their rationalization for these deeper motives the explanation that they did not want the teachers to set a bad example for the children.  This incident focused the attention of many people on the teachers, who henceforth were watched more carefully.  The teacher who really or allegedly violated the code laid down by the community immediately aroused latent emotions in persons in need of another scapegoat.

### The social structure and attitudes toward the schools

When this study was started, the action of the North Central Association was a live issue, and people readily voiced their opinions on what they thought about the high school.  It was soon apparent that the attitudes expressed by different Elmtowners reflected, in large measure, the speaker's position in the social structure.  About 8 out of 10 class I adults believed the community had been treated unfairly; the school was more than adequate; the charges against the school were trifling matters and did not mean much.  Four former presidents of the Board were interviewed on the subject, and each defended the way he had administered the affairs of the school system.  None could see that anything was seriously wrong with the high school.  They argued that its graduates had gone away to some of the finest colleges and universities and acquitted themselves well.  This, they believed, demonstrated that the quality of the teaching was as good as any in the country and that the curriculum offered was good enough to equip these graduates to meet the tests of college competition.  One admitted that the building was a fire hazard, then asked:

But why should the school lose its rating because the building is a fire hazard? I don't see it. I think that the high school is a better than average school, and I don't see why it should be condemned because of the building.

With our President running the School Board and our Superintendent, I think we have a very superior situation. I think we should leave the system as it is.

Not a single class I person was found who accepted the North Central Association's criticism. An elderly businessman came nearest to agreeing with it when he remarked, ". . . we have a pretty good school system here, but it's just pretty good. In fact, you might say it is the main weak spot of the community." On the whole, class I persons were willing to ignore the snub from the North Central Association and wait to see what the state authorities would do.

Class II persons were divided in their loyalties. They were close enough to the reality of the situation to admit that the charges were sound, but they were close enough to class I in their interests to side with it until the whole thing was settled one way or another. Privately, practically every person placed the blame for the condition of the school system on the "propertied interests" who had controlled the Board of Education for so many years. According to class II persons, the owners of the factories, mines, banks, and extensive farm lands were concerned only with keeping tax rates low. This could be achieved through the control of the Board of Education. By refusing to remodel the old building, by buying only what was necessary, by allowing pupils to quit school when they desired, and by keeping teachers' salaries low, it was alleged that taxes could be kept low because support of the school system was the major cost of government.

Class III persons commonly blamed both classes I and II for the situation since the great majority of the Board members through the years had come from class II. Optimistically, these people generally believed that the high school was better than average, but that something ought to be done about the building. Few knew how this could be accomplished since "the Board will do what the bankers and the big landowners want." Class III persons felt impotent before the power the two higher classes possessed and knew how to use. The owners of small businesses feared that a new school building would raise taxes. The problem of making profits balance the costs of operating their businesses under severe competition was a constant pressure on them, and, if increased taxes were to cut their profits, they were not sure that they wanted a new school. Owners of medium-sized farms appeared to be strongly opposed to a proposal which the Board was seriously considering to include the rural territory in an enlarged high school district that would cover the entire community. They were working against the proposal through a secret Farm Bureau Committee. Clearly an adequate high school for Elmtown was not to be purchased at the expense of the small owner of a business or a farm. Yet this class looked to education as the principal avenue open to its children for success in adult life, but it did not think of the high school as an educational institution. It thought of college and advanced vocational training as the open sesame to success. Few class III's comprehended the need for adequate preparation for these higher goals—certainly not if they had to pay so much for it that their own success was jeopardized. Their struggle for success placed them in an ambivalent position on this issue. To have a good high school would cost them more money in taxes, and this would cut down on the family's utilizable income, but to have one might enhance the children's opportunity in life.

The dilemma of the little business people may be illustrated by the statement of a class III woman who did the office work for her husband and helped wait upon trade in their store.

> The high school is horrible. The halls are narrow and the stairs so worn children are hurt on them every so often. The floors squeak so bad when a person moves, they can be heard all over the room. If they ever have a fire in there, it is going to be awful. Why, it's a crime to use a building like that.
>
> Now they are talking about a new building. This is no time to build with costs going up by leaps and bounds. Why, here in the store we never know when we order something whether we are going to get it and how much it is going to cost. Our costs are going way up, and we can't raise prices or the people will go somewhere else. If they build a new building, our taxes will be doubled, and we just can't pay them the way things are now. No! We can't do anything right now, even though that building is so overcrowded you can hardly walk down the halls.

I think we ought to have a community high school. Then a lot of these big landowners would have to help educate the children. As it is now, it costs us too much to run the school system. But I suppose something will have to be done now the school is taken off the accredited list.

Probably three out of four class IV adults were unconcerned over conditions in the school. They knew that the school was overcrowded and the building old, but they were not discontented, nor did they think that something had to be done. Indifference best characterizes their reaction. There was, however, an unorganized minority who felt bitterly about the high school and the way it was run. These people criticized the Board, the Superintendent, the principal, and the teachers. They believed that the school was operated for the sons and daughters of the three higher classes, particularly those of the two upper ones and against the interests of their children. Their criticism was directed toward the social system, not the school alone.

The building has been condemned twice by the state men, but they go on using it. It's all the School Board's fault.

The Board's always on the inside ring. The Courthouse Ring and the Lawyer Ring decide who's going to run on the School Board. They pick out someone who belongs to their group, and then they run them. It's easy enough for them to always elect the people they want to have in there because practically no one will stop work to go vote in the piddling school election. You think these people down at the Mill are going to take off two or three hours from work and get docked and go out there and vote? No, they stay at their work and only those that are inside the ring vote.

A few years ago, we had a hot school election, but the ring, they knew how to take care of things. When they saw their enemies were going to their election, they went to the telephone and got out their cars and rounded up their friends and beat us easily. This inside ring is just like a Chicago gang. They're organized. It's organized around the newspaper and the courthouse. The banks and lawyers and the big landowners, they're in on it too. The Republican machine and this newspaper run this town.

The high school's rotten all the way down to the building. People get on the School Board who want to see their children make good grades and so they hire the teachers, and only those teachers who give the children the grades, well, they're the only ones they keep.

The grammar school teachers and most of the high school teachers play the School Board's game.

These attitudes were representative of a discontented minority of 20 to 25 per cent of class IV, scattered throughout the communal area.  Generally, they were ambitious people who had tried "to climb the social ladder" and had run into effective opposition.  They were often called "radicals" and "trouble makers" by persons in the higher classes and by many persons in class IV.  Most of them spoke more or less openly after they learned that we could be trusted not to "pack tales" or condemn them.  But in their initial contacts they were careful not to express themselves too frankly, as careless words could be costly to their personal affairs.  One mother emphatically stated, "We have learned from bitter experience that some of the things we've said have been carried into the school and they haven't done the children any good.[4]  A misspoken word could have resulted in the dismissal of the parent from his job.[5]  This fear of what might happen to them if they spoke frankly might have restrained some persons in their comments about the high school.

Class IV, as a whole, believed that nothing could be done to challenge the position of "the inner ring."  The discontented minority thought that outside pressures from the State University and the State Superintendent of Public Instruction alone could do it.  In a vague way, these people looked for help from "the government" without knowing how it could be effectuated.  Perhaps more important, there was no apparent leadership in this stratum.  Its criticism of the school system was basically negative, destructive, and on a vituperative plane.

Class V people were almost entirely disinterested in the question.  They were so far removed from the main current of community opinion and so much preoccupied with their own affairs

[4] Later experience verified this statement. On numerous occasions, the Superintendent, the high school principal, and two teachers who acted as "bird dogs" for the Superintendent attempted to elicit statements from me about what certain parents, who were suspected of being critical or were known to be critical of the school and the Board of Education, had said about the school.

[5] The specter of years of unemployment, during the depression of the 1930's, still weighed heavily upon the memories of class IV people.

that they took little interest in things of a civic nature. They knew that their children were discriminated against in the school system by both the teachers and the pupils, but they did not openly voice hostile attitudes toward the School Board and the large property owners such as were found in the vocally critical minority of class IV. On the whole, they tended to personalize discrimination within the school itself rather than in the community, individual parents blaming teachers for specific acts they considered hostile to them or their children. They used these as excuses to justify the withdrawal of the child from school. Any occurrence in the high school which these people could use to explain why a child dropped out of school was used. For instance, one mother stated:

> The place is overcrowded. They have over 400 there and only room for 300. They took them off the list this year. The kids can't go to college now, so why send them to a school like that?

Another one reported, "After that teacher died last year, I was afraid to send the girls. They might catch something." [6]

Class V's isolation from the respectable classes probably accounts for its relative apathy on a question vital to the property owners and the people who looked to education as a channel leading toward success in life. Class V parents were indifferent to the future; they did not look forward to anything better for themselves or their children than they had known. Their school experience had been limited almost exclusively to the elementary grades. Dropping out of school by the end of the eighth grade was the rule, and to go beyond this point was not approved generally by the class culture. Therefore, few families urged their children to continue on into high school. To be brief, the desire for a high school education was not a part of the class folkways. If it had been, it is probable that these parents would have shown more concern over the loss of accreditation.

[6] The teacher referred to had died after an operation that was variously reported as being for cancer of the stomach and visceral tumors, but many class IV and class V persons placed a lewd interpretation on her death.

# 7

---

# THE ADOLESCENT IN THE COMMUNITY

PARTICIPATION IN THE CULTURE brings the maturing person into contact sooner or later with almost every aspect of social life in a community the size of Elmtown. By the time the teens are reached, boys and girls are aware of the essential functions of each institution. They know more about the family, the school, the church, the grocery and meat market than they do about the county government and the big gray brick bank on the corner of Freedom and First Streets. Most high-school-aged boys and girls have a good understanding of the class system. As John Bingham said, "These high school kids know what is what, and who is who; we don't fool them any." This observation was borne out many times by the remarks and actions of adolescents in the study group. These young people know "there are not supposed to be any classes, but there are." They have learned that the sheriff arrests people and that law breakers are put in jail—at least some of them are. They have learned also that the class to which the offender belongs determines whether he is arrested and whether he goes to jail. In short, they have a good working knowledge of the formal and informal aspects of the culture.

## Status and role

*Elmtown's culture does not provide any community-wide procedures to help the adolescent define himself as an adolescent in the transition from child to adult.* Of course, there are no rites or ceremonies, such as are found among many preliterate people, to signify the end of childhood and the beginning of adulthood.

But what is more important, the culture has developed very few substitutes; so neither adults nor adolescents have group-wide conventions to guide them in their definitions of what to expect from either youth or adult.  Moreover, the culture has few definitions either relative to the borders or divisions within the period called adolescence.  Consequently, both age groups function in an ill-defined no-man's-land that lies between the protected dependency of childhood, where the parent is dominant, and the independent world of the adult, where the person is relatively free from parental controls.  This no-man's-land is a place where the maturing person works out the extremely important developmental tasks of freeing himself from his family, making heterosexual adjustments, selecting a vocation, gaining an education, and—for a considerable percentage of young Elmtowners—establishing a home of his own.

The high school is the principal institution the culture has developed for this purpose, and it is so integrated with the class system that it functions more as a device to prolong dependency on the family within the three upper classes than as a training ground for adult life for all adolescents.  The few services which the community provides emphasize protection from knowledge about the inner workings of adult society rather than orientation to it.  By segregating young people into special institutions, such as the school, Sunday School, and later into youth organizations such as Boy Scouts and Girl Scouts for a few hours each week, adults apparently hope that the adolescent will be spared the shock of learning the contradictions in the culture.  At the same time, they believe that these institutions are building a mysterious something variously called "citizenship," "leadership," or "character" which will keep the boy or girl from being "tempted" by the "pleasures" of adult life.  Thus, the youth-training institutions provided by the culture are essentially negative in their objectives, for they segregate adolescents from the real world that adults know and function in.  By trying to keep the maturing child ignorant of this world of conflict and contradictions, adults think they are keeping him "pure."

The adolescent's ambiguous position in the society may be a product of the loss of function for this age group in our culture. The increasing expectancy of life coupled with the harnessing of physical energy and the development of mechanical techniques on the farm and in industry have turned society from its direct dependence on the adolescent in the productive process.[1] The establishment of high schools during the late nineteenth and early twentieth centuries may have been a response to the loss of economic functions of adolescents in American culture. Although this movement developed under the guise of the need for more training for adult life, the training given has been limited largely to intellectual pursuits; practically, it has extended the period of dependency on the family for four or five years in the "middle classes," and increasingly in the "working class."[2] So far as Elmtown is concerned, the high school has never been integrated into the communal culture; neither has it segregated many more than one-half of the adolescents out of direct participation in the economic process.

The nearest the culture has approached the problem of defining the borders of the no-man's-land between the dependency of childhood and the independence of adulthood is in law. But the law, like other aspects of the culture, is contradictory in the way it defines what an adolescent can or cannot do, what is expected of him, and what he can expect from the law. For instance, males and females in Home State cannot vote until they are 21 years of age, but when they are 14 they can enter the economic world with the approval of an employer and a duly authorized school official but without the consent of parents or guardian. The school law provides for compulsory school attendance for both sexes until the sixteenth birthday, except for young people who procure an employment certificate after their fourteenth birthday; full employment maturity is reached at age 16. Both males and females are regarded as mature by the motor vehicle act when the fifteenth birthday is reached. The

[1] For a discussion of this point in considerable detail, see: Robert S. and Helen M. Lynd, *Middletown*, Harcourt, Brace and Company, New York, 1928, pp. 39–52; and *Middletown in Transition*, Harcourt, Brace and Company, New York, 1937, pp. 49–55. The detailed changes in Elmtown's economy in the period from 1890 to 1940 have been omitted here because of the nature of the problem under discussion.

[2] Edward B. Reuter, in "The Education of the Adolescent," *Journal of Educational Sociology*, Vol. 14 (1940–1941), pp. 67–78, developed this point.

law has a different view of matrimonial maturity.  A male cannot marry without his parents' or guardian's consent before he is 21 years of age, and only with their consent after he is 18 years of age.  A female may marry without parental consent at age 18, but she can marry after 16 with this consent.  Where bastardy is involved, no age limits are recognized for either the man or the woman.  The law apparently regards biological capacity for parenthood as *prima facie* evidence of maturity, but interestingly enough, if bastardy is the point at issue and the parties are under the legal age for marriage, the law does not provide for their marriage, even though they wish to marry, without falsifying their ages.  The civil code states that a female reaches her majority at 18 and a male at 21, but in the realm of torts the courts have ruled that a person above 14 years of age has the same responsibility as an adult.  However, from the viewpoint of criminal law, different definitions are laid down.  Males under 17 and females under 18 are treated as delinquents rather than criminals.  They are tried in juvenile rather than criminal courts, and their records are kept separate from those of adult offenders.  Likewise, their punishment is meted out in terms of the concept of juvenile delinquency rather than of adult crime.  When dependency and neglect are involved, a male reaches maturity when he is 17, but a female not until she is 18.

A further illustration of the ambiguous position of the adolescent in the community as defined by law is his relation to taverns and places where alcoholic beverages are sold or served.  One statute prohibits the sale of intoxicants to minors and states that they shall not be allowed to approach the bar.  Another stipulates that minors shall not be allowed to draw, mix, or serve intoxicating drinks, but it allows the wife of an alcoholic beverage licensee to draw, mix, or serve drinks.  Nothing is said about her age.  This point was brought to our attention by a minister who complained bitterly about a tavernkeeper's wife, age 16, who acted as barmaid in her husband's tavern.  The prosecutor, he claimed, refused to act because the law was not violated.  The wife's younger sister worked in the barroom as a waitress.  It was illegal for her to work in the taproom, even though she did not approach the bar; but, in fact, she substituted as barmaid when her sister was not there.  The law was contradictory, and the girls did not obey it; probably they did not know of its existence. Even if they did, the definitions of the southern European culture they had learned from their parents and associates approved this behavior.

Clearly there is no consistency between the way the law defines immaturity and maturity for either sex. These conflicting definitions complicate growing up, for in one aspect of life the adolescent is considered an independent adult, whereas in another he is a dependent child.

Inconsistent definitions of personal status, rights, responsibilities, duties, and roles are encountered constantly between parents and children. The boys and girls generally consider themselves capable of exercising adult judgment, whereas their parents and other adults usually view them as "immature children." Again, parents often present their adolescent children with conflicting definitions of their role in the community and the family within a single hour. A common complaint of the adolescents is that their parents expect them to perform the same work around the home as the parents do, yet they deny them the right to select the clothes they wear. Some parents do not worry about their daughters' working until ten o'clock at night in the theaters or restaurants, but they refuse to allow them to go to young people's meeting at the church on Sunday evening; the reason most commonly given is that they do not want their children on the streets after dark. Yet a girl is allowed to walk home alone from work between ten and eleven o'clock six nights a week. The same type of inconsistency is experienced in school, where teachers expect students to accomplish their homework without the help of other students, but do not trust them to leave the area during class hours without a written excuse from home or the principal's office.

### Institutional competition

Institutions compete with one another for the time and loyalty of the adolescents. They also operate independently of one another, and often at cross purposes, for each is interested in furthering its own ends rather than in aiding in the development of the boy or girl. The institutional leaders, however, are convinced that the contribution of their particular effort is of the utmost importance to the young people with whom they come in contact. Consequently they heap condemnation upon institutions whose programs compete directly with theirs, especially if they believe that the competing program undermines theirs. For instance, the Superintendent of Schools and the high school principal severely criticize the Lutheran minister as well as the owner of the theaters. Each time the school has a dance, play, or party in the evening, the Lutheran minister organizes a church party to keep the Lutheran students away from the high school affair. The minister admits that he does this because "their souls are damaged by secular pleasures." The theater owner allegedly puts on a double feature at half-price to attract high school students away from ball games, dances, and parties. He maintains that his action is not deliberate or perverse, but merely a product of booking practices by motion picture rental agencies. He asks, "Do the high school people expect me to close up when they have a party?" The incongruity in his argument is that double features and reduced prices occur on the nights the high school holds its affairs and at practically no other time.

Underlying the apparent surface cordiality among institutional officers is a broad area of questioning of motives, program content, and goals, if not downright distrust of one institution by another. School teachers do not see eye-to-eye with ministers on their religious programs for the high school students. The ministers in turn severely criticize in private the school authorities for being irreligious and sponsoring dances in the school gymnasium. A few are so sure of their positions that they preach sermons against "godless educators," dancing, and "unclean recreation." One minister in particular so distrusts the influence of the high school that he asks devout pupils in his congregation to report to him irreligious statements made by high school teachers in their classes. He records the alleged remarks in his files and calls them to the attention of the church board. In the spring of 1942, one high school teacher was accused of blasphemy through this information system. The minister discussed the matter with his board, and the decision was reached to take the matter up with the teacher directly rather than with the Board or the Superintendent, as these were godless men. The minister said:

It is useless to go to them. This thing has happened time and time again. They only laugh at us. No, we must go directly to this man and make him feel the power of God. We will give him one chance more. Then he must go.

The evening after these remarks were made to me, the minister and a committee of churchmen went to the teacher's home and stated their bill of particulars. The teacher was told that if he made any more heretical statements he would be run out of town. The teacher in turn reported the incident to the Superintendent. The Superintendent said to him, "Be careful of what you say. We are all being watched. I think the Board will understand, but be careful of what you say from now on."

There is no coordination between the programs of the different youth-training institutions with regard to either content or objectives. Each institution—school, church, job, recreation, family—has a self-defined set of objectives and a program presumably designed to attain them. Furthermore, each one is sure of the worth of its program and the contribution it makes to the adolescent's development. The program of each is centered around the continuation of cherished institutional values which adults believe the young should learn and respect. The high school is concerned with educating the adolescent; the church with imparting spiritual and moral truths; the youth organizations teach character; the recreational people claim that they are teaching the rules of the game, the need to be a good sport, the way to relax; and the storekeeper believes that he is teaching the boy he hires after school and on Saturdays to become a businessman or to know the value of a dollar. In this process, each institution goes its own way. There is no coordination among their general objectives or of the effects of this disparate training on the adolescent. The net effect is community-wide unconcern about the training of all adolescents; however, there is great concern about the training of a particular one, or a segment of the total group, but not adolescents as adolescents, as is the case in many preliterate societies.

Training adolescents to be "good citizens" is the professed objective of all institutional functionaries. However, in the administration of their offices emphasis is placed on the institutional program rather than on the effect it has on the adolescents subjected to it. Little effort is made to determine whether or not the program presented is doing what it is presumed to do. The assumption followed by the adults in charge is that the program is good because it represents established beliefs and practices. If the adolescent does not accept the program, he is at fault, not the institution. Since each institution functions independently, and each is convinced of the need for its program in the development of good citizens, there are inevitable conflicts in the several programs presented to the adolescent. In addition, each tends to overemphasize its own importance and to demand greater amounts of their time and loyalty than boys and girls can possibly give to it and still participate in the others. This overemphasis combined with competition between institutions and class groups for favorable prestige positions in the social structure produces differential opportunity among adolescents in their efforts to adjust to the demands the culture makes upon them.

Another complicating factor faced by the adolescent in his adjustment to adult life is the official denial of the existence of the class system. None of Elmtown's institutional leaders admits officially and publicly that the community's institutions are integrated around classes. Yet each one privately says that classes exist and proceeds to indicate explicitly how this fact has to be taken into consideration in the administration of the functions of his office. Formal definitions of institutions are built around the idea that all men are born free and equal; Elmtowners publicly maintain this position, but in actual situations they conveniently forget the formal protestation and act toward one another on the basis of differential evaluation of persons and behavior far more consistently than they do in terms of the formal definitions of the culture.

The school, the job, and leisure time pursuits are the greatest competitors for the time and loyalty of adolescents in Elmtown. In these areas of the culture the adolescent faces the greatest amount of conflict. Also, it is here that the factor of class operates with the greatest force and clarity, for these functions demand the best hours of the adolescent's day. The high school year lasts from early September to early June of the following year. Its scholastic program begins at eight o'clock in the morning and lasts until three-fifteen in the afternoon five days a week. In addition, there are the inevitable extracurricular activities that begin immediately after school and last until five-thirty or six o'clock; many start after the supper hour and continue until ten or eleven o'clock at night. These of course are the hours the work world and recreational centers also use in the daily round of activities.

The alternative of school or work is faced by the vast majority of young Elmtowners sometime between their fourteenth and eighteenth birthdays. The choice between work or school is a parting of the ways for the adolescent, for his social relations with practically every institution in the community throughout the adolescent years, possibly on into adult life, will be associated significantly with this decision. If he takes the school road, he will move into an entirely different social world from the one he will traverse if he takes the work road. A middle road between the two is traveled by those who combine school with part-time work out of school hours.

Confusion and conflict in the state labor and school laws enable local officials to compromise easily with the demands the school and the job make upon adolescents. The school law requires all children, except the grossly abnormal, to attend private, public, or parochial schools between their seventh and sixteenth years at least 130 days a year. This is nullified to a large extent by a paragraph which states:

> Children over fourteen who are necessarily and lawfully employed may be excused from attendance at school by the county superintendent or the superintendent of the public school which the child should be attending on the recommendation of the board of education of the public school district in which such children reside, and said board shall certify the facts in all such cases.

The state labor law is tied in with this excuse provision in the school law. It states that any boy or girl may obtain an employment certificate provided the minor can read and write legibly simple sentences in the English language and has ". . . attended school at least 130 days during the year previous" to the issuance of the certificate "or between his thirteenth and fourteenth birthdays." To obtain an employment certificate, the applicant has to certify to the issuing authority that employment has been promised and to furnish the name of the prospective employer. There is no provision in either the labor law or the school law which requires the consent, either verbal or written, of a parent or guardian before an employment certificate is issued. Neither is the issuing authority required to verify the claim of the applicant that he has been promised employment by the avowed employer. A boy or girl over 14 years of age presumably is considered mature enough by the law to decide whether he shall go to work or continue in school. School officials seemingly have little choice in the matter; actually, they may exert considerable influence to keep the adolescent in school or make it easy for him to enter the work world, for the loose wording of the school and labor laws places the responsibility for their enforcement on local officials. If community pressures require the boy or girl to attend school, the school law may be used as authority. On the other hand if, as in Elmtown, local interests are concerned more with keeping educational costs to a minimum, they may do so with impunity by issuing employment certificates to almost any boy or girl over 14 years of age who asks for one, or, as happens more generally, simply allowing the youngster to drop out of school.

The dominant conditioning factor in the choice between school or work, as well as the combination of school with part-time work, is the adolescent's need for money. Long before a young Elmtowner is able to earn money, he knows that he must have it to buy the things his culture teaches him he must have if he is to be "successful." He has to pay a nickel before he can go to a two-reel motion picture show in the second grade. When the little boy (or girl) goes to Sunday School, he is expected to put a penny in the box that is circulated before the class is over. When the fascinating world of stores is entered, the child is surrounded by things he desires and the storekeeper wants him to have, for a price. Little Elmtowners, by the time they are 7 years old, have learned two fundamental principles about pecuniary values and the prestige structure: (1) some people are rich and others are poor, and his family can or cannot afford stipulated things because of the amount of wealth it possesses;

and (2) high prestige is attached to the rich and low prestige to the poor. By the time adolescence is reached, pecuniary values are firmly impressed upon the boy or girl. In fact, it might be said that the need for and the power of money is the central focus in adolescent experience in Elmtown, particularly in the three lower classes.

Whatever an adolescent boy or girl does, aside from merely walking around town, requires money. Constant demands for money by every institution he comes in contact with—Boy Scouts and Girl Scouts, the picture show, the high school basketball game, the hamburger stand—place him in the position of needing money to do the things his peers are doing. His clique may or may not have money; but, to do the things they want to do, they must have it. In this culture, the ability to pay one's way is a general symbol of one's maturity and competence; to be a success, one must meet the economic demands made upon him.

To the adolescent, money comes from two sources: it is either earned by his own efforts or given to him by his family. The need "to pay one's way" presents the adolescent who cannot obtain from his family the funds necessary for his participation in the peer group's activities, no matter what his class position is, with a dilemma: Should he enter the work world or stay on in school? The more severe the economic drain on the family, the more likely the boy or girl is to choose or be forced by circumstances to drop out of school and find a job.

Although a family might be able to afford the constant drain of dollars, half-dollars, and quarters for their children's activities, the parents generally do not approve of the practice. Moreover, they are prone to question each request. This leads to friction between parent and child, and each party is likely to feel "put upon." The healthy solution to the problem from the adolescent's viewpoint is to earn his own money. In classes IV and V, one measure of male adequacy is to earn money by holding "a man's job at a man's pay." In the adolescent's world, money is indispensable if one is to do things and have a good time.

Boys and girls who receive their spending money from their families regard themselves as superior to those who have to work for it. This does not mean that work is not a positive value in the culture; it is, and to earn money is good, but to receive it from the family is better.  Boys and girls whose families give them from one dollar to ten dollars a week look down upon the boys and girls who have to earn their money by part-time jobs. The adolescent with a part-time or a full-time job is excluded in large part from the activities and the free and easy life of his peers who receive their spending money from parents.  The gainfully employed adolescent often is forced to help with the family budget, buy part or all of his clothes, and scheme to save enough for his own pleasures.

The family sets the stage upon which the adolescent is expected, if not compelled by subtle processes and techniques, to play out his roles in the developmental tasks he faces in the transition from child to adult.  As he moves into the community, he carries his family's station in the prestige structure with him. He is identified by his family name, and the heritage of the family is his heritage.  To be sure, he is a personality separate from his family; however, sociologically, he is an inseparable part of it since he has not had an opportunity to emancipate himself from it and establish a station of his own in the community's prestige structure.  Consequently, when an adolescent leaves his home and goes into the community, his family goes with him in a very real sense.  Elmtowners know the history and reputations of families, as well as their mannerisms and traits.  The boy or girl who has matured in a family learns these things from his ancestors for better or for worse, since the type of behavior that has marked his family is expected from him.  A successful businessman epitomized this process when he said, "My dad used to tell me, 'Get out of town; you can't cross the railroad tracks here.'  But I showed him.  Sometimes, though, I think Dad was right."

The 535 families in this study furnished the human material the youth-training institutions relied upon to keep them functioning. The 735 adolescents left the parental home, in most cases, to participate a few hours daily or weekly in the program of the school, the work world, the church, or recreation, and returned in a few hours once more to merge with the family.  While they were away from home, they continued to be identified with their families, although they might not have been aware of this tie, and, in many cases, they might have tried consciously to escape it, but could not.

While the adolescent is living in a world composed of formal protestations and behavior which contradicts them, he must adjust to the situation in some way. He does it in the same way his parents and other adult Elmtowners do. From his association with family, friends, and community institutions, he has learned a verbalized public code, and from his associates he has likewise learned an unofficial, informal set of conventions which he follows. He makes a practical adjustment between the two which enables him to work out his major developmental tasks of adjusting to adult life in a manner generally approved by his sex, age, and class, if not by adults. Although adults may not approve of the way he makes his adjustment to the problems which confront him, he does it the way he has learned from them. In familiar Elmtown usage, "He is a chip off the old block," but with the modifications introduced by the dynamics of the culture as they apply to adolescents in the different classes.

# THE HIGH SCHOOL STUDENTS

PART III TRACES THE RELATIONSHIPS between the class position of 390 high school students in the social structure and the way they participated in selected aspects of community life—the school, cliques and dates, the church, the job, recreation, and pleasure.

From the beginning of the field work, it was apparent that the sharpest line of demarcation between adolescents was whether or not a person was enrolled in high school. As the work progressed, more and more evidence appeared which indicated that the data should be divided into an in-school and an out-of-school series. The criterion used to differentiate which series a youth was placed in was whether he finished the 1941–1942 school year in Elmtown High School. Those who were in school for the entire year were put in the in-school series. Those who were not in school that year or who quit high school during the year were placed in the out-of-school series. In May, 1942, the 735 adolescents studied were divided rather equally into these two categories: 390 (53 per cent) were in school, and 345 (47 per cent) had withdrawn from school.

# 8

---

# THE HIGH SCHOOL IN ACTION

### Our school

*This School of Ours:* It's sure grand to be a part of Elmtown High, because the kids greet you with smiles, and not frowns, and one thing certain is if you need any help you are sure to get it (even if it isn't such good help).

We have an affectionate feeling for our narrow old halls and little rooms because we're used to them, although we know they are long outgrown and dangerous. Our school isn't perfect any more than anything or anyone is perfect, but it is our school and we'll defend it and assist it. We're happy when we see our friends doing a good job at the business of learning things from books and life.

ELMTOWN HI, October 31, 1941

AN OBSERVER WALKING ALONG THE STREETS between seven-thirty and eight o'clock on a typical weekday morning from early September until the following June, may see two, three, four, or five boys or girls walking, riding bicycles, or driving automobiles toward the high school. Now and then a couple may be seen; rarely will an adolescent be seen alone. A tour of the several residential areas indicates that these boys and girls carry into the school situation certain rather obvious traits which have a bearing on their group relations and on participation and performance in high school.

If the observer starts on the south side of town, he will be faced with the continuous barrier of the canal. There the town seemingly ends, but, if he follows along Canal Street he will soon see a few boys and girls climb the canal bank and walk along the abandoned tow-path until they come either to a sagging, swinging bridge or to an old wagon bridge. They will

163

cross the canal and thread their way through the maze of ram-
bling mud and cinder paths leading to the business section with
its checkerboard of concrete sidewalks. Careful notation will
reveal that the ratio of girls to boys who cross these bridges is
about three to one. These youngsters walk slowly as if they are
not in a hurry to meet the day's demands at the high school.
They are poorly dressed in drab-colored garments that have been
worn a long time; perhaps the original owners took the sheen off
and the press out. They carry few books, but most have a lunch
wrapped in a newspaper or a used paper bag. Careful scrutiny
reveals that the boy's hair is either in need of a trim or has been
cut by some inexpert person, probably at home by a member of
the family or by a neighbor. If the weather is fair and the girls'
heads are not covered, their straight hair, sometimes not too
carefully combed, will be held in place by cheap barrettes from
the local "five and dime." Closer observation will reveal that
their hands are often dirty or stained; if the wind is right, faint
odors may be detected which might lead one to believe they had
not heeded advertisements for a well-known soap. The girls
cross the bridges most frequently in twos, with now and then a
threesome. Generally a boy crosses alone or with a smaller boy
who leaves him at the high school while he goes on to Central
School. These boys and girls are the few of the many living
in the strip between the canal and the river who have not quit
school.

If the observer swings around to the other side of town and
watches students cross the railroad tracks on the two crossings
that enter the main part of Elmtown from Ixnay and Frog Hollow, he will see many more boys and girls than he saw down
by the canal. The girls walk in twos and threes and the boys
likewise, but the sex ratio is not so one-sided. Still, there are
more girls than boys. If the observer stands where the traffic
from Ixnay passes, he will note that the adolescents are blond,
blue-eyed, and fair-skinned, for most of them belong to families
of Norwegian ancestry. An occasional dark- or red-haired child
may pass; he comes from one of the few Irish or "American"
families who live here. Many have a neatly packaged lunch
tucked in with their books; they live too far from school to go
home at noon, and there are no cafeteria facilities in the high

school. Their clothes are better in quality, newer, cleaner, and neater, on the whole, than those observed on the youngsters from "across the canal." The boys look as if their hair had been cut in a barber shop, and their hands are fairly clean. The girls' hair is brushed carefully, arranged in a loose flare around their shoulders, braided into pigtails tied with brightly colored ribbon, or pinned into a "biscuit" over their ears or at the nape of their necks. Few have permanent waves, for their parents do not believe in "vanity." Boys and girls walk by in twos and threes, with an occasional group of four or five. Perhaps the observer is imagining it but they appear to be gayer, to walk faster, and with more of a purpose than those he watched cross the canal.

The boys and girls from Frog Hollow are the children and grandchildren of the "Polish" immigrants who settled the area some thirty years ago. They are not so well-dressed or so neatly groomed as the youngsters who cross the tracks four blocks away; neither are they so shabbily clothed or disheveled as those from "below the canal." Practically all carry lunches in bags; now and then a lunch is wrapped in newspaper. More girls cross the tracks than boys. The girls pass by in twos and threes with now and then a stray.

Observation of the other residential areas is difficult for the rest of the town is not set off by natural barriers. Nevertheless, if the observer is curious and desires to see students from all sections of town he may station himself on the corner of Freedom and Elm Streets and watch the boys and girls from the 400 area go by. As he looks down Elm Street, he may see young Frank Stone come out of his father's near-mansion and go across the street to Joe Clayton's home. In a few minutes young Frank and Joe appear dressed in clean white shirts, brilliantly hued ties, tweed trousers, gray worsted sweaters, with soft kid leather jackets over them. Their hair is cut close, "crew" fashion. They do not carry lunches or books. As they walk around the house to the two-car brick garage Joe explains, "We will have to take the La Salle today. Dad has a board of directors meeting in the city, and the folks are going to drive the Cadillac." The two boys drive off to get their friend, Paul White. Then they cruise the five blocks to the high school. By the time they reach it, the convertible will be filled with several more boys from this area.

Most of the boys and girls from the 400 area walk the four to eight blocks to school. On the whole, they are well-dressed, carefully groomed, and pleasant-mannered as they hurry by. Now and then, a snatch of animated conversation is heard about what someone did last night, or what the group plans to do at the forthcoming high school or Country Club dance. Generally, only one youngster emerges from a house, but he or she soon meets a friend, often a third or fourth, and they walk by in a group.

Many boys and girls converge on the high school from the industrial side of town where the Foundry, the Mill, and the Factory are located. A survey of several streets indicates that no clearly definable type emerges from this direction. The adolescents come in groups segregated by sex and age, as from the other areas, but their dress and grooming are not distinctive. A well-dressed group may catch the eye as often as a poorly dressed one. However, a count of boys and girls will show that there are 15 to 20 per cent more girls than boys. Most of them carry books and notebooks; few pack lunches, as they will go home at noon.

While the observer is noting the characteristics of the town boys and girls, he will see a number of old, mud-spattered automobiles filled with boys and girls of high school age. Occasionally, a shiny new coupé or roadster will drive by with only the driver in it. Their occupants are farm boys and girls. These cars more often than not have been purchased for the express purpose of transporting the children to school. Boys and girls in the old, well-filled cars live in the neighborhood of the driver. The new roadsters and coupés, from the country, are owned by the children of wealthy farmers, and no effort is made to fill them from the neighborhood. As the country cars park in front of the high school, it can be seen that the boys and girls are dressed similarly to those observed in town. Some are well-dressed and carefully groomed, and others are somewhat dowdy. Most of those who come in old cars and in groups carry lunches along with their books. However, those who come in the new cars do not pack lunches. They will either eat lunch with relatives in town or go to a restaurant, whereas the lunch packers will eat theirs in the Commons Room in the basement of the high school.

As the several streams converge on the high school, they are divided into sex groups by custom and the location of the toilet and cloak rooms. The girls' toilet and adjacent coat room are at one end of the basement, the boys' toilet and cloak facilities are at the other end, and the Commons Room is in the center. Hook and shelf space in the cloak room is determined by traditional usage; usage has decreed that a given hook and shelf belongs to a student throughout the year. Careful observation indicates a close relationship between the hook a youth uses, where he lives, and who his friends are. The least desirable hooks, those in the path of traffic, are used by youngsters from below the canal and Ixnay; the most desirable ones by those from the 400 area. This differentiation is broken down further into a number of sub-areas on the basis of who associates with whom. If the observer knows the boys and girls well enough to understand the internal organization of their social relationships, he will see that close friends have adjacent hooks in six cases out of eight, and in five out of eight the members of a clique occupy a row of hooks.

If these students are observed throughout the school day, one will see them divide themselves into little groups composed of either boys or girls of approximately the same age and class in school. They may be seen in the halls talking animatedly to one another about what they have done, or what they plan to do. They will go to classes together and sit in adjacent seats unless the teacher breaks up the group. In the halls, talk between the sexes usually will be in this group. This is particularly true among freshmen and sophomores where the dating process has not matured to the point where boys and girls stand off as couples. Pairing off, however, is frowned upon by the teachers and most students; so there are few couples who set themselves off from the rest of the students during school hours by open amorous behavior. Group action is at its height during the last quarter-hour of the noon period. Then the Commons Room, the cloak rooms, the halls, and the study hall are alive with noise and activity, as the groups come together to talk, banter, gossip, ridicule, and plan their activities for the remainder of the day. At the close of the school day, the groups tend to break into sub-groups as students wend their way home, go to a part-time job, or head downtown for a good time.

### The curriculum

The high school curriculum is organized around three courses: college preparatory, general, and commercial.[1] Enrollment in each course is related very significantly to class position; [2] that is, each course acts either to attract or repel students in the different prestige classes. In 1941, the class I's and class II's concentrated on the college preparatory (64 per cent) and ignored the commercial course. Fifty-one per cent of the class III's were in the general, 27 per cent in the college preparatory, and 21 per cent in the commercial course. The class IV's entered the general (58 per cent) and commercial courses (33 per cent) and avoided the college preparatory; only 9 per cent were in it. The pattern for the class V's was similar to the class IV's, except that 38 per cent were in the commercial and 4 per cent in the college preparatory course.

The prestige bias in the different courses is particularly clear among the girls. For instance, 12 of the 14 class II girls (86 per cent) enrolled in the college preparatory course; none in the secretarial division of the commercial course; and only one in the general-commercial course, and one in the general course. Sixty-two per cent of the girls from class IV and 38 per cent from class

---

[1] The college preparatory course is designed to meet the entrance requirements of Home State University. It prescribes 4 years of English; 1 of United States history; 2 of mathematics; 2 of physics, chemistry, or biology; and 2 of foreign language. The general course requires six units: 3 of English, 1 of United States history, 1 of mathematics, 1 in some kind of science, and allows 10 units of electives. The commercial course is divided into two sections, general-commercial and secretarial-commercial. Both require 3 years of English, 1 of United States history, 1 of practical mathematics, and 1 of general science. The remaining units are in specialized subjects, such as bookkeeping, shorthand, typing, and commercial law.

[2] Specific enrollment figures by class and course are given in Table X of the Appendix. In the tables and discussion the four class I boys are combined with the class II's and treated as class II's in all but a few special incidents.

III were concentrated in the commercial course, particularly in the secretarial division. Since most girls trained in the secretarial division find jobs as secretaries and clerks in Elmtown's offices after graduation, the high school provides these girls with specialized terminal education.

The elementary curriculum trains children on the assumption that they will enter high school, and the high school in turn is oriented principally toward the preparation of students to enter college. Neither educational level is looked upon as terminal by the school administrators and teachers, yet one-third of the potential pupils never reach the high school, and of those who start less than one-half finish. Between 1935 and 1942, one-third of the adolescents who reached 18 each year graduated from high school, and, of this group, only from 15 to 18 per cent left Elmtown to pursue some form of additional training. Less then one-half of the latter group went to a college or university. The remainder entered nurse's training, or took secretarial courses, business, Diesel-engine, air-conditioning, photographic, or other specific vocational training. Thus, although the high school represented the end of formal education for at least 4 out of 5 of its graduates, the curricular emphasis was on the college preparatory student.

This condition undoubtedly is related to the values assigned by students and teachers to the college preparatory course in contrast to the general and commercial courses. A senior girl summarized the prevailing views of the college preparatory students when she said:

> If you take a college preparatory course, you're better than those who take a general course. Those who take a general course are neither here nor there. If you take a commercial course, you don't rate. It's a funny thing, those who take college preparatory set themselves up as better than the other kids. Those that take the college preparatory course run the place. I remember when I was a freshman, mother wanted me to take home economics, but I didn't want to. I knew I couldn't rate. You could take typing and shorthand and still rate, but if you took a straight commercial course, you couldn't rate. You see, you're rated by the teachers according to the course you take. They rate you in the first 6 weeks. The teachers type you in a small school and you're made in classes be-

fore you get there. College preparatory kids get good grades and the others take what's left. The teachers get together and talk, and if you are not in college preparatory you haven't got a chance.

The students may reflect the attitudes held generally by the teachers, but we believe that the favorable prestige assigned to the college preparatory course is connected functionally with the fact that the majority of class II youngsters were enrolled in it. If a person wants to "rate," especially among the girls, it is wise to enroll in the college preparatory course. The following interview materials indicate how the process works.

Alice White (class III) and Nellie Anderson (class IV) were clique mates in Central School during the seventh and eighth grades. During the summer following their graduation from grammar school, they informally planned their high school years. Alice's father and mother expected her to go to high school, then on to college, so she had no other idea than to enter the college preparatory course. Nellie's father had deserted the family the spring she finished the seventh grade, leaving her mother with Nellie and two smaller children. Although Mrs. Anderson did not consider it necessary for Nellie to attend high school, she did not wish to violate the law; so she started her, telling Nellie many times of sacrifices necessary to send her to school "now that Daddy has run away." Nellie's mother wanted her to take the secretarial course so she could "get a job" when she was old enough to quit school.

On the first day of the fall semester, Nellie went to Alice's house, and the two girls started to school together. On the way, they met Anne Parker (class III), a third clique mate, whose mother had told her to be sure to take home economics. Anne, however, wanted to enroll in college preparatory, because most of her girl friends intended to. The three girls discussed the situation on the way to school and decided that all three would enroll in the college preparatory course.

That evening Alice reported to her parents what she had done, and her father commented, "Fine! Now I expect you to work hard on Latin and algebra. The rest will be easy." Her mother was happy until Alice told about the girls' discussion on the way to school. Then she exclaimed:

I don't think Anne's mother realizes the girls in the home economics course are looked down upon by the girls from the better families. Alice, you did wrong in getting Nellie to sign up for the college preparatory course. Her mother can't send her to college, and the poor girl will be snubbed by the other girls in there. Why can't you ever learn you can't manage the lives of other people? Water will seek its level. Let Nellie take the secretarial course and go her way.

Anne's mother objected to her enrollment in the college preparatory course, but let her continue it with the comment, "If you do real well in your studies, your father may help you go to college, but it will be hard for us."

Nellie's mother was explosively angry with Nellie and with the high school authorities for allowing Nellie to enroll in the college preparatory course.  She immediately told Nellie that she must change to the secretarial course.  Nellie cried most of the night, but her mother went to school the next morning and changed Nellie's course herself.  Nellie continued in school for a year and a half, but dropped out of her old clique, and then left school to work in the "dime" store.

Because the academic teachers believe that college preparatory students have more ability, are more interested, and do better work than those in the general course, they prefer to teach the former group.  Although these contentions may be true, more probably teachers of the college preparatory group satisfy their desire to see the students reflect the academic values they hold. These teachers look upon students in the general course as persons who have nothing better to do with their time, are mediocre in ability, lack motivation and interest.  Students in the commercial courses are believed to be lower in ability than those in the general course.

Ten teachers are in the academic and five in the vocational group.  The vocational teachers differ from the academic teachers in their estimates of student ability, as they do in most things relative to the school; they believe that students specializing in their courses are as bright as the rest of the lot.  These divergent beliefs between the two groups are in part a defense of their own interests and in part a result of the thinly veiled animosity that prevails between the academic and the vocational teachers.  Each teacher in the vocational subjects—agriculture, home economics, shop, band, and secretarial science—has an especially equipped room.   Teachers in the traditional subjects—English, algebra, geometry, Latin, French, chemistry, physics, and history—believe that too much money is spent out of the limited school budget to equip these rooms.   They are correct in their argument that more money is invested in this equipment than in all the rest of the school; moreover, it is comparatively new, whereas the academic teachers have to use equipment that dates as far back as 1890.   Salary differences between the two groups is another potent source of friction, since the highest salaries are paid to the vocational and the lowest to the academic teachers. The cleavage between the academic and non-academic interests enter into every aspect of school life—curriculum, grades, student government, athletics, and the cliques in which one participates.

GRADES AND GRADING PRACTICES. The Superintendent in his Annual Report to the Board of Education in June, 1942, analyzed the grades students received the preceding year.   In connection with this report he stated:

> No effort is made arbitrarily to conform to a normal distribution curve, but it is surprising how nearly the total marks do approach the normal curve. The accompanying charts indicate an excellent job of grading.

The semester grades do approximate a normal distribution, but the Superintendent's report does not reveal that high grades went to the students from the "better" homes and the low ones to the pupils from "inadequate" or "unfortunate" homes.   This fact becomes apparent when the grades of each student are averaged, and average grades tabulated by class on a three-division scale. The results stated in per cents follow.

| | Per Cent with Mean Grade of | | |
| Class | 85–100 | 70–84 | 50–69 |
|---|---|---|---|
| I and II | 51.4 | 48.6 | 00.0 |
| III | 35.5 | 63.2 | 1.3 |
| IV | 18.4 | 69.2 | 12.4 |
| V | 8.3 | 66.7 | 25.0 |
| Total | 23.8 | 66.3 | 9.9 |

This distribution is not a matter of chance; neither is it "normal" in the sense in which the Superintendent used the term. On the contrary, strong biases were at work. The class I and class II students received more than twice as many grades in the 85–100 category as probability indicated they would have if chance factors alone were operating.[3] On the other hand, class V boys and girls were given about one-third as many grades between 85–100 as they should have received if no bias had been present (8.3 per cent observed against 23.6 per cent expected). If these figures are stated in terms of opportunity, it is clear that, on the average, the higher an adolescent's class position, the better his chances are to receive high grades. Conversely, the lower one's position in the prestige structure, the more likely the adolescent is to receive low grades. To be sure, a real differential factor in the home environment may be conditioning the child's response to the school situation in each class, but this does not invalidate the relationship between class and grades.

Failures are biased toward lower class pupils in an even more striking way than all grades, as the following tabulation of the 29 students who failed one or more courses in 1941–1942 shows.

| Class | Number of Students | Number of Failures | Per Cent of Failures |
|---|---|---|---|
| I and II | 35 | 1 | 2.9 |
| III | 146 | 4 | 2.7 |
| IV | 183 | 18 | 10.0 |
| V | 26 | 6 | 23.1 |
| Total | 390 | 29 | 7.4 |

$$X^2 = 13.4154. \qquad p < 0.01.$$

When we discovered this relationship between failures and class position, we analyzed the grade records of 495 adolescents who had completed at least one semester of high school.[4] Class II had only 1 failure; this student repeated the course. There were 8 failures in class III (5.5 per cent); 5 of the 8 repeated the

[3] $X^2$ analysis was used to determine the probability statements given here.
[4] The grade records of 105 students in the out-of-school group as well as the 390 high school students are included in this analysis. By class, the 495 adolescents were divided as follows: I and II, 35; III, 155; IV, 233; V, 72.

course, 2 took substitutes, and 1 was in the out-of-school group. There were 63 failures in class IV (27 per cent); 38 students failed one course; 14, two; 7, three; and 4, four.  Twenty-one of the 63 failures in class IV continued in school, and 42, exactly two-thirds, dropped out after they received a failing grade in one or more subjects.  Of the one-third in school, 39 per cent repeated the course failed, and 61 per cent took a substitute.

Sixty-four of the 72 class V boys and girls (89 per cent) who completed one or more semesters of high school had failed one or more courses; 62 of the 64 left school the subsequent semester, the two exceptions being freshman girls who took a substitute course.  Thus, no class V adolescent repeated a course.

Is failure in the lower classes linked with lack of intellectual capacity?  We tried to answer this question objectively by comparing intelligence test scores with class position.  The *Otis Group Intelligence Test, Advanced Examination: Form A* was given to all students by the high school principal shortly after they enrolled.  The scores 507 adolescents made on this test were obtained.[5]  These intelligence quotients averaged considerably higher than the general population of the United States, as the following comparison shows.

| | Elmtown | | General Population |
|---|---|---|---|
| I.Q. Range | Number | Per Cent | Per Cent * |
| 120–139 | 38 | 7.5 | 9.0 |
| 111–119 | 180 | 35.5 | 16.0 |
| 91–110 | 269 | 53.0 | 50.0 |
| 70– 90 | 20 | 4.0 | 23.0 |
| Total | 507 | 100.0 | 98.0 |

* The top and bottom of the scale, usually given for the general population, namely 128 or more, 80–90, and 66–79, were merged with the adjacent groups in our data owing to the small number of cases. Then, too, we had no scores below 70, so the normally defective 2 per cent with scores below 70 do not appear in the calculations. This is why the third column totals only 98 per cent.

In this connection it is interesting to note that the Elmtown sample has a slightly lower percentage in the 120-and-above

[5] In the following discussion the total group is used rather than the 390 in school, because it provides a broader comparative base between intelligence test scores in class V with failures in high school than would have been possible if only the in-school group were included.

category than the general population, but more than twice as high a percentage in the 111-to-119 range, and only about one-sixth as many in the 70–90 group. If we assume that those with an I.Q. below 90 were unable to do high school work, a very doubtful assumption, then there were only 20 with this arbitrarily asserted inability. Eighteen of the 20 belonged to classes IV and V, as Table IV shows.

TABLE IV

INTELLIGENCE TEST SCORES BY CLASS

|  | Class | | | |
| --- | --- | --- | --- | --- |
| I.Q. | I and II | III | IV | V |
| 120–139 | 8 | 19 | 11 | 0 |
| 111–119 | 15 | 72 | 82 | 11 |
| 91–110 | 12 | 59 | 128 | 70 |
| 70– 90 | 0 | 2 | 8 | 10 |
| Total | 35 | 152 | 229 | 91 |

$X^2 = 79.6145.$     $P < 0.01.$     $C = 0.37.$     $\bar{C} = 0.44.$

In so far as class V was involved, only 11 per cent of the adolescents for whom we had scores had an I.Q. below 90, but 89 per cent of those who completed a semester or more of high school failed at least one course. Although intelligence was associated significantly with class position, the degree of association was not high enough to account for the concentration of failures in class V. Neither was it great enough to attribute the high grades in classes I and II to the intellectual capacity of this prestige level.

Behind the stark figures of grades received in courses and scores made on intelligence tests lies the Elmtown social system. The culture complex associated with classes I, II, and III trains boys and girls to respond positively to competitive situations such as that presented by examinations and intelligence tests. Experience imbues them with a need for personal achievement that is expressed in their constant search for success, teaching them from infancy to face each new situation aggressively and to overcome it to the best of their ability. When they take a test, whether it is arithmetic or intelligence, they normally try to do their best on it, for their ego is on trial and they must make good, and they generally do. On the other hand, the class V adolescent has been subjected to a family and class culture in which failure, worry, and frustration are common. He has not been trained at home to do his best in school. His parents have not ingrained in him the idea that he must make good grades if he is to be a success in life. Moreover, the class system as it functions in the school does not help him to overcome the poor training he has received at home and in the neighborhood. We believe that such factors as these have as much influence on the differences observed in the test scores as "native intelligence," but this is essentially an impression—an impression, however, based on evidence accumulated in Elmtown.

The motivation of the adolescents toward high school and education in general is related, we believe, in a direct way to the grades they receive, but this relationship was not measured. This educational motivation is derived from the student's experiences in his class and family culture. The class I and II boys and girls know that high grades are necessary if they are to achieve the educational goal set for them by their family and class. Parents, friends of parents, brothers, sisters, and relatives who have been outstanding students in Elmtown High have set precedents they are urged to follow; for most, high school is merely a preparatory step for college. Then too, parents and relatives, who have achieved prominent positions in the community, expect them to be leaders. Stimulated by this interest and these examples, they generally respond by aiming for greater achievement. A by no means negligible element is a teacher's expectation that the class I and II child will "make good"; and she helps him realize this goal for, after all, his parents may "help" a teacher or cause "trouble" very easily. These factors react in subtle ways to produce high grades and leadership in extracurricular activities in classes I and II.

Class III children tend to come from families who are either in relatively prominent, secure positions or who are insecure "climbers" who have achieved their positions within recent years after a long period of hard work. The latter group of parents normally are anxious to see their children achieve more in life than they have; consequently they place great emphasis upon grades and extracurricular activities. They would like to see their children go to college, at the very least into nurse's training, business school, or some type of short, direct training beyond high school. The secure parents do not have such strong desires for their children as the "climbers," but they want them to have a high school education. Approximately one-fifth of the parents in both groups realize they will not be able to send their children to college; these parents assume that the high school will give their children the last formal training they will receive. Class III children who aspire to climb the social ladder take the same courses as the class I's and class II's, groom themselves in a similar manner, join the same clubs, try to work into their cliques, and follow the same leisure time activities. Some two-thirds, however, are content to drift along, associate with other unambitious class III's or with the class IV's. They are not particularly interested in good grades, extracurricular activities, or training beyond high school. In passing, we may note that these children do not exhibit the tensions the ambitious upwardly mobile ones do.

Class IV students carry into the school situation attitudes they receive from their parents. A prevailing attitude in this class is: "No matter what you want to do or would like to do, the children from the 'rich families' and the teachers won't let you do it." The great majority of their parents did not attend high school, and a goodly segment of these people have little appreciation of the work the school is doing or what the child will get out of it. To many parents, high school is a needless drain on family finances, and they think that the boy and girl ought to be working. For a small majority the high school provides their children an opportunity to receive at relatively little expense to them some type of vocational training. The children from these families tend to enroll in the secretarial, agriculture, shop, and homemaking courses. Some of these parents have a blind, almost pathetic, faith that education will enable their children to gain something from life that was denied to them.

For instance, Mrs. Ellis Johnson, who worked as a scrub woman to supplement the family income, largely earned by her truck driver husband, spoke to us on three different occasions about her son.

Please talk to Jim, and try to get him to stay in school. His Paw had to drop out. I couldn't finish, and neither could his older brother and sister and they don't seem to be getting any place. Jim's a good boy, but he's not interested in school. He doesn't think it is doing him any good.

Jim lackadaisically walked from class to class, often without his notebooks or textbooks. He sat in study hall daily, dreamily looking out the window. When the teacher told him to get to work, he would slowly reach into his desk, take out a Western magazine or a comic book, and read it for the rest of the period. Jim thought the best thing for him to do was to join the Navy. He said he was going to do this just as soon as he was 16; after the outbreak of war, he was more convinced than ever that this was his destiny. The day he was 16, he quit school; the day after, he joined the Navy. Jim believed his mother had to work too hard for him to achieve a high school diploma; besides, "What good is it? I know a lotta guys at the Mill; they ain't finished eighth grade." His father didn't care whether he went to school or not, but he thought in a vague way that it would "be a good thing if Jim finished" high school.

A high school education is outside the experience of class V parents, and beyond the expectancy of most of their children. The principal ambition of the class V child is to grow up and escape from the authority symbolized by his parents and teachers. For him growing up means quitting school, getting a job, and doing as he pleases. Six of the 8 class V boys in school were freshmen, 2 were sophomores; none expected to finish high school, for all wanted to quit by the time they were 16. They were all enrolled in the general course, and none was actively interested in whether he passed or failed. Although the 18 class V girls in high school showed more interest in their studies than did the boys, they believed generally that they would not graduate, about 3 out of 4 girls expecting to quit at the end of the year or as soon as they were 16. Thus, there was little incentive to work for good grades. Only three class V girls were seniors; one withdrew before the second semester was over, and the other 2 graduated in the lowest quarter of the class in June, 1942.

TEACHERS' REPORTS. The teachers' *weekly reports* to the principal provide some objective evidence of the relationship between a student's position in the class system and the way he is re-garded by his teachers. Among other things, this report requires the teacher to name the parents of students counseled during the week, and the nature of the counsel. In the course of the year, the parents of 77 students were reported as having been counseled, either as to the work of the child or the discipline of the child. Although some parents from all classes were coun-seled about the work or the discipline of their children, the num-ber counseled about work in the two higher classes was in direct contrast to the figures on discipline in the two lower ones, as the following figures show.

| Class | Parents Counseled Work of Child | Discipline of Child |
|-------|--------------|---------------------|
| I and II | 5 | 2 |
| III | 16 | 4 |
| IV | 11 | 28 |
| V | 2 | 9 |
| Total | 34 | 43 |

$$X^2 = 19.4113. \quad P < 0.01. \quad C = 0.45. \quad \bar{C} = 0.62.$$

It is paradoxical that the teachers are so much interested in the work of the children in classes II and III when on the whole these students are the ones who receive the better grades. Lower class children, on the other hand, are given poorer grades, but the teachers consult the parents about discipline far more fre-quently than they do about the child's work.

Other categories on these reports require each teacher to list students doing poor work, failing work, and students receiving aid out of class. It seems reasonable to assume that, if a teacher recognizes that a pupil is doing poor work or failing work, she will give him aid out of class, but what seems reasonable is not what happens; on the contrary, the students reported for poor and failing work are not listed as having received help outside of class. For instance, 27 per cent of the class II's were reported at one time or another for poor or failing work, and 92 per cent of the class V's; the other classes were distributed between these extremes; conversely, 63 per cent of the class II's received aid outside of class, but only 8 per cent of the class V's.

We might infer several things from these figures: First, class II boys and girls are more interested in their work than the lower classes, and they receive more help; also they may ask for the help they receive; likewise, the teacher may volunteer. Second, the class V adolescents may have little interest in school; therefore, they may not ask for help, and the teacher does not give them any voluntarily. The one certain conclusion is that the class V's are named most frequently for doing poor and failing work, but they receive the least outside help; however, when the parents are involved, if we accept the reports, the subject discussed is discipline, not the child's work.

FAMILY INFLUENCE, GRADES, AND PRIZES. In the Elmtown social system the school is used on occasion by ambitious parents to further their own designs. The two upper classes generally assume that good grades, school prizes, student offices, and prominence in scholastic affairs are their natural due. New teachers soon learn from their associations with other teachers, townspeople, parents, and adolescents "who is who" and what one should or should not do to avoid trouble. Trouble, a constant fear among the high school teachers, takes many forms which range from adverse reports by students to their parents to threats in Board meetings to dismiss so-and-so for such-and-such. Teachers, if they are successful, act judiciously in their relations with the children of the powerful; on appropriate occasions they look the other way. Teachers experienced in the system warn newcomers about this boy or that girl. Narratives, gossip, a hint here, a warning there, remarks in faculty meetings, give the teacher some understanding of the situation.

When controls implicit in the class system do not suffice to give persons in the two higher classes what they desire for their children, direct pressures are applied. A family struggling to maintain favorable prestige relies upon the children to bring home good grades, and, if the family is in a position to exert pressure on the school, it sees that they do receive high grades. Dozens of stories were told by Elmtowners of occurrences of this kind, not once or twice, but repeatedly. Two members of the Board were accused of bringing direct pressure on certain teachers to give their children high grades. Another member suggested that the President of the Board fire a certain teacher because he had made his daughter stay after school to complete an assignment.

It is believed widely in classes IV and V, and to a somewhat lesser extent in class III, that the grades a student receives are determined by the position of his parents in the social structure rather than by his ability or his industriousness. This belief is not without foundation, as is generally the case when one encounters a persistent belief illustrated by one story after another, over a number of years of questionable grading practices in relation to the children of prominent families.

A girl from one of the most prominent class II families had been given a scholarship to college the year before the field work started. Gossip had it that she had been given the scholarship because of her father's influence. Many versions of this story were told in all strata, but the family of the girl was criticized only once in classes I and II for allowing such a thing to happen. A few class I's and class II's justified the alleged action on the ground that the selection was made on all-round ability rather than grades. Persons in the lower strata were enraged, but accepted the award as another illustration of "the way things work." Four different versions of this story follow, plus the Superintendent's reactions when the family put direct pressure on him the next year to push another child to the front.

1. A class I male's comment on the alleged action:

Sending the kids to college is going to be pretty expensive, especially when I'll have two of them in college at the same time. Helen was really never a good student; so I did not expect her to get a scholarship. The fact is, if Helen had received a scholarship, I don't think I'd have let her take it. I'm not one of these people who think that you ought to get a scholarship for your kids just for prestige purposes. Now, that's what happened this last year. Willa Cross received the "Special College" scholarship. In my opinion she should not have received that scholarship. She kept that Brummit boy from going to college. Joe Brummit is a brilliant boy, and I think in many ways he was brighter than Willa Cross. My own personal opinion is that Henry Cross had his nerve to let Willa accept that scholarship if her work didn't actually justify it. I know positively Henry Cross could have sent Willa to college without hurting himself any, but no, he would have Willa get a scholarship just for the pride of the thing.

## 2. A class II girl graduate of 1941:

Joe Brummit was the brightest student in the class. He was a whiz at mathematics and science. He was awfully good in mechanics. Joe worked his last two years in high school in a gas station. He wanted to go to the university and study aeronautical engineering; now he is down at the Mill. His father's a carpenter, so he is not in a position to send him off. I suppose he should have been given the "Special College" scholarship, but it was given to Willa Cross. I guess when you compare the two, Willa is more of an all-round person than Joe.

## 3. A class IV father whose son graduated in 1941:

The School Board's children and children of prominent people around town always have the inside track. They seem to be in everything, and it's difficult for other students to get into activities and offices and things like that. Joe—that's my son—graduated last year. He's a reader. I guess he's read most of the books over here in this library, and he knows what's in those books. He made good grades over there at the high school, but he couldn't get into things. The principal seemed to have it in for him. Of course, it goes back to the school strike and what happened then. All the kids who went out on the strike were never treated the same afterwards, so he never got a scholarship to college.

## 4. A class IV mother whose daughter graduated in 1937:

The grammar school teachers and most of the high school teachers play the School Board's game. People get on the School Board who want to see their children make good grades. They hire the teachers, and teachers who give students grades, well, they're the ones they keep. Jean [the speaker's daughter] and the older Sweitzer girl were in the eighth grade together. Jean had better grades than the Sweitzer girl right up until the last month. Then one of her teachers gave her a "B." There had been some gossip around here that they were going to let that teacher out. Mr. Sweitzer was on the School Board; so they gave his girl all "A's" that month. Well, she graduated with the highest honors, and our girl was second. They didn't fire the teacher either.

Jean was the brightest girl in high school. When she graduated, she was number one in the class. The Hopkins boy was number two, but they recommended the Hopkins boy for a college scholarship. They are some of the big people in town, and we aren't. Just think, those people kept my girl from having four years of college. They gave the Hopkins boy the scholarship, but he couldn't pass the examination. Then it was too late to do anything for Jean. Last year, about the same thing happened. Joe Brummit and Willa Cross were pretty close together in scholarship. Joe really got the best grades; I know because I've seen them. [The last statement is very questionable.] I won't say that Willa isn't a nice girl. You'd like her better. She's a nice appearing girl. Her dad's in that Inner Ring. They recommended Willa for the "Special" scholarship. Joe's working down at the Mill for about eighteen or twenty dollars a week—he'll probably be there for a long time. His father's a carpenter, and he can't afford to go away. You see, that's the way things go around here. If you're inside the ring, you're all right, but if you're outside, they keep you out.

## 5. Superintendent of Schools—situation self-explanatory:

You run into some funny things in school administration. You know Marian Cross [Willa's mother]. She has some queer quirks. Just now, she came over here and jumped all over me. Alice Joyce [class II] is going to the state contest to play in the violin solo group, and Marian wanted Elsie [Mrs. Cross's third daughter] to accompany her. The truth is Elsie isn't much of an accompanist, and Alice isn't strong enough to carry a poor accompanist, and Elsie isn't good enough to help her. We were going to send Marcie Long to accompany Alice, but Marian thought that Elsie should have been sent. I tried to explain it to her, but I didn't do much of a job. She got sore and cut loose, and told me we'd been discriminating against Elsie all year, that we have been sending out the violin trio, and we had sent out the singing trio. We pushed those girls. We wouldn't let Elsie go out, and she didn't like it. The fact of the matter is, Elsie is so poor on the piano she has made a number of embarrassing performances.

She's under terrific pressure to succeed as well as Willa did, and the kid is trying too hard. Last year, Henry Cross put a lot of pressure on me to see that Willa got the things they thought she should have. Henry Cross is a funny fellow, and it's taken me a long time to learn how to get along with him.

[The Superintendent sat for a minute or two, leaned back in his chair; then went on in a whimsical way.]

I used to be a reformer and stood for strict ideals, but as I've grown older I've learned you have to give a lot and take a lot in this business. I don't mean to say I have abandoned all principles, but you have to work with people, and so at times you just have to wink at things. It's a hard thing to meet all the criticisms that are brought to bear on a person in a position like this. It used to make me mad, and I'd really blow up; but now I just keep still and let things take their course.

If the stories which circulated can be believed in their entirety, the honors in the graduating classes from both the elementary and high schools are deliberately given to children from the prominent families. According to these stories, the winner is not entitled to the honor under the rules of fair competition; but under the unfair rules imposed by some parents and teachers, these children are sure to win. It is charged that grades are changed, teachers threatened with dismissal, and examinations rigged to achieve this result. A class IV girl epitomized this process in her account of the awarding of the American Legion Award while she was in Central School.

> Many of us did not think Madge Thomas earned the American Legion Award. Of course she was a prominent girl, but her father has a lot of money and he used to be prominent in the Legion. I think he was a Commander or something. There were many girls who deserved the award more than she did; so we thought it was funny. Then the next year when her sister Virginia won we knew something was wrong.

Several families in classes I and II are alleged to have brought pressure from time to time on the Superintendent or principal to have grades changed after graduation so the child could enter college. We doubt that this pressure was as deliberate as we were led to believe by some parents, but the principal stated that it had happened in "a few cases."

There is little doubt that many of the stories are rooted in facts, for the teachers do cater to the prominent families. The one teacher who had been in the high school more than four years was highly regarded by the parents in classes I and II, but hated and distrusted by many in classes III and IV. They were convinced that she graded with "one eye on the social register and the other on her own advantage." An old lady often referred to as the most powerful person in Elmtown once told us, with reference to this teacher, that the town was very fortunate to be able to keep Miss X. "She is such a wonderful teacher. She teaches every child in a different way; she knows each one's background and treats it accordingly."

DISCIPLINE. The administration of discipline laid bare the dynamics of the class system in a way that is directly observable but difficult to quantify. We were in an advantageous position to see the school as it was administered from the principal's office because we sat in one corner of the office to do our formal interviewing. In the course of the year, the principal, teachers, and students became so accustomed to us that they came and went about their business seemingly oblivious of our presence. From this vantage point, we watched the school function and attempted to comprehend some of what we saw.

The teachers handle minor infractions of the folkways, such as talking in class, passing notes, lack of attention, in their own way. The school's three basic rules, however, are administered from the principal's office. These are:

1. Students have to attend classes unless excused in writing by the principal and the teacher.

2. Students have to be inside the classroom or study hall door when the bell rings. Any tardy pupil is supposed to go to the principal's office for an admission slip. If he cannot explain why he was late, his name is placed on a detention list, and he is required to spend one hour in the detention room after school.

3. Students expelled from class have to go to the principal's office.

The second rule is violated most frequently by the students as well as those responsible for its administration; it is also the source of the majority of the school's disciplinary problems. Three critical incidents which were observed involved this rule; they will be discussed at length because they are indicative of the way the school functions on this point. They reveal further that the Superintendent is very sensitive to pressures from families who are in a position to influence Board members and that he pays scant heed to criticism from persons in lower positions in the class structure; at times, he appears to expect it. As he said, he had learned one had to follow "the line of least resistance or move on every year or two. You can't do that very long." Thus, discipline is administered in such a way that powerful families are satisfied, and at the same time the school can boast it is training its citizens to obey the law. The effect upon student morale, particularly in classes IV and V where the onus of the practices followed is felt, appears not to have entered the consciousness of the Superintendent, principal, or most teachers; however, two teachers guardedly criticized the way discipline was administered.

The administration of the tardy rule is complicated by the principal's absence from his office during three, four, and often five periods each day. His supervisory duties require him to patrol the high school building, as well as the area between it and Central School; in addition, he teaches three classes regularly and substitutes whenever necessary. Then, too, school or personal business takes him downtown occasionally. When he is away, the office is run by four girls who receive credit for office training. There is always one girl in the office, and she assumes the principal's function in so far as school routine is concerned.

These girls know who was or was not likely to be in trouble, who should be given admission slips as a matter of policy, and who should be denied them, if they, the office assistants, are to maintain their positions in the office. They know that certain class II and class III students may be excused and that a few others, mostly class IV's (but there are a few class III's in this group), should not be, without consultation with the principal. This "office gang" is feared and hated but respected by the other students because of the power they wield. These girls often save their friends by issuing admission slips and trap their enemies by withholding them. The principal tries to enforce the tardy rule, but it is practically impossible with the office gang in charge of the office routine so much of the time.

The situation deteriorated so badly shortly before Thanksgiving that a teachers' meeting was called to discuss the question. After an hour of discussion, the teachers voted unanimously to send all tardy students to detention; no excuses were to be accepted. In the course of the discussion, the Superintendent objected to the no-excuse proviso the teachers insisted upon but voted with them. After the meeting, he left the building with us; on the way home, he remarked:

You cannot make a rule like that stick in this town. There are students who simply cannot be sent to detention. Their families will not stand for it. I look for trouble from this. Mr. [Principal] will try to enforce that rule to the letter, especially on students he does not like. I will have to watch this *very* carefully.

The next day, the principal lectured the office gang privately and the student body publicly in a special assembly. The Student Council held a meeting that afternoon and voted approval of the new detention rule. Many students were scared and some defiant—they did not believe that the teachers meant what they said. The principal started his campaign with vigor and dispatch. Each evening he checked the detention list with the teacher in charge of the detention room. If a student was missing, he telephoned his home, if the family had a telephone; if it did not, the student was called into his office the next morning for a lecture; a sentence of five hours in detention usually followed.

The second week of the new regime, the daughter of a prominent class II family did not go to detention. Instead, she kept an appointment with a beauty parlor to have a permanent wave. The next morning the Superintendent walked into the principal's office, diffidently fingered the mail in the teacher's boxes, sauntered over to the windows with his hands in his pockets, looked at the autumn leaves moving across the yard, and in a disinterested way asked, "How is the detention room working?" The principal answered:

All right, except we are running into the old stall of some students who think they can do as they please!

[Superintendent] Yes, I know. The idea is all right, but I do not think it will work in every case. Last evening, Mrs. Newton called Evelyn [the Superintendent's wife] about the church supper next week. She mentioned that Kathy [her daughter and the girl in question] was at the hairdresser's last night!

[Principal] That is just what I had in mind. Last evening I called Mrs. Newton and told her Kathy was not in detention and I wanted to know where she was. Mrs. Newton told me she had to have her hair fixed for the dance at the Country Club tonight. When I get Kathy in here, I am going to tell her a thing or two.

[Superintendent] Now, be careful, Alfred. I do not think there is a thing we can do in this case.

The principal sat silently at his desk and shuffled excuses. The Superintendent walked out of the office.

When Kathy came in for her lecture, she was dressed neatly in a brushed wool sweater and tweed skirt. She walked coyly to the principal's desk and asked in a naive voice, "Did you want to see me last night?"

The principal looked up and quietly asked, "Did you forget about detention?"

. . . A pause. "No, I had an appointment at Craig's to have my hair set."

. . . "Did you have to go last night?"

. . . "Yes, tonight I have to go to Mrs. Nettle's to get my dress for the dance."

. . . "All right. Go on to class, but don't let this happen again."

After Kathy left the office, the principal threw a pack of excuses on the desk and muttered, "There it goes again! The next time one of these prominent families puts pressure on me, I am going to raise hell!"

The following Wednesday morning, Frank Stone, Jr. (class I), parked his father's Cadillac in front of the high school at a quarter after eight, climbed out leisurely, picked up his notebook, and walked into the office and casually remarked, "I guess I'm late again."

The principal looked hard at him and spoke firmly, "What's the story this time?"

. . . "I didn't wake up, I guess."

"This time you are going to detention like everyone else." He wrote young Frank an excuse, placed his name on the detention list, and, as he handed him the excuse said, "This means one hour in detention. I want to see you there at three-fifteen tonight."

When the principal checked detention at three-thirty, he noted that young Frank was absent. He walked down the hall to the Superintendent's office where the one telephone in the building was located and called Frank Stone, Sr., at his office. He told Mr. Stone that young Frank had been late that morning and he had not come to detention. He ended with, "I want him down here right away."

The Superintendent heard the telephone conversation from his partially enclosed office. As the principal hung up the receiver, he walked into the outer office and asked, with a studied effort to be calm, "What did Mr. Stone say?" The principal replied, "He is going to get young Frank down here right away. I have to leave now to practice my solo for this Sunday with Mrs. Henderson, but I will tell Mr. White to check young Frank in when he comes." (The principal sang in the Methodist choir "for policy's sake.") The principal returned to detention, spoke to Mr. White, then came back to his office, locked his desk, put on his coat, and left.

About a half hour later, Mr. Stone drove to the high school with young Frank. The Superintendent waited in his office with an eye on the street. As Frank came into the building, the Superintendent slowly walked down the hall toward the principal's office. The two met at the head of the stairs, and the Superintendent asked in a pleasant voice, "Haven't you gone home yet?" Young Frank, burning with rage, retorted, "Mr. [Principal] made me come back for detention. Dad is really sore."

"Frank, come into my office, and let us talk this over." The two walked into the Superintendent's office and discussed the matter. After ten or fifteen minutes, the Superintendent told Frank to sit in the outer office for a while and not go to detention. Some days after this, he said to us:

> I did not want to put young Frank in the detention room with the rest of the kids; so I sat him there in the outer office, and I deliberately worked around in my office until about five-thirty. Then I came out and said, "Frank, I guess you have been here long enough. You go on home and let's not have any hard feelings." I talked to his father later about the whole thing, and I think we have come to an understanding.

The principal was enraged when he learned what had happened, but he could do nothing. This practically ended uniform enforcement of the new detention rule. Thereafter, class I and class II students and many class III's flaunted it on the least pretext; the office gang returned to its old ways. However, it was enforced more rigidly for many others.

Three weeks after the Frank Stone, Jr., incident, "Boney" Johnson, a 15-year-old class IV boy came late one morning, and the English teacher refused to admit him to class without an excuse. As "Boney" walked into the office, the principal was sitting at his desk. Before "Boney" could say a word, he barked, in a sarcastic tone:

> So my pretty boy is late again! I suppose it took you half an hour to put on that clean shirt and green tie! [The principal arose from his desk, walked around, and looked at Boney's trousers and shoes and went on.] Ha, you have your pants pressed today! I suppose you took a bath last night, too. New shoes, and they're shined.

"Boney" said nothing, but his face flushed and he bit his lips. The principal walked back to his desk, sat down, and wrote out an admission slip. He put "Boney's" name on the detention list and handed over the excuse with the remark, "I want to see you in detention tonight. Now go on to class and show the girls what a pretty boy you are."

"Boney" turned, and as he walked toward the door, said in a low voice, "I'm not going to your damned detention room tonight or any time."

The principal apparently did not hear him as he went on with his work. In a few minutes, he walked across the room and said:

> Now there's a hot one. He's one of our wise guys. He thinks he's a hotshot. His old man is a laborer out at the fertilizer plant, and the kid thinks he's someone, umph! He'll be on the W.P.A. if they have one twenty years from now. There's one guy I'm going to see put in detention.

When school was out that afternoon, the Superintendent stood in the hall near the side exit, Mr. White, a teacher, watched the front door, while the principal patrolled the building. Mr. Gardner, another teacher, was in the detention room.[6] After the building was cleared of students and most of the teachers had gone home, the Superintendent walked back to his office, but the principal stood outside the front door. Suddenly the door was thrown open from the outside, and angry voices were heard.

[6] The principal relied upon these two teachers to help him enforce discipline. They were hated by most students because they were known to carry tales to the principal. A number of students referred to Mr. White as "Bird Dog," and Mr. Gardner as "Pussy Foot."

The Superintendent rushed out of his office and stood at the head of the stairs. The principal pushed and shoved "Boney" up the stairs as he repeated, "You can't get away with that stuff." As they neared the top, "Boney" broke from his grasp and started down the hall toward the side door. The Superintendent blocked his path, and "Boney" ran upstairs. The principal leaped and grabbed him by the coat collar with his left hand. "Boney" turned and started to fight. The principal spun him around, seized the visor of his cap with his right hand and yanked it down over his eyes. While "Boney" was fighting to get the cap off his face, the principal hit him three times with the heel of his hand on the back of the neck near the base of the skull. "Boney" cursed, struggled, and hit in all directions. Soon he broke free and ran toward the Superintendent, who shook and slapped him three or four times. Both men then grabbed him by the arms and shook him vigorously. The Superintendent angrily screeched, "You're going out of this building. You're never coming back until you bring your father and we talk this over." By this time, the three had reached the front door. "Boney" was shoved outside. He stood there, cursing and threatening both men with violence. In a few minutes he composed himself, straightened his clothes, and walked away, muttering to himself.

The principal and the Superintendent came upstairs and walked into the Superintendent's office. The Superintendent dropped into his swivel chair and said, when he had caught his breath, "I can stand a lot of things from kids, but one thing I can't stand is a sassy kid. No kid's going to sass me." He puffed a few minutes more. The principal said nothing, and the Superintendent resumed, "That boy is a trouble maker. I've had my eyes on him all year. Look at the gang he's running with."

"Yes, I know. They're trouble makers around here. I had trouble with them all last year, and they're starting out again this year. If he wasn't that type, he wouldn't be running with that bunch."

After a pause, the Superintendent composed himself and remarked, "That boy will have to bring his father back here, or he'll not get in this school." The principal agreed, "Yes, I'll stand with you on that. We have got to stop this thing some way."

After the principal had walked out of the office, the Super-intendent slumped wearily in his chair and said:

> I ought to know better than that. I would have really liked to smack that boy, but that's one thing I've learned. You can't pop these kids even though they deserve it. The hardest thing I have to fight all the time is to keep from popping these smart kids. I shouldn't have lost my temper but, damn it, sometimes it gets too much for me. When a kid sasses me, I see red and that's all there is to it. I don't think anything will come of this, his back-ground being what it is.

The Superintendent was right; nothing came of it, except—"Boney" quit school.

Stories about special applications of the tardy rule passed through the student body and on into the community. Resentment was general among the lower class students, but few dared openly to defy it since it had been ratified by the Student Council and was enforced by the teachers. Some class IV boys and girls threatened among themselves to catch the principal out some night and "beat him up." Nothing like this happened, but the students expressed their feelings in other ways. Derogatory pictures of the Superintendent, principal, "Bird Dog" White and "Pussy Foot" Gardner circulated freely around the school. Student resentment was indicated also by uncomplimentary jingles passed around about the Superintendent and about the way certain teachers favored the "rich kids."

## Extracurricular activities

An elaborate extracurricular program brings the school's activi-ties before the public on a broader front than its teaching func-tions do, since this, the "circus side" of school, entertains students, parents, and Elmtowners in their leisure time. The entertainment features are emphasized by the Board of Education, the Super-intendent, the principal, teachers, and students. They want their athletic teams to win games, their musical organizations to per-form publicly at all possible times in a creditable manner, and their dramatics group to produce plays that will not be criticized but enjoyed. Extracurricular activities without spectator appeal or broad public relations value, such as girls' athletics, student government, and departmental clubs, receive little active support from the Board or the community.

ATHLETICS. There is far more public interest in the football and basketball teams than in all other high school activities combined.[7] The team has come to be a collective representation of the high school to a large segment of the community. Business, professional, and working men not only expect but also demand that the Board and the Superintendent hire a coach who can develop winning teams. The Superintendent knows he will be judged publicly in large part by the number of games the team wins in their contests with neighboring communities. The Board pays the maximum salary to the coach, and it expects him "to deliver the goods." A coach knows his "success" is determined wholly by the number of games he wins—particularly in basketball and football.

*The Bugle* keeps its readers informed on what has happened in the local sports realm and what is likely to happen in the next game; when the team loses, it often presents a brave apology. The "dope" column is widely read by the sports enthusiasts, adolescent and adult. At least two sports stories are carried each week throughout the school year; frequently a third or fourth one is built around the past or expected play of the "stars."

During the basketball season, enthusiasm mounts until it reaches crescendo in the three-game series between the Elmtown Indians and their arch rivals, the Diamond City Jewels. A coach may lose the majority of the games played with other schools in the sports circuit, but if he loses to the Jewels he knows that he will have to look for another job in a year or two. Furthermore, the Superintendent is faced with the problem of explaining the school's failure to the Board of Education, adult fans, and *The Bugle*. Baseball, by way of contrast, receives little attention from either the students or the public. A few faithful Cheer Club rooters, the band, and about a dozen other students go to the games. Little excitement occurs and general apathy is shown toward who wins or loses: even the games with their traditional enemy school are rather routine. The baseball team can lose all its games, and few people will criticize it, the coach, or the

[7] High school teams provide spectators with the only organized athletic events within a radius of sixty-five miles of Elmtown.

school. A measure of the relative popularity of the three sports in 1941–1942 is the number of paid admissions to the different games; basketball averaged 450, football, 300, and baseball, 24.

Community pride is the issue in basketball games. Elmtown is approximately two and one-half times larger than Diamond City, and it reflects the usual belief in American culture that bigger is equivalent to better. Besides, Elmtown considers itself a "cleaner" town than Diamond City. Elmtowners for generations have associated immorality, vice, and crime with Diamond City. Thus, when the Indians and the Jewels meet on the athletic field more is at stake than winning or losing the game—particularly if the game is basketball.

The 1941–1942 sport season was disastrous for the Indians. They lost seven of the eight football games played, and one was to the Jewels. The three-game basketball series with Diamond City was a complete failure—the Indians lost every game. This was a galling load for the school authorities to bear; the school's critics seized upon these defeats as one more illustration of "incompetency" in the school. After the second defeat the desire to win the third game was so strong in some citizens that they offered rewards to the players before the game, if they won—theater tickets, merchandise, and in some cases money. One wealthy man offered a dollar a point to each boy who made a point; two fathers of team members added another dollar to the reward for each of their sons. Thus, these boys received two dollars for each point they made in the game. In the closing minutes of the third game, the referee called fouls on the Superintendent, the coach, and the Elmtown rooters; two team members were barred from the game for unnecessary roughness. One Elmtown boy knocked a Diamond City boy to the floor, and the referee sent him to the showers immediately. This cost his team two points, but one enthusiastic fan gave the boy five dollars after the game for his "good work."

Athletics attracts boys from all classes in about the same proportion. Specifically, 3 of the 4 class I boys, and 3 of the 8 class V boys turned out for football and basketball, and two played on the baseball team. Before the football and basketball seasons were over 2 of the 3 class V's dropped out, turned in their suits, and were rated as failures by the coaches. There is little doubt that if they had been larger and heavier they would have been used, for the coaches are scrupulously honest in their relations with these class V boys, but there is evidence that boys in the other classes are not. One quit football because, he said, "They ran the plays over me all the time." This was true in part, as on several occasions a clique of popular football players was heard discussing, with great hilarity, how they had mussed "Plug" up in scrimmage. The other boy turned in his suit after he carried a black eye and bruised cheek home. His father and mother blamed the school for the accident and made the boy quit the game. One of these boys played on the scrub basketball team throughout the season and enthusiastically reported that he was going to make the varsity next year.[8] The two baseball players made the team, and, although they were rated as good players by the coach and the boys, they were not acceptable socially.

Student attendance or non-attendance at athletic events is associated very highly with class position. A glance at Table V will show that all the class II's attend some games whereas 31

### TABLE V

#### ATTENDANCE AT ATHLETIC EVENTS BY CLASS

| | Class | | | |
|---|---|---|---|---|
| Level of Attendance | I and II | III | IV | V |
| Attended no games | 0 | 17 | 44 | 12 |
| Attended few games | 2 | 20 | 58 | 14 |
| Attended most games | 2 | 25 | 58 | 0 |
| Seldom missed a game | 31 | 84 | 23 | 0 |
| Total | 35 | 146 | 183 | 26 |

$X^2 = 152.9250.$     $P < 0.01.$     $C = 0.53.$     $\overline{C} = 0.63.$

out of 35 seldom miss a game. Almost one-half of the class V students do not attend a single game, and none claim to have attended more than a few. Even the class V boys who turn out for a team do not attend games other than the ones their teams play at home. The two baseball players accompany the team,

[8] The urge to quit school and join the Paratroopers was too great in the summer of 1942; he entered the Army three years under age and went through the European campaign in 1944–1945.

but this can hardly be called attendance in the way the word is used here.[9]

It may be argued this is what one should expect since the games are held in the late afternoon and early evening when many boys and girls have to work, or since the children from the lower classes cannot afford to go. Neither argument has too much relevancy, first, because the games cost students only twelve cents and, second, few students work in both the afternoon and evening. If they work, they have the money, but they use it for things other than football, basketball, and baseball games.

DANCES, PARTIES, AND PLAYS. The school year is filled with carefully planned student parties of one kind or another. Early in the fall, the freshmen are invited to a "mixer" where group games are played, everyone is introduced to everyone else, and the high school orchestra plays for a dance. The mixer is followed, a week later, by a dance open to all students. Once each month thereafter the Student Council sponsors a Friday night dance. Between Thanksgiving and Christmas, the sophomores hold their annual dance. In the spring, the juniors give a dinner and dance for the seniors. During commencement week, the seniors have their senior ball. In addition to these traditional affairs, several clubs sponsor dances in the intervals between the major affairs; the "E" Club, composed of varsity athletes, has a dance at the end of the football, basketball, and baseball seasons; the Cheer Club girls hold a formal late in the winter; and the Future Farmers give an annual dinner followed by a dance.

To dance or not to dance is an old issue. Shortly after World War I, a group of students, backed by their parents, succeeded in breaking down resistance to dances in the high school. They convinced the Board that it was all right to have a dance in Central School's combination gymnasium and auditorium. Early dances were held in the face of stern objections from church groups, but the young people who originally sponsored them belonged to influential families in classes I and II; therefore, they were able effectively to overcome opposition. This old cleavage

[9] In Table V the players on a particular team were excluded from the individual tabulation; spectators only were included.

between the "aristocrats" and the "church people" is still observable. Although most ministers and some church members disapprove of high school dances, organized opposition is centered in the Norwegian Lutheran minister. This minister has argued the matter on religious and moral grounds many times with the Board of Education. When the Board voted for the dances, the Lutherans retaliated by holding prayer meetings and church entertainments on dance nights, either at the home of the minister or at that of a prominent Lutheran layman.

In addition to the Lutherans, and to a less extent the Methodists, unorganized hostility is encountered in some class III families, but more often in class IV, for economic rather than for religious reasons. These critics believe that the dances, particularly the formals, place an undue emphasis on clothes and grooming. It is charged that those who can afford expensive clothes, a car, and a good time after the dance talk in front of those who cannot and make them uncomfortable. It is clear that in many cases a child wants to go to the dances, but the parents object, usually because they cannot afford a new dress or suit. In this way, tension for which the high school receives the blame develops between the parent and the adolescent over the question. The "tradition of lovely formals" which has prevailed at "grand balls" among "the aristocracy" for a century is criticized most bitterly and frequently by lower class parents. The tradition was carried into the high school in the early twenties by the dominant class I girls who started high school dances. These girls set a pattern that has been maintained proudly by successive generations of high school girls. Although there were no girls from "the great families" in school, the other girls had heard stories of the kind of gowns belles of earlier years wore, and they worked hard—ably aided by ambitious mothers—to keep the tradition alive. Mothers without the means to furnish three or four "dramatic formals" a year for their daughters often take out their frustration on what was essentially a class question by a critical attitude toward the high school.

From the viewpoint of attendance, dancing is the least acceptable extracurricular activity sponsored by the high school; 53 per cent of the students do not attend any dances. Although some non-attendance exists in all classes, it is concentrated disproportionately in classes IV and V. No class V boy attended a single dance; only one girl reports that she went to one. This girl went to the freshman mixer with a class IV boy. She said that she did not have a good time. "The kids treated me so I didn't want to go anymore." Table VI shows that the level of

TABLE VI

ATTENDANCE AT HIGH SCHOOL DANCES BY CLASS

| Level of Attendance | Class | | |
| --- | --- | --- | --- |
|  | I and II | III | IV |
| Did not attend | 5 | 60 | 115 |
| Attended a few | 3 | 17 | 44 |
| Attended most | 3 | 24 | 14 |
| Seldom missed one | 24 | 45 | 10 |
| Total | 35 | 146 | 183 |

$$X^2 = 95.4086. \qquad P < 0.01. \qquad C = 0.46. \qquad \overline{C} = 0.58.$$

attendance differs significantly from one class to another, with the most intensive participation in class II, where 6 out of 7 youngsters attend some dances and 2 out of 3 seldom miss one. Class IV presents a sharply different pattern. Here only 10 students out of 183 report that they seldom miss a dance. These young people belong to cliques largely composed of class III youngsters, but a few very popular, upwardly mobile class IV's manage to cross class lines through the possession of personal talents valued in the culture—physical beauty, a pleasant voice, a sparkling personality, athletic prowess, careful grooming, a sense of humor.

The attendance pattern for club parties and plays is very similar to that of the dances. Every class II boy or girl attends at least one party or play held in the evening, but no class V boy or girl attends a single one. Even the 2 class V boys on the baseball team do not come to the baseball team's party. The highest level of participation occurs in classes I and II, the lowest in class IV, where 6 students out of 183 report that they seldom miss a play or a party; no one in class V participates. The situation is summarized in Table VII.

## TABLE VII

ATTENDANCE AT EVENING PLAYS AND PARTIES BY CLASS

| | | Class | |
|---|---|---|---|
| Level of Participation | I and II | III | IV |
| Attended none | 0 | 39 | 110 |
| Attended a few | 4 | 25 | 51 |
| Attended most | 8 | 41 | 16 |
| Seldom missed one | 23 | 41 | 6 |
| Total | 35 | 146 | 183 |

$X^2 = 131.2455.$    $P < 0.01.$    $C = 0.51.$    $\overline{C} = 0.66.$

MUSIC AND MUSICAL ACTIVITIES. Music is stressed heavily in the extracurricular program as a part of the school's public relations program. Local organizations rely on the high school for free entertainment on special occasions, which range from the American Legion's Armistice Day Dinner to the Rotary Club's Annual Ladies' Night. In 1941–1942 the school furnished 131 programs out of the 140 requests received. Fifteen different musical groups were supported and used in these programs: marching band, concert band, girls' chorus, mixed chorus, swing band, violin ensemble, brass quartet, cornet trio, girls' glee club, and three girls' and three boys' quartets. The larger groups, such as the marching band and the mixed chorus, included practically all students able to play an instrument or sing well enough to do chorus work. Seventy-nine students (20 per cent of the student body) carried the load of this extensive activity.

Participation in musical activities is associated highly with class position. Twenty-three class II's, 31 class III's, and 25 class IV's belong to either an instrumental or a vocal group; no class V's belong to any groups.

The ubiquitous arms of powerful families reach into this phase of extracurricular activities in devious ways to guide and push their children to the center of the stage where they will receive the attention due those of their status. Demonstrated musical talent is highly prized in the two upper classes, and parents are not averse to bringing direct pressure on the Superintendent to push their children to the front, as we saw in the Cross case.

This type of pressure was exerted 15 different times, that we heard about, in the course of the year.

THE STUDENT COUNCIL. The Student Council is composed of 33 representatives elected by secret ballot from the home rooms, each school class, and the student body. The two or three candidates for each office are nominated several days before the election without any noticeable interference from the teachers or school officials. The election proper is patterned as closely as possible after a regular adult election to give the students an idea of the workings of the electoral machinery in our society. Since the ballot is secret and adult pressure is not exerted to elect a particular student to a given office, we may assume that there will be no relationship between a student's position in the social structure and election to a student office, if ability alone is involved.[10] Conversely, we may expect, if the class hypothesis has validity, to find students from classes II and III disproportionately represented on the Student Council, whereas those from classes IV and V will not have so much representation as their numbers in the student body indicate. Actually the percentage of officers elected from class II is well over twice as great as its representation in the student body. On the other hand, class IV, with almost one-half of the student body, has less than one-third of the offices, and class V, with nearly 7 per cent of the student body, does not have a single representative. The figures on this point are summarized below:

| Class | Per Cent of Student Body | Per Cent of Elected Representatives |
|---|---|---|
| I and II | 9.0 | 21.6 |
| III | 37.3 | 46.2 |
| IV | 47.0 | 32.2 |
| V | 6.7 | 00.0 |
| Total | 100.0 | 100.0 |

[10] Eighty-two per cent of the students believed that their elected representatives were leaders—they had to have ability to get things done, personality, character. Athletic stars, "social butterflies," and "little cuties" were not elected to the Student Council, according to student beliefs, but it was commonly accepted that they were popular.

The election of a disproportionately large number of officers from classes II and III is an illustration of the paradox inherent in the class system. Boys and girls in classes IV and V, and to a less extent in class III, resent the dominance of class II students in student affairs, cliques, and clubs. They cite instance after instance to show that these boys and girls receive favorable consideration and that those of their own status are discriminated against; yet, when they have an opportunity to exercise authority by electing members of their own class to student offices, they turn to classes II and III for two-thirds of their leadership. Then, after they have elected them as their representatives, they complain about the "rich kids hogging all the offices."

SUMMARY OF EXTRACURRICULAR PARTICIPATION. Twenty-three extracurricular activities that range from organized athletics to the school paper are supported actively by the student body. Potentially a boy can belong to eleven different organizations and a girl to twelve. In spite of the number of activities and the wide range of interests they represent, one student out of three does not participate in any extracurricular activity. The percentage of participation or non-participation is associated very strongly with class position, as the following tabulation shows:

| Class | Participation | Non-Participation |
|-------|---------------|-------------------|
| I and II | 100.0 | 00.0 |
| III | 75.3 | 24.7 |
| IV | 57.4 | 42.6 |
| V | 27.0 | 73.0 |
| Total | 65.9 | 34.1 |

Adolescents from the higher classes are in far more activities than those from the lower classes, and the girls are in more than the boys. Eighteen girls are in six or seven activities. Nine of the 18 come from class II, 6 from class III, and 3 from class IV. Since there are only 14 girls in class II, but 73 in class III, and 111 in class IV, it is easy to see that a much higher proportion of class II girls enter as many activities as they desire and give the impression to the other girls that "they are in everything" as they, indeed, tend to be. The hyperactive class III girls represent only 9 per cent of the girls in this class; moreover, they tend to be scattered in more activities so their presence in an activity is not so conspicuous. The three class IV girls in either six or seven activities represent less than 4 per cent of the girls in the class; therefore, the roles they play are really different from those the average girl in this stratum plays. Boys do not become involved in as many activities as girls. No boy participates in more than four, and only two are in this many—one a class II, the other a class IV member. The class II boys average almost twice as many activities as the class III boys, as Table VIII shows.

TABLE VIII

MEAN NUMBER OF EXTRACURRICULAR ACTIVITIES PARTICIPATED IN BY SEX AND CLASS

| Class | Boys | Girls |
|-------|------|-------|
| I and II | 1.8 | 3.9 |
| III | 1.1 | 2.0 |
| IV | 0.8 | 1.0 |
| V | 0.6 | 0.1 |
| Total | 1.0 | 1.4 |

Participation in all extracurricular activities, except boys' athletics, is biased in favor of some classes and against others. Moreover, each club is class-graded. For example, the Home Makers' Club is composed predominantly of class IV girls (60 per cent). Class II girls avoid it; two, or 4 per cent, of the membership, are in it. The French Club, in contrast, is essentially a class II group, 60 per cent, whereas only 2 class IV girls belong to it. The Library Club is weighted heavily with class III's, 71 per cent. The Future Farmers of America is its counterpart among the boys—60 per cent from class III.

A class IV girl summarized the effect of the class system in the high school on the lower ranking boys and girls, in so far as it pertains to extracurricular activities, when she said:

Frankly, for a lot of us there is nothing here, but just going to classes, listening to the teacher, reciting, studying, and going home again. We are pushed out of things. There is a group of girls here who think they are higher than us. They look down on us. I won't mention any names, but they are a group of girls from the higher families. They have a club that is supposed to be outside of school, but it's really in the school.[11] They just go from one club to the other and hog all of the offices. They're in all the activities. They talk about what they're doing, what they're going to do, and they won't pay any attention to us. They snub us and they won't talk to us. Some of them will speak to us sometimes, but most of the time they just ignore us. I'd like to be in the school activities and the school plays, go to the dances, and things like that, but they make us feel like we're not wanted. I went to some of the activities when I first started high school. Last year, I was in the Home Makers' and the Cheer Club, but they ignored me. Now I'm not in anything. If we go to the high school dances, nobody will dance with us. They dance among themselves and have a good time and we're nobody. If we go to the football games, it's the same way. Those Cheer Club girls are supposed to sit together at a game and root, but they don't. They break up into little groups and, if you're not in one of the groups, you're left out of things.

As she said this, she turned her palms upward, shrugged her shoulders and said, "Well, why go? We're made to feel out of place and that's the way it is."

[11] This club and its activities will be discussed in Chapter 9.

# CLIQUES AND DATES

### Cliques and clique relations

This school is full of cliques. You go into the hall, or the Commons Room [between classes or at noon], and you will find the same kids together day after day. Walk up Freedom Street at noon, or in the evening, and you'll see them again. These kids run in bunches just like their parents. This town is full of cliques, and you can't expect the kids to be any different from their parents.

THIS OPINION, EXPRESSED BY A HIGH SCHOOL TEACHER, is also expressed by many Elmtowners. Frequently, the question is asked, "Have you run into those bunches in the high school?" Another common comment is, "You can't understand those kids unless you can get into their gangs."

Systematic observation over a six-month period confirmed these and similar remarks. Persistent study revealed the vast majority of a particular boy's or girl's waking hours are spent in the company of a few pals. When he leaves home in the morning he generally walks or rides to school with them. In and around the high school he can be seen talking, laughing, walking, playing with them. Through the day he is with them whenever some formal demand on his time, such as classes or the job, frees him for informal activities. Before school opens in the morning little groups of friends can be seen talking together, laughing over some joke or prank, planning future activities, or reliving past ones through talk and shared memories. Later the same little band of boys or girls can be seen going to class together. At noon they may be seen going to or from lunch, and usually together; if they pack their lunch they may be grouped in a corner of the Commons Room or in the Central School gymnasium.

After school two or three out of a group of five or six may go uptown to the pool hall if boys, or to the drug store or bowling alley if girls. The same two or three boys or girls may be seen early in the evening on their way to a show or a friend's home. This persistent relationship between a few boys or a few girls which carries over from one activity to another throughout the day, and day after day, is the most obvious thing about the behavior patterns of the high school pupils.

These small, informal groups, which we shall call *cliques*, consume most of the interest, time, and activities of the adolescents. We shall call the more or less permanent ties the members of a clique have with one another a *clique relation* to differentiate it from other kinds of social relationships. The clique relationship exists only through the social relations the members of a clique maintain with each other. A clique relationship lasts as long as a person is a member of the clique, whereas social relationships in the clique are ephemeral, multiform, and almost infinite in number.

A clique comes into existence when two or more persons are related one to another in an intimate fellowship that involves "going places and doing things" together, a mutual exchange of ideas, and the acceptance of each personality by the others. Perhaps the most characteristic thing about the clique is the way its members plan to be together, to do things together, go places together. Within the clique, personal relations with one another involve the clique mates in emotional and sentimental situations of great moment to the participants. Confidences are exchanged between some or all members; often those very personal, wholly private, experiences that occur in the family which involve only one member may be exchanged with a best friend in the group. Relations with the opposite sex, with adults, and with young people outside the clique are discussed and decisions reached on the action to be taken by the clique, or by a particular member involved in a situation.

Membership is voluntary and informal; members are admitted gradually to a pre-existing clique and dropped by the mutual consent of its participants. Although there are no explicit rules for membership, the clique has a more or less common set of values which determines who will be admitted, what it does, how it will censure some member who does not abide by its values.

As the clique comes to be accepted by other cliques as a definite unit in the adolescent society it develops an awareness of self, a "we feeling," sentiments and traditions which impel its members to act and think alike. Its members frequently identify their interests with the group in contrast to the interests of the family, other cliques, the school, and society. Generally clique interests come before those of the individual member or any outside group or interest. This attitude often results in conflicts between the clique and the family, between the clique and the school, or between the clique and the neighborhood. If this conflict element becomes the *raison d'être* of the group, the clique develops into the gang.[1]

The impact of clique controls on the adolescent produces a sense of his personal importance in his relations with other members, as well as with persons outside the clique, for the clique has a powerful emotional influence on him which he tends to carry over into outside social relations, using it to bolster his own conception of himself. Each member has a group status derived from his ability to achieve some thing or to contribute some thing to the well-being of the clique. This group-derived status is often valued very highly by the boy or girl. Thus, the clique is a powerful influence in the life of the person from its formation in the pre-adolescent years until it is dissolved by the development of the dating pattern.

Outsiders, especially parents and teachers, often fail to realize the meaning which the clique has for its members; consequently there is a tendency for them to deprecate it. This may produce more resistance and withdrawal into the sanctuary of the clique on the part of the adolescent, for, in a conflict situation that in-

[1] The clique and the gang are closely related social forms, the essential difference between the two being the importance placed upon predacious activity that almost invariably leads to conflict in the gang. The clique is a socially accepted group which normally does not develop conflict relations to the point where an undeclared war exists between itself and society or, for that matter, other cliques.

volves him as a member of the group, the youngster tends to
look to the clique for support. The adolescent, bolstered by his
sense of belonging to a group that backs him in his efforts to
emancipate himself from adult and institutional controls, feels
a sense of power, of belonging, of security, and consequently
makes decisions in collaboration with his clique mates he would
never make alone, as long as his decisions meet with clique approval. Each member of the clique, reinforced by the presence
of his "pals" and their agreement that some line of action is desirable or undesirable, that something must be done or undone,
produces a cohesive social situation in which the clique acts
as a unit. Controls operating in the clique tend to produce uniformity of thought and action on the question at issue. Individuals who do not go along with the decision of the majority
are coerced into acquiescence or ostracized, since deviation is
tolerated only within narrow limits. Adherence to the group
code is guarded carefully by the clique's members, for cliques
develop reputations and have favorable or unfavorable status
attached to them by other cliques, parents, teachers, preachers,
and adults on the basis of their membership and activities.

### Number, type, and size of cliques

The 259 cliques we studied are divided into three types on
the basis of where they functioned. *School cliques* are composed
of either boys or girls who associate with each other around
school. Their membership can be seen between class periods,
during the last quarter hour of the lunch hour, or immediately
after school, participating in the activity of the moment. There
are 106 school cliques which have from 2 to 9 members for boys,
2 to 12 for girls; the modal size for both sexes is 5 members.
*Recreational cliques* function in various situations away from
school. Their members are only slightly different from the
school cliques, but in a typical recreational clique some members
of the school clique are missing. The place of the missing boy
or girl may be taken by a person who belongs to another school
clique, but for recreational purposes this person participates
with a clique with which he does not associate around school.
Sometimes a large school clique splits into two recreational
cliques. The 120 recreational cliques are smaller than the school

cliques. They range in size from 2 to 7 members and have a modal membership of 4 for both the boys and the girls. *Institutional cliques* are seen in specific non-school situations such as Sunday School, young people's meetings at the churches, Boy Scouts, and Campfire Girls. Thirty-three institutional cliques are known to exist, 13 of boys and 20 of girls. They are smaller than the others, ranging from 2 to 5 members each. The modal membership is 3 for the boys and 4 for the girls.

Exactly one-fourth of the students live in the country, but only 15 cliques (6 per cent) are composed exclusively of rural boys or girls. These cliques tend to be neighborhood- as well as school-oriented because of the distance they live from school and from each other. The rural cliques are smaller in size than the cliques made up of town or mixed town-country adolescents. They average (mode) 3 members, whereas the others have 5 members. However, what the town adolescent does with his 3 or 4 pals, the country youth does with 1 or 2, for the quality and function of the relationships entailed in the smaller cliques are not different from those in the larger ones. Moreover, since in general the interests of the country youth are not essentially different from those of town dwellers, we shall dismiss the town-country dichotomy without further consideration.[2]

### Who cliques with whom

Evidence accumulated from parents and children indicates that parents consistently try to limit their children's friendship ties to certain boys or girls, usually, however, without too much success. Social pressures in the adolescent group operate far more effectively, and with greater subtlety, to channelize friendships within limits permitted by the social system of both the adult and the adolescent social worlds than the hopes, fears, and admonitions of anxious parents. This dual process is illustrated in the materials given below.

Joyce Jenson, class III, was discussing her friend Gladys Johnson, class III, when she laid bare a number of factors which regulated the group relations of the adolescents.

[2] All cliques were analyzed by $X^2$ to determine if any significant difference exists between (1) size and class in school and (2) size and prestige class. None was found.

We influence each other a lot. She influences me almost as much as my parents do. I listen to them, especially when it comes to choosing friends, but I don't agree with everything they tell me. I've had them really give me the dickens about going around with some girls I wanted to go with or maybe Gladys did. Most parents don't want their kids running around with certain other kids, and they'll give them advice and they'll follow it or they won't, but when my folks put the foot down on me I listen.

I know that the folks give me good advice, but sometimes they just don't understand what kids want to do, and they think we ought to act like they acted twenty years ago. My parents, especially my mother, influence me in what I do, but Gladys probably influences me as much or more.

I don't want to run any of the kids down, but there are certain girls here who are just not my type, and they're not Gladys' type; they'd like to run around with us, but we don't let them.

Pauline Tryon [class IV] and her bunch would like to run around with us, but we turn our backs on them because they run around all night, cut school, and hang out down at the Blue Triangle.

There are some kids we'd like to go around with, but they don't want us to go with them. Gladys and I would like to go around with "Cookie" Barnett [class II] and her bunch, or the G.W.G.'s, but they snub us if we try to get in on their parties, or dances, or date the boys they go with.

Gladys revealed the close reciprocal relation between these girls, and how they reacted upon each other in different situations when she said:

I have one very close friend, Joyce Jenson. We met four years ago and we've been going around together since. We plan our clothes, we talk about what we're going to do, and we study together. We come to school together, we take the same courses, we visit each other at home, we go to church together, we plan church parties, and so on. Of course, we don't agree 100 per cent on everything, but we've made up our minds when we don't agree that one is going to dominate the other. Sometimes she dominates me and sometimes I dominate her. If we decide we want to go to a church party, well, maybe I won't want to go, but I'll go because she really wants to go. Then maybe we'll decide to go to a show. Sometimes she won't want to go because she doesn't like the show, but she'll go because I've gone to the church party with her.

This is typical of the interaction between adolescent personalities in the intimate relationships of the clique and the still closer, and more pervasive, ties that hold best friends together.

High school boys and girls maintain few clique ties with adolescents in the out-of-school group. Of the 1,258 clique relations recorded for the student group, 91 per cent of the boys' and 93 per cent of the girls' are with other high school students.[3] Clique ties between the students and non-students are confined largely to classes IV and V; the exceptions are limited to 4 cliques.[4]

As we shall see presently, clique ties are strongly associated with an adolescent's position in the class structure. Since all class II's and 12 out of 13 class III's are in school, whereas 2 out of 5 class IV's and almost 9 out of 10 class V's are out of school, it is normal for class II's and class III's to clique with their in-school peers and for the lower class youngsters in school to have clique ties with their peers who have withdrawn. This is true especially in the case of class IV boys and girls who are not connected with any extracurricular activities in high school. They, together with class V's, associate far more frequently with persons in the out-of-school group than their class peers who are involved in school activities. Boys and girls with clique ties outside the school group are oriented emotionally and socially outside the school.

The clique structure is very highly correlated with the formal division of the student groups into high school classes—freshman, sophomore, junior, and senior. A corrected coefficient of contingency of 0.86 for the boys and 0.90 for the girls was found

[3] Clique relations by sex and class were analyzed by $X^2$ for significance of difference; none was found. This indicates that our observations are not out of proportion for the number in each stratum and sex. The number of observed clique relations by sex and class is given in Table XI of the Appendix.

[4] Five high school boys, 2 class II's and 3 class III's, maintain clique relations with 2 class III's in the out-of-school group. Three class III's in school are in a clique with 2 class III's who left school. There are 2 class III girls in a clique with 3 class IV girls who graduated from high school in 1941. The fourth clique is made up of 1 class II boy, 1 class III, and 2 class IV's in school and 2 class IV's out of school. This clique is bound together by its members' common interest in gambling, poker, pool, dating out-of-town girls, drinking, sex play, and "aceing around."

when the clique relations of each sex were correlated with class in school.[5] These coefficients indicate that clique ties are limited in large part to a boy's or girl's class in school, but not wholly.

The high correlation between class in school and clique ties does not throw light upon the crucial question of our hypothesis: Is an adolescent's position in the social structure related to the formation of clique ties within the limits of his class in school? The clique relations of a given adolescent, viewed in terms of this question, may be tabulated 16 different ways, since there are four school and four prestige classes. But for our purpose they are combined into four categories: (1) clique relations within an adolescent's school class and prestige class; (2) clique relations within school class, but outside prestige class; (3) clique relations outside school class, but within prestige class; (4) clique relations outside both school class and prestige class. The results are summarized in Table IX.

TABLE IX

DISTRIBUTION OF CLIQUE RELATIONS BY PRESTIGE AND SCHOOL CLASSES
FOR EACH SEX

| Combination of Clique Relations | Per Cent | |
|---|---|---|
| | Boys | Girls |
| Within school and prestige class | 54 | 60 |
| Within school class but outside prestige class | 32 | 26 |
| Outside school class but within prestige class | 12 | 13 |
| Outside both school and prestige class | 2 | 1 |
| Total | 100 | 100 |

A glance at Table IX will show that 54 per cent of the boys' and 60 per cent of the girls' clique relations are within the limits of prestige and school class, and 32 per cent of the boys' and 26 per cent of the girls' clique ties which crossed a prestige class line are with their classmates. When a youngster's clique relations extend beyond his school class, they are with a prestige class equal rather than one unequal in school or prestige class. The crossing of class lines is related very closely to a youngster's class in school. For example, freshmen girls and boys cross prestige

[5] The distribution of clique relations within and between school classes by sex is given in Table XII of the Appendix.

class lines 4.5 times more frequently than do seniors in their clique relationships. As a boy or girl progresses in school, school class lines are crossed more frequently than prestige class lines. Moreover, the more a boy or girl dates in the junior and senior years, the greater the likelihood is that the clique mates will be in the same prestige class rather than in the same school class. The concentration of clique ties along prestige lines among class II and class III girls (and, to a lesser extent, boys) during the junior and senior years is noticeable particularly in the "socially conscious" portion of these two prestige and school classes.

The figures presented in Table IX show that clique ties are concentrated along prestige class lines in some 2 cases out of 3 among both the boys and the girls. That is, boys and girls select their clique mates from among their prestige equals within their class in school in a highly significant manner.

Analysis of the 1,258 clique ties when the factor of school status is ignored reveals that approximately 3 out of 5 are between boys or girls of the same prestige class, 2 out of 5 are between adolescents who belong to adjacent classes, and 1 out of 25 involves persons who belong to classes twice removed from one another. In specific terms, this means that the typical clique of 5 is composed ordinarily of 3 adolescents from one class and 2 from another. The chances are only 1 in 25, as Table X shows,

TABLE X

CLIQUE RELATIONS WITHIN AND BETWEEN CLASSES BY NUMBER AND PER CENT FOR EACH SEX

| Clique Relations and Class Position | Boys | | Girls | | Total | |
|---|---|---|---|---|---|---|
| | Number | Per Cent | Number | Per Cent | Number | Per Cent |
| Equals with equals | 302 | 59 | 490 | 66 | 792 | 63 |
| Across one class line | 190 | 37 | 224 | 30 | 414 | 33 |
| Across two class lines | 22 | 4 | 30 | 4 | 52 | 4 |
| Total | 514 | 100 | 744 | 100 | 1,258 | 100 |

that a clique will be composed of three prestige classes. For example, a predominantly class III clique may have 2 class IV's in it, but the chances are that it will not include a class II person. On the other hand, it may be basically a class III group with a minority of class II's in it. When class II's, class III's, and class IV's are found in the same clique, the class IV's are upwardly mobile adolescents who possess very unusual personal traits which enable them to function well outside the normal limits of their class. There are 4 cliques among the boys and 2 among the girls like this, but in every case the class IV person is the object of comment. For instance, "Ziggy" Moran was one of 3 class IV girls who crossed two class lines successfully; she participated almost exclusively in a clique composed of girls from classes II and III. She also dated 1 of the 4 class I boys in school, much to the consternation of the boy's parents. They were afraid "something would happen," as it had years before with "Ziggy's" older sister in a similar situation. "Ziggy's" success was so unusual that Elmtown adults and teachers often spoke of her as being "out of her element." Such remarks as, "She is flying too high," "After high school she is going to take a bad fall," "Ten years from now she will be taking in washing like her sister on Beacon Street," were common.

The detailed study of "who cliques with whom" discloses that from 49 to 70 per cent of all clique ties are with class equals. It also reveals that the polar classes in the social structure are isolated one from another in so far as intimate, personal, time-consuming, ego-involving, face-to-face relations are concerned, for there are no clique ties between the class II's and the class V's. When a boy's or girl's clique ties cross a class line, and about one-third do, a member of an adjacent class is involved. Inevitably, when a class I clique tie crosses a class line it crosses to a lower group; conversely, a class V goes up. This results in the class I youngster functioning in cliques composed predominantly of class II's and class III's, with a few class IV's. The class V adolescent, on the other hand, associates mostly with other class V's, some class IV's, very few class III's, and no class II's. Adolescents in the intervening classes follow the same general pattern, except that about 3 out of 5 of their clique ties are with class equals, with most of the remainder from the adjacent classes. Theoretically, an adolescent in class III or class IV should have an equal chance to associate with adolescents in the adjacent class, but the process does not operate this way. By reading across the rows of Table XI, it can be seen that the class III's, both boys and girls, have a significantly higher percentage of clique ties with the class IV's than they do with the class II's, but the class IV's avoid the class V's.

TABLE XI

PERCENTAGE OF CLIQUE RELATIONS OBSERVED WITHIN AND BETWEEN
CLASSES BY SEX *

BOYS

| Class | I and II | III | IV | V |
|---|---|---|---|---|
| I and II | *49* | 38 | 13 | 0 |
| III | 11 | *61* | 27 | 1 |
| IV | 5 | 33 | *60* | 2 |
| V | 0 | 13 | 31 | *56* |

$X^2 = 156.7688$     $P < 0.01.$     $C = 0.48.$     $\bar{C} = 0.61.$

GIRLS

| Class | II | III | IV | V |
|---|---|---|---|---|
| II | *56* | 26 | 18 | 0 |
| III | 7 | *64* | 28 | 1 |
| IV | 4 | 21 | *70* | 5 |
| V | 0 | 4 | 36 | *60* |

$X^2 = 578.9209.$     $P < 0.01.$     $C = 0.65.$     $\bar{C} = 0.79.$

* This table must be read across the rows. The figures in italic type are clique associations within each class.

It should be remembered that the numbers in classes II and V are much smaller than in the intervening classes; therefore, when one reads in Table XI that 1 per cent of the boys' clique ties in class III are with class V boys, but 13 per cent of the class V boys' ties in class III are with class V boys, he must realize that the difference in numbers in the two classes produces this apparently anomalous situation. From the viewpoint of class III, there is little clique contact with class V; only 2 boys out of 73 are in cliques with class V boys, but from the standpoint of the class V's this is important, for 2 of the 8 class V's in school associate with class III boys. The clique ties between the 2 class III boys and the 2 class V boys are in the freshman class and the baseball team. From the broader viewpoint of all class

III boys in contrast to all class V boys in the community, there is practically no association between the two classes.

"BEST" FRIEND. Within the clique some members are more closely tied emotionally, and in their common activities, to some other member than they are to the rest. These closer, more intimate sub-groups within the clique represent a closest-friend or best-friend combination that is found in practically every clique which has more than 2 members; in the case of a twosome, the combination of clique tie and best friend are the same. The cliques were watched carefully to determine who appeared to be associating with whom within the clique more frequently than with the other members, and these observations were recorded on the personal cards of the boys and girls involved. Later, each boy and girl was asked to name his best friend or closest friend.[6] *In every case* the listed best friend was known to be a member of the clique of the person who listed him. Furthermore, 78 per cent of the girls and 71 per cent of the boys listed as their best friend a person who belonged to the same prestige class as they did. These figures indicate that these adolescents seek their best friends in their own class oftener than they do their other clique mates; that is, the choice of best friend is associated more closely with class position than the selection of one's other friends. This can be seen if the percentages of Table XII are compared with those of Table XI.

The naming of best friends is a two-way process. A student may name another student as his best friend, but that student may name a third person as his best friend, or the naming may be reciprocal; that is, the mutual acceptance of best-friend status. Mutual acceptance of best-friend status is general when the namer and the named belong to the same class. Rejection of the namer by the named occurs in each case when the namer belongs to a lower class than the named. To be specific, Paul Stout, class IV, was the President of the Student Council and in a clique with

---

[6] The listed best friend and the observed best friend combinations were analyzed by $X^2$ for each sex and prestige class to determine significance of difference. None was found at the 0.01 level. That is, the correspondence between the observed and the listed best friend was so close that the variations within each class and sex were attributable to chance rather than to significant differences in the two lists.

### TABLE XII

CLASS OF SELF AND CLASS OF LISTED BEST FRIEND BY NUMBER AND PER CENT *

#### BOYS

Class of "Best Friend"

| Class of Namer | I and II Number | I and II Per Cent | III Number | III Per Cent | IV Number | IV Per Cent | V Number | V Per Cent |
|---|---|---|---|---|---|---|---|---|
| I and II | 15 | 71 | 6 | 29 | 0 | 0 | 0 | 0 |
| III | 8 | 11 | 51 | 70 | 14 | 19 | 0 | 0 |
| IV | 1 | 1 | 15 | 21 | 54 | 75 | 2 | 3 |
| V | 0 | 0 | 0 | 0 | 3 | 37 | 5 | 63 |

$$X^2 = 77.0815. \quad P < 0.01. \quad C = 0.55. \quad \bar{C} = 0.74.$$

#### GIRLS

Class of "Best Friend"

| Class of Namer | II Number | II Per Cent | III Number | III Per Cent | IV Number | IV Per Cent | V Number | V Per Cent |
|---|---|---|---|---|---|---|---|---|
| II | 10 | 71 | 4 | 29 | 0 | 0 | 0 | 0 |
| III | 3 | 4 | 58 | 80 | 12 | 16 | 0 | 0 |
| IV | 1 | 1 | 18 | 16 | 88 | 79 | 4 | 4 |
| V | 0 | 0 | 0 | 0 | 4 | 22 | 14 | 78 |

$$X^2 = 110.0172. \quad P < 0.01. \quad C = 0.58. \quad \bar{C} = 0.78.$$

* This table is to be read across the rows. It includes all named best friends whether the named best friend is in or out of school.

2 class III and 3 class II boys. He named a class II clique mate as his best friend. The latter, however, named another class II clique mate as his best friend. The case of "Ziggy" Moran was identical. She named a prominent class II girl as her best friend, but the latter did not reciprocate. Surprisingly, there were only 8 such cases among the girls (4 per cent) and 4 (3 per cent) among the boys. These lower class boys and girls who make friendship claims that are rejected are clique mates of the person named. It is believed that these claims are made in good faith and the boy or girl who lists a higher class boy or girl as a best friend really considers that person his or her best friend. Probably, if the namer knew he did not enjoy the reciprocal evaluation

of best friend by the person he named as best friend, he would have been shocked.

Approximately 10 per cent of the students list as best friend an adolescent in the out-of-school group. This is related directly to the class position of the person doing the naming, as Table XIII shows. This relationship between school status, best friend,

TABLE XIII

Class Position of Persons Who Named as "Best Friend" a Person Not in School

| | Boys | | Girls | |
| Class of Namer | Number | Per Cent | Number | Per Cent |
| --- | --- | --- | --- | --- |
| I and II | 0 | 0 | 0 | 0 |
| III | 5 | 7 | 3 | 4 |
| IV | 9 | 12 | 12 | 11 |
| V | 3 | 38 | 5 | 28 |
| Total | 17 | 9 | 20 | 9 |

and class might have been expected since an adolescent's clique ties tend to be with class equals. In the case of the class II's, since all adolescents in the class are in school, the opportunity to associate with a class equal who quit school does not exist. In addition, association with an out-of-school boy or girl is frowned upon by adolescents and adults because withdrawal from school is considered reprehensible. On the other hand, adolescents from the three lower classes drop out of school in numbers that are related directly to class level.

## Reputation in the student group

Once an adolescent is identified as a member of a particular clique, the reputation of the clique tends to be attached to him by adolescents outside the clique, by teachers, and by other adults who know the youngster and his clique mates. Cliques develop their reputations through the extracurricular activities their members participate in, as well as through what they do away from school, particularly in their leisure time. The students use dozens of clichés to categorize a particular boy's or girl's reputation, or clique affiliation; but they have one common element, namely, they are symbolic of the esteem or disesteem in which the person or his clique is held by the speaker. Often this evaluation is shared commonly in the adolescent group. The function of these clichés is to place a clique in the informal structure of the adolescent social world. Some of these referential statements are given here to indicate their nature; some apply to individuals, others to cliques.

Bill is a trouble maker, and his gang is just like him.

Perk's a good, ambitious kid, but Plug's kind of dumb. He comes from an unfortunate family.

Hank is one of our leading playboys; he belongs to the elite.

Bob's in a wild gang; they have rotten reps. No respectable girl will go with them.

John's bunch are "clippers"; none of our group [Lutheran girls] will go with them.

Sleepy's a "grubby," I don't know whether he's dumb or just not interested in school.

Joe's a "lone duck." His only friend is a "bush ape" from east of town.

Those kids have gone to the dogs. [Said in reference to a clique of class IV girls who attended public dances, drank, and petted indiscriminately.]

"Doc" has a bad rep. He works in a carnival in the summer; from what he says, I don't imagine he'd feel out of place in one.

Eleanor's one of the faster girls.

They're all nice kids in Mary's bunch.

Little Butch's gang are "grubbies."

That's the big-bang athletic bunch; they belong to the elite around here. [The reference is to the clique of Frank Stone, Jr.]

Those kids are all jerks. [Said by a class IV girl in reference to a clique of class IV girls of whom she did not approve.]

The G.W.G.'s are our "four hundred."

Ola's bunch are nice, harmless kids who don't have many dates.

Kink runs with the kids who are never much of this or much of that. [This is in reference to a large clique of class III boys.]

You know, they're good kids. [A clique of class IV girls in Home Makers.]

They are awfully sweet kids but not active in school. [Another group of III's and IV's.]

They are pretty fast, and we leave them alone. . . . Those kids are not accepted at all. [These comments apply to a mixed clique of class III and class IV girls.]

Gabby acts like a wild animal; I guess she just hasn't been told or raised. [A class V girl.]

Some of the kids think Pansy is crazy, but I think she is just queer. [Statement made about a class V girl by a representative of class III.]

The athletes rate tops with everybody. You see, they're our heroes! [A class IV girl's estimate.]

The Polish kids live across the tracks and have bad reps. Annie and Romine are "Poles" but they're different. Annie is a nice kid; she's pretty, dresses slick, and she's bright. [From a class III girl who lived in the older residential area.]

Everything is wrong with the kids May runs with. First, they live down by the old tannery. They're not clean, they don't dress well. Their hair isn't fixed right. Then May can't live her sisters' reps down. [Said by a class III girl with reference to a class V girl and her clique.]

Jane's a Lutheran that's gone wild.

Janet's a big girl [class IV] and she doesn't dress right; so she just isn't accepted. [Said by another class IV girl.]

Emma's another one that's isolated. She has a rotten "rep" too.

That's the Lutheran crowd. Those kids stick together like glue.

Jerry belongs to the Catholic bunch.

Nadine is a farm kid.

There are two kinds of farm kids—those who associate with anybody, and those who stick with the farm kids.

Careful grooming, proper language, and character traits such as honesty are accepted by the vast majority of students as desirable qualities. Other personal traits, such as "Jim's a swell fellow: he'll never pass you up without speaking," "Tom'll help anybody with their math," "Alice won't cheat, but she won't tell on you if she sees you copying an answer," are rated as valuable characteristics by most students. Participation in athletics rates high among both boys and girls. However, if a boy on an athletic team breaks training rules, he is generally condemned, but he does not lose the rating of a "big bang" unless he is singled out as the scapegoat for the loss of a game. Other extracurricular activities have various ratings. To be a member of the Drama and Debating Club places one among the elite, but to be a prominent member of the Home Economics Club means little, except that the girl is probably a "good kid." Actually, the "Home Ec" girls occupy a lower rating than they might otherwise enjoy simply because they are identified as "Home Ecs." Personal behavior such as carrying tales, malicious gossip, drinking, or smoking in public, among the girls, places the individual in an unenviable category among most of the other students.

The informal values the adolescents attach to one another were quantified by student raters to determine if the various status-giving values assigned to each student were associated with class position. A representative boy and girl from each school and prestige class, a very popular class III senior girl, the president and vice-president of the Student Council did the rating in private conferences with us. These students were asked to evaluate the members of their school class and all other students they believed they knew well in terms of their *reputation* in the student group. We stressed that we wanted them to tell us how a particular student was regarded generally by other students. After the field work was completed, two graduate students in sociology at Indiana University categorized their comments. Originally seven categories were used, but these were combined into three when it became evident that there was little beyond a verbal difference between the categories dropped—"farm kids," "the Lutheran gang," "the Catholic bunch," those who were "never this or that"—and "the good kids" category. The way each student was categorized on the basis of the remarks of the

19 raters was then weighted on a 1, 2, 3 scale and punched on Hollerith cards. The mean rating was then calculated and assigned to the ;udent in the same way we assigned class position to his family.[7] The final reputational categories may be described as follows.

1. THE ELITE. The elite is composed of leaders in extracurricular student activities, as well as in church work, in the youth groups, and in social affairs. The teachers, ministers, and adult leaders rely upon them for help in the formation and promotion of organized adolescent activities. These students conceive of themselves as leaders. Students who do not belong to this group view them as those who do things and think they are somebody.

2. THE "GOOD KIDS." In adolescent language the "good kids" are "never this or never that." They come to school, do their work, but do not distinguish themselves with glory or notoriety. Some two-thirds of the students are in this category.

3. THE "GRUBBY" GANG. "Grubbies" are set off from the other students for many reasons—unfortunate family connections, personality traits, lack of cooperation with teachers, living in the wrong part of town. Boys and girls identified as grubbies are "nobody" in the eyes of the non-grubbies. To be rated a grubby is comparable to being blacklisted. According to student beliefs, grubbies have no interest in school affairs; besides, they are trouble makers. They are not believed to be clean personally; certainly they are not well groomed. Some are alleged to be cheaters, school skippers, and sassy and uncooperative. About a dozen girls are rated as grubbies because they are believed to have broken the sex taboo; some admit the truth of the gossip. One girl bluntly said, "The girls I run around with are not nice." Another, while talking about her clique, stated, "We go with out-of-town kids. We ride in cars, and have fun with our boy friends. We're hated by the other girls because we've broken the taboo." Her clique is shunned by girls who are not engaged in similar activities, no matter whether they are "elite," "good kids," or "grubbies." Girls who disregard the sex taboo are placed beyond the line of respectability among even the grubbies.

---

[7] This procedure is described in some detail in Chapter 2, pp. 25–40. The coefficients of correlation of the 19 raters ranged from $r = 0.67$ to $r = 0.87$; the mean $r = 0.76$.

A class IV "grubby" illustrated this one day when she stated, "Lucille [a class III girl who rated among the elite] will speak to me sometimes, but she won't let me walk home with her. You see, I don't rate with her." She was then asked about her relations with Esther, a neighborhood girl who confessed she had sex relations with "boy friends." She almost hissed, "I wouldn't be seen dead with her bunch. They drink, smoke, and run with fellows from Wahoo and boast they're not virgins."

A very strong association is found to exist between the class position of a student and his peer group reputation. No class II adolescent is rated as a grubby; conversely, no member of class V was among the elite, and only 1 out of 6 was in the "good kid" category. The chances are 4 to 1 that a class II will be rated among the elite. The odds are 6 to 1 against a class V being rated anything but a grubby. The class III's enjoy a comparatively favorable position, for only 2 out of 146 (1 boy and 1 girl) are rated as "grubbies." Their chances of being rated among the elite are approximately 1 in 5. A class IV possesses only 1 chance in 20 of being rated among the elite, but 1 in 5 of being classed as a "grubby." Obviously the positions of the class III's and class IV's are inverted with respect to the elite and the "grubbies." The figures in Table XIV indicate that

### TABLE XIV

#### PEER RATING OF STUDENTS AND CLASS

| Peer Rating | I and II Number | I and II Per Cent | III Number | III Per Cent | IV Number | IV Per Cent | V Number | V Per Cent |
|---|---|---|---|---|---|---|---|---|
| The elite | 27 | 77 | 30 | 21 | 9 | 5 | 0 | 0 |
| The good kids | 8 | 23 | 114 | 78 | 133 | 73 | 4 | 15 |
| The grubby gang | 0 | 0 | 2 | 1 | 41 | 22 | 22 | 85 |
| Total | 35 | 100 | 146 | 100 | 183 | 100 | 26 | 100 |

$$X^2 = 222.3532. \quad P < 0.01. \quad C = 0.60. \quad \bar{C} = 0.77.$$

the rating a child receives from his fellows is a function on the whole of his family's position in the community's prestige structure rather than of any position he creates in the peer group for himself. The corrected coefficient of contingency of 0.77 shows rather conclusively that the symbolic referents the adolescents used to categorize one another were carried over in large part from the adult social system.

### Dates and dating

Local folkways define picnics, dances, parties, and hayrides as date affairs at which a boy is expected to pair with a girl. The testimony of many students demonstrates that the vast majority have their first formal date on these occasions. Individuals recalled vividly whom the first date was with, where they went, who was there, and other details which marked this important step in the transition from childhood to adolescent life. The first date is often a cooperative enterprise which involves the members of two cliques of the opposite sex. Two illustrations will be given to illuminate the process; both were taken from autobiographies of seniors. The first was written by a class III girl.

> I began to date in the eighth grade with boys I had played with all my life. I ran with a group of girls, and there was also a group of fellows we liked. At all social functions where boys and girls mixed, these two groups came together. We started running around in the fifth grade at Central School, but we did not date yet. We were always together at all school parties, and by the eighth grade we were having our own private parties to which these two groups and no one else was invited. We held these parties at the homes of the girls fairly frequently, usually on a Friday or Saturday night, sometimes on Sunday, but not often. We still did not have any regular dates until the end of the eighth grade.
>
> [Then] Marion Stowe's mother had a party for us. She invited all the kids in both our groups. The fellows got together and decided they would have dates. Tom Biggers asked me to go to the party with him. I was so thrilled and scared I told him to wait until I talked it over with Mother. Mother thought I was too young to start having dates. I argued with her for two days. Dad couldn't see anything wrong with me going to the party with Tom; so Mother let me say "Yes." Tom's dad came by for us in their car and took us to the party, but we walked home. My next date was with Joe Peters during the summer before I started to high school.

Eddie Parker, a class IV junior, believed that his interest in dating went back to the seventh grade, when he and his friends began "to feel shy in the presence of girls," whereas they had been indifferent, aloof, or hostile to them before. His clique talked "a lot" about dates, girls they would like to date, and "women" in general, but no one was bold enough to make a date. This went on until the spring "we were in the eighth grade when all of us [his clique] decided one Saturday we would make dates with the girls in our class who lived in the neighborhood. We went around to their houses and asked them if they would go to the show with us. We made dates with five of them, and that night we all went to the show together." In this case, it would appear that the boys, and probably the girls as well, derived support from one another. If we accept student reports, common characteristics of these first dates are shyness, fear of doing the wrong thing, of making statements the other person will resent, and overcautiousness in the physical approaches of one partner to another. Both persons have been filled with so much advice by parents, usually the mothers, about how to act and what to expect from the date that both play their roles clumsily. They are told precisely what to say and do, when to come home, what they should not do, and what the consequences will be if they violate their instructions. As one class III girl said:

> I was so scared by what Mother told me Jim might do I did not like the experience at all. He did not even try to hold my arm. I knew I was supposed to "freeze up" if he did and I was so ready to "freeze up" we walked all the way home without saying much. I knew he was afraid of me so we just walked along. I was so disappointed in that first date I did not have another for a year. I had several crushes on boys, but I couldn't bring myself to say "Yes" when they asked me for a date. In the latter part of my sophomore year, I had a crush on Larry Jacobs, and when he asked me for a date I said "Yes." We went together a few times when Frank Stone asked me for a date. I went to the Junior Play with him. After the play we went to Burke's [a popular restaurant] with the rest of the kids and then home. Oh, we had fun! Since then, I have had a lot of dates, and now I really enjoy them.

The more adventurous youngsters begin to date when they are 12 years of age—at picnics and family group get-togethers—and the parents are usually present. A definite dating pattern becomes clear during the fourteenth year; 20 per cent of the girls and 15 per cent of the boys report that they had their first dates when they were 13. A much larger number begins to date in the fifteenth year, and by the end of it approximately 93 per cent of both sexes are dating with some regularity. Among the sixteen-year-olds, dating is the accepted procedure, and the boy or girl who does not date is left out of mixed social affairs. Our data make it clear that between the beginning of the fourteenth and the end of the sixteenth years the associational pattern of these adolescents changes from almost exclusive interaction with members of their own sex to a mixed associational pattern similar to that found in adult life. In this period, certain activities, such as girls' "hag parties" and hunting and baseball among the boys, are organized on a single sex basis; and others, such as dances and parties, are almost exclusively mixed.

Forty-three per cent of the boys and 58 per cent of the girls report that they experienced the thrill of their "first date" before they entered high school. Dating before entry into high school is not related significantly to age, town or country residence, or class. On the contrary, it is associated with clique membership. Some cliques have a much higher ratio of dates than others, but we did not search for an explanation of this fact either within the cliques which dated or those which did not. The discrepancy between boys and girls with dating experience prior to entry into high school continues throughout the freshman year. This differential disappears in the sophomore year, and by the time the junior year is reached more boys than girls report dates. At this level only 1 boy out of 13 and 1 girl out of 10 claims they have never had a date. All senior boys report they have had dates, but 3 girls are still looking forward to this event.

About 51 per cent of 553 dates the students reported during April, 1942, were with other students who belonged to the same school class; that is, freshman with freshman, and so on.[8] When

[8] All statistical data on the dating pattern unless otherwise indicated, such as the figures on dates and no dates before high school, are derived from the analysis of the dates the students reported they had during April, 1942. April was selected as our sample month because by that time we knew the students personally and had asked them so many questions that we

the dating partners belong to different school classes, the pattern is significantly different between the boys and the girls.
One-third of the boys' dates are with girls who belong to a
class *below* them in school, whereas 31 per cent of the girls'
dates are with boys *above* them in school. This gives the freshman girl a wider opportunity for dates than the freshman boy,
for she can be dated by a freshman or a boy from the sophomore, junior, or senior classes. Freshmen and sophomore boys
are reluctant to ask a girl who belongs to a class above them
in school for a date. Many girls do not like to date younger
boys unless they possess specific prestige factors, such as athletic
prowess, "family background," or "good looks." Only 15 per
cent of the boys' dates are with girls from a higher school class
than theirs. Almost two-thirds of these mixed dates (62 per
cent) are between senior girls and junior boys; the remainder
are between sophomore boys and junior and senior girls.

These figures bring out the effects of two customs on the
dating relations of these young people. In the first place, the
folkways of courtship encourage a boy to date a girl younger
than himself. The complement of this is that the girl expects
to date a boy older than herself. The operation of this rule
results in boys' dating girls either the same age as themselves
or younger. With the school classes graded principally along
age lines, this means that the boys date girls from their own
class or a lower class in school. Thus, the freshman, sophomore, and junior girls have more opportunities for dates than
the senior girls. In the second place, the senior girls' dating
chances are limited still further by an administrative rule which
restricts to high school students any high school party at which
there is dancing. This rule severely restricts the senior girls'
dating field, and to a less extent the juniors', particularly in
class IV, because boys at this level drop out of school sooner

assumed, and correctly, that they would give us information about their
dating behavior. A second reason for choosing April was the belief that
by this late in the year the dating pattern of the student group would be
well established. We also believed that it was better to attempt a complete
study of dating behavior for a single month than to trust student memories
over a longer period.

than girls. Thus, a shortage of senior boys, combined with the school rule that only students may attend high school dances, forces the senior girls to ask junior boys for dates or let it be known that they would like to go with a junior boy or not date at school affairs. Another effect of this aspect of the dating system is the limited opportunity open to the freshman boy to date girls. Within the high school, the only girls he can date readily are freshmen, and here he competes with sophomore and junior boys who have more prestige in the eyes of the girls than he does. Then, too, the older boys are more sophisticated, more experienced in the arts of love, usually have more money, and give the girls more status in their own eyes than a "green kid" whom they have known through years of close contact in elementary school. The net effect of these factors on dating is a significantly lower ratio of dates among freshman boys in comparison with freshman girls, and of more junior and senior girls dating younger boys or boys outside the student group.

## Dates within and without the student group

Slightly more than 4 girls out of 5 (81 per cent) report that they dated in April, 1942, in contrast to 69 per cent of the boys. The girls likewise have on the average more dates than the boys. The mean number by sex is: girls, 3.6; boys, 2.9. However, there is no difference in the mean number of different persons dated; the figure for both is 1.7. Class II boys and girls date largely within the student group; this is true also for class III boys and girls. Class III girls, however, date outside the student group to some extent, but slightly less than one-half as often as might be expected if chance factors alone impinged upon their dating pattern. The class IV boys date outside the student group twice as frequently as expectancy indicates; and the class IV girls date out-of-school boys 71 per cent more frequently than chance factors would indicate. Actually, 60 per cent of the class IV girls date non-school boys, and 75 per cent of the class V girls date outside the student group.[9]

[9] Figures on dates within or outside the student group are given in Table XIII of the Appendix.

The association between the number of dates within or outside the student group by sex and class is significantly higher than it is for the number of different persons dated who are either students or non-students. The corrected coefficient of contingency between the number of dates within or without the student group is 0.45 for the boys and 0.61 for the girls. For the number of persons dated either within the student group or outside it, this coefficient is 0.37 for the boys and 0.52 for the girls. These coefficients mean that there is a very significant relationship between a student's class position and the practice of dating students or non-students. In brief, the class II's and III's have many dates within the student group; the class IV's and class V's have fewer dates proportionately, and more of them are with non-students. This tendency to date outside the student group is far more prevalent among the lower class girls than the boys. The boys in all classes date within the student group more consistently than the girls. For instance, 79 per cent of the boys' dates are with high school girls, but only 45 per cent of the girls' dates are with high school boys. This disparity is related in part to the unbalanced sex ratio in the high school, 174 boys to 216 girls. It is connected also with the class system, since the excess of girls over boys in the student group is concentrated wholly in classes IV and V. And it is in these two strata that most of the dating with non-students occurs in both sexes.[10]

The few non-students dated by the class II's are all Elmtown High School graduates. Fifty-two per cent of the non-students dated by the class III's are Elmtown High School graduates, 34 per cent are in the out-of-school group, and 14 per cent are persons whose class status is unknown. The class IV's date high school graduates in 23 per cent, persons out of school in 47 per cent, and persons of unknown status in 30 per ent of the cases. The class V's do not date any high school graduates. Their non-student dates are split between persons who quit school, 80 per cent, and persons whose status is unknown, 20 per cent. When a class II dates a non-student, the person dated

---

[10] The number of dates students had with non-students by class is given in Table XIV of the Appendix.

is usually a former fellow student, often a person dated when both were in school. By way of contrast, when the class V's date non-students their dates are with persons in the community who quit school or out-of-town persons. The intervening classes date "across the board," but the class III's tend to date high school graduates rather than those who had quit school or out-of-town persons. The class IV's, however, date predominantly in the out-of-school group or out-of-town young people.

The number of dates reported by boys and girls varies significantly from one class to another, but the greatest differential occurs among the girls. The class II boys and girls report more dates with more persons than the other classes do, as a glance at Table XV will show. The volume of dates and the number of different persons dated are sharply lower in class III, but the

TABLE XV

NUMBER AND PERCENTAGE OF STUDENTS WHO DATED IN APRIL, 1942,
NUMBER OF PERSONS DATED, AND NUMBER OF DATES BY CLASS

BOYS

| Prestige Class | Number Dating | Per Cent Dating | Number of Girls Dated | $\overline{X}$ Number * of Girls Dated | Number of Dates | $\overline{X}$ Number * of Dates |
|---|---|---|---|---|---|---|
| I and II | 18 | 86 | 36 | 2.0 | 61 | 3.4 |
| III | 53 | 73 | 87 | 1.7 | 145 | 2.8 |
| IV | 43 | 60 | 69 | 1.6 | 126 | 2.9 |
| V | 7 | 87 | 10 | 1.4 | 15 | 1.9 |
| Total | 121 | 70 | 202 | 1.7 | 347 | 2.9 |

GIRLS

| Prestige Class | Number Dating | Per Cent Dating | Number of Boys Dated | $\overline{X}$ Number * of Boys Dated | Number of Dates | $\overline{X}$ Number * of Dates |
|---|---|---|---|---|---|---|
| II | 14 | 100 | 37 | 2.6 | 73 | 5.2 |
| III | 54 | 74 | 93 | 1.7 | 174 | 3.3 |
| IV | 90 | 81 | 155 | 1.8 | 303 | 3.4 |
| V | 15 | 83 | 23 | 1.5 | 70 | 4.6 |
| Total | 173 | 81 | 308 | 1.8 | 620 | 3.6 |

* $\overline{X}$ = the mean number of boys or girls dated during April, 1942.

pattern of the class IV's is almost the same as that of the class III's. The class V's date, on the average, the smallest number of persons in both sexes, and the boys have less than one-half as many dates as the girls. It is worth noting that the class V girls have almost as many dates as the class II girls, 4.6 as compared with 5.2, but their dates are with fewer boys, 1.5 against 2.6 for the class II's. This indicates that the class V girls tend to "go steady," certainly more often with the same boy, than the class II's, even though they are on the whole a year younger than the class II girls. This figure is, thus, an indirect reflection of the early marriage pattern so characteristic of the class V girls. (This point is elaborated in Chapter 16.) The class II girls are "popular" as measured by the number of dates they have and the number of boys they date. It is said often in the high school that the elite girls (mostly class II's) "play the field," that is, go with a number of different boys. We shall soon see, however, that "their field" is limited largely to the boys from their own class and from class III. The scarcity of dates among the class V boys may be accounted for by the pressure of economic circumstances and by the competition of males out of school for the low class student girls rather than by age. Although all these boys are under 16 years of age, this is of small moment, for the same fact applies to 14 of the 18 class V girls. A more pertinent factor was expressed by a class V boy who summarized the situation neatly: "Hell, how can I have a date? I'm broke. The old man hasn't given me a red cent in five years. I only make a dollar a week at the junk yard and dates cost money!"

### Intra- and interclass dating patterns

Intra- and interclass dating relationships closely parallel the clique pattern. Sixty-one per cent of the daters belong to the same class; 35 per cent belong in an adjacent class; and 4 per cent are separated by one intervening class. There are no dates between the class II's and the class V's. The social distance between these classes is too great for boys and girls to come together in intimate relationships such as cliques and dates, even though they all attend high school and live in the same small

community. The association of class with class on dates is
graphically illustrated in Chart I.

The corrected coefficient of contingency of 0.60 for the boys'
and 0.76 for the girls' dates shows that dating class equals is the

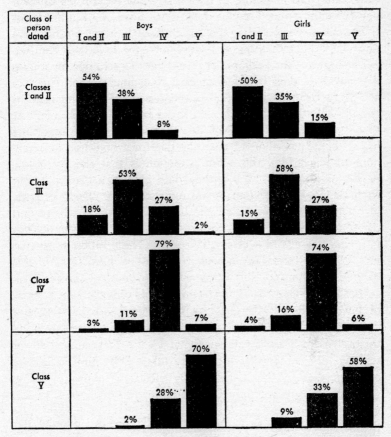

Chart I.   Intra- and Interclass Dating Patterns of Boys and Girls, April, 1942.
(All dates reported by the Student Group are included.)

dominant factor in the patterning of this relationship. When a
boy crosses a class line, the chances are 2 to 1 that he dates a
girl from a class below himself (64 per cent of 107 cases); reciprocally, the girl dates above herself. This ratio applies to

dates which cross either one or two class lines, but only 11 cases crossed two class lines.

These figures indicate either that a boy is approximately twice as willing to date a girl lower than himself in the prestige structure than a girl is willing to date a boy lower than herself, or a boy has more opportunity to do so since he is in a bidding position. When we say that the boy is in a bidding position, we must not forget that the girl does not have to accept the bid. A corollary of this is that a boy is always free to ask for a date a girl who belongs to a higher class than himself, and she may accept or turn him down in as theoretically free a manner as the girl who is asked for a date by a boy from a class higher than herself. Irrespective of the abstract argument about the boy's freedom of choice to ask the girl for a date and her freedom to reject him, the actual situation is that the boys date equals or unequals. When they date girls in a class different from their own, the chances are approximately 2 to 1 that the girl belongs to a class below the boys. Conversely, when a girl dates an unequal, the chances are about 2 to 1 that she dates a boy who belongs to a class above her. These ratios, translated into practical terms, mean that it is twice as hard for a boy to date above himself as it is for a girl to do so. Thus, a high school boy confines his dates to girls of his own class or to those of lower classes. The girls, on the other hand, have greater opportunities to associate with boys of higher prestige than themselves on an intimate, personal level. This enables lower ranking girls, if they have mobility talents, to climb at least a few rungs of the social ladder by means of personal charm, whereas the boy not only finds it more difficult to rise in this way, but he has also to use other talents to elevate himself over the barriers of class.[11] Another suggestive factor in this complex is the tendency of Elmtown's males to look upon a girl from a lower class as "fair game"; that is, she is an object for sex exploitation by boys "on the prowl."

INTERRELATIONS BETWEEN CLIQUES AND DATES. Dating is a very personal affair, but who dates whom, as we have shown, is

[11] Figures on intra- and interclass dating by sex are recorded in Table XV of the Appendix.

associated strongly with the daters' membership in the class structure. It also is connected very closely within the limits imposed by class and school class to the clique structure, and to the values and practices that are part of the adolescent social code. A prominent element in the clique-date complex is the practice of dating persons from another clique approved of by the members of one's own clique. This practice results in an overlapping of clique and class patterns with the dating pattern. How this regulates the dates of particular boys and girls may best be shown by a few illustrations. The Cadet Club and the G.W.G. are the two dominant clubs in the high school. The Cadet Club is composed of boys and the G.W.G. of girls. The membership of both comes predominantly from class II, but there are a few class III's and one class IV in each. A G.W.G. wrote in her autobiography:

One comical situation which consistently appeared and reappeared in my dating schedule was that of boys not on this preferred list [a list of boys from the Cadet Club] asking me for dates. My parents, Mother especially, had pounded into my mind most firmly that I was to be nice to everyone regardless of who they were, socially speaking. Everytime I attempted to put this into practice, I ended with a bid for some social event with someone with whom I did not care to go. And it was always these individuals who asked me so early that logical excuses were difficult to give. The incongruity of society! Be nice to people only to a certain restricted degree unless you are anxious to cultivate their friendship.

The boys we dated had to meet with each other's approval [her clique mates in the G.W.G.]. . . . I easily recall different instances in which some unexpected person asked one of us to some dance. Before we accepted, we usually found out the others' reaction to such a date. It was desirable to be seen with a boy who was liked first by the girls and secondly by the boys themselves. Any divergence from the prescribed list was avoided at all cost.

A Cadet Club member revealed the complementary aspect of this process in somewhat different words:

The Cadet Club is allied with the G.W.G.'s. . . . A majority of the Cadets date girls within this group, and there is some rivalry among the men for the attentions of one of the girls. In several instances, when it was decided at a Cadet meeting to have a dance or other sort of party, there was an immediate rush to the telephone by two or three fellows to be the first to ask this one girl for a date for the affair. The losers in the race are invariably short-tempered with the winner until the event has taken place.

In one instance, the winner of this race a week or so later decided he did not want to go with the girl. His decision was based on the news that an old flame would be receptive to a request for a date. Throwing good taste and respect for unwritten rules out the window, he broke the date and took the other girl to the dance. It is needless to say that strained relations within the groups [each club] were apparent for a few weeks. For the most part, the men did not mind it so much. . . . The girls were more intense in their like or dislike of the affair. But it was soon forgotten and normal relations with everyone were soon resumed.

These groups very carefully control the dates their members have with one another and with outsiders; moreover, the girls especially watch what their members do when they are not on dates. For instance, one G.W.G. was expelled for going to the skating rink and accepting a date while there; another was ostracized for dates with a boy who was not on the approved list. One member of the Cadet Club said to us the day after Joan Meyers (the girl in the latter case) had accepted a date for a high school dance with a class IV boy who was not approved by either the G.W.G.'s or the Cadets, "If Joan goes with Melvin Swigart her social position in the high school will be jeopardized." Joan was given the "cold shoulder" at the dance. She "sinned a second time" two days later by going for a ride in Melvin's jalopy during the noon hour. Joan was "cut" by the other G.W.G.'s and several Cadets after this happened. About a week later Mary Skelton, a G.W.G., was asked casually at a group get-together where Joan was. She replied, "We do not have anything to do with her *now!* There's a wall there." As she said this she raised her hands, with fingers touching, in front of her face.

Joan soon realized she was "in the dog house" with her clique mates and the acceptable boys. She was given the "silent treatment" for a few weeks, then allowed to come back into her old social circles, but her position in the group was never as solid

after the "Melvin Swigart affair" as it was before.  She realized
this and commented upon it as follows:

> You see, I'm in the G.W.G.'s, but I don't run around with the
> G.W.G.'s all the time. I'm kind of in-between the G.W.G.'s and
> the other kids. I was out of the G.W.G.'s for a while because they
> made me mad. They drew the social line too fine. I dated a boy
> they didn't like. We went to a dance, and they just ignored me. I
> just couldn't stand that. It hurt me, so I pulled out of there; but
> now I've more or less started to go back with them.

A class IV girl, commenting on this incident stated, "Joan
should not have dated Melvin if she wanted to run with those
upper kids.  A girl like her cannot do that kind of a thing."
(Joan was a class III, in a predominantly class II club.)

The rank and file of the class III and class IV students know
that the G.W.G.'s and the Cadets exist, but, since they are
organized outside of the high school, the teachers officially do
not know that they are clubs or who their members are.  To
many ordinary students this "combine," as it is often called, is
one group.  A class IV boy in describing the "combine" indicated this when he said, "The sons and daughters of the social
register are in it.  They're the social elite around here.  They
have money, that is, they really have it or put up a good front
except for one girl, 'Ziggy' Moran.  She has personality plus.  The
rest are in the Country Club set; they're way up in the clouds."

The Catholic and Lutheran groups are as tightly knit as the
Cadets and the G.W.G.'s, but they do not enjoy such high prestige.  The "Lutheran gang" is made up of devout Lutheran
boys and girls whose social life is centered in their church rather
than the high school.  They are predominantly from class III,
but there are a number of class IV's on the fringe.  A class II
Lutheran girl who made the G.W.G. and dated in the Cadet
Club had both withdrawn from and been ostracized by the
Lutherans.  The year before, another class II Lutheran girl
had been pledged to the G.W.G.  Like her successor she valued
the G.W.G.-Cadet Club identification more highly than that of
the "Lutheran gang."  In commenting on her in particular and
the Lutherans in general, this girl remarked, "She's like me.

The Lutherans will not allow us to run around with their crowd."
On another occasion she explained:

> Those kids gang together except for me. They stick together like
> glue. I was ostracized because I danced, went to shows, played
> bridge, and drank beer. Every time we have a high school dance
> they throw some kind of a party at the church and try to make
> the kids come. Those who don't come are ostracized.

A class III girl wrote in her "life history" relative to her clique
and date pattern:

> There are two main rival groups running the high school . . .
> the God We're Good girls with the Cadets, and the Jeeps, and I
> am not a member of either one. I guess I have lost some friends
> and gained some by being in the Catholic group. I am not a Catho-
> lic, but I went to parochial school and many people think I am. My
> girl friends are Catholics. . . . All the boys I have dated went to
> parochial school with me. By the end of my freshman year, I was
> a member of a click [sic] of boys and girls. All of them went to
> parochial school with me. There are 7 girls and 8 fellows. Very often
> we have parties as a group, and some home dates. Last year we
> began to date. Now my mother wants me to make friends in my
> own church [Methodist]. She is afraid I might fall in love with a
> Catholic.

Religious and parental factors constantly impinge upon certain
aspects of the dating and clique patterns. For instance, late in
the spring of 1942 a very popular class III freshman girl who
was practically certain to have been "bid" by the G.W.G.'s in
her sophomore year "crossed the last line." Her clique immediately expelled her, and she dropped into a very low-rating
clique of class IV girls with one from class V in it. Her offense,
in the words of an outraged former clique mate, was, "She
started running around with Sammy Sinkowitz. He's one of
these lousy Sinkowitzes we have here in town. I don't see what
her folks are thinking about. As another Hebrew said about
them, 'They are just Kikes.'" The girl's mother was emotionally distraught, and she appealed to us "for guidance in this
horrible affair." She summarized the girl's social position first
in terms of its effect on her and the father and secondly in terms

of its effect on the girl. "I am disgraced. Her father is broken-hearted. Mabel must be made to see the folly of her foolish actions. She simply must be popular; every girl has to be popular. Now the boys and girls have isolated her."

Parental guidance in the selection of friends and dates is the rule in classes II and III. It is attempted in class IV, but not so self-consciously and probably with less success than in the higher reaches of the prestige structure. A class III girl showed how parents deliberately blended cliques and dates into a socially acceptable manner at her "coming-out party."

> When I was 15 years old, my parents gave a party for me. They saw to it that only the right boys were invited—children of their friends. Having started out with this group of boys, I have continued in that group. These boys are my Sunday School acquaintances. The friends at my party were my high school bunch, except for one girl and two boys my parents disapprove of. [These youngsters came from class IV; their fathers were mill hands, and this girl's family owned a retail business.] They did not think they rated well enough to come.

THE "STEADY DATE." Many parents disapprove of young people keeping "steady company," for normally after they have been doing so for a few months they start to think about getting married. Other parents voice a suspicion that young people "going steady" are likely to become "too intimate." Both of these fears are grounded in the solid knowledge of experience. Teachers openly disapprove of "steady dating," for the young people often develop into discipline cases because their very personal interests are substituted for school interests. The students deride the "steady daters" as "sappy," "moony," "sleepy," "in love," or "dopey." When people are afflicted with these emotional states, they separate themselves from their fellow students, lose interest in normal clique activity, the school, and the opposite sex except the "boy" or "girl" friend. For all practical purposes, they are lost to the adolescent world with its quixotic enthusiasms and varied group activities.

The key to the disapproval attached to the steady date appears to be fear of the power that aroused sexual desires have over physically mature persons who have their sex drives focused on a particular member of the opposite sex by frequent association in a dating situation, which in the society is defined as a private, secluded relationship apart from the constraints imposed by the presence of others. Past experience has demonstrated to parents that social taboos against normal sex relations outside marriage are violated all too frequently by young people who date steady; for it is popularly believed that love, steady dates, and sex go together.

Fifty-four students, 15 boys and 39 girls (18 per cent of the students who dated in April, 1942) reported that they were dating a single person of the opposite sex regularly.[12] The steady date involves students with non-students far more frequently than students with students. Eight of the 15 steady boy-daters were "going steady" with high school girls, and 7 with non-students; but 31 of the 39 steady girl-daters were dating non-students. For the steady daters as a whole, 70 per cent of the dating partners were non-students. The steady daters were 9 months older, on the average, than the boys and girls who dated several different adolescents, and 18 months older than the non-daters.[13]

The sex taboo is violated by many students, but the percentage was not ascertained, for even to talk of such things was tabooed. If Elmtowners had learned that we had even the remotest interest in the sex activities of the adolescents in the study, we are convinced we should have had to terminate our research abruptly. Therefore, we had to be most discreet in our observations on their intimate love life and very oblique in the questions asked about it. Although we realized that the subject was delicate and the risk of community tensions great, we collected as much data as possible by indirect techniques about violations of the sex taboo and the parties thereto.

As we became acquainted with the students, gossip and rumor reached us about this boy who was alleged to have had sex rela-

[12] The practice of dating steady was not associated significantly with class position.

[13] The mean age of the steady daters was 16.3 years on January 1, 1942; 15.5 years for ordinary daters; and 14.8 years for the non-daters. There were no essential differences in the ages of the boys or girls in any of the three groups.

tions with that girl, or about a particular girl who was reputed to be "putting it out" to her friends. That some of these stories were true we had little doubt, but verification was well-nigh impossible.

In so far as sex relations were known, the picture may be summarized in these terms: 8 student couples dated steady. Three of the 8 admit having sex relations, and 3 others were alleged by other students to have done so. The other two were not innocent of suspicion, for, as the best friend of one of the boys stated, "Jack is getting his, I know, but he has everyone else fooled." Of the 6 who admitted the sex act, 3 girls and 1 boy were class IV's; the other boys were class III's. Twenty-nine of the 38 students dating non-students regularly stated "very confidentially" they were having sex relations with their dates. Twenty-two of the 29 were girls; 7 were boys. From the viewpoint of class position, 17 were class IV's, 4 were class V's, and 1 was a class III. Four of the boys were class IV's, 2 were class III's, and 1 was a class V. Although the number was very small, we believe it significant that there was such a high concentration of class IV's and class V's who admitted sex relations. These figures confirmed a general impression that the sex mores were violated far more frequently by adolescents in classes IV and V than they were in class III, and more in class III than in class II.

Although the few figures given here involve about four times as many girls as boys, we do not want to leave the impression that high school girls are more likely to have sex relations than boys. The contrary is the case, as Kinsey has indicated.[14] In this particular situation, four times as many girls as boys "dated steady" out-of-school persons of the opposite sex. Furthermore, these girls were almost all from classes IV and V, and they were dating, in the main, young men from classes III and IV. These young people came from the "social levels" Kinsey has demonstrated to have a high incidence of pre-marital sex experience.[15]

[14] Alfred C. Kinsey, Wardell B. Pomeroy, and Clyde E. Martin, *Sexual Behavior in the Human Male,* W. B. Saunders Company, Philadelphia, 1948, p. 223.

[15] *Ibid.,* pp. 347–351.

Finally, the ratio of girls to boys (3 to 1) who were having sex experience with companions was a product of the folkways which decrees that a girl should date boys older than herself. A second folkway pertinent to this discussion was the tendency of boys in the two lower classes to drop out of school some years before girls in the same classes. With the biased student sex ratio, many girls in school, especially in the two lower classes, had to date out-of-school companions or not date at all. Thus, the sex experience figures given here have little relation to sex experience in the study group. This will be brought out in Chapter 16.

The question may be raised, Was class a factor in this aspect of the adolescent's behavior? It appeared to be, but the number of known cases of sex experience was very small, probably too small to be more than provocative. In 23 of the 29 cases where one of the steady daters admitted sex relations with the companion, the class position of both parties was known. In 82 per cent of these cases the girl belonged to a class below the boy, and in 18 per cent the partners were class equals. No case was found in which the boy belonged to a lower class than the girl. Clearly in this small sample there was a strong tendency for young Elmtown males to exploit lower class females sexually. The boys in these cases ranged all the way from class II through class IV. There was but one class II boy involved who was "going steady," from the girl's viewpoint, with a person in class IV. From the boy's viewpoint the relationship was not likely to lead to marriage. He boasted to us once that he was ". . . the hell out of that little Henderson gal." Class III males, high school graduates, and former classmates of the class IV girls they were dating steady dominated this cross-class sex picture; 13 of the 17 boys whose class position was known were class III's. Some undoubtedly were sincere in their relations with the girls with whom they were intimate, but many were merely "having fun," or "taking them for a ride." The 3 class IV boys who had liaisons with class V's were probably in the same category. Irrespective of the number of cases, the available figures throw a narrow beam of light on the question of whom young males in our society seek out for sex thrills. Adequate research needs to be done on this question before more can be said on this point.

## Summary of clique and date patterns

A typical clique is composed of either 5 boys or 5 girls. Four of its members belong to the same class in school. From the viewpoint of its members' prestige class position, 3 ordinarily belong to the same prestige class. The chances are 25 to 1 that the others belong to an adjacent class, or to one on either side of the prestige class to which the 3 boys belong. However, if the core of the clique is composed of class IV boys, with some class III or class V boys, the chances are 38 to 1 against one being a class V. On the other hand, if class III's are mixed with class IV's, the chances are 1 to 3 that the cross-class clique ties will go from class IV to class III. These ratios make it plain that class IV's avoid clique ties with class V's. On the contrary, class III's do not disparage class IV's in the same manner as the class IV's do the class V's. When a class III boy or girl crosses a class line in a clique relationship, the chances are only about 4 to 1 that it is with a class IV rather than a class II. The dating ratios are not significantly different from the clique ratios as to the number of dating relationships within or between classes.

The parallel between clique and date ratios within and between classes is an important factor, we believe, in the maintenance of the class system. For, the majority of clique and dating relations takes place between persons who belong to the same prestige class. When cross-class ties are established, they tend to involve persons from an adjacent class, except that persons in each class try to develop relationships with persons a class higher in the prestige structure than themselves. Conversely, the higher class person, on the average, tries to limit his contacts with persons of lower prestige than himself in order that he not be criticized for "lowering himself." This process operates in all classes, but it is especially noticeable in contacts with class V. This class is so repugnant socially that adolescents in the higher classes avoid clique and dating ties with its members.

The fact that only 1 clique and dating tie out of 25 crosses two class lines, and none crosses three, is indicative of the mutual isolation which exists in the adolescent group between the polar strata in the prestige structure. The class V youngsters occupy a position too far removed from the class II's for intimate association to occur. The class III's tolerate a few ties with the class V's, but they are avoided in most instances. The class IV's are tolerated by the class III's just as the class II's tolerate the class III's. Thus, since the class III's are in an axial position they clique with and date the two adjacent classes, but the lower of the two—that is, the class IV's—approximately 50 per cent more frequently than they do the class II's. The class IV's, in turn, avoid the class V's. Intimate associations between the two strata do occur; however, this is not the preferred pattern, nor the dominant one. Thus, the class V adolescents clique and date more frequently in their own stratum than do those in any other class. This is one way of stating that the class V's are differentiated more definitely in their clique and dating relations than are the members of any other strata. Finally, it is clear that the adolescent clique and dating patterns are a reflection in large part of the adult social structure.

# 10

## RELIGION AND RELIGIOUS BEHAVIOR

### Religious beliefs

YOUNG ELMTOWNERS ACQUIRE RELIGIOUS BELIEFS from their parents in the same way as they learn that the parental home is their home. If the parents are devout Catholics, the children are introduced into the ritual and instruction of the church very early in life. Likewise, a good Methodist family imparts to its children the traditional attitudes and beliefs inherent in Methodism; or if a family is Methodist by tradition and not by practice, the children may be told that they are Methodists, but their connection with the local church may be tenuous. When there are religious differences between the parents, the child hears them mentioned, argued about, and quarreled over from his earliest years. He also learns in his home that to be Catholic, Methodist, or Pentecostal is desirable or undesirable socially. Thus, the young child has no more choice in the matter of religious beliefs than he does in the language he learns or the bed in which he sleeps. Finally, as is well known, religious attitudes learned in the home are carried unconsciously into the neighborhood, the school, and other areas of community life.

Formal religious training for the majority of Elmtown's children begins in the Sunday School when the child is 4, 5, or 6 years of age. In the Protestant churches, instruction is carried on by a few mothers assisted by one or two high school girls; in the Catholic Church, nuns are charged with this work. Sunday School classes are maintained in all churches for children of elementary school age, and in the Protestant churches for adolescents of high school age; after confirmation—usually near the end of the eighth grade—young Catholics are required to attend Mass and the earlier instruction by nuns ceases. There are few, if any, denominational pressures brought to bear upon Protestant parents, other than the Lutherans, to send their children to Sunday School. The decision to attend or not to attend religious services is left to the parents, and in many cases to the children themselves.

The impression gradually grew that religion to these adolescents is comparable in a way to wearing clothes or taking a bath. It is something one has to have or to do to be acceptable in society. The youngsters also assume that Christianity is the one right and true religion. In a vague, almost incomprehensible way, they know of the existence of other religions, but only a few can readily name one of the great historic religions other than Christianity. Moreover, it is rarely that a student understands the difference between a religion and a denomination. This became clear as student after student named a denomination with a local congregation when he was asked what his religion was. Occasionally, a student would volunteer the information, "We are Christians, but there isn't a church here." Here and there is a student who stoutly maintained he did not belong to a church and neither did his family. Such students were asked, "Do you have a religion?" Reactions to this question varied, but, in general, the response was to the effect, "I am a Christian, but I don't belong to any church." This way of thinking was impressed upon the child in such an informal way that he assumed he was religious and a church member, when in fact neither he nor his family were affiliated with a church.

Religion to the vast majority is an amorphous body of beliefs symbolized by a number of awesome words, God, Jesus, Christ, Sin, Salvation, Satan, Heaven, Hell. It is given form in a book that embodies all sacred truth, the Bible. The church is built on *the* Bible and Sunday is *The* Lord's Day. One can believe *the* Bible without reading or understanding it; just to know about *the* Bible makes one religious. To the great majority, the sacred words associated with religion through long usage have taken on a magical quality, and one respects them for this reason. To a few, God, Satan, Heaven, Hell, Sin, and Salvation are real entities that surround them at all times like the air they breathe; for them, everyday experiences are manifestations of spiritual reality, and life is a testing ground for the Hereafter. But to about 90 per cent of the boys and about 80 per cent of the girls, religion does not have this compulsive quality. These youngsters believe that a person ought to be religious, but the word does not have any very specific content or meaning except a vague belief in God confirmed by the assertion that they are Christians or belong to a church.

Church in Elmtown is an inclusive term that embraces dogma, doctrine, theology, edifice, members, and beliefs about one's own faith and the faith of other churches. To be labeled a church member is very important, for it tells people where one belongs in the rather complex denominational structure. One may label himself a Methodist with approval and seldom, if ever, worship with the congregation; it is sufficient to be known as a member of an approved church. One can refer to himself as being of any Christian faith without inciting outright opposition, but, if he identifies himself as a Hebrew, a subtle web of distrust, suspicion, and possibly hate will be spun around him. However, if he blandly says that he is an atheist, barriers will be erected around him by the devout, for atheist and communist are two labels an Elmtowner must avoid if he desires to be accepted as a respectable member of society.

In preceding paragraphs we have implied that religion and religious ideas are largely negative elements in the life organization of these adolescents without giving precise evidence for this impression beyond our subjective reactions to the way the students answered questions in interviews. This impression is bulwarked objectively by the results of two tests given to the students at two widely spaced intervals. The Bavelas Test,[1] which was given first, is a semi-structured association test designed to reveal a person's moral ideas. The person taking it is told to make a list of a series of good things to do and of those who will praise him for doing them, and a list of bad things to

[1] Alex Bavelas, "A Method for Investigating Individual and Group Idealogy," mimeographed manuscript, Iowa State University, Iowa City, Iowa. This test was given by me at the suggestion of Professor Robert J. Havighurst of The Committee on Human Development.

do and of those who will censure him for doing them. We
directed the students to list nine good activities and nine bad
activities and the corresponding praisers and blamers. The test
was given in the study hall during two successive periods; consequently the students had no opportunity to discuss the test with
one another. A total of 3,306 different things were mentioned as
"bad" and 3,305 as "good" things to do. Some 0.9 of 1 per cent
of the students listed disrespect for the church as a bad thing;
slightly less than 1 per cent of the girls and 0.7 per cent of the
boys listed God, Jesus, the minister, or the church as an agency
that would praise or censure them if they did some good or
bad thing.

The Mooney Problem Check List,[2] which is divided into eleven
areas, was given three months after the Bavelas Test. One area
is designed to reveal religious and moral problems of the person
taking it. Of the 383 students who took this test, 26 per cent
did not check a single item in the religious and morals problem
area; 55 per cent checked from 1 to 4 items; 14 per cent checked
from 5 to 9; and 5 per cent checked 10 or more. This was significantly lower than the problems checked in the other 10 areas.

The results of these tests agree with one another and with
our observation that to most students the church is a community facility like the school, the drug store, the city government, and the bowling alley. To them, the church is a place
where one goes to Sunday School, to young people's meeting, to
a church party, and, to a small segment, it is a place to worship
or to hear a sermon. It is not something special or supernatural
as the ministers and some elders would have them believe. It
is plain that about 7 out of 8 young people are not troubled by
religious questions or problems. The small minority troubled
by religious problems are largely Norwegian Lutherans. The
Lutheran minister, aided by a handful of elders, attempts to
bind "my young people" to the church through a comprehensive
socio-religious program organized in opposition to the high
school, fraternal orders, and commercial recreation.

[2] Ross L. Mooney, "Problem Check List, High School Form," Bureau
of Educational Research, Ohio State University, Columbus, Ohio, 1941.
This test was administered by Bernice Neugarten of The Committee on
Human Development with my assistance.

Adolescents who seek an answer to religious questions which trouble them are faced with confusion and contradiction in other areas of the culture.  In their formal contacts with the church, they are taught to pray to God for an answer to their prayers when faced by a personal problem.  In tneir high school science courses they are taught cause and effect relationships.  The clash of these two thought systems lies at the bottom of most of their religious worries.  The Free Methodist minister said to the Sunday School early in February, "Rely upon the infinite wisdom of God; He will show you the way.  Follow His path and trouble will never overtake you."  The following week, a teacher in the science class of the high school stressed cause and effect relationships in nature and used the weather as an example.  The weather is of vital importance in this farming community where an early frost may do thousands of dollars' worth of damage to late-maturing crops, or a severe blizzard may kill livestock in unprotected areas.  In late January, 1942, an unseasonal thaw accompanied by torrential rains produced a sudden flood on a tributary to Indian River.  Several hundred livestock on low ground were stranded and many were drowned; one family lost $12,000 worth of cattle in a few hours.  This event was fresh in the memory of the children in the science class when the aforementioned discussion of cause and effect took place.  At that time a devout Lutheran boy stated that he believed the flood was punishment for our entry into the war. A Free Methodist girl believed the flood could have been averted by prayer.  In the course of the discussion, the teacher was alleged to have stated, "There are no miracles," in response to an earnest Lutheran girl's observation that a miracle could have saved the cattle, hay, and grain.  This discussion resulted in confusion and some disillusionment for the girl, who later asked the minister, "If there are no miracles, what good are my prayers?"  The minister defended his position, and attacked the high school for teaching blasphemous "rot."  A Baptist girl was puzzled by a similar experience.  She related, "I was taught when I was a little kid that Christ was conceived by the Virgin Mary.  Then in general science [freshman course] I learned there must be fertilization before life begins.  A bunch of us kids talked about this the other day.  We could not understand it: so I asked Mrs. Block in Sunday School, 'How could Mary have given birth to Christ if she was a virgin?' She was kinda confused for a minute, and she changed the subject. So I still don't know."

It is difficult for the serious student to reconcile the contradictions between what he learns in the religious compartment of his culture with what he is taught in school. His doubts on religious questions are increased particularly when representatives of the church deny facts taught in school without providing any proof beyond assertions that what they believe is "true" and the "facts" of science are "untrue," or when in a shamefaced manner they turn from the question the child asked to some other topic.

The high school is the target of conservative critics in all churches, but the Lutherans, Free Methodists, and the small evangelical churches take the lead. The ministers of these churches systematically question young people about statements teachers made in class relative to the Bible and religion. If a teacher is reported for "radical" or "irreligious" statements, this teacher is watched, and, if two or three unfavorable reports are brought in, the matter is taken up with the Board of Education. This is usually sufficient warning to the teacher that all is not well, for the Superintendent attends Board meetings. Later, the teacher is called into the Superintendent's office and warned. If additional offenses are brought to the attention of the minister, he may raise the question with his church council; after discussion, the council may formally request a teacher's dismissal. The Board of Education listens to these requests sympathetically, but more often it sidetracks them. If a church cannot achieve its ends through the Board, sometimes its representatives wait upon an offender personally and lay down its demands.[3]

### Religious affiliation

Although every student claims that he believes in God and says that he is a Christian, 9 per cent are either unable to name or refuse to name a denomination or a church with which they

[3] A case of this was described in Chapter 6, pp. 153–154.

are affiliated. Two-thirds are boys and one-third girls. From the standpoint of class position, the lower the level the higher is the incidence of non-affiliation, as the following figures show:

| Class | Percentage without Any Church Affiliation |
|:-----:|:-----------------------------------------:|
| II    | 3                                         |
| III   | 5                                         |
| IV    | 13                                        |
| V     | 16                                        |

None of these boys or girls is listed on any type of church roll; moreover, only three are known by ministers. One is a class II, the others are class III's; it is evident that the prominence of their families in the community rather than the children themselves bring the family to the attention of a minister.

The 91 per cent of the students who claim affiliation with a local congregation are distributed among the different denominations almost exactly like their parents.[4] In the adolescent group as among their parents, the Federated attracts class II's, tolerates class III's, repels class IV's, has no class V's. The Methodist attracts class III's, tolerates class IV's, and repels class V's. The Catholic and Lutheran parishes represent all classes, but the bulk of their membership comes from classes III and IV, and it is divided equally between these classes; both have twice as many affiliations from class V as from class II. Like the Federated, the Baptists and Free Methodists are in a category by themselves; they are definitely class IV churches. They attract the class IV's, tolerate the class V's, and repel class II's and class III's. In the Baptist Church, class III's and class IV's play the same roles and occupy the same positions the class II's do in the Federated, but here they do not compete with them for leadership positions.

When these claimed affiliations were compared with the membership rolls of each church, the Sunday School books, the rosters of the young people's organizations, and information the ministers supplied about each boy or girl, we found that 21 per cent were not on any church list, nor were they known to the

---

[4] See Table VI of the Appendix for the denominational affiliation of the family; Chapter 5 for discussion of parental religious participation; and Table XVI of the Appendix for the distribution of the high school students.

minister.  An additional 30 per cent were on a church list, or
known by a minister, but, from the evidence of membership lists,
statements of ministers and adult lay leaders, it is clear that they
have dropped out of Sunday School, do not attend church
services, young people's meetings, or church parties.  Thus, 51
per cent of the high school students have no active connections
with Elmtown's churches.

## Types and levels of participation

THE CRITERION OF PARTICIPATION.  Participation in at least one
organized activity sponsored by the churches was used as the
criterion to test our hypothesis in relation to religious behavior.
The completion of a *church schedule* for each adolescent, at
least four interviews that lasted from one to six hours with each
clergyman,[5] and consistent attendance and observation at church
affairs were relied upon to learn the way the adolescents participated in organized religious activities—Sunday School, church
services, young people's organizations, parties, choir practice,
altar guilds.  The specific test of participation was whether or
not a given boy or girl was known to have come to at least *one*
church service, Sunday School class, party, or other gathering
between September 1, 1941, and May 31, 1942.

Participation in religious activities is influenced by class and
denominational factors.  In the Federated Church, for instance,
two-thirds of the class II's, one-half of the class III's, but only
one-third of the class IV's participate in one or more kinds of
religious activities.  In the Lutheran Church, emphasis is placed
on ethnic unity and participation in the church program, but
even here participation is associated with favorable class position
(78 per cent of the class III's were active) and non-participation
with unfavorable positions (48 per cent of the class IV's were
inactive).  Two of the 3 class V's who claimed to be Lutheran
were participants; one was a non-participant.

The cleavage between participation or non-participation and
class is not apparent among the Catholics until class V is reached.
At this level none of the 6 class V's who reported that they were
Catholic participated in religious affairs.  These adolescents

---

[5] All Elmtown ministers had been in the community two or more years,
and they were thoroughly familiar with their congregations.

were Poles, the priest was aware of their inactivity and he de-
plored the friction between Irish and Poles which existed in his
parish.  None of the 7 class V's in school who reported themselves as Baptists participated in their church.  Fifteen of the
18 active Baptists were class IV's.  This relatively homogeneous
group was composed basically of four cliques, two of each sex,
who ran the young people's program with an iron hand.  These
cliques isolated any adolescent of whom they did not approve
and drove him out of their activities; it was not coincidence
that those discriminated against were class V's.

The percentage of non-participation in religious activity by
class is: class II, 26; class III, 42; class IV, 57; and class V, 81.
Since the participation figures complement these, the shift is
very striking, and we shall go into the dynamics of the situation
in later paragraphs.  In passing, it may be well to state that no
significant differences were found for participation or non-participation by sex; the girls, however, have a higher percentage
of participation than the boys in each class, but these differences
are insignificant.

Sunday after Sunday,[6] about 125 young people, about 90
Protestants and 35 Catholics, attend Sunday School or Mass.
A smaller group, approximately 75—65 Protestants and 10 Catholics—go about one-half the time.  Sunday School attendance
differs significantly from one class to another, as the figures in
Table XVI show.  Briefly, the higher the class level, the larger
is the proportion of attendance, whether regular or irregular, and
the lower the class level the smaller is the proportion active in
Sunday School.

The 11 A.M. worship service attracts about one-half as many
young people as the Sunday School.  Sunday School attendance
is limited primarily to freshmen and sophomores, whereas the
older students are more likely to attend the worship service.
Approximately one-half of those who attend church also attend

---

[6] Each student's attendance record was abstracted from the Sunday School
rolls in the Protestant churches, and the Catholic priest estimated the attendance of his young parishoners. His estimates were combined with the
Sunday School count, and the two are equated in this discussion, even
though some question may be raised about the comparability of the count
versus the estimates.

### TABLE XVI

PARTICIPATION OR NON-PARTICIPATION IN SUNDAY SCHOOL BY CLASS

| | | | Class | |
|---|---|---|---|---|
| Level of Participation | I and II | III | IV | V |
| Not on Sunday School rolls | 8 | 38 | 85 | 20 |
| On rolls—no attendance | 4 | 9 | 21 | 1 |
| Irregular attendance | 5 | 30 | 38 | 3 |
| Regular attendance | 18 | 69 | 39 | 2 |
| Total | 35 | 146 | 183 | 26 |

$X^2 = 45.9778.$　　$P < 0.01.$　　$C = 0.32.$　　$\bar{C} = 0.40.$

Sunday School. Three-fourths of these are girls from the three higher classes, with classes II and III contributing a disproportionate number who sing in the choirs. To be exact, 5 of the 11 girls in class II active in church work are in the Federated choir; 11 of 43 class III girls active in the churches are in Protestant choirs, and 7 of the 52 religiously active class IV girls are in Protestant choirs. One class V girl sings in the Free Methodist choir. Most of the boys who go to church are content to listen to the sermon and sing from the back pews; only 5 are members of church choirs, 2 are Methodist, and 3 Baptist.

YOUNG PEOPLE'S ORGANIZATIONS. The Federated, Methodist, Lutheran, Baptist, and Free Methodist churches support young people's organizations which meet either in the church or the minister's home early Sunday evening. Ministers and adolescents are in perfect agreement on one point, namely, merely to hold a young people's meeting is not enough; the group has to be organized into a local chapter of the denomination's national organization. Membership cards, constitutions, pledges, oaths, pins, dues (local and national) are integral elements in this complex. To participate as a full-fledged young Baptist, for example, one has to be initiated into the local chapter of the national Baptist Young People's Union at the semi-annual candlelight service at which the sacred ritual is administered to the neophyte by the members. Although these organizations are integrated nominally around religion and religious objectives, they in essence promote primarily the clique interests of their members; the objectives of the denomination are secondary.

Fourteen different organizations, ten for girls and four for both boys and girls, are sponsored by the churches for young people of high school age. This heavy emphasis on female organization is probably related to the adult pattern which emphasizes many women's organizations in the churches. Among the women there are numerous quasi-social, quasi-religious clubs, circles, guilds, and sororities built upon age, prestige, and social interests in each denomination; but few men's groups.

One-third of the students belong to one or more of these clubs, and 101 of the 130 (78 per cent) are girls. Membership in the young people's clubs is related significantly to class level as well as to sex. Specifically by class and sex the percentage in young people's organizations is:

| Class | Boys | Girls |
|-------|------|-------|
| II | 33 | 71 |
| III | 18 | 52 |
| IV | 11 | 43 |
| V | 0 | 28 |

It is easy to see that the lower a boy's or girl's class position is, the higher the probability that he or she does not belong to a religious club.

Boys and girls in these clubs differentiate rather sharply between those with whom they do or do not want to associate. The Federated Fellowship takes considerable pride in the fact that the leading high school students are in "their club." Its nucleus also belongs to the elite *sub rosa* high school club, the G.W.G.'s. These girls deliberately make any girl of whom they do not approve feel so uncomfortable that she will attend neither young people's meetings nor Sunday School. A girl may be acceptable to this clique on the basis of family background, but if she does not dress, talk, think, and act like them, they exclude her ruthlessly from the little band. A popular member of this clique said of a class II sophomore girl:

> Judy doesn't go out. She would like to, but her folks won't let her. The kids tease her all the time. They say she is tied to her mother's apron strings. You can't be tied to your mother's apron strings and be told you have to be in at ten o'clock and you can't wear lipstick, and you can't do this, and you can't do that, and be

popular. Judy's not popular. She could be. The kids don't like her just because she does what her folks tell her.

The Methodist minister felt strongly on this point and confessed that he had tried to organize the Methodist students into "one happy family working for Christ and the Church," but had "failed utterly." He related that there were two girls' clubs in the church when he came to Elmtown in 1939. One, a Greek letter group, was composed predominantly of girls from classes II and III; girls in the other club came from classes III and IV, with one faithful class V girl. He did not think this was a "wholesome condition," as the Greek letter group looked down upon Esther's Circle and successfully kept its members out of the choir and Sunday School offices. The Greek letter girls organized parties, picnics, and in all, as the minister said, "ran the show." For their part, the girls in Esther's Circle accepted their subordinate position, organized their own parties, and ignored "the Greek girls."

The minister allowed the two clubs to continue until the end of that school year. But when the young people's activities were organized in the fall for the next year, he tried to convince the girls and boys that there should be but one fellowship in the church and the right one was, of course, sponsored by the national church. The new program was planned as a religious discussion group composed of *all* Methodists of high school age, and outsiders who could be interested in the idea. The Methodist Board, the Ladies' Aid, and Missionary Societies enthusiastically approved the plan. The discussion theme for the year was announced as a militant Christian fellowship working for peace, democracy, and the furtherance of Christian welfare.

Fifteen to 20 young people, 10 to 15 girls and 4 or 5 boys, came to the first few meetings. Gradually, attendance among the boys dropped off to 1 or 2, and the girls who had been in Esther's Circle quit coming, except the class V girl who had no other social or recreational outlets. This situation continued week after week; it reached a climax one cold, midwinter night when only the class V girl from down by the Canal, who had walked across town in weather 15 degrees below zero, reached the church. The minister and the girl waited for more than an hour before they gave up hope that anyone else was coming. Finally, the minister decided to take the girl home in his car. On the way to the girl's home, he passed the home of the girl who had been the last president of the Greek letter sorority. The shades of this girl's living room were not drawn, and the minister saw about a dozen girls sitting in a circle as he drove by. The minister drove the class V girl home, went back, and looked the group over carefully from the street. "The lights were on, and I saw it was that group of Greek letter girls." He learned later that these girls had met in this way by prearrangement as a protest against his idea. The next year he suggested that the girls might like to reorganize their former clubs. They did so, and along the old lines.

Parties sponsored by the young people's groups in each church are announced from the pulpit by the minister, or a notice of the time and place is posted in the church bulletin. Presumably they are open to all young people in the church, their friends, and guests, but it is generally understood by the adolescents that the active members of the group are the only ones wholly welcome, except on special occasions, such as the Young Baptists' truck ride and wiener roast, when every person who can be sold a ten-cent ticket is welcomed as "a good fellow" irrespective of his religious affiliation. An outside boy or girl who attended ordinary parties was condemned as "a jackal interested in free eats." Consequently, attendance is limited mainly to the regular members and their dates. Members "in the swim" organize and run the parties, and the less active members come, at least part of the time. Less than a third of the students (32 per cent) attended any of these affairs, 13 per cent said they went to "a few," and 18 per cent were regular participants. Like other aspects of participation in religious activities, attendance is strongly biased in favor of the class II's and against the class V's. The percentages by class are: class II, 77; class III, 42; class IV, 20; and class V, 4. These figures are further evidence, if it is necessary, that organized social affairs are not an important trait in the activity pattern of the typical adolescent of class IV or class V.

MINISTERS' JUDGMENT. Each minister rated the adolescents who claimed affiliation with his church on a five-division scale:

(1) unknown; (2) known, but does not attend services; (3) a good Christian child; (4) a church leader; (5) an unreliable person. Twenty-three per cent of the students were unknown; an additional 27 per cent were known, but they did not come to any services, and, from his experience with the boy or girl, the minister had reached the conclusion that the church had lost its hold on him. Almost exactly one-half of the 49 per cent who participated in church affairs were rated as good Christian children. That is, they came to services, did not create any disturbance or give the ministers any excuse to worry over them; neither could they be relied upon to accept leadership in religious activities. The remaining one-half was divided almost equally between church leaders and the unreliables. Adolescents rated as "unreliable" did things the ministers considered out of character for "a good Christian child" or "a church leader," yet they came to church, Sunday School, or young people's meetings. Their transgressions ranged from repeatedly broken promises, dancing, wild driving, lying, gambling, drinking, stealing, profanity, and smoking to violation of sex mores. The ministers' ratings were moderately associated with class position. The class II's and class III's received a disproportionate number of "church leader" and "good Christian child" evaluations, whereas the class IV's tended to be rated as "unreliables," and the class V's were unknown.[7]

MINISTERS' WORRIES. All Protestant ministers were concerned over the "loss" of their young people, its effect upon the future of the church, and the salvation of individual souls. The Lutheran pastor was most acutely troubled on emotional, doctrinal, and moral grounds; the Free Methodist minister was exercised about "godlessness in boys and girls today." The Baptist pastor expressed his impotence in the situation, "The young people are beyond me. I have a small group of active youngsters. Most of the high school kids, though, have no interest in the church or what it stands for." The Methodist preacher was jealous of the "fine attendance among the Federated boys and girls. I simply do not see how Reverend Dodge keeps his young people. I do the same thing for my boys and

[7] See Table XVII of the Appendix.

girls, but they are not enthusiastic. I sometimes think Dodge runs a dating bureau. We cannot have that sort of thing here." Reverend Dodge, comparatively, had the highest level of adolescent participation of any church; yet he would have liked to have more young people active in the church. The ministers believed that Sunday motion pictures, nation-wide radio programs, Sunday afternoon automobile rides, sports of one kind or another, and dates "led young people away from the church."

In their relations with adolescents, these ministers fail to realize the following three facts about the churches they lead and the cultural system in which they function: first, no church has adapted its services to the needs of this age group; second, the adolescents have transformed the young people's groups into semi-private clubs, and the students who run them extend the class system into the churches on the adolescent level; third, the ministers by their attitudes toward the behavior of the adolescents build a barrier between themselves and their adolescent members.

Regarding the first point: The young people's meeting, held between six and seven-thirty in the evening, is the one concession the Protestant churches have made to the teen-age group. It is not popular, but it gives many who come an acceptable excuse to have a date on Sunday night without parental objections. However, the boys who attend church socials and young people's affairs are often looked down upon by the boys "wise in the ways of the world" as "old-fashioned," "a bunch of Christers," "sissies," "panty waists," or "pansies." Among the girls, particularly in classes II and III, this feeling is not so pronounced, since going to church and participation in church work is an admired role. A girl who wants to be socially correct places considerable stress upon her church activities. The "church girl," in turn, looks down upon girls who do not go to church, but to maintain her exclusiveness she draws the social line very carefully against the girl trying to participate in religious clubs who has "lost caste" through misbehavior or who comes from a low-ranking family.

Adolescents deeply involved in church groups are interested in their clubs for social rather than religious reasons. The really vital element is whether other boys or girls in the Sunday School class and the young people's group accept or reject them as persons in the group's activities, not the religious values which the church emphasizes. This may best be given point by quoting the words of a few who were rejected.

1. A class IV sophomore girl from a Methodist family who started to attend the Federated Church and left it.

> I used to go to Sunday School, but I don't any more. I went to the Methodist, but I don't like the kids over there any more, and I don't like our class [sophomore girls in the Federated Church]. Mrs. Belden teaches it, and I don't like her and I don't like those kids either. They make you feel like you don't belong there. They think they're better than me. They talk about the things they do; we sit there and they just ignore us kids.
>
> [She was asked, "Who are 'us kids'?"]
>
> All of us that dropped out of [the Federated] Sunday School. My cousin Josephine dropped out first. That was about a year ago. Then Alice dropped out next, maybe it was the first part of last summer. Katie dropped out next, and I dropped out about a month ago. Three weeks ago, Virginia dropped out, and that's all of us. All this bunch dropped out this summer and fall. We don't go around with those kids [the ones who continued in the Federated Sunday School], and they don't go around with us, so we didn't want to go there any more. [The girls named were the speaker's clique mates, all sophomores, and in class IV, from Federated families.]

2. A class IV junior girl, Federated:

> I have quit going to church because that group of girls who think they are higher than us look down on us. They have a club [the G.W.G.] that is supposed to be out of school, but it's really in school. This same group of girls go to the church I used to go to [Federated] and there's only one girl who goes there that is not in that group. I do not feel I want to go to church any more. Those girls snub us; they will not talk to us. They speak to us sometimes, but most of the time they pass us by.

3. A freshman boy, class V, Baptist:

> Those kids are all snobbish. They snub us and I quit going, that's all.

A subtle set of social cues operate in interpersonal relations that tell people whether or not they are acceptable to the people with whom they are associated, cues which are a part of the social code the child learns from his associates as he participates in group life. When these cues are called into action, a person knows he is either not acceptable to the other members of the group or "in the dog house" temporarily for some misstep. On the other hand, a smile, an arm around the waist or across the shoulders, and a hearty "Hi ya!" "Come on, join the gang!" are attractive cues that tell him he is "in the swim." Friendly acceptance by the group "in the swim" is what these adolescents crave, not religious values extolled by the minister. If an adolescent derives pleasure from association with his clique mates in the church situation, he attends Sunday School, young people's meeting, and church parties without being more than nominally influenced by, or interested in, the religious aspects of the situation.

Rejection or acceptance of the boy or girl by other boys and girls active in a church program is related to the culture complex associated with each class. For instance, active participation and leadership in both church and secular affairs are in the folkways of classes II and III. Church attendance, supplemented by Sunday School teaching, acting as ushers, singing in the choir, missionary work, and service on the church board are important elements in the action pattern of the adult class II's and class III's. These people resent the intrusion of persons with lower prestige than themselves into areas they consider rightfully theirs. Adolescents active in these churches follow the pattern set for them by their elders. The young people active in the Federated and Methodist churches welcome class equals and "turn the cold shoulder" on those who rank below them. Thus, boys and girls from the lower classes either go to churches where they feel comfortable or drop out entirely because they are not accepted by the clique in control. The few exceptions are so noticeable that they excite comment from students and ministers. A low-ranking class IV girl was snubbed frequently by the Baptist girls, yet she continued to come to Sunday School, B.Y.P.U., and some parties. When she was asked about her religious beliefs, she piously stated:

> My church has definite laws which are given to the members by the church. I have to follow the laws of the church or be put out of it. To me the church is the highest law.

To her, participation in religious activities was a part of this law; so she withstood the insults of the group stoically.

Ministers are aware of the prestige differences in the community, and they know in a general way where their church belongs in the structure, but they do not connect class position with attendance or non-attendance on the part of their congregation. The Methodist minister, in particular, worries about why his young people do not participate in church activities, yet he denies the influence of class on religious behavior when the question is raised.

The deprecatory view taken by ministers of behavior enjoyed by the students acts as a barrier between them and the church. If a youngster wants to do the things his friends do, such as dancing, and his church disapproves, he either withdraws from the church or dances and keeps that fact from the minister. Many withdrew, but a not inconsiderable group both participate in tabooed activities and remain silent. This is only one aspect of *the conspiracy of silence which exists between adolescents and adults.* In this case, the minister, because of his calling and position in the value system, is isolated by the young people, and every effort is made to keep him ignorant of what is actually happening in the adolescent world.

By the ministers' own admission these youngsters do not come to them with their problems because they believe that they would be condemned rather than understood since the ministers are interested in the traditional other-worldly values associated with the Christian religion rather than with the views and values of the adolescents. The ministers do not know what their young people are thinking or doing, and the young people very carefully preserve this gap between themselves and their ministers.

A very amusing case of this type of thinking and acting involved a class II girl who was believed by the Methodist minister to be a paragon of virtue. She taught in the Sunday School, sang in the choir, had held all offices in the Greek letter

club, and never used cosmetics or curled her hair when she
came near the church. The minister on numerous occasions
referred to her to bolster his belief that a person could be "a
devout Christian, popular with the young people, and not sin."
This girl was known in the elite high school set as a "smooth
number." She belonged to five different school clubs and the
G.W.G.; she went to all the dances and after the dances participated in the post-dance petting party pattern followed by the
typical couple; on occasion, she smoked, drank a cocktail, and
petted heavily. The minister would have been horrified had
he known these things. This girl's popularity was derived from
her ability to adjust to the demands her social life made upon
her. She was not condemned by the high school leaders or her
religious friends simply because she divided her loyalties and
had a good time. This was the success pattern of the popular
class II girl; she followed it avidly, and knowledge of her activities was kept from the minister.

Many Lutheran boys and girls hide their participation in
"sinful pleasures of the flesh" systematically and successfully
from the sight and knowledge of their minister. This clergyman
believes that all things the church abhors are sinful. In his
scheme of thinking, the function of the church is not only to
provide a way of salvation, but also to prevent the individual
from "destroying his soul through the satisfaction of earthly
pleasures." Therefore, most things the young people enjoy are
condemned as "immoral devices" which "corrupt the soul." If a
boy or girl is caught in one of these activities, the minister gives
the culprit an impassioned lecture; if the act is "dangerous to
the soul," the minister goes directly to the parents, and an unpleasant family scene results. The vigor of these methods keeps
many students active in church, but it drives others away and
produces duplicity on a broad scale.

The Lutheran minister categorically denies his adolescents
dancing, cosmetics, curls, permanents, bobbed hair, motion pictures, alcoholic beverages, automobile rides—especially on Sunday—bowling, cards, pool, high school parties. In fact, almost
every recreation approved in the non-Lutheran, non-holiness
portion of the community comes under the ban. The only sanc-

tioned pleasures are short educational films of religious shrines or foreign missionary work, shown in the church basement, and church-sponsored parties and games.

The minister realizes that he cannot deny all pleasures to his young people; so he encourages the members of the Luther League to organize roller skating parties. However, he does not sanction their skating in either of the local rinks because they are run by "Godless men." One is owned by a Catholic, and to be seen in this rink, from the viewpoint of this minister, is an abomination in the sight of the Lord. The other rink is city-owned and -operated, and the minister cannot approve of it because the city is a secular institution. The approved rink is owned by a Norwegian Lutheran in another community. Although the minister urges his young people to go to this rink for "good, clean fun," he does not attend skating parties himself since he believes that his presence in a commercialized public place, where the one function is pleasure, places the stamp of the church's approval on the activity carried on in the place. He justifies his private, informal, approval of roller skating at this rink in these terms, "It's a good, clean place run by a Norwegian gentleman."

This rink has a reputation among non-Lutherans, adults, and adolescents as the toughest place in the vicinity. Class II and class III girls do not go there because of its unsavory reputation; it is, however, a favorite place for many boys "on the prowl." A young professional man, who knew the rink and its history from his adolescent days, reported "we always went there for hot pick-ups." A youth in his late teens related, "They used to have some rousing times over there. Every Saturday night, there was at least one fight, and when it was over they had to chop a hole in the floor to let the blood run out." This is obviously an overstatement, but it indicates the way the rink was viewed by young non-Lutheran males.

Did the minister know this rink was a center of conflict? Bluntly, yes! He explained it away by saying, "All that is outside. No rough stuff is allowed in the pavilion." This was not true, for we saw two fights start in the pavilion. They were stopped immediately by the owner, but the boys and their adherents merely moved outside to settle the fights.  Incidentally, the minister's approval of this skating rink illustrated the often-alleged clannishness of the Lutherans.

The Lutheran minister characterized high school dances in these terms.

> When a boy or girl, the purest creatures of God's creation, dances over at that high school, the Devil dances behind each one. When the boy holds a girl in his arms, the Devil takes the place of his soul, and he doesn't see a sweet, clean, pure creature in front of him. No, he only sees a scarlet woman there. Dancing makes a boy or girl into a fiend. That's why I will not allow my young people to go to those high school dances.

To this minister's way of thinking, roller skating to music is not dancing, but the young people often waltz or fox-trot on skates, holding one another as closely as they do at the high school dances.  There are no chaperons present, and it is not at all unusual for the young people to pause and fondle one another, not too delicately, in the darker corners of the rink and to slip away together.  This part of the skating party is beyond his knowledge, simply because the boys and girls know that if they tell him this pleasure is likely to be denied them.

A folk saying in Elmtown is "The better Lutheran a girl is, the more likely she will have to get married sooner or later." The minister confessed, "I can't understand why so many of my devout girls stray from the teachings of the church." The minister's approval of this roller rink, coupled with the type of behavior which takes place there, spells trouble for many a Lutheran adolescent.

Open warfare exists between the Lutheran minister and the class II youngsters in his congregation.  The social ritual in this stratum tolerates and in many instances requires such tabooed things as cocktail parties, dances at the Country Club, bridge, poker among the men, dinners in the home on Saturday night, and a visit to the motion picture theater.  Other class traits are memberships in the Country Club, the Masons, Rotary, the Friday Morning Club.  These secular behavior patterns of the parents have their counterparts in the activities of the class II boys and girls.

In this situation the class II Lutheran child is faced with making a choice between the various Lutheran adolescent groups and withdrawing from high school extracurricular affairs and the youth groups in town, such as Job's Daughters and the Greek letter clubs. The adolescents' adjustment to the conflicts presented by the religious versus the secular elements in the class culture range from withdrawal from the church to a nominal attendance on Sunday morning. In the preceding decade, four or five families had left the Lutheran Church and gone to the Federated; they were criticized severely by the Lutherans as "social climbers." One Lutheran girl who was castigated for dancing dropped out of the Luther League and some two months later with her parents' approval started attending the Federated Fellowship, where she was accepted.

Another was caught in this conflict and left the church. One Sunday she went to the evening service wearing a white scarf to cover curlers in her hair. There she sang in a girls' quartet, and as soon as the service was over went home to remove the scarf and the curlers. Some of the older women who thought that wearing a scarf in church was rather singular began to gossip. When the minister demanded an explanation for the girl's headdress from the girl's mother, she told him the girl had gone out with some other girls that night. The minister learned later (quite by accident according to his story, but a class III girl claimed he "pried it out of one of his stool pigeons") that this girl had curled her hair and gone to the picture show with her boy friend after the church service. The next Sunday, the minister's sermon was on the evils of deceit and the corrosion of the soul by the motion picture. In the course of the sermon, he pointed an accusing finger and told the congregation what had happened the preceding Sunday night. The girl went home and cried the rest of the day and most of the night. Her father, who was only nominally a Lutheran, took the girl's side and told her that she did not need to go back "to that church."

The Lutheran sin-and-salvation complex is in marked contrast to the view of their young people taken by the Federated and Methodist ministers. These ministers are not worried so much about what their young people are doing in the afternoons and evenings, but why they do not come to church, Sunday School, or young people's meetings.  It is only in the grossest cases of outright immorality on the part of a boy or girl that they show real concern, and then they are fearful over the effect it will have on the adolescent's reputation rather than its effect on his soul. For instance, a class IV Federated girl who came from a broken home was suspected for several months of stealing in the high school and in the church before she was actually apprehended rifling purses at a young people's party.  This girl's mother was known in the community as "common property around town," and the girl was known among the young people as a "pretty hot number who will go all the way with the right guy—and practically anybody is right."  The minister had heard the stories of her stealing and sex behavior, but he did not believe them until the girl was caught; then he became exercised over the way the girl was isolated by her peers.  We discussed this girl's behavior several times with the minister, but he never expressed any worry over her soul or the effect this would have upon her ultimate salvation.  He was concerned wholly about the effects the situation had on the girl's standing in the high school.

The members of the Catholic faith were largely descendants of European immigrants who had not been fully assimilated to Elmtown's culture, but the church's relation to its young people was in sharp contrast to that of the Lutheran's.  The priest believed the adolescents were "no better or worse than young people everywhere.  A few are fine young men and women, and a few are wayward.  The run of them are a good lot."  He was careful to emphasize that he spoke unofficially.  As far as he was concerned, the role of the church was not to suppress human desires, but to provide young persons with a solid anchorage upon which they could base their hopes for salvation in the hereafter.  As an institution, it did not condemn secular activities, such as dancing, cards, and motion pictures.  He likened the church to an indulgent mother who guided, suggested, and provided for her children rather than as a stern disciplinarian who admonished, threatened, and harangued if they deviated, even the slightest, from her conception of right and wrong.

By way of summary, we shall point out again that, although practically every student believes in God and thinks he is a Christian, only one-half of the high school students participate in religious activities. Non-participation is very strongly associated with lower class positions and participation with higher class positions. The students who participate in religious organizations carry the class system into the church; consequently religious clubs are definitely class-biased. Finally, a barrier exists between the adolescents active in the churches and the ministers. The young people band together and do what their class and age groups do; if they are caught in their actions they usually withdraw from the church. More generally they hide their activities from the minister, as they do from their teachers and parents, and happily go with the crowd.

# 11

# JOBS AND IDEAS OF JOBS

### Part-time jobs

THE ELMTOWN ECONOMY has relied upon the labor of boys and girls since frontier days. The language is sprinkled with descriptive terms indicative of the roles boys have played in the mines, mills, stores, and offices: grocery boys, butcher boys, mine boys, water boys, engine boys, barge boys, stable boys, donkey boys, printer's devils, office boys, dray boys, ash boys; all attest to the association of boys with particular kinds of jobs. The working girls' roles have been limited traditionally to housemaid, nursemaid, ribbon clerk, office girl, waitress, seamstress, and barmaid. The farms have not provided so wide a variety of jobs as the town, but the roles of the chore boy and the hired girl are well developed in the farm culture, and prosperous farmers have furnished menial, low-paid jobs to numerous boys and girls through the generations. In the era before a high school education absorbed some two-thirds of the time of about one-half of all adolescents in their middle teens, farms, businesses, and industries assimilated all adolescents in the community, except the sons and daughters of a few wealthy business and professional families, as soon as a youngster was old enough to do farm work, help an adult in some manufacturing process, drive a grocery wagon, or (in the case of a girl) perform the simple, routine tasks involved in caring for children and housework.

Although Elmtown's economy has changed radically in the last two generations, especially in the production of raw materials and manufactured goods, its reliance upon and need for the labor of adolescent boys and girls has not disappeared as

267

have the gas-pipe hitching racks from the courthouse square. Although unions no longer allow thirteen- and fourteen-year-old boys in the coal mines, the Mill, or the Foundry, there are no union pressures to keep them out of any small business, or off the farm, nor has the union closed the door to girls who wish to work in restaurants, stores, and homes. Today, the distributive and service aspects of the economy have as much need for adolescent employees as in an earlier era, perhaps more. The one uniform, restricting current factor operating against the employment of boys and girls in Elmtown's business establishments, on its farms, and in many homes is the compulsory school law. This law is only a third of a century old, and it is not accepted as either a necessary or a good thing by many parents in the two lower classes; neither is it accepted by all manufacturers or all businessmen as socially desirable. From the frontier days to the present, *the economy has had need for the labor of adolescents; and, just as important, the vast majority of the adolescents need the jobs the economy provides to earn the money they all have to have in order to participate in the commercialized forms of recreation available to them.*

The great depression of the 1930's affected the adolescent in his relation to the job in two ways. On the one hand, while it lowered family incomes for everyone, for many heads of families it resulted in unemployment or underemployment. Thus, since there was less money in the family budget to give to adolescents, the need for the teen-aged boy or girl to earn money was greater than in the lush years of the 1920's. On the other hand, the scarcity of jobs resulted in adolescents being forced out of the labor market by adults. When the field work began, the depression complex still prevailed in Elmtown, although there were many more jobs available than there had been a few years earlier. Nevertheless, competition was very keen because the number of young people wanting jobs was much greater than the number of jobs available. Over 39 per cent of the class II students and 86 per cent of those in the three lower classes said they would like to have a job. With the rise of war industries and the acceleration of the draft after the outbreak of war this condition changed rapidly.

The demand of the retail trades and services for part-time employees synchronizes well with the high school students' needs and desires. The high school work load is so light that very few students have to study more than an hour or two a week outside of school hours. And since very few town families have enough work at home to occupy a high-school-aged youngster three or four hours in the afternoon or evening and all day Saturday, the typical youngster has several hours of free time on his hands. During these same afternoon and early evening and Saturday hours the business peak in the retail stores is reached; therefore, through the years the custom has developed of employing high-school-aged youngsters to work in these establishments part-time. Practically every store has at least one student who works two or three hours in the afternoon or early evening, and from twelve to fifteen hours on Saturday. Saturday's hours are always long, for the stores remain open until nine or ten o'clock at night to take advantage of the evening trade. In addition to the stores, the theaters, bowling alley, skating rink, hamburger stands, and short-order cafés utilize student help in large part, because their business is transacted mainly between four o'clock in the afternoon and ten in the evening. Many housewives who cannot afford a full-time servant turn to high school girls for help with the housework and "minding the children."

There are several reasons for the keen competition among the town adolescents for part-time jobs. It is linked closely, first, with the high value the culture placed upon work and earning one's way and, second, with their need for money. One class IV boy wrote in his autobiography, "When I had entered my thirteenth year, I discovered that it was expected that boys of that age would begin to show some after-school job enterprise." A class III boy wrote, "I wasn't told to do it, nor were any of my friends, to the best of my knowledge. It was accepted as the thing to do when you reached high school." To grow up and get a job is one of the strongest folkways in the adolescent group. Jobs mean money and—for that great majority outside of class II who have no allowance—freedom from the embarrassment of asking father or mother for money.

Furthermore, family incomes in the two lowest classes are so meager that most parents find it expensive to send a child through high school. The incomes of class IV parents generally cover the necessities of life, but they do not allow for the extras they like to have. Most parents in classes III and IV believe that a child should help all he can. Many of them frequently view their children as economic burdens which prevent them from closing the gap between what they desire of the material things which advertising campaigns have educated them to expect in the American way of life and what the family income actually can buy. In some cases it is necessary for the children to work in order to stay in school. Class V parents are so poor the child is practically forced to leave school to make his own way in the world by the time he is 14 or 15 years of age. Therefore, in the three lower classes there is both a sociological pressure for and an economic need of jobs by the adolescent.

Mrs. Jensen, class IV, the mother of seven children and the wife of a mill worker who earned $120 a month, epitomized this feeling of family need when she said:

> Joy simply has to work to help out. We're a large family, and we have to watch the pennies to get along. If Joy did not buy her own clothes and earn her spending money, we couldn't keep her in school. I wish she didn't have to work, but I guess work never hurt anybody.

Curley Burke, a furnace tender at the Factory, stated:

> I want to see that all four of my kids finish high school and I'd like to send them to college, but I'm afraid this can't be done on $110 a month. The oldest one, Martha, graduated a couple of years ago. She started working in the dime store the summer she graduated from Central School. At first she put tags on stuff in the basement and kept the stockroom clean for ten cents an hour. She kept right on working there after school started. She worked up front as a clerk. After a while, she learned bookkeeping and typing, and the manager put her in the office. The last two years she was in high school she earned five dollars a week. That was pretty good when they were only paying the clerks ten dollars [a week]. At night, she used to take care of kids when people went out. We never bought Martha any clothes or gave her any money while she was in high school. She used to give her mother two or three dollars a week to help buy the groceries.

Dan [the eldest son] has earned all his own money since he was in the seventh grade. He started delivering meat for Sommer's market on his bicycle. He learned how to help around the market. Now he cuts meat every afternoon and Saturdays. He buys all his own clothes, has his own money, and supplies us with most of our meat. He wants to go to college, but we can't help him. He might be able to work his way, but that's mighty hard.

Ben [the second son] works in the A & P as a stock clerk. He started to work there this fall. He only makes three dollars a week, but he buys his own clothes and has his own money. That's not bad for a freshman. In a year or two, he hopes to work up to the checking counter where he'll make six dollars a week. The baby's only ten, so we don't expect her to work.

Some parents, particularly in class III but a few in class II, believe that their children should work in order to learn the value of money and to acquire a sense of responsibility even though the income earned by the youth is not needed to supplement the family income. This position, however, is not so typical, especially in classes III and IV, as are the numerous cases of boys or girls who work from necessity. In cases where the youth is made to work, he is often unhappy and feels that his family is taking advantage of him. Then, too, the family is criticized generally for urging the youth to work when it does not need the money. Class II and class III parents whose children do not work cannot understand why such parents bring pressure to bear to have their sons or daughters work. Furthermore, such parents are criticized by class IV parents who believe that they are deliberately "hogging" the jobs.

Although students from the farms are as eager for jobs as the town dwellers, they have little opportunity to work away from home, since their parents expect them to come home as soon as school is out to help with the chores. "There is always room for one more hand around the farm." That "hand" is more often than not the high school girl who works around the house, or the boy who does the farm chores. Farm boys and girls are not gainfully employed away from home to any extent; only 4 boys and 1 girl have jobs in town. But about 90 per cent report they work at home an average of 2.5 hours a day on school days and

9.3 on Saturday.[1] Farm parents believe that their children should help at home; "they owe this to their parents." The farm adolescent performs a role in the farm economy comparable to that of the town adolescent who acts as a supplementary labor force in the retail business houses of the community. He helps with the farm work by feeding livestock, cleaning out the barns, feeding the chickens and gathering the eggs, hauling hay, repairing fences, and doing other maintenance chores. Many farm boys are practical mechanics, and they are expected to take a major role, if not the chief one, in the repair of tractors, trucks, farm engines, and machines in general. John Olson, a prominent farmer, estimated that his son, a junior in high school, saved him from $250 to $300 a year in repair bills and machinery costs. "Joe understands engines and I don't. He can take our Farmall and make it work when I can't even get it started." Although the father bragged of his son's ability, he limited him to fifty cents a week outside of gasoline for his car, which was pumped out of the farm's storage tank. Joe, however, like many another farm boy, had more cash income than the half-dollar his father gave him, for he carried four to five dozen eggs to town each week and sold them for cash. If a "special deal" called for extra money, it was easy to bring a cockerel or two to market in a sack. Or now and again he could beg an extra dollar.

### Jobs and class

Desirable part-time jobs usually are obtained by arrangement between adults rather than through the adolescent's own efforts. The employer knows the youngster's family in practically all cases before the adolescent is hired; reciprocally, the employee and his family have some appreciation of the employer's personality, business methods, and reputation. In this situation, non-economic factors have as much, or even more, influence upon

[1] The comparable figures for the town dwellers are: 77 per cent, 0.8 of an hour on week days and 1.2 hours of work on Saturday. The girls report as much work at home as the boys, but their work is confined to domestic duties, whereas the boys care for the furnace, wash dishes, garden, cut and haul wood, cut the lawn, work on the car, paint. No significance of difference appears in the amount of work reported at home by the four classes.

the relationship between employer and employee as strictly economic ones, for everyone involved in the relationship is a person functioning in a social system in which the economic is only one phase of the total situation.

Jobs open to students have assigned values similar to those which prevail in the adult work world. Office work in the stores, in the Mill, and for doctors and lawyers rated highest; clerical work in locally owned department, hardware, jewelry, and grocery stores is next. Then comes work in the chain stores and stores owned by Jews. Work in service stations, garages, and in the theaters is respectable, but it does not carry as much prestige. Housework, paper routes, and the care of children in the afternoons and evenings are looked upon as necessary but hardly dignified. Waiting on table in local cafes and carrying and washing dishes are definitely menial and viewed with disfavor by the adolescents and many of their parents. Janitors, junk yard, garbage, and ash haulers are at the bottom of the job hierarchy.

That place of employment is connected with class position can be seen by noting who is employed at the various establishments. Stores locally owned by Gentiles are able to select their employees with care. The two class II girls who work are employed in the misses' and young ladies' wear section of the most respectable department store. Three of the 4 gainfully employed class II boys hold jobs as follows: 1 works in the payroll department of the Mill office; 1 is a clerk in his father's jewelry store; the third does office work and helps wait on trade in a great uncle's hardware store. Forty-seven per cent of the gainfully employed class III's work in locally owned stores and offices; very few class IV's, however, are able to obtain one of these better-paid and higher prestige-bearing jobs because more often than not they are procured by parental arrangement with the proprietor.[2] The pay in chain stores is about a dollar a week less; therefore, students prefer to work in a "home" store because of the prestige and the pay, but some class III's and many class IV's work in chain stores, and some in establishments owned by

---

[2] "Good, needy" adolescents are sometimes placed in these desirable jobs by interested adults; in the course of the year the Methodist minister made three placements of this type.

"Jews." Class V's work at menial work such as washing cars, waiting on table, janitorial work, and hauling garbage, ashes, and trash.

The percentage of students gainfully occupied part of the time is not significantly different in the three lower classes. The work pattern of the class II's, however, is radically different from that of the other classes. By class the percentage employed is: class II, 17; class III, 61; class IV, 57; class V, 61. For the student group as a whole, 64 per cent of the boys and 49 per cent of the girls have jobs which give them a regular cash income.[3]

The significantly low percentage employed in class II is a reflection of the class folkways which emphasizes the father's ability to support his wife and minor children. To confess that the family needs money earned by children for its partial support would be a blight upon its prestige. The class evaluation of leisure dovetails into the behavior patterns of the class II adolescents during the high school years. Like their parents, they are involved deeply in various activities which, in addition to many extracurricular organizations in the high school, include, in the non-school area of social life, the Cadet Club, the G.W.G.'s, the Campfire Girls, the Senior Boy Scouts, the Federated Fellowship, the Tenderfoot Club, bowling leagues, and Country Club parties. If a person has to work, he does not have the time to devote to these activities; consequently, he tends to be isolated from his class peers, both by the fact that he works, and also by his lack of knowledge of what they are doing, have done, or intend to do. To be "in the swim" one has to splash in the social whirl with his fellows; or, as one frequently heard, "fish or cut bait." The 17 per cent of class II students who work tend to "cut bait"; the other 83 per cent "fish."

The two girls and four boys in class II who work are "looked down upon" by most other class II's, and their families are openly criticized by class II parents and by several in class I. All these adolescents belong to families which moved into class II during

---

[3] Wages range from 15 to 35 cents per hour; the mean is 22 cents. Weekly earnings range from $2 to $6 per week with a mean of $4.26. The amount earned differs significantly in the three lower classes. The class III's report an average of $4.67 per week; the class IV's $4.07, and the class V's $3.45.

the lifetime of the parents, largely through their own efforts. These fathers and mothers are ambitious, hard-working persons who have learned the value of self-help, frugality, enterprise, and planning. Each of these families has plans for its children, and the child's part-time job advances the parents' ambition and future hopes. These parents undoubtedly carry the idea of the necessity for hard, unremitting toil into their present class position from the lower classes. They have not been in their class position long enough to have acquired the beliefs and practices of the class to which their own efforts have carried them. The mother of one of the two girls made this plain in her discussion of the family's struggle for success:

Mr. Martindale and I started out with very little. He was not able to finish high school, and I had to quit after my second year and learn business training. I worked in a millinery store days and went to school nights. I finished my secretarial course and was working for the Home Insurance Company when I met Mr. Martindale [he was an agent for the company]. I liked the way he worked on correspondence school courses whenever there wasn't anything to do around the office. After two years we were married. For the first few years, we both worked very hard and saved everything we could. We kept books on every penny we made so that we knew where we were going. When Alice was born, I quit work and I have been raising my family since. Mr. Martindale kept working hard, and we have made a few good investments. Fortunately, we had several thousand dollars saved when the depression came. We were going to buy a home at first, but one day I said to Mr. Martindale, "I believe we better buy a farm or a business building." We started looking around and found two good farms at a reasonable figure. I hated to do it. Oh, but I was worried. We bought both farms. Now they are paid for, and we are buying this house. The last few years Mr. Martindale's income has been better, and we've been able to give the girls advantages and buy nice things for the home, and things have been just a little easier.

We did not want the children to have to work the way we did, and they haven't had to, but two years ago this Christmas Mr. Martindale was in the hospital and I was worried about the costs and everything. One day I was talking to Mrs. Horton about it, and she suggested that Alice might like to work in their store during the holidays. Alice was wild to earn some money, and I was happy that she could. She has been working in the store on Saturdays ever since. Mr. Martindale thinks it is all right for her to work, but I am not so sure. Mrs. Frank Daniels and I have talked it over a number of times. She thinks families in our circumstances should not allow our children to work. I know we are criticized for letting Alice work, just as the Freemans are for letting Lewis, Jr., work in that Greek place. I see these things, but Mr. Martindale does not. He just does not have any perception about social things.

He wants Alice to go to college, and I do too. He thinks she will appreciate things more if she helps earn them, but I want her to be happy, and I am afraid she isn't sometimes when she has to go to work in the store and her girl friends are going to a party or on a hike or planning a picnic.

The Martindale family was frequently the object of biting remarks from persons who did not believe that it was necessary for Alice to work. It was well known in classes I and II that the family's annual income approximated $6,000. The same type of criticism was aimed at the Josephs, the other class II family whose daughter held a job on Saturdays. The boys' families were not criticized so openly for allowing or making them work as were the Martindale and Joseph families. The community expects boys to work, even class II's if they want to do so.

Open censure was focused on the Lewis Freeman family by many class I and class II parents, some high school teachers, Protestant ministers, and a number of low-ranking families, because Lewis Freeman had placed his son Lewis, Jr., as a fry cook in Harry's Café. Harry, the Greek's, as it is familiarly known, is a highly respectable short-order hamburger stand, extensively patronized by high school students and young adults. In addition to working there himself, Harry hires student boys exclusively. His six or eight employees work every afternoon and evening, in shifts from three to seven, and from seven to eleven o'clock on week nights, later on week ends. Lewis Freeman, Sr., had earned his way from the time his father died, when he was eleven. He had worked at many trades as a young man, acquiring an intimate understanding of the ways of the world, and had started to work his way through the State University when the first World War interrupted his schooling. He volunteered, went to Officers' Candidate School, was commissioned, sent overseas, fought in three campaigns, and was wounded. He returned to civilian life as a captain and finished Home State University on veterans' benefits.  In the early 1920's, he married a young woman who had graduated from the University with him, and at that time was teaching high school in a small city near Elmtown.  She had inherited two farms in Home County on the edge of Elmtown community.  The young couple moved to one of them and began to feed livestock and to farm scientifically.  By means of good management, hard work, and shrewd trading in farms, livestock, and machinery, they prospered rapidly; however, they overextended their operations in the late 1920's and took severe losses in the depression years.  Early in 1930, they moved to Elmtown to occupy a home Mrs. Freeman had inherited from a "half-greataunt."  By 1941, the family had more than recovered its former financial position through consolidation, a few daring deals in farm lands, and a speculative "fling" in coal land.

Mr. Freeman believed in "throwing" his son "into life"; so he arranged with Harry to give him a job behind the counter. Lewis, Jr., took his turn at the early and late shifts along with the other boys; and on Saturdays and Sundays he worked twelve to fifteen hours.  After a few weeks Lewis, Jr., was made foreman, and his wages were raised to 30 cents an hour, whereas the other boys received 20 cents.  Some of them had worked for Harry for two years without a raise or a promotion.  Harry explained the promotion and raise by saying, "Godda-damma, I trusta thata keed; his olda man know how to handle da money." Of course, it does not follow that because Lewis Freeman, Sr., knew how to handle money his son also had this knowledge. However, Harry believed that he did, and that was the important factor.  The rapid promotion was resented by the other boys who believed Lewis had been raised in pay and position because of his family's prestige.

Mrs. Freeman was disturbed greatly.  She was afraid that the associations of Lewis, Jr., with the class IV boys in the shop would "undermine his social position" with the boys and girls in his own class.  She said:

My friends are ashamed to have their daughters go with a cook. I can see what's in the future, but Mr. Freeman believes if a boy has the stuff in him he will not be harmed by working there. I can't see it at all. That is a Greek place, and a cheap restaurant. I have always been taught to look down upon foreigners. I do not hate them, but I might as well be honest with you and with myself. Foreigners have a place in this life, and they should keep that place, just as we should. I don't think we should put ourselves in the place of a foreigner and I don't think they should be coming over to our place. You just don't mix races, and you can't mix classes. Classes should mix with classes and not with other classes. You just can't mix people. That's what Mr. Freeman is doing with Lewis.

Mrs. Freeman's fears were more than justified. Lewis' clique relations shifted, within a month after he started working, from the group he had belonged to for years, mainly class II's and class III's, to a new clique composed of 2 class IV boys who worked for Harry and a class III boy who delivered milk for a dairy. His dating pattern also shifted from the class II and class III girls he had formerly dated to a mixed one that included some class III's, but more class IV's (some of them out of school). He soon bought a jalopy and started to make trips to Diamond City for pick-ups. Lewis learned to drink with his new clique, and, as the Superintendent of Schools put it, "carouse like a common bum; he has lost interest in school and his studies. Sometimes I believe it is my duty to talk to his father."

Shortly after his father forced him to work or quit school, Lewis referred to his father as a tightwad. But in a few months he had adjusted to his new role, friends, and personal freedom. Then he was not so critical of his father: "The old man opened my eyes to a few things. I know how to take care of myself now, anywhere, any time!"

Although the percentage of part-time workers in the three lower classes is not significantly different, the types of jobs in which they are employed differ sharply from one class to the other. Class III boys and girls are employed in office and clerical jobs one-fourth more frequently than probability indicates; the class IV's do not follow these jobs so frequently as we might expect if chance factors alone are operating; the class V's

are represented in this type of work less than one-third as often
as probability indicates.   On the other hand, the class III boys
avoid odd jobs and paper routes.   These are largely the property of the class IV boys.   No apparent selective factor appears
to operate, in so far as class is concerned, on the garage, service
station, and farm machinery jobs.   Care of children is a popular
afternoon and evening job for the class III and class IV girls,
but most parents will not trust their small children to class V's;
therefore, class V girls report this type of work one-half as frequently as might be expected.   Housework is regarded as low
class work; so the class III girls prefer baby tending.   Only 2
class III girls admitted that they did housework, and both
asked us not to tell their teachers.   The girls in classes IV and V
did not reveal any embarrassment over the fact that they did
housework, and the class V's gave the impression that they believed housework was the proper type of work for them.[4]

Being a waitress is rated as the lowest type of work a girl can
do.   The belief that waitresses are beyond the pale is widespread, and a high school girl who takes a job in any restaurant
except the Crystal Palace, which is known as the society place,
can expect to be snubbed by her peers.   The 11 class IV and
the 2 class V girls who work as waitresses are isolated from the
girls in classes II and III and from the majority of those in class
IV.   Through the years girls who have worked as waitresses have
tended to drop out of school after they have been in the restaurants a few weeks or months.   This is not unrelated, we
believe, to the stigma attached to the work.

A class IV girl who dropped a former clique mate after she
started to "hash" nights in Monk's Café said, "My friends said
Marge stank; I had to drop her.   They'd of left me out too."
Marge was deeply hurt by the silent wall she felt the girls had
erected around her.   At first she appeared to be indifferent;
gradually she quit coming to Home Makers, the one club to
which she belonged.   She was caught cutting English class while
*Idylls of the King* was being read and discussed.   She broke
down and cried to us when we asked her why she cut class.
"That snob Julia Jackson [class III] whispered to Marcia Slocum

[4] Figures on the type of jobs students held by class are given in Table
XVIII of the Appendix.

[class III], 'Marge is our scullery maid.' That was the day before I left. I won't go back there again." Marge did return to the class, but not until after her mother came to school and the teacher promised to change her seat to another part of the room.

Another class IV girl, Pauline Tryon, prepared sandwiches and fountain drinks and waited on tables in the Blue Triangle in the afternoons and evenings. Like Marge, she dropped out of all participation in high school affairs, and before the year was over she tried to quit school, but her mother refused to allow her to do this. Mrs. Tryon was aware of the implications of her daughter's job and the reputation of the place, but the family's economic position was such that there was little she could do.

We know the Blue Triangle is not a good place. It doesn't have a good reputation. Pauline and her father have talked that over, and I have talked to her. I don't want Pauline working down there, and Jim doesn't want her working there. That place has had a bad reputation for several years. The C.C.C. boys used to go there, and girls with questionable reputations hung around the place. Now when fellows come into town late, they're likely to go in there, a lot of them will be half drunk, and it's not the place for a girl like Pauline to be working. Twice recently the police have had to be called to take rowdies out of there and quiet the place down.

I would like to have Pauline work in some other place. I have been down to see Mrs. Willoughby in the notion store, and Dad [her husband] has talked to Mr. Peterson over at the theater. I have talked to Mr. Harmes [owner of a local department store]. I know him well, as I worked there for several years. He has promised to do all he can to help us place Pauline, but I don't know. I found out there was going to be an afternoon and Saturday job in the bakery. I went right down and talked to Mr. Schroff, but he said he had already promised it. [The job was filled by a class III girl whose father was a friend of Mr. Schroff.] The A & P manager has promised to put Pauline on when he has another opening. I have talked to the manager of the Prescription Drug Store, and he said he could use Pauline when trade picks up.

Both Dad and I want her out of the Blue Triangle as soon as possible. As I told you, we have seven children. There are five children younger than Pauline and one older. Dad works steady, but his salary isn't large enough to buy us the things we need, let alone the things we'd like; so Pauline has to work to earn a few extra pennies so she'll have spending money and to help buy her clothes. Sally should be working to help out, but both Dad and I have decided not to let her start working until we can find a suitable place. We don't want her to just start working.

Pauline was an attractive girl with a good personality. However, she had "two strikes against her," as one merchant said, because she worked as a waitress at the Blue Triangle, and because of her family. Her father was "only a night watchman," her mother took in roomers and boarders, and the family was large—a symbol of low status in the Elmtown value system. The Tryons, like many other low class parents, tried to help their children find desirable jobs, but to no avail. The merchants were courteous when they were asked for a job, but they put the applicant off with hollow promises: "We don't have an opening now," "When things pick up I will remember you." The merchant knew that these were empty promises, but, the class system being what it is, courtesy demanded that he make the promise or claim that he had just filled the job. When business did pick up, the job was filled more likely than not by a relative, a friend, or an adolescent in the same class as the merchant. Pauline's case is typical of the class system in action, in so far as it applies to the job opportunities open to a youngster who comes from this type of family background.

Summarizing the Elmtown economy as it affects the adolescent, we may say that job opportunities are strongly associated with the class position of the applicant. The class I family places its young men—the women do not work—in strategic positions which will lead to financial, managerial, and legal control of the major portion of the community's wealth. This process does not enter into our data because none of the 4 class I boys works; neither are they likely to enter the labor market until after they have finished college. As a rule, class II adolescents do not work, but if they do the work has to be dignified, that is, physically clean, and apart from such socially contaminating odors as hamburgers and onions. When a class II adolescent works, his parents feel apologetic and give an excuse for this departure from the class folkways; they, too, arrange for their children's positions.

Work is an essential element in the class III complex; there-fore, little stigma is attached to adolescents working part time. The parents urge them to do so, and, what is important here, a large part of the jobs these boys and girls obtain are procured for them by their parents.  Complete success in the selection of good jobs by parents and adolescents is limited by their scarcity and the oversupply of boys and girls who desire these jobs.  In this process, the class III boy or girl is given preference by the owners and managers of local business houses; but the class IV's are without much influence.

The great majority of the class IV's take what they can get. Their parents try to help them in many cases; however, their influence is negligible, as the Tryon case indicates.  When a class IV parent asks a businessman to give his child a job, his relation to the businessman is generally across a class line, for practically all business families in the community are rated as either class III's or class II's.  But when a class III parent asks a businessman for a job for a child, or a relative, he asks a favor from a class equal in many cases.  However, if the establishment is owned by a class II family, he too petitions a superior for favorable consideration.  In this case, other things being equal, the social equal (the class III) or the superior (the class II owner) normally gives the job to the class III child rather than the class IV.

The class V youngster is not helped by his parents in the pro-curement of jobs; he gets what he can after the higher class children have taken the desirable jobs.  He is discriminated against many times because of his family's reputation.  The net result of this system, in which family influence counts so heavily, is the assignment of the good jobs, such as office and clerical work, to the class II's and class III's and the respectable jobs to the class IV's; the class V's get the bad jobs, such as helping in the junk yards and hauling garbage and ashes.

### Ideas about jobs

Each adolescent in the study was asked to name the job or occupation he would like to follow when he reached maturity. This question was designed to enable us to determine if there was a relationship between their ideas of desirable vocations and class position. We realized that a very large proportion of these young people would not do the thing they thought they would like to do, but for our purposes this was beside the point. What we were interested in learning was whether or not adolescents' social perceptions of vocations were conditioned by the class culture in which they had been reared.

The vocational choice question gave a clear picture of the effects class position has on the desires and hopes, if not the ambitions, of these young people. Class I and class II adolescents in the main (77 per cent) want to be business and professional people; the remainder believe they want to be farmers, clerks, or craftsmen, in that order. Girls want to get married. This strong preference for business and the professions is reflected indirectly in the courses these students have selected. As we have seen earlier, these classes are oriented toward college and university, and their desires encompass the professions (law, medicine, engineering, architecture) and technical knowledge such as chemistry, physics, industrial management. All these vocations are within the horizon of their experiences, either in Elmtown or through family and class contacts.

Class III has somewhat the same vocational interest pattern, but it is weighted only one-half as heavily on the professional and business end of the scale, 36 per cent in contrast to the 77 per cent of the class I's and class II's. Clerical vocations are attractive to 20 per cent; 12 per cent are interested in becoming craftsmen; 10 per cent farmers; 8 per cent miscellaneous semi-skilled workers; and 14 per cent are undecided. The vocational patterns exhibited in these figures are indicative of the rising interest in vocations other than the professions and business at this level of the social structure. The interest in clerical positions and the crafts is undoubtedly a reflection of the influence of the adult vocational pattern that prevails in a large segment of this class. The large percentage increase between class II and class III of adolescents without a definite idea of their future likes is indicative, perhaps, that these youngsters have more personal responsibility to determine their future and are unable to reconcile their desires with the ability of their family's financial condition to fulfill them. By way of contrast, the class II's are expected by their families to become professional or business people. The class II family also is able to help the child accomplish his vocational objective; therefore, he has little indecision or conflict about his future if he conforms to the class and family patterns.

More class IV's want to enter the professions or business than any other occupational group, but the percentage is only 23 in contrast to 77 for the class II's, and 36 for the class III's. Twenty-one per cent of the class IV's want to be clerks, and 17 per cent craftsmen. The sharp increase in the undecided group should also be noted: 20 per cent among the class IV's in contrast to 13 per cent in class III. The farm has few attractions for these youngsters; a mere 6 per cent believe that they would like to spend their life on a farm.

The class V's present a vocational choice picture that is almost the opposite of that of the class II's. The uncertainty with which these youngsters face the future is revealed by the high percentage who have no idea about a vocation (41 per cent). Others list highly dramatic, romantic, and freak jobs, such as wild animal trainer, bareback rider in a circus, six-day bicycle racer, juggler in a carnival, which we placed in the miscellaneous group (25 per cent). The largest percentage with definite ideas of a potentially realizable job are in the craftsman group (14 per cent); 11 per cent want to be clerks, and 7 per cent want to enter business or a profession. The class V's have one thing in common with the other classes—they do not want to be farmers; only 2 per cent do.

The girls as a group and by class have more definite ideas about what they would like to do than the boys, but peculiarly enough being a housewife is not a desired vocational aim. Since we were interested in obtaining the youngsters' idea of their vocational future, the incongruity between what they said they wanted to do and what they would probably do was not raised, and to admit that one would like to get married was taboo among the girls in classes III and IV.

The girls' preferences are rather equally divided between business and the professions (44 per cent) and clerical work

(39 per cent). Only 9 per cent report indecision about their vocational futures. The remainder express interest in a wide range of miscellaneous pursuits. The girls are oriented toward occupations that require some or much technical training. Most of them will not obtain it, but the motivation is present. The boys, on the other hand, have a much wider range of interests. More than one-fourth, 29 per cent, want to go into business or enter the professions, and almost a fourth, 24 per cent, desire to become craftsmen; but one-fifth, 20 per cent, express no idea as to what they want to do. This indecision is concentrated for both the boys and the girls in classes IV and V. Clerical positions have little attraction for the boys (5 per cent), but farming has more (15 per cent). Miscellaneous jobs are listed as desirable by 7 per cent.

The pattern of vocational choices corresponds roughly with the job patterns associated with each class in the adult work world. Therefore, we believe that the adolescents' ideas of desirable jobs are a reflection of their experiences in the class and family culture complexes. These adolescents are not only aware of the differential prestige attached to vocations, but they also know the position of themselves and their families in the prestige system, and they understand the connection which exists between the father's occupation and the family's economic and prestige positions.

In this system, if the traditional American myths that every boy may become a millionaire, president of the company, or at least wealthy and that everyone who wants to can climb the socio-economic ladder prevailed equally in the four classes, the students might have been expected to name vocational desires which reflected the operation of the myths on their thinking. If this had occurred, the vocational choices would not have varied significantly from class to class. As it was, the adolescents in each class tended to name the types of vocations with which they were familiar. The class II's knew most about business and the professions; they also realized that these vocations would insure them at least as much prestige as their parents enjoyed. The class III's, on the other hand, were more familiar with small businesses, clerical pursuits, and the crafts; the class IV's were

(To be read down the columns)

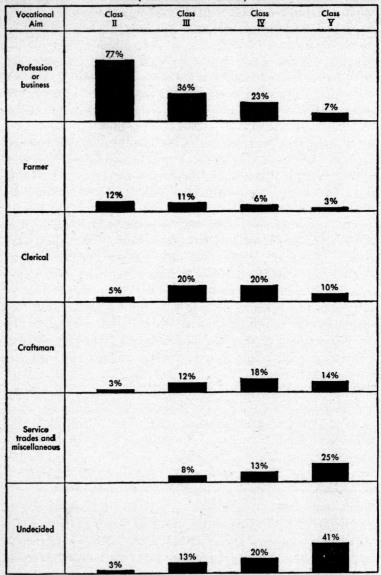

Chart II.   Vocational Choices of Adolescents by Class and Occupational Groups.

interested in clerical work and the crafts mainly, whereas the class V's were oriented toward the service trades and indecision.[5]

The relationship between class and vocational desires for the entire study group is depicted in Chart II. All cases are included in Chart II in order that an overall picture may be presented in one place for both students and non-students. The surprising thing to us is not the high percentage of youngsters in class II who want to go into business and the professions, but the low percentages in classes IV and V. Apparently these lower class youngsters, on the average, have adjusted their job desires to what they may hope to achieve. By so doing, they have limited their horizons to the class horizon, and in the process they have unconsciously placed themselves in such a position that they will occupy in the class system the same levels as their parents. The indecision in the two lower classes, especially in the out-of-school group which we shall discuss later, is clearly indicative of the limited job horizon which prevails in these classes. Finally, the jobs the adolescents have and their ideas about desirable jobs reflect significantly their family's position in the class structure. This is made evident by the corrected coefficient of contingency of 0.51. In short, they are either being forced to accept or they are willing to accept the vocational patterns the class system holds out to them.

[5] See Table XIX of the Appendix for the figures on vocational desires by class.

# 12

## RECREATION AND TABOOED PLEASURES

GENERALLY APPROVED LEISURE TIME PURSUITS, reading of good books, participation in religious organizations, membership in the Boy Scouts, are dignified by the culture as recreation and are encouraged by "enlightened elements" in the community. Depending to some extent upon the viewpoint of an individual, such things as bowling, roller skating, attending motion pictures, and dancing are defined as recreation. By way of contrast, smoking, drinking, gambling, and sex play come under the heading of forbidden pleasures in the views of most adults. Because these things are considered to be bad, they are officially denied to adolescents, and all experience with them has to be hidden in the clandestine area of behavior. These pleasures are commonly viewed as immoral, destructive of character, unhealthy, or sinful.

The clandestine pursuit of pleasure is fostered, in opposition to official protestations, by a set of conspiratorial rules which encourage the breaking of these taboos by adolescents as well as by adults. What we called the *conspiracy of silence* in Chapter 10 represents the central working principle which organizes behavior in this area of the culture. It may be summarized in the following way: One must not admit publicly the existence of tabooed behavior traits except in condemnatory terms, for to recognize their existence is bad, to condone them is abhorrent to respectable people, and to admit any knowledge of their violation is wicked. Finally, to have any interest in learning about the way the latent patterns work and the participants in them is the worst social error a person can commit. In other words, to violate a taboo is "bad"; but to talk about it is "vicious."

The boys and girls have long since learned that one talks only about the approved recreational pursuits in which one has participated to persons outside the clique. Participation in tabooed pleasures is carefully masked or denied to all but one's intimate associates, and if sex is involved not even to them. Another element in this complex is, when talking about activities which involve both recreation and tabooed pleasure one mentions only the recreational aspects to persons outside the clique. To illustrate, picnics are an approved recreation for boys and girls, and petting is generally an important activity some time during the picnic. The "necking" may be the most interesting, if not the most important, thing about the picnic, but, since it is pleasurable and involves sex play, the adolescent ignores this when he says he had a "swell time" at the picnic.

This division of adolescent leisure time behavior into public and private segments makes doubly difficult the investigation of participation in tabooed pleasurable pursuits. In the first place, many adults resented our interest in and association with adolescents in the evening hours; and, in the second, the adolescents have long since learned they might commit wrongs with impunity if they "keep their mouths shut." On the other hand, accumulation of information about the publicly approved "character-building," institutionally sponsored recreational programs is all that adolescents and adult Elmtowners expected from us. For example, the leader of the 4-H Club criticized the project in the first six weeks because we did not "consult him" about what was being done to "build character" in the farm boys and girls. The mayor stopped us on the street one day in October and invited us to come to his home and talk about the city's park and playground program, especially its swimming pool and skating rink. The spirit was different in the field of commercialized recreation. Dance hall operators and owners of low-ranking hangouts, where the boys and girls from classes IV and V spend many hours, were very suspicious of our presence and attentions until they learned that we did not care who came in to dance, loaf, work the punch board, buy a ticket in the numbers lottery, or flirt with the waitresses or factory girls who frequent the several different places in the evening. Their attitudes were connected with the fact that they sell forbidden pleasures as well as approved recreation; they allow adolescents to mix whiskey with their cokes, and some play poker in the back room for small stakes. Paula, however, stoutly maintained to the end that she does not allow high school boys in her "house," but that is not true. It is in the questionable centers of business, such as soft drink places where dancing to a "juke box" is permitted, that approved recreations, drinking sodas for instance, and forbidden pleasures, dancing combined with petting, are joined. In consequence, such places are not viewed by most parents, ministers, and teachers as "wholesome."

## Adolescent organizations

The approved character-building organizations especially for teen-aged youngsters are sponsored by the churches, the American Legion, and the Farm Bureau. Membership in each is theoretically open to any boy or girl in the age range we studied with the exception of two lodge-sponsored groups, which are restricted to youngsters who can meet fraternal requirements.[1] Since they are restrictive in their membership, we shall not discuss them further.

BOY SCOUTS. After a lapse of several years, the Boy Scouts were reorganized in May, 1937, by an influential class II boy and his father. The boy and his 6 clique mates, 3 class II's, 2 class III's, and 1 class I, composed the troop's nucleus. Five of the 7 belonged to families prominent in the Federated Church, the other 2 came from leading Lutheran families. As a result, the Federated Church sponsored the troop. A young class II professional man, also in the Federated Church, was asked to become Scout Master. A rival troop was organized in the Methodist Church in the fall of that year. The latter troop selected its members from families prominent in the Methodist Church,

---

[1] The Order of Eastern Star sponsors a chapter of Job's Daughters for high-school-aged girls. By class its membership is: class II, 4; class III, 8; class IV, 3. The Woodmen of the World foster a small group of boys in an athletic club that has its headquarters in the lodge hall. Only 4 high school boys are in it.

that is, largely from classes II and III; the Scout Master was a Methodist who came from class II. Early in 1939 the Baptists organized a third troop to "take care" of their boys, and in 1940 the American Legion was induced by the adult leaders of these troops to sponsor a troop of older boys from the three junior troops. This troop was composed of boys from 15 to 17 years of age. Its Scout Master was a popular, civic-minded, young non-legionnaire from class II, but a Rotarian.

The Boy Scouts are not looked upon as a cross section of young teen-age Elmtowners either by the boys, their adult leaders, or Elmtowners in general. The president of the district Boy Scout Council summed up the official position in these words: "Scout officials represent the better type of people. They have to—they are in scout work." On the other hand, the organization is criticized severely by members of the mill workers' union and many parents in class IV as "a wealthy boys'" group.

This criticism is in large part valid, for the Boy Scouts are very selective in their membership. In 1941–1942, 41 high school boys belonged to the Boy Scouts. By class the membership was: class II, 32 per cent; class III, 44 per cent; class IV, 22 per cent; and 1 class V, 2 per cent. These figures show the proportion each class contributes rather than what each might contribute if all the boys in each class belonged to the organization. All boys in the study are theoretically eligible for membership by age, so we may assume that they are all potential members; that is, if all other factors are equal. When the number of members is compared with the number that might join, the picture has very different dimensions. For instance, 13 of the 21 boys in class II (62 per cent) were Boy Scouts; however, only 1 of the 116 boys in class V was a Boy Scout. Obviously, the chances for a class V boy to belong to the Boy Scouts are not the same as for a class II boy.

An index of membership was constructed to measure the difference between potential and actual membership. In this index, if each class belongs in the ratio that is theoretically possible, the index for each will be 100. If a class belongs more frequently than its proportion of the total group indicates, the index is above 100; if its membership is less than proportionate the index is below 100. The bias for or against membership in each class as revealed by the index of membership is given in the last column of the following tabulation.

| Class | Number of Boys * | Number of Boy Scouts | Index of Membership |
|-------|------------------|----------------------|---------------------|
| I and II | 21 | 13 | 549 |
| III | 80 | 18 | 203 |
| IV | 152 | 9 | 54 |
| V | 116 | 1 | 8 |
| Total | 369 | 41 | 100 |

* The total number of boys in the study was used here rather than the high school group, because the Boy Scouts were supposed to be community wide, not merely for students. Actually, however, only students belonged. When a boy left school he left the Scouts.

The index of membership shows that the class II's are attracted very strongly to the Boy Scouts, the class III's to a less extent, whereas the class IV's, and particularly the class V's, are repelled. If the class II's and the class V's are compared, it is evident that the chances of a class II boy belonging are 69 to 1 as compared to the chances of a class V boy. Clearly, there is a very strong class factor at work in the Boy Scouts.

The Boy Scouts, although sponsored nominally by three churches and the American Legion, are controlled by a tightly knit clique of class II civic leaders, all members of Rotary, who take great pride in "their" movement, "their" camp, and "their" campaign for funds. In the spring of 1942, they organized a financial campaign and raised over $1,200 to support the Boy Scouts. Four of the five members of the financial committee were class II's; the chairman belonged to class I. The financial chairman told how he "put the pressure" on some people "who could not see this thing at all."

When I first started raising money for campaigns, I used to ask people to help, but I soon learned that doesn't do any good; so now I call them up and I say, "I want you to give ten dollars to the Boy Scouts, and I want ten dollars from your firm."

Last year I had the tough ones to handle. John Austin and the Townsends were the worst. I called up John and said, "I want you to give ten dollars, and I want ten dollars from Mary [his wife] and ten dollars from John, Jr., and, do you hear, I want twenty-five dollars from the Hummer Corporation!"

John hemmed and hawed around, and I said, "You rich tightwad, you can afford to give a lot more than that. I'm not going to take no for an answer." He came through, but it hurt him.

Now Jim Townsend is really a tight boy. I called him up and said, "I want twenty bucks from you and twenty bucks from Tom [Jim Townsend's brother], and twenty bucks from each of your wives. And I want fifty bucks from the company." He tried to put me off. Then he said, "Let me talk it over with Tom. I'll drop the checks in the mail in two or three days." The two or three days went by, and then I called up the cashier and said, "Billingsley, write out two twenty-dollar checks to the Boy Scouts from the Townsends' personal accounts and one for fifty dollars to the Boy Scouts from the company's accounts, and take them to Tom, and tell him I said for him to sign them, and you get them in the mail today." Tom just wouldn't back out. He's not small enough for that, and the checks came through. But I'd never been able to get the money out of them without having Billingsley put the squeeze on.

CAMP FIRE GIRLS. Two "maiden ladies" organized the Camp Fire Girls shortly after the Boy Scouts were reorganized. These women (one was on the fringe of class I; the other was in class II) knew how to organize a club with the "right kind" of support. Therefore, when they decided "to do something for the girls," they privately discussed the idea with old Mrs. Woodson and Mrs. Homer McDermott. After they had gained the approval of these worthies, the idea was presented to the Friday Morning Club. The Club voted its approval, and several members became unofficial sponsors. Inevitably the Federated Church offered its parlors to the girls for their meetings; gradually the group became identified with this church, although members of the Friday Morning Club continued to finance its activities. Originally, membership was by personal invitation rather than by sex and age groups as it had been in the Boy Scouts. This policy more or less limited membership to girls from the first three classes, with a heavy emphasis upon the upper two; but in 1939 the ranks were opened to any girl 10 years old or older who desired to join. The girls already in the organization, however, exerted informal pressures to restrict the membership to class II and class III girls and within these classes to a few cliques.

Adults in the three upper classes believe that the Camp Fire Girls is "a fine organization." They are also in general agreement that the two women who worked with these girls are doing "a remarkable piece of work." The high school girls in the group are very sure of themselves and smug in their awareness that they belong to the "right" organization. However, the girls who do not belong hold other opinions. Some are indifferent, others envious, and a minority vocal in their criticism of these girls as "snobs" and "social climbers." The Camp Fire Girls, like the Boy Scouts, really represent the girls in the upper one-fourth of the prestige structure rather than the whole, as the index of membership reveals. (No class V girl belongs or has belonged to the Camp Fire Girls.)

| Class | Number of Girls * | Number of Members | Index of Membership |
|-------|-------------------|-------------------|---------------------|
| II | 14 | 8 | 772 |
| III | 78 | 15 | 260 |
| IV | 160 | 4 | 34 |
| V | 114 | 0 | 0 |
| Total | 366 | 27 | 100 |

\* The total number of girls in the study by class.

GIRL SCOUTS. Although only 10 girls, 3 class III's and 7 class IV's, belong to the Girl Scouts, this organization merits considerable discussion, for it reveals the difficulty encountered by an organization which has the "wrong kind of leadership." It was organized about the same time as the Boy Scouts and the Camp Fire Girls. Its original sponsor was a civic-minded young woman in class III who believed that the community should do "something constructive" for its boys and girls. She was convinced that the ones to be reached were "those whose families could not help them understand what was going on around them." She got permission from the Methodists to use a room in the church as a meeting place for the proposed troop. She broached the idea to the Women's Club, the Sunday Schools, and the public schools, stressing the fact that this was a "wholesome organization" open to any girl between 10 and 14 years of age. After several months of hard work, she managed to organize a small troop, largely among the Methodist girls. This woman carried on practically alone for two years, then gave up, and the troop disbanded. One girl who did not want to see the organization die wrote to the national headquarters and asked what she could do to keep it going. The national office sent her a set of instructions and a form to be filled in by a prospective leader. When these materials arrived, she showed them to several of her clique mates who had been members. The group decided the first girl's mother would make a good leader; so they asked her to take over the troop. Even though she said she had "no qualifications," she became the leader.

The Girl Scouts never had the backing of the women from the two upper classes, nor that of the class III's until the fall of 1940, when a class III Girl Scout was able to interest her mother and a nun in the parochial school in the organization. The nun later interested a prominent Catholic class III mother. This woman was a close friend of a third woman who was influential in the American Legion Auxiliary. Through the latter woman's efforts the American Legion Auxiliary became involved. These women were instrumental in the organization of a Girl Scout Mothers' Club. This interest and activity produced a lively troop of 40 girls from the seventh and eighth grades of the parochial school and the Elmtown Central School.

The Girl Scout leader and the Mothers' Club in the fall of 1941 attempted to organize a Senior Troop among the high school girls. Their efforts, however, were quietly and effectively blocked by the high school principal and the Superintendent of Schools, with the tacit approval of certain members of the Board of Education. The principal was the son of a Presbyterian minister; he had been taught to hate and fear Catholics, so he had "his guard up" against the Catholics. When he learned from a high school teacher who had been asked to lead the proposed senior troop that the invitation had been extended by a leading Catholic woman, his deep-seated prejudices became active. He questioned the teacher closely as to "who is behind this anyway." The teacher told him the new troop was to meet in the Methodist Church, but it was sponsored by the nuns of the parochial school, the American Legion Auxiliary, and the

Mothers' Club. After he had listened to the teacher's explanation, he gave her a number of reasons why she should not take
on "such a responsibility in her first year."

The next day the principal consulted the Superintendent and
asked his advice about what the teacher should do. His story
to the Superintendent was different from the one he gave the
teacher. He explained that his teachers were busy, but he
thought that Miss X could take on the work if the Superintendent deemed it advisable; the Superintendent did not think it
advisable "under the circumstances." The principal returned
to his office and notified the teachers that they should consult
him before they entered into any community activities which
might "interfere" with their school work. The Superintendent
later told us that he believed the decision not to allow the
teachers to lead the Senior Girl Scout Troop was "wise." He
then went on to explain that he did not want to give "the
Board" the idea that he was trying to set up a "rival organization" to the Camp Fire Girls. (Two members of the Board had
daughters in the Camp Fire Girls; the Superintendent's daughter
was also in this organization.)

An old personal quarrel between two members of the School
Board and certain Legionnaires, one that had nothing to do with
educational policy, was also a factor in this action.[2] Several
years before, a former Legionnaire on the Board had been the
leader in an acrimonious squabble with the clique which was in
control of American Legion affairs in 1941–1942. The Superintendent, aware of this hostility, believed that by encouraging
the Girl Scouts in the high school he would run into trouble with
his Board because the Auxiliary of the American Legion was
helping the movement along with the Catholics. The members
of the School Board were aware of the moves the Girl Scout leaders were making, and two of them were in private severely
critical of these efforts. One Board member said:

They are just trying to copy what we did last spring in the Boy
Scouts, but you can't organize the class they have in that outfit.

[2] Five of the 7 members of the School Board had been Legionnaires, and
the President of the Board was formerly Commander of the local post, but
none of them was active in the American Legion leadership at this time.

Last year they tried to go in with us when we raised our budget, but I said, "Nothing doing." [3]

One Board member was instrumental in blocking the efforts of the county judge to organize a Big Brother movement in Elmtown. He said he did not want to see the judge "build a political machine in that class"; yet he claimed on numerous occasions that "you can't organize that class." The boys and girls in the lower classes are the victims of these personal rivalries, jealousies, and efforts of a handful of community leaders, largely in class II, to maintain prestige. The latter are in control of the schools, churches, and adolescent organizations; thus, they are able to use the institutional machinery they control to block any movement of which they do not approve.

The girls understand the sharp differences between the prestige rating of the Girl Scouts and the Camp Fire Girls. A class III girl, who had belonged to the Girl Scouts in another town and whose family had moved to Elmtown in 1939, summarized the situation neatly when she related how the Girl Scouts rated in her old home town and how active she had been there. When the family moved to Elmtown, she joined the Girl Scouts and took up where she had left off, only to drop out in three months; "Mother did not think the kids were socially what they should be. She thought the kids looked crummy." The following year she joined the Camp Fire Girls. "They are much nicer."

4-H CLUB. An active 4-H Club, which was sponsored by the Farm Bureau and led by the county agent, had 30 student members, 16 boys and 14 girls, drawn mainly from the farm population. The 4-H Club was far more popular among rural boys and girls than the Boy Scouts, Camp Fire Girls, and Girl Scouts were in town. Nevertheless, its members were drawn disproportionately from classes II and III. Since the number of rural dwellers was small in classes II and V, the class II's were combined with the class III's, and the class V's with the class IV's for purposes

[3] From the time the Girl Scouts were organized until the Mothers' Club was formed, the girls and the leader raised all their own funds by soliciting their families and by conducting cookie sales. In 1941, the American Legion Auxiliary donated $10, and the Woman's Relief Corps in the Catholic Church gave $3.

of measuring the potential membership against the actual in the index of membership. After these combinations were made, the index of membership for the boys in classes II and III was 202; and for those in classes IV and V, 54. The index for the girls was little different from that for the boys; for classes II and III it was 282; and for class IV, 88. (There were no class V girls in 4-H.)

The objectives of the 4-H Club are similar to those of the Boy Scouts, Girl Scouts, and Camp Fire Girls, but they are implemented with a very different program. The Boy Scouts and Girl Scouts and Camp Fire Girls hope, through directed recreation and study for about two hours at a weekly meeting and an annual two-week summer camp, to teach boys and girls to use their leisure hours constructively. The 4-H Club leadership has the same conception of its function, except that it reflects rural beliefs that leisure should involve the production of something useful. This is expressed in the statement of a class III farmer, "My father used to say when I wanted to play baseball, 'While you're resting, chop wood.'" The 4-H Club builds its program around this philosophy; thus, instead of meeting once a week to play games or to simulate living on a long-dead frontier, its members are engaged in individual projects.

The county agent, who is interested keenly in county, regional, and state livestock-growing contests, favors calf, hog, and chicken projects rather than a balanced program for both boys and girls. Although the woman who runs the Home Bureau in the county agent's office works with the girls on homemaking projects, stock-feeding projects are of major interest to most of the young people. All the boys and 5 of the 7 class IV girls in the club, but none of the class III girls, are engaged in livestock-growing projects. Class II and class III girls do not approve of a girl's feeding stock; this is considered a boy's job. Consequently, they are occupied with needlework and canning projects. The class III boys, however, are avid stock feeders; this is a man's role, and they fill it ably. Year after year, Elmtown farm boys bring home their share of blue and red ribbons from the State Fair in 4-H and adult competition. In 1941, a class III boy won the state junior championship with a Hereford

steer and went on to win in open competition at the International
Livestock Exposition in Chicago.

## Informal recreation

In spite of the emphasis public-spirited adults place upon the
Boy Scouts, Girl Scouts, Camp Fire Girls, and 4-H Club, only
28 per cent of the students belong or have belonged to them.
Even among the most active members they never occupy more
than a third of a youngster's free time. The informal, largely
unsupervised, activity of the clique consumes from 64 to 99 per
cent of the students' leisure hours. The percentage spent in the
different kinds of recreation and pleasures, discussed in successive paragraphs below, varies significantly from class to class.
The total amount also varies inversely with class position, as the
following percentages indicate:

| Class | Boys | Girls |
|---|---|---|
| I and II | 77 | 64 |
| III | 86 | 78 |
| IV | 95 | 87 |
| V | 99 | 96 |

These figures tell us that, even though most of the class II's and
many class III's are members of clubs, these boys and girls believe that from two-thirds to seven-eighths of their leisure time
is spent in informal group activities. Practically all the free
time of adolescents in class V is whiled away with other adolescents far from the eyes of adults who might constrain their
activities. The activities of adolescents in these leisure hours
sometimes give rise to trouble—primarily those stimulating sensa-
tions connected with the illicit violation of taboos: smoking,
gambling, alcohol, driving automobiles fast, and sex.

VISITING. Visiting in the homes of one's clique mates is a popular pastime that occurs twice as frequently among the girls as
among the boys; 26 per cent of the boys and 52 per cent of the
girls report that they visit in a friend's house once a week or
oftener. Practically all others say that they visit in their friend's
home about once a month.[4] Boys in all classes are far more

[4] The percentage of boys visiting their friends' homes by class is: class II,
38; class III, 27; class IV, 20; class V, 25. These figures are not statistically
significant.

likely to spend their leisure time away from their own or a friend's home than the girls, for they are more or less free to wander around town and to go to other towns in search of adventure and pleasure, whereas the culture places limits on a girl's freedom away from home.

The girls' visiting patterns differ significantly from class to class. The class II girl's free hours are oriented around a series of activities which involve the clique in extracurricular affairs at the high school, church parties, or music. When she is free of this round of work and fun she is usually getting ready to go to a dance or a party where she will participate once more with the clique. When the clique, or a part of it, is not busy in these ways, its members are very likely to be visiting in a clique mate's home. The same pattern applies to the class III's, except that the percentage of girls engaged in such activities is significantly lower. The class III girls in this whirl are generally members of the same clique as the class II girls. These girls appear to be lost when they are alone. If they are not engaged in some group enterprise, they are probably talking to a boy or girl friend on the telephone. These telephone visits are usually very long, and they often end with plans for a visit to continue the discussion. Perhaps a second pal is called, and the "gang" goes to some girl's house to talk, to lay future plans, to discuss something or someone, to listen to records, and inevitably to raid the refrigerator. It is not unusual for a few boys to drop in for a while, but the boys are always from the cliques the girls date. These are gay times; indeed, a pleasant way to while away the hours.

The non-social portion of class III and most of the class IV girls visit in the homes of their friends once a week or oftener, but these visits are between best friends and only one or two clique mates. The long telephone conversations are not so prevalent; neither are the record-playing sessions, raids on the ice box, and visits from the boys. The class IV girls' families do not have so many telephones, few have record players or records, and kitchen raids and spontaneous parties are not allowed in most of these homes. Thus, the home visits tend to be on a smaller scale and to take the form of discussions between close friends.

Frequent visits between girls in class V are the exception; 17 per cent report visits to friends' homes once a week or less. This level is characterized by a high degree of anonymity and individuality both within the class and in its relations to the community. Each person tends to go his own way without paying attention to his neighbors, or often even to his family. The young people belong to few, if any, community associations; they are inclined to distrust and fear, if not to hate, society; so they both isolate themselves from the other classes and are isolated by them. Their clique and recreational contacts occur on the street, in a tavern, or a hangout rather than in the home.

MOTION PICTURES. The motion picture show is the most popular recreation participated in by the students. Any night of the week some boys and girls may be seen going in or coming out of one of Elmtown's movie theaters. The peak attendance for the students who do not attend high school affairs is reached on Friday night, when they go to the ten-cent show at the Silver Bell.[5] The high school authorities believe that these ten-cent shows are presented in direct competition with plays, parties, dances, and athletic games sponsored by the school. This may be true, but it is doubtful whether the students who go to the movies would go to the high school parties even if this counter-attraction were not present because most of the Friday theater goers are from class IV, and the non-participants in extracurricular activities from class III. Saturday is the big show night for the many class II's and class III's and the few class IV's who participate in high school activities on Friday nights. The favorite theater is the Elmtown, particularly of those who have dates. Students who work on Saturday generally take advantage of the half-price matinees between one and five o'clock on Sunday afternoon. The current picture attracts some to a particular theater, but the guiding factor week after week is the

[5] The best and most popular theater, the Elmtown, located in the center of the business district, shows first-run pictures, news, and shorts. The Silver Bell, two blocks away, features westerns, second-run films, and double features on Friday nights. The Bright Star specializes in second-rate shows and sensational sex films. Local values place the theaters in a hierarchy with the Elmtown at the top, followed at some distance by the Silver Bell, and the Bright Star a very low third.

show where one's friends go. This means that the class II's and class III's and a few upwardly mobile class IV's go to the Elmtown, whereas the majority of the class IV's and class V's go to the Bright Star or the Silver Bell.[6]

Ninety-six per cent of the boys and 91 per cent of the girls attend motion picture shows with some regularity; 68 per cent of the boys and 73 per cent of the girls go to at least one show a week. More than one-fourth (28 per cent of the boys and 27 per cent of the girls) attend two or three shows a week. Three is the normal maximum, but occasionally a boy or girl goes to four in one week. The frequency of attendance differs significantly from class to class in both sexes.[7] Class II boys attend far more shows than might be expected on the basis of chance, whereas class IV's, particularly the boys, go to fewer shows than probability would indicate. Another way of stating the differences in the attendance patterns for the four classes is to say that the modal figure for class II's and class III's is two or three shows a week, for class IV's the mode is one show a week, and for class V's less than one a week.

The boys and girls who stay away from motion picture shows are principally Lutherans. The minister is so fanatical on this question that he made his young people pledge that they would not "contaminate their souls" in a commercial motion picture palace.

DANCING AND DANCES. Dancing, like the motion picture, is the center of controversy in some churches and in many homes. The Lutherans, Free Methodists, and Methodists condemn dancing on moral and doctrinal grounds. The Baptists are opposed to

---

[6] Class I, class II, and class III adults normally go to the Elmtown, occasionally to the Silver Bell, but seldom if ever to the Bright Star. Many class IV's but few class V's attend the Elmtown. The majority of the Silver Bell's patrons work in the mines and the mills, but a generous sprinkling of farmers is attracted by the westerns. The difference in admission may exert an influence, as the Elmtown charges 40 cents, and the Silver Bell 25, but we suspect custom is more important. The Bright Star is located near the railroad tracks on the poor end of Freedom Street, and the admission is 20 cents. Its patrons are almost exclusively drawn from classes IV and V, the scale being tipped toward class V's rather than class IV's.

[7] Figures on frequency of attendance are given in Table XX of the Appendix.

dancing but not so openly as the churches named above.  Many parents, who object to public dances, approve of high school dances and dances held in private homes.  Some parents who fear that dancing will corrupt their children's morals find their prejudices bolstered by religious beliefs.  Others do not want their children to stay out late at night.  Another segment, largely in class IV, is hostile to dancing since dancing and dating go together; to these people the close physical contacts of boys and girls at a dance is tantamount to the arousal of sexual desires. The persistence of these prejudices about dancing and fears of what it might lead to is marked; the young people, however, dance.  Where they dance, how often, and under what circumstances are very closely associated with their family's position in the class structure.

Periodic private parties and dances are held during the year by 7 out of 8 students in class II, by 1 out of 3 in class III, but by only 1 out of 13 in class IV, and by none in class V.  Home dances at which the boys and girls dance to music furnished by the radio or records are the most popular type of party in class II and the social segment of class III; however, seven private dances were given at the Country Club in the spring of 1942.  A total of 27 different boys and 37 girls attended these Country Club dances.  The sex disparity between the boys and the girls resulted from the tendency of girls to invite older boys they had dated in earlier years, boys who had finished high school and were going to college and were home for a week end or during vacation.  (The older girls who had graduated from high school a year to two before and were either in college or in town considered the dating of a high school boy beneath their dignity.)  The percentage of boys and girls from each class who attended one or more of these Country Club parties was: class II, 63; class III, 21; class IV, 7.  The 4 boys and 8 girls from class IV, who were included within the narrow circle of Country Club party guests, were "smooth," and active in extracurricular high school affairs—athletics, student government, music, and dramatics.  These were the same young people we mentioned earlier as being upwardly mobile persons in cliques composed of adolescents from the two higher classes;

thus, they were able to participate in activities not commonly associated with their class position.

The boys and girls who attend these Country Club parties represent "the society bunch," but to some they are "the snobs." The youngsters in this little band not only attend these Country Club affairs, but also private home parties, as well as the high school dances and games. To them, life is one party and gay time after another. The pace setters within this elite group belong to the very exclusive Tenderfoot Club, which is sponsored by two mothers of class I boys and a socially ambitious mother of a class II girl. Its membership is composed of 7 boys and 7 girls who are also in the G.W.G.'s and the Cadet Club. Twelve of the 14 belong to families in four adult cliques among which there is little intercourse, but this does not preclude their children from uniting into the most exclusive association in high school. This is the "silk stocking" younger set which John Bingham says runs the high school, and in large part he is right. Although it is not a secret group, its members operate so unobtrusively that several teachers and the majority of the students do not know of its existence. It is one of "those things one does not mention" outside the charmed circle of "we few." Those who are aware of its existence and affairs are largely class II's and class III's; the few class IV's who know about it often refer to it as that "snob bunch—they have a club and think they are somebody."

The Tenderfoot Club was organized two years before as a dance group by two mothers who controlled its membership and managed its affairs. In 1941–1942, its membership by class was: class I, 3 boys; class II, 3 boys and 6 girls; class III, 1 boy and 1 girl. The real leader of the group, the mother of a class I boy, explained its membership in this way:

> Those boys and girls are about William's age, and it just happened most of them are the sons and daughters of the girls I knew as a child.

William traced its membership to the neighborhood where he had lived since he was five years old (the 400 area).

> We lived out on the ranch until the folks built this house in 1929. I was five when we moved here and I started running with this

bunch of kids. We were together when we went to Washington School. We picked up a few new ones there. All through the first four grades we ran in a bunch. When we moved over to Central, we picked up a few more. Some moved away and some were added, but we had about the same crowd when we finished grammar school. When we got in high school, we picked up four new ones, Cliff Hendricks, Bill Warren, George Simonds, and Marge Whitney. Wilbur Sorenson [class IV] dropped out when we were freshmen. He had always been kind of on the edge though. Now he doesn't run with us at all. Then Catherine Alexander [from a class II family that moved to Elmtown when Catherine was in the seventh grade] came into the group while we were freshmen.

We started to have parties around at one another's house when we were freshmen. Then in the fall of our sophomore year Mr. and Mrs. Strayer let John [class I] have a dance at the Country Club. We had such a swell time we decided to organize into a club. The folks said it was all right, and mother agreed to sponsor us. We have lost three members in the last two years and added one. We used to have sixteen members, but we only have fourteen now. A member may invite a guest to a dance if the kids and the sponsor approve. At the annual Country Club dance, each member may invite one non-member, but that person's family must belong to the Country Club.

The Tenderfoot Club transfers the exclusive, private club idea so characteristic of the class I's and to a less extent of the class II's from the parental to the adolescent generation. There is also a hint of the "old family" tradition in its membership.

Public, Saturday night dances at Morrow's Hall on the lower end of Freedom Street are the complementary lower class form of the elaborately planned, closely supervised private dance at the Country Club. Few adolescents have the opportunity to attend the Country Club dances, but every boy with seventy-five cents, and any girl by her presence, may participate in the fun at Morrow's. But do all avail themselves of this opportunity?

Class II girls *do not go to Morrow's,* and only 4 class II boys go there regularly—to "pick up a babe." Class III boys and girls, in general, avoid Morrow's and other public dance halls, but 9 per cent, 7 boys and 6 girls, go either to Morrow's Hall or to some other public dance place in the community. The favorite non-high school dance of the class III's is the semi-private, semi-public lodge party. The class III's, however, avoid the Mill union's dances unless they are sons or daughters of skilled workers.

In the main, the public dances at Morrow's Hall and at the several dance barns scattered over the countryside are patronized by post-high school and out-of-school persons, but 33 per cent of the class IV boys and 44 per cent of the class IV girls attend them at one time or another. The comparable figures for the class V's are: 75 per cent for the boys and 61 per cent for the girls. The reputation of public dances is decidedly unsavory in the upper half of the social structure and among many conservative class IV parents. The chief criticism directed at the public dance from the "better elements" is the sale of liquor either on the premises or nearby. Even if liquor is not sold in the dance hall, it is drunk there more or less openly. Another criticism is that the dance halls are "common"; anyone may go there. Frequent fights start there, and public brawls are not a part of the action pattern of the three higher classes. A tangible effect of these attitudes is the significantly low attendance at public dances by students from classes II and III and the disproportionately high attendance from classes IV and V.

The lower class boys and girls do not have access to the Country Club, and, in large part, they cannot attend lodge dances, because few of their parents belong. They could participate in the high school dances, but they are not "comfortable" there. This self-feeling is very important in the determination of where an adolescent goes and what he does. If his friends go to a certain place and do a given thing, he feels "comfortable." If his friends are not there and the activity is outside his action pattern, he feels "uncomfortable." The boys and girls in classes IV and V who attend the dances at Morrow's Hall or Scrugg's Tavern would be uncomfortable at the Country Club, because experience has not prepared them to go to the Country Club in any capacity other than as caddy, waitress, janitor, garbage collector, or workman. Conversely, the "Country Club crowd" would be morally outraged to be invited to a dance at Scrugg's. The net effect is the segregation of the young people along class lines at the private, semi-public, and public dances.[8] The corrected coefficient of contingency of 0.62 demonstrates that there is a very real relationship between a high school boy's or girl's class position and his or her attendance at private, semi-private, or public dances.

READING. Reading of newspapers, magazines, and books is not an important trait in the students' leisure hour activities. A youngster who is known as "a reader" is looked down upon by the non-readers, and in a sense pitied, for he is left out of the group activities which form such an important part of "life" in this age group. The front page of *The Bugle* is scanned hastily, the reader often reads nothing more than the headlines and local news of personal interest, but the comic page is read carefully. To be well informed, a high school boy has to know the standing of the major league baseball teams in the summer and fall, the major college football teams in October and November, and the basketball scores in January and February. When spring comes, his attention turns to track, and baseball again. Boxing is of considerable interest; wrestling, however, is hardly noticed. Local high school sports news in *The Bugle* is read avidly to see what the local sports writer thinks of the team and the individual players. Adverse comments are criticized severely the next day by the boys around the high school.

Girls read the women's page and the society column with almost as much relish as the boys read the sports page. Their concern is focused upon clothes, cosmetics, hair styles, publicity on motion picture stars, pictures, and novels carried serially in *The Bugle,* rather than the bridge, food, and household columns.

Picture magazines such as *Life* and *Look* are the most popular items in the periodical field. They are followed by the popular weeklies—*Collier's, Saturday Evening Post,* and *Liberty.* The home monthlies—*Woman's Home Companion, McCall's, Good Housekeeping*—are next in order. Farm periodicals are looked over by most of the farm youth, but not read to any extent. Sex, screen, comic, western, and detective stories are read more widely than the above-mentioned magazines that are taken in the home on a subscription basis. This group is purchased by

[8] The distribution of non-high school dances by class and type of dance is presented in Table XXI of the Appendix.

the copy from one of the local news stands and circulated clandestinely from student to student. Their circulation is not limited to any class, but one gained the impression from months of observation that there is more reading of sex and adventure stories among the youngsters in classes IV and V than in the two upper classes, but this is only an impression.

A more adequate picture of the students' reading habits was obtained from a study of the way the high school group used the public library. The withdrawal cards for each person for the six months from September through February were copied.[9] These cards show the number of books each boy or girl borrowed, but not the name of the book. Therefore, our figures are on volume, presumably read, rather than on content. In the period covered, 54 per cent of the boys and 34 per cent of the girls did not borrow any books. To borrow or not to borrow is associated significantly with class position among the boys, but not among the girls where the percentage of non-borrowers shows little variation from class to class: class II, 29; class III, 36; class IV, 33; and class V, 39. The percentage figures of non-borrowers among the boys are: class II, 43; class III, 45; class IV, 65; and class V, 88.

The (roughly) two-thirds of the girls and one-half of the boys who borrowed books in this six-month period did not read extensively. The girls averaged 2.2 and the boys 2.1 books each. Sixty-three per cent of the boys and 36 per cent of the girls borrowed one book each. An additional 25 per cent of the boys and 22 per cent of the girls withdrew two books. Thus, only 12 per cent of the boys and 42 per cent of the girls took more than three books from the library. The class II boys who borrowed books withdrew exactly twice as many, on the average, as the girls in the class; in the other classes, the girls borrowed more books than the boys. The book-borrowing habits of the boys and girls in classes III and IV were little different from one to the other. The picture was radically different between the sexes in class V, where 1 boy borrowed one book, but 11 of the 18 girls (61 per cent) borrowed 3.3 books each. The class II boys

[9] Miss Marchia Meeker of The Committee on Human Development co-operated with us in this task. Her help is gratefully acknowledged.

and the class V girls borrowed almost the same number of books on the average.

The inverse relationship between the number of books borrowed by the boys and girls in the several classes is interesting and suggestive. If we assume that the books borrowed from the library are read, it appears that different factors are operating in each sex in the opposite directions. We might suggest that the class II boys read for information, whereas the class V girls read to escape. Although these are only hints, they are based upon inferences derived from observations of the overall behavior patterns of the two groups. The class II boys tend to take their school work seriously, because they look forward to college and professional preparation. The class V girls are isolated in the high school and to a large extent from their out-of-school peers. Although their overall prestige position is low, they are a highly select group within their class; the fact that they are in high school is indicative of their singular status within class V. By reading, they can occupy their time, amuse and possibly improve themselves. The same type of argument may be applied to the class IV girls, who read on an average more than the class II girls, 2.4 books in contrast to 1.6 books each. Although more class II than class IV girls borrow books, they borrow fewer per person. Going to the library is popularly approved on this level, and a gesture of one's search for culture, but to read one has to sit down alone, a trait these girls, busy with their school work, extracurricular affairs, church meetings, clubs, dances, and parties, have not developed.

The librarian estimates that about 75 per cent of the books borrowed by high school students are used in connection with their course work. The school library has less than a hundred reference books, a dozen periodicals, one encyclopedia, and a large dictionary. Therefore, books needed for outside reading have to come from the public library. Civics, current problems, American history, and English courses require the student to read one outside book each. A popular trick used by many students is to borrow a book from the library, read it, and then tell the story to clique mates. Another clique mate reads another book and outlines the material. In this way, a student might read one book but receive credit for three or four. This system appears to be most widely used among the hyperactive students who have little time for their studies; this is also the group which borrowed relatively few books but received the best grades. Students who read for pleasure or information are in a distinct minority. Moreover, they are generally isolated from the popular crowd who skim the surface of the newspapers, magazines, and books and then go gaily on to their many time-consuming pleasures in the company of their pals.

BOWLING AND ROLLER SKATING. Bowling is a popular indoor sport in the higher classes, as roller skating is in the lower classes. These sports are related inversely to class position in both sexes, as the following tabulation indicates:

| Class | Percentage of Boys Who | | Percentage of Girls Who | |
|---|---|---|---|---|
| | Bowled | Skated | Bowled | Skated |
| I and II | 52 | 9 | 64 | 14 |
| III | 23 | 18 | 30 | 38 |
| IV | 17 | 23 | 20 | 48 |
| V | 00 | 50 | 00 | 69 |

A second interesting thing that became evident in this phase of the study was the small amount of overlapping between these sports; that is, the skaters do not bowl, and the bowlers do not skate, except in classes III and IV where the overlap is 6 and 9 per cent respectively.

Bowling occupies the highest prestige position in the socially correct list of winter sports, as golf does in the summer, among the elite students in classes II and III. These students look upon roller skating as "low class stuff," "a cheap sport." Skating is a much cheaper sport than bowling, a fact which appeals to youngsters who have little money, and it is not coincidence that these young people come disproportionately from classes IV and V. A boy or girl can skate from four to six o'clock in the afternoon for 10 cents and all evening for 20 cents, whereas it costs 15 cents to bowl a line in the afternoon and 25 cents in the evening. This does not appeal to very many youngsters with only 10 or 20 cents to spend in an afternoon or an evening. Such persons have more fun at the skating rink where they skate to the music of an electric gramophone with an oversized loud-speaker. There they may waltz, fox trot, speed-skate, crack the whip, or skate with a date and neck in the corners, for hours on end, cheaply.

The high school authorities frown upon students' skating, except Tuesday afternoon and evening, when all other patrons are barred. Young people in classes II and III, particularly the girls, if they do not want to be suspected of loose morals, avoid the skating rink, for many young men go there to pick up dates; and frequent quarrels, which end in fights, are common. Most students skate on Tuesday afternoon and evening, but 14 boys (2 class III's, 10 class IV's, and 2 class V's) and 45 girls (5 class III's, 34 class IV's, and 6 class V's) skate regularly on Friday and Saturday nights. All these adolescents are rated as "grubbies" by their peers. One clique of 5 girls (4 class IV's and a class V) in this larger group skate four or five nights a week. All of them have shady reputations; they are known as "easy marks" among the boys and as "fast numbers" among the girls. The other girls ignore them in school and around the skating rink. The boys even avoid them around school, but on Friday and Saturday nights the "clippers" and "wolves" hang around them like flies around sugar on a summer's day. These girls are often the center of fights between lower class high school boys and boys in the out-of-school group. That sex is the object of attack and counter-attack is understood in the adolescent world. Three of the girls admit that they have had sex relations with their "boy friends"; another one said, "We've gone all the way lots of times." Questioned as to the meaning of this she explained circuitously, in conformance with the linguistic usages associated with the sex game, that all five girls in the clique had sex relations with the "right fella."

If a high school girl hangs around the bowling alley in the evening, she invariably has a bad reputation among her peers. After eight o'clock the alley is taken over by couples (mainly young adults who work in Elmtown's stores and offices) and middle-aged businessmen. Women from classes I and II who bowl in the afternoon in teams and cliques do not go to the alley in the evening, because the proprietor allows players and spectators to drink hard liquor after eight o'clock. He has a small corner room where customers mix whiskey, gin, or rum, which they bring with them, with the "cokes" they buy there, or drink from the bottle. Those who "spike" their cokes drink openly in the spectators' gallery or on the players' benches. The association of illegal liquor, commercial pleasure, and innuendo combine to taboo the alley for most girls at night.

HUNTING, FISHING, AND TRAPPING. Hunting, fishing, and trapping are strictly male activities. All the boys report that they fish some time during the spring and summer in Indian River or a tributary creek. Boys in classes I, II, and III fish almost exclusively on property owned by their families or friends or in the area controlled by the Fish Club; boys in classes IV and V fish wherever and whenever they can. Since there are abundant nearby waters, little attention is paid to where a boy fished except around the Fish Club.

Hunting for pheasants, rabbits, and ducks is general among the boys in the fall and early winter, but it is not so easy to find a place to hunt as to fish. During the hunting season, most farms are posted against hunters, but it is easy for a local person who is not a class V member to get permission to hunt on a farm that belongs to a relative or friend. The class V's are largely town dwellers, and since they are distrusted generally it is difficult for them to gain permission to hunt on a given piece of land, even if they take the trouble to ask the owner.

The younger town class IV's and almost all class V's do not bother to ask anyone if they may hunt on his land. They fish with impunity and consider it their right to do likewise in the hunting season. They also generally know where the game hides much better than the other boys, because a good bit of their free time is spent on or along the river; so they go directly to these places without regard for farmers or livestock. The game wardens and irate farmers who occasionally catch teen-aged poachers normally run them off the property, but some are brought to town and warned by the district attorney after a lecture that a second offense will result in a possible fine and probation.

During the winter, trapping muskrat, fox, skunk, coon, and weasel is a popular sport and part-time occupation of 13 per cent of the boys. Most farm boys trap some while they are in elementary school, but the trait is not carried over into high school to any extent, except in classes IV and V. Seventy-five per cent of the boys in class V, 20 per cent in class IV, 5 per cent in class III, and none in class II trap. Trapping is a "low class" and a "young boy" trait; 16 of the 23 trappers are freshmen, the remaining 7 are sophomores. These boys are also non-daters, except in class V, where two boys date girls of the same class.

Dating and trapping do not go together for various reasons. The trappers are rather uncouth in their manners and grooming; their faces and hands are grimy, their clothes rumpled and stained, and the odor acquired in handling and skinning wild animals pervades the area where they sit in school. When a skunk is caught, the whole school knows of the trapper's good fortune.

By the time a boy reaches the sophomore year, he is usually ready to date, and, through subtle controls exerted by his peers, he learns that the trapper is a marked man. To avoid the condemnation of his fellows and to appear in a favorable light to the girls, he quits trapping if he is in class III or class IV. The class V boy quits trapping and school about this time. Rearing rabbits, guinea pigs, pigeons, and pups is another younger boy pastime found in all strata, but with greater frequency in classes III and IV than in classes II or V. Rearing of pets, like trapping, fades out when a boy grows old enough to start dating.

TEAM GAMES. Baseball, football, field hockey, and basketball are common pre-adolescent activities without a significant association with class which carries over into high school among a considerable number of the freshman and sophomore boys. Although 41 per cent of the boys report that they play the team game in season with pals once a week or oftener, the distribution is skewed definitely toward the younger boys. Almost two players out of three (64 per cent) are freshmen, and an additional 17 per cent are sophomores. Three factors produce this situation: First, unless he is highly skilled or large for his age, it is difficult for a younger boy to "make the team"; if he has free time (and most younger boys manage to find some a few times each week), he rounds up his pals or they look him up, and an informal game is started. Second, younger boys do not have equal opportunity with older boys to find part-time work. Finally, they are not so likely to be interested in girls, pool, bowling, or high school extracurricular activities.

The shift from informal team games played in the open to team games carried on inside buildings is part of the maturation process that occurs during the middle years of high school. Since the culture frowns upon the big boy who acts like a youngster, the approved role in the junior and senior years is to watch the highly skilled, carefully trained varsity team play. We believe that the subtle process of identification of self with the team enables the non-player to play the game vicariously and simultaneously to enjoy its thrills through deep ego involvement. After the game, he experiences the warm glow of glamorizing the players with those who shared the experience with him. This process was evident to us as we went to the shower rooms with the players after the games, and then on to the "coke spots" with "the gang," where the players were the center of attention.

POOL. The pool hall is strictly male territory, and the taboo against a female entering it is never broken. If a female has to communicate with a male in the pool hall, she either sends in a man with a message or goes next door to the drug store and telephones. Even tapping on the window or calling through the door is never done. Yet, the pool hall is a respected establishment. The proprietor does not allow any "rough stuff," profanity, loud talk, or vulgar stories; even petty gambling between the players is carried on in a discreet way.

The pool hall is a center of gossip, news, and story telling. If a boy does not play, he is always welcome in the gallery if he is not a recognized member of class V. The owner of the pool hall discourages this class from frequenting his place for he does not want it to become, as he said, "a hangout for such bums." Part of the pool hall's popularity among the young men may have grown out of the fact that it is the most convenient place for a boy to go to get out of the weather. It is always warm inside, and any sober man is welcome there as long as he behaves; few middle-aged or older men frequent the place. This is the favorite hangout of farm boys when they are in town. During the week, if a country boy has to wait for a member of his family, he usually goes to the pool hall. On Saturday night, from 25 to 30 farm boys may be found there some time during the evening. They drift in before a date, after the show, and sometimes after a date.

Pool is the most popular male game in all classes; 63 per cent of the boys play. In addition, it is not associated with class position except in class V; no class V boy plays pool.

Eighty per cent of the pool players play once a week or oftener, about a fourth of this group play four or five times a week, and an additional third two or three times a week. The remainder play once a week; the minority, 20 per cent, play two or three times a month. Frequent play or none is encouraged by the custom which prevails that the loser pay for the game. Each player knows the relative ability of the others; if one is a poor player, it is to his advantage to improve, move to another clique, or stop playing. The unskilled boy, if he likes the game (and under the competitive conditions most do) works to improve. The only way he can do this is to play as often as his finances permit. The boys who try to win at all times are ostracized by their pals, and the "pool shark" who lies in wait for the unwary novice is soon unmasked. The boys simply refuse to play with him; so he is forced to play the game like the rest or move into the older youth group where skilled players keep him in check. Pool, like other games, is played by cliques, and there is little social interaction other than casual stray remarks between the different groups. For instance, one clique of boys from classes II and III play almost daily at the front table, and another composed of boys in classes III and IV play at the back table; but there is practically no interaction between them.

### Tabooed pleasures

Law and the mores deny high school students the right to enjoy the pleasures derived from tobacco, gambling, and alcohol. However, the mystery with which adults surround these areas of behavior lends them a special value which seems to act as a stimulus to many young people who desire to experience the supposed thrill of pleasures their elders deny them. *The conspiracy of silence* which is an essential part of the clandestine violation of the mores has already taught them how easy is to avoid restrictions imposed by law and taboo if they are discreet about how, where, and under what circumstances it is done.

Acquisition of knowledge of the means of transgressing against alcohol, tobacco, and gambling taboos without being caught and the thrill of violating these taboos take place for the most part in the clique. For instance, little boys as young as five years of age privately experiment with smokables, in association with other boys, and sometimes with little girls who are perhaps only a year or so older. As they grow older, they become bolder about smoking and turn to tobacco almost entirely. By the time high school is reached, the smoking pattern has narrowed down to cigarettes, with an occasional try at a pipe or cigar. Elmtown boys rarely chew tobacco except to see how it tastes. If one's clique smokes, one is almost compelled by the pressures inherent in the group to smoke, but if one belongs to a clique in which smoking is frowned upon, one loses personal status by smoking; and if the violation of the clique code continues, one will be expelled. To be in a clique in which socially tabooed activities are a part of its action pattern, one has to participate in them. The reason is that one's membership is dependent, first, upon the conformity to the values held by the majority of the group and, second, upon how congenial the activities participated in by the group are to him.

SMOKING. The 77 per cent of the boys and 29 per cent of the girls who smoke [10] know when and where to smoke. Boys approve of smoking for boys in the pool hall, the hangout, in a private car, on the street after dark, on dates, and out of town. Smoking is taboo around the high school, at high school athletic games, dances, church, and Boy Scout meetings. Girls may smoke in the clique and on dates, but not on the street. Freshman girls lose face with both boys and girls if they are known to smoke. This rule is violated by a few girls, both in their cliques and on dates, but if the violation becomes known, the offenders are gossiped about, snubbed, left out of parties, and generally treated with contempt. Two sure ways for a freshman girl to "lose caste" with her peers is to date out-of-school and

[10] Smoking is associated in each sex with particular cliques throughout the class structure. There is no significant difference in the number who smoke from class to class among the boys, but the number of girls in classes II and V who smoke is significantly higher than the number in classes III and IV.

out-of-town boys and to flaunt openly the anti-smoking taboo. Six freshman girls are known to have violated the rule in one way or another; one is in class II, three in class IV, and two in class V. The class IV and class V girls belong to a clique that is known for its wild behavior on dates and at public dances. We have mentioned them before and we shall have occasion to refer to them again.

Girls who smoke in their cliques when they want to act sophisticated have to be careful about where they do it, especially if the place is public or semi-public. A few cliques smoke in the back booths of student hangouts after school, early in the evening, or on Saturdays. Smoking on dates is approved if the boy smokes, but a girl does not smoke if the boy is a non-smoker. Smoking and drinking usually occur together on dates. Those sophisticated enough to go into a tavern for a drink believe they are mature enough to smoke while they visit over their drinks. This trait is limited rather severely to the seniors, and the pattern appears among the juniors with increasing frequency as the school year advances. The dating-drinking-smoking pattern is observed also among sophomores who associate with the elite juniors and seniors.

A trip to the Cloverleaf, a night club on the highway some twenty miles away, or to Cherry's, in Elmtown, after the show, game, or a dance is routine among the elite seniors and most juniors. The class II freshman girl mentioned above who ignores the no-smoking rule associates with this sophisticated elite; she drinks and smokes with the crowd at the Cloverleaf, or in Cherry's, at the expense of her reputation both within her school class and clique ranges. Her ability to stay in this crowd stems from her family position, and her attraction for the older boys. She always has dates with the most popular boys in the crowd— when the girls have parties for which they can control the invitations she is cut from the list. Her tactics with the boys are resented by every girl in the elite group. The fact that she violates the taboos against freshman drinking and smoking is justification enough for them to ostracize her whenever they can; in addition, she is known to be a "date stealer."

This girl has mastered the glamour role in the culture; she knows how to groom herself so that she is sought after by the boys. To be seen with her adds to a boy's prestige in the elite peer group; to have a date with her is "something." She pets with her dates discreetly—never goes too far, just far enough to make them come back again. Part of her success with the elite boys rests on her known rule to accept the first boy who asks her, but she limits her dates to the boys acceptable to the elite coterie. She lies to boys not on her approved list with impunity and refuses them dates no matter when they ask her. Boys outside the circle resent her actions, but she has plenty of dates within it. The girls gossip about her "boldness," but she successfully violates the rule against a freshman girl's smoking and still maintains her prestige with the boys.

GAMBLING. Gambling is primarily a male activity, although the girls on special occasions, such as a basketball game, bet one another a sandwich, soda, or a coke on the outcome. Betting in this more or less spontaneous manner is not viewed in the same light as gambling. Gambling is defined in the adolescent group, as in the adult culture, as deliberate wagering of money on some test of skill or strength or on the outcome of a game. Student mores condemn deliberate public gambling, but it is approved tacitly; moreover, it is not so immoral for boys as for girls. Girls sometimes play slot machines in out-of-town taverns at the invitation of their date; however, it is not good form for a girl to ask to play the machines or to use her own money on them.

Gambling is concentrated disproportionately among the boys in classes II and III who have more time and money for this pastime than those in classes IV and V. Sixty per cent of the boys, in contrast to 5 per cent of the girls, are known to gamble, in one way or another, at almost any time and in any place, and 77 per cent of these gamblers are class II's and class III's, whereas only 59 per cent of the student boys belong to these classes. Unlike smoking and drinking, there are no tabooed areas for the gamblers. Although it was forbidden around the school, frowned on in church, and prohibited everywhere by law, to those who gambled none of these restrictions is complete or observed. Penny matching is a favorite game in the Commons Room of the high school during the noon hour; some boys toss coins to a line on one end of the room when no teachers are near; a few boys even match pennies in Sunday School.

Anyone may gamble in service stations, drug stores, the pool hall, the bowling alley, and in most cafés, either on punch boards or the numbers; in addition, slot machines are located in a number of taverns and some out-lying cafés. The pool players and bowlers usually gamble on the outcome of the game; low man pays for everyone's game. In addition, side bets—a coke, a nickel, or a dime—are made between the players, often by a "kibitzer," on a particular shot. Poker players are the most frequent and persistent gamblers. Poker is played regularly, once a week or oftener, by about 20 per cent of the boys, and about two or three times a month by an additional 20 per cent. The regular poker players regard gambling as a part of the game; the irregulars admit they gamble part of the time.

"THE DEMON RUM." Adult Elmtowners realize there is some drinking among high school students, but they officially dodged the issue and frowned upon our efforts to find the facts. Perhaps they feared that more violations of the mores would be discovered than they liked to think existed among the students. This reluctance to learn the extent of young people's participation in tabooed behavior sometimes stemmed from anxiety that investigation would prove to be embarrassing, as it did in several cases.

Elmtowners support 14 taverns, a wholesale liquor distributor, and three private bars inside the city, five taverns outside the city limits, and an additional private bar in the Country Club. This is a ratio of one public bar to each 525 inhabitants; if all liquor outlets are included, the average is one to 435 persons. In Home State, a tavern is not required to sell food. However, 11 of the 19 are combination restaurants and bars, and 18 provide their patrons with some gambling device to help them enjoy their drinks, food, and leisure.

Taverns are prohibited by law to sell alcoholic beverages to minors, but nearly all tavern keepers sell liquor to high school students and ask no questions. The members of the Board of Education know that high school students can buy liquor locally, and that many of them do. One member, under the urging of the Lutheran and Methodist ministers, is eager to enforce the law. His fellow members sensibly point out that those who want liquor will get it by going to other towns or by having an older boy buy it. The Superintendent and the principal know that a number of students have obtained liquor on different occasions. They take the same position as the majority of the Board, namely, that drinking among the students is "no concern of ours so long as it does not occur while the students are under our control." The high school dances are patrolled as carefully as possible to detect the presence of alcohol, and only three students have been known to drink before coming to a high school affair. The peer group mores do not sanction this behavior, and a student who violates the code out of bravado loses status with his fellows, even if the school authorities do not detect his violation.

Drinking is approved by the majority of boys as long as it is done away from the school, the church, and generally away from parents, but there are exceptions. A rule strictly followed within the peer group when alcohol has been taken is: Do not talk around teachers, preachers, or parents; if they start questioning you about who is drinking, do not admit anything. Nevertheless, some students talk from time to time about certain students' drinking, often only after the person gossiped about has drunk to excess. But if adults try to track these stories down they invariably encounter denial after denial; no one knows anything.

Thirty-nine per cent of the boys and 19 per cent of the girls drink alcohol in some form during the school year, usually away from home, and always away from church and school.[11] Drinking in both sexes is associated significantly with class [12] as well as with age. Where, when, and with whom one drinks are more strongly associated with class than the mere fact of drinking or abstinence, as we shall point out in later paragraphs. Abstinence is significantly greater among the fourteen-year-olds than among the seventeen-year-olds in both sexes, and among all classes, except among the boys in class V, none of whom is in

[11] These figures are not essentially different from those reported recently for high school students by Raymond G. McCarthy and Edgar M. Douglass, "Instruction on Alcohol Problems in the Public Schools," *Quarterly Journal of Studies on Alcohol*, Vol. 8 (1948), pp 609–635.

[12] The $X^2$ for the boys is 17.2569 and for the girls 15.1453 between class position and drinking or abstinence; 3 degrees of freedom. Both figures are significant at the 0.01 level.

school.  A corrected coefficient of contingency of 0.76 between
class and age among the fourteen- and seventeen-year-old boys
in classes II, III, and IV who abstain from or drink alcoholic
beverages shows that age and alcohol are connected one with
another in these groups.  In this case, the drinkers are mainly
the seventeen-year-olds and the abstainers the fourteen-year-
olds.  The girls reveal somewhat the same pattern, but the association is much lower (the corrected coefficient of contingency is
0.43); both coefficients are significant.  These figures tell us
that sometime between the fifteenth and the eighteenth years,
or between the freshman and the senior years of high schools,
two-fifths of the boys and one-fifth of the girls begin to participate illegally in the clandestine pleasures of alcohol.

Drinking is surrounded in most Elmtown homes by so many
constraints that strong pressures are necessary before an adolescent overcomes emotional blocks against alcohol which result
from his early family training.  Some adolescents have been
allowed to have a drink occasionally with their families; most,
however, take their first drink away from home, usually with
their "best friend."  The stimuli which motivate a boy to violate
alcoholic taboos are often provided in the peer group, in rare
cases by older persons with whom he is in close contact.  If a
boy starts to drink with a companion who is not a regular member of the clique, and the other clique mates object to alcohol,
the drinker is ostracized.  In such cases, the drinker often is
incorporated into a clique in which drinking is common.  However, if the drinker is "swell" or "O.K.," it is not long until he
initiates the group into the mysteries of alcohol.  When the
majority of a clique learns to drink, and one boy resists, he, in
turn, is compelled to seek companionship in a clique more com-
patible with his beliefs on this question.  Clique drinking, once
it has begun, continues throughout the high school years.  Drinking among the boys sometimes begins in the freshman year,
but more generally in the sophomore year.  By this time most
boys are fifteen, and the peer culture defines one of this age as a
"man."  To prove it he should have at least tasted liquor, or
claimed, in his clique, that he has.

If the drinking stories can be trusted, some four out of five
boys start drinking with their pals when the clique gains the

nerve to buy a bottle of wine, whiskey, gin, or some beer, and carries it to the woods, out to the park, into the country, or some other place where the group can drink in relative secrecy. On these occasions the boys wait to see what happens; since they have been trained by previous experience in the culture to associate rowdiness with liquor, they expect to "whoop it up." The boys believe a few drinks will make a person "noisy," "mean," and "unable to control himself." By going to some out-of-the-way spot they take the precaution of being able to react to expectancy and not be caught. Although this is the general pattern, a minority go out of town, boldly enter a tavern, and order a drink. This occurs usually when a younger boy is with an older one who has already been initiated into the alcoholic ritual.

Excessive drinking generally results from a celebration or a boy's attempt to impress his clique mates that he can drink and "hold it like a man." It is not unusual for a boy to take a few drinks, then deliberately go to the clique's hangout where he hopes to be seen by his pals. To properly impress one's peers, it is good form to overact the part. Sometimes the pseudo-drunk's real condition is diagnosed; then the boys belittle him and accuse him of acting drunk. A common reaction to this scepticism is to start drinking to prove one's "real" ability. Once a group has a boy on the defensive, and he starts drinking to justify his ego before his tormentors, the boy is given drink after drink to see how much he can hold. In this way, older boys often talk a younger boy into getting so drunk the victim loses control of himself, becomes sick, and has to be taken home. A variant of this type of excessive drinking is the attempt of a clique's members to impress one another with the amount each can hold. By circular stimulation and response, the drinkers talk themselves into one drink after another until they become intoxicated.

Clique drinking was the accepted way to celebrate special events—the end of the football season, a high school victory or defeat, a birthday, a holiday, a thwarted love affair, a parental dressing-down. Such occasions justify the clique's "chipping in" for a bottle. On such occasions the boys are more likely to drink to excess than at any other time; the stimuli which motivate the party may contribute to the overdrinking. A secondary factor is the excitement created as the bottle is passed around in the men's room of the pool hall, the court house, in a service station, down the alley, or in a car.

Saturday night is the most popular time for a celebration. Every Saturday night between 11:30 P.M. and 1:30 A.M., from two to seven or eight cliques in various stages of intoxication can be observed in the Blue Triangle drinking strong, black coffee and eating sandwiches before they go to their respective homes. Usually about a half dozen, class IV boys mainly, become so intoxicated every Saturday night they have to be taken home by their pals. The standard routine in these cases is to get the boy over his sickness by walking him or plying him with black coffee, then taking him to the door of his home and leaving "fast."

Drinking on Saturday night is more widespread in the athletic crowd both during and after training than in any other group in high school. Only two boys on the football and one on the basketball team are total abstainers. The others vary in the amounts they drink—a few boys take a drink or two to be "sociable" and some become fully intoxicated. The heaviest drinking takes place immediately after the end of the football, basketball, and baseball seasons, when practically the whole team goes to another town for a dinner and an informal bout in the taverns. Some stag drinking is indulged in on Friday night by the athletes, but this is unusual since the high school dances are held then and the athletes generally attend the dances.

The coach knows his players are drinking, but he feels that he can do nothing to stop them. He disapproves of it, lectures them on the need to keep in training, and on the consequences for them personally, for the team, and for the school if they do not, but it does little good. He discusses the question with the Superintendent and the principal, who decide to say nothing and do the best they can because the most flagrant offenders are class II and class III boys.

Clique drinking is supplemented by couple drinking when boys start to date, borrow the family car, and move freely about the countryside. Couple drinking begins on a very experimental scale late in the sophomore year and becomes more general in the junior year. By the time the senior year is reached, some four out of five boys take their dates after a high school dance to Cherry's or drive to the Cloverleaf.

No evidence was accumulated that the girls do any drinking in their cliques. Usually a girl begins to drink at a party with her date. Generally, these first social drinks are taken in a roadhouse or an out-of-town tavern. After the first thrill, excitement, and fear of drinking has passed, the couple often slips into Cherry's and orders a mixed drink. Couple drinking is usually of a very mild nature; ordinarily it consists of one cocktail or a bottle of beer. There are some exceptions, but they are so spectacular that student gossip overemphasizes their importance. For instance, a class II boy driving home one Saturday night from a neighboring town, where he and his girl friend had attended a party, ran off the road and smashed his car. Two other couples who had been to the party saw what happened and brought them to town. A wrecker was sent back for the other car, and the incident was hushed up by the families and the insurance agent. The clique involved talked among themselves in a very guarded manner about the party. Gradually the gossip spread among the elite group. After the excitement had passed, it was learned that the boy had had seven Scotch and sodas in the course of the evening and the girl had taken two Manhattans. When such incidents happened, the students exercised censorship in their discussion of the matter with outsiders.

Drinking at private parties is limited almost exclusively to the students in classes II and III and the few in class IV who "make the grade." Punch "spiked" with gin or whiskey is the customary beverage at these parties. "Spiking" the punch is done discreetly by the mother of the host or hostess of a house party, or by the manager of the Country Club at the direction of the parents when the parties are held there. It is not good form to have a bottle at either home or Country Club parties, although one boy on one occasion brought a flask and hid it in the men's restroom at the Country Club. He and a few close friends tapped it throughout the evening. They became slightly unruly and objectionable and were asked by the host to leave. This was so unusual that it was gossiped about for weeks, and the guilty boy was snubbed for the rest of the year.

During the Christmas holidays, a half-dozen private parties were held by different class I and class II families for their children and friends; the punch was spiked at four of them. Two mothers openly related that they had mixed gin with the fruit juices and they defended their behavior by saying that they knew the young people liked "zip" in their punch. Holiday dances at the Country Club are either preceded or followed by cocktail parties at someone's home, and it is not unusual at this level to serve high school students in a different home from adults. For instance, one class II mother invited to an eggnog party after the New Year's dance at the Country Club 8 couples who ran around in the clique her daughter dated. This mother related that the group drank two gallons of eggnog and called for more, but she was out of brandy; so she gave them coffee.

Outside of the Country Club crowd, couple drinking is limited to the public taverns, for private cocktail parties are not part of the culture complex in classes III and IV. Drinking in these strata occurs on Saturday nights before, during, and after the public dances in four or five taverns in neighboring communities and two in Elmtown.

Public drinking among the girls in class III is relatively light except in the case of two cliques composed predominantly of class IV's, but there are 2 class III's in one and 1 in the other who are known for wild behavior and excessive drinking. These girls are avoided by other high school girls; even the high school "wolves" and "clippers" do not date them. They are dated almost exclusively by boys from out of town, and it is not unusual to hear of their Saturday night escapades on Monday.

# THE OUT-OF-SCHOOL ADOLESCENT

PART IV IS AN EXAMINATION of a few of the interrelations between the class system and the activities of the 345 young people, 47 per cent of the study group, who had begun a full-time adjustment to adult life. Four major topics are emphasized: withdrawal from school, the job, recreation and pleasure, courtship and marriage.

Important blocks of data on high school life were missing, perforce, from the experience of youths in the out-of-school series. The out-of-school youngsters were scattered in the community, and most of them followed adult pursuits. Their social and leisure time activities were different from those of the adolescents in high school. The high school group, by way of contrast, was concentrated in one area for seven to eight hours a day under institutional control. This concentration enabled us to watch them, to talk to them, and to participate in their activities. Thus, we came to know them in a very personal way, whereas our contacts with many adolescents in the out-of-school group were more formal and of a touch-and-go nature.

The high school group was the major *obvious* interest for a very practical reason: The community expected us to spend our time with the students rather than with the out-of-school adolescents. Early in the study, tension was detected among school officials and community leaders when interest was expressed in *all* youth in the community, not just those in high school. Some possible explanations for this may become clear when the process of leaving school is analyzed in Chapter 13.

It was very difficult to collect the data we desired from all out-of-school youths. Extensive, systematic observations of their behavior on the scale used on the in-school group was impossible simply because they did not operate in the same areas of social interaction as the adolescents in high school. A considerable number left the community and visited neighboring towns for their recreation and amusement; moreover, very few high school students associated with them.

# 13

## LEAVING SCHOOL

### Folklore versus facts

MEMBERS OF THE BOARD OF EDUCATION and the school administrators, when they learned that we were interested in adolescents out of school as well as those in school, hastened to point out that we would find that "some" boys and girls of high school age had left school. They then went on to explain that country boys and girls drop out to work, for country people, especially the Norwegians, do not believe in education beyond the eighth grade. They emphasized that the school law, which requires attendance until the sixteenth birthday unless a boy or girl has a work permit, was enforced. The implication of these painstaking interpretations of policy was that we would find "a few kids" who were neither country dwellers nor above sixteen years of age who had employment permits and who were not in school.

If the explanation that country boys and girls drop out of school and town dwellers continue to attend were true, we should expect to find the proportion of rural dwellers to be high in the out-of-school group and that of town youngsters to be low. The facts, however, reject this explanation. Actually three-fourths of the 735 adolescents in the study group live in town and one-fourth in the country. What is important here is that three-fourths of the high school students live in Elmtown and one-fourth in the country; and three-fourths of the withdrawees live in town and one-fourth in the country. Thus, there is no relationship between place of residence and persistence in or dropping out of school. The second assertion, namely, that boys and girls under 16 years of age are required to attend school, except in "unusual" cases, does not fit the facts, for 74 per cent of the 345 young people out of school in the spring of 1942 withdrew before they were 16 years of age, and so far as we were able to determine employment certificates were issued to only a small proportion.

Since continuation in school and withdrawal from it were not in accordance with beliefs about place of residence and age, some more adequate explanation of the facts had to be sought. In passing, it may be well to mention that Elmtowners, neither within nor outside the school system, were aware of the number or the proportion of high-school-aged young people who were out of school.

An analysis of the relationship between class position and continuance in or dropping out of school produced the following results:

| Class | In School | | Out of School | |
|---|---|---|---|---|
| | Number | Per Cent | Number | Per Cent |
| I | 4 | 100.0 | 0 | 00.0 |
| II | 31 | 100.0 | 0 | 00.0 |
| III | 146 | 92.4 | 12 | 7.6 |
| IV | 183 | 58.7 | 129 | 41.3 |
| V | 26 | 11.3 | 204 | 88.7 |
| Total | 390 | 53.1 | 345 | 46.9 |

$X^2 = 294.0954.$    $P < 0.01.$    $C = 0.53.$    $\bar{C} = 0.73.$

Obviously class position is associated very strongly with whether an adolescent is in or out of school. All the young people in classes I and II were in school, over 9 out of 10 of those in class III, 6 out of 10 in class IV; but only 1 out of 9 in class V. We must conclude that the class to which a child belongs is a really significant factor in his relations with the school.

This is believed to be, at least, a two-way relationship. On the one hand, the class and family cultures furnish the child certain beliefs about the school system, and perceptions of what it has to offer him. On the other, the Board of Education, professional administrators, teachers, and Elmtowners in general provide pupils in the several classes with differential attitudes toward the school system. The beliefs and perceptions the child learns in the family relative to education and the school combined with those he develops from his direct school experiences result in distinctly different response patterns in the school situation in the different classes. They appear to act as agents which keep adolescents from the three higher classes in school long after legal requirements have been met and to drive many in class IV and particularly in class V from the school before they have met the educational standards prescribed by law.

## The withdrawal process

Withdrawal is a complex process which begins well down in the elementary grades. The effects of the factors which condition it come into focus in the upper elementary grades as the child becomes aware of the way in which he is regarded by his peers, teachers, and the community in general; from then on the process is intensified. If his family regards education lightly, is unable or refuses to contribute small sums to meet increasing financial needs, or has "a bad reputation," the youngster develops stronger motives to escape from school than he does to continue. The attitudes and actions of teachers may accelerate his decision. Conversely, the teacher may help to keep a student in school, but if he comes from a lower class family the chances are against this. Moreover, the lower the position the child's family occupies in the social structure the less his chances are of being helped by a teacher, and, equally important, of accepting the help if it is offered. The latter aspect of the situation should not be minimized, for the class IV's and class V's commonly resent teachers who "meddle" in their affairs.

AGE. Some class V youngsters from very low-ranking families start dropping out of school when they are 12 years of age; and once the process has begun, it accelerates gradually during the fourteenth and fifteenth years, until it reaches a peak in the sixteenth. By the end of their fourteenth year, approximately one-third of the youngsters in both classes IV and V have quit school. *Before* the sixteenth birthday is reached, 64 per cent of the class IV's and 75 per cent of the class V's have left school.[1] The drop-out pattern is definitely different in class III (11 of the 12 withdrawals took place *after* the sixteenth birthday).[2]

[1] Mean age when class IV quit school is 15.2 years, standard deviation 0.4 year; the mean age for class V is 14.9 years, standard deviation 0.37 year.

[2] The age at time of withdrawal in each class is given in Table XXII of the Appendix.

SEX. Boys are more likely to leave school than girls, especially in class IV, where 62 per cent of the withdrawees are boys and 38 per cent girls. Class IV boys drop out faster than the girls at all age levels, especially at the end of the eighth grade, when the number of drop-outs is nearly three times higher among the boys than among the girls. In class V, 53 per cent of the withdrawees are boys and 47 per cent girls. Both boys and girls drop out in almost equal numbers until they reach age 16; after 16, the boys drop out faster than the girls.[3]

GRADE COMPLETED. All class III youngsters completed the eighth grade, and 11 of the 12 withdrawees *started to high school.* In class IV, 92 per cent *completed the eighth grade,* but only 46 per cent went on to high school. A similar break appears in class V. Here, however, *the first sharp decline of those in school comes between the sixth and seventh grades,* when the percentage falls from 98, who complete the sixth, to 79, who finish the seventh grade. A second series of drop-outs comes between the seventh and eighth grades, when the completion figure falls from 79 to 57 per cent. The largest break in class V, as in class IV, comes between the eighth and ninth grades, when the percentage of completions drops from 57 to 23, a difference of 34 percentage points. The consistent tendency of class V youngsters to drop out of school at a lower grade level than those in class IV is shown in Table XVII.

### CLASS XVII

PERCENTAGES OF WITHDRAWEES IN CLASSES IV AND V WHO COMPLETED A GIVEN GRADE BEFORE DROPPING OUT OF SCHOOL

| | Class | |
| Grade Completed | IV | V |
|---|---|---|
| Fifth | 100.0 | 100.0 |
| Sixth | 99.2 | 97.6 |
| Seventh | 96.1 | 78.9 |
| Eighth | 92.2 | 57.4 |
| Ninth | 45.7 | 23.0 |
| Tenth | 31.0 | 14.7 |
| Eleventh | 12.4 | 6.4 |
| Eleventh plus | 3.9 | 0.0 |

[3] In class III, 7 boys and 5 girls have left school.

If the in-school is combined with the out-of-school group and some projection of trends is hazarded, certain conclusions relative to the educational pattern in the different classes may be reached. These are: (1) Members of classes I and II attend high school, as do 9 out of 10 in class III; all class I, II, and III youngsters complete elementary school, and 157 out of 158 in class III complete the ninth grade. (2) Class IV children complete elementary school (302 out of 312, 97 per cent), but about one-fifth do not attend high school (only 78 per cent start). (3) Class V boys and girls leave school as soon as they are old enough and large enough to find a job. Furthermore, they are almost as likely to quit before the eighth grade is completed as they are afterwards (43 per cent did not complete it, and 21 per cent left school before they reached it). Less than one-third, 32 per cent, start to high school and only from 2 to 4 per cent graduate; clearly, a high school diploma is outside the expectancy of between 96 and 98 per cent of the class V's.

THE SEASONAL FACTOR. Nearly one-half (48 per cent) of all withdrawees leave school between the end of one school year and the beginning of the next, and an additional 23 per cent drop out within the first six weeks of the fall term. Withdrawal during the summer is facilitated by the vacation period, and the fact that the children usually change teachers at the end of each year. Since the school loses track of pupils during the summer, it is easier to avoid a compulsory return then than at any other time. Then, too, a child may have found a job and used it as a justification for not returning in the fall. During the first six weeks of the school year, the withdrawal rate is about three times higher than during any other six-week period. If a youngster is able to stay in school through these weeks, he has a fair chance to continue for several months more, possibly the rest of the year. A few withdrawals occur week after week, but there are no concentration points, such as corn-picking, Christmas, or spring-plowing time. Furthermore, there is no significant association between sex or class and the time of year the withdrawals occur.

THE WITHDRAWEE'S SCHOOL RECORD. The records of all class IV children who attended Central School from grades five through eight were analyzed to see if the in-school group makes a better adjustment to the demands of the school than the out-of-school group. This analysis was limited to class IV, because all except 5 of the class III graduates of Central School were in high school, and all but 11 of its class V graduates had left school. We found that the out-of-school class IV's had significantly poorer scholarship and attendance and deportment records than the in-school class IV's.[4] The in-school class IV's received, while they were in Central School, a disproportionate number of A's and B's in comparison with their out-of-school peers; concomitantly the out-of-school group received a significantly higher proportion of C's and D's. The number of grades repeated was startlingly different in the two groups; 10 per cent of the in-school group had repeated one or more elementary grades, in comparison with 34 per cent of the out-of-school group. Attendance during the elementary years followed the same general pattern as scholarship and grades repeated; the out-of-school group was absent far more frequently than the in-school group. In addition, the deportment of the withdrawees was judged by their teachers to have been worse than that of those who were in high school. These four measures agree with one another that the class IV withdrawees made significantly poorer adjustments than did the group in school. In terms of the educational values held by the higher classes, the group in school were successful, and the withdrawees were failures.

Adjustment to the formal demands of the high school by the 11 adolescents in class III, the 70 in class IV, and the 72 in class V who started high school but later withdrew was a continuation of the pattern laid down during the elementary years. The grades the withdrawees received in these three classes were consistently lower than those in school received, but we tested this difference for significance only in class IV.[5]

Intelligence quotients of class IV's in school and class IV's in the withdrawee group who had received all elementary training in Elmtown's schools and had enrolled in high school were com-

---

[4] The $X^2$ for scholarship was 27.0213, 3 degrees of freedom, $P < 0.01$; for attendance, $X^2 = 25.3053$, 4 degrees of freedom, $P < 0.01$; for deportment, $X^2 = 35.1221$, 4 degrees of freedom, $P < 0.01$.

[5] In class IV, the grade distribution for the two groups yielded a $X^2$ of 24.3502, 4 degrees of freedom, $P < 0.01$.

pared to see if they differed significantly. It was found that the in-school class IV's had significantly higher I.Q.'s than the out-of-school class IV's,[6] but there was no significant difference between class V's matched in the same way.[7] However, we do not believe that the lower intelligence scores of the withdrawees in class IV are an adequate explanation for these youngsters' withdrawal from school before their class equals, even though Elmtowners often say (and many sincerely believe what they say), "A kid never quits until he learns all he can." Nevertheless, this belief will continue to be resorted to as justification to gloss over the facts of class distinctions and their effects on a child's adjustment to the demands of the school. Clearly, differences in intelligence do not explain withdrawals in class V, where the I.Q.'s of the withdrawees are not significantly different from those of class V adolescents in school.

FAMILIAL FACTORS AND WITHDRAWALS. Within class IV, a family's formal educational experience was the most significant factor in an adolescent's continuation in or withdrawal from school. Twenty-two per cent of the class IV fathers in the student group had completed one or more years of high school, in contrast to twelve per cent of the fathers in the out-of-school group of class IV adolescents. The difference was greater among the mothers: 34 per cent of the mothers of class IV students had had some high school training, whereas only 12 per cent of class IV withdrawee's mothers had attended high school.

The mean educational level of brothers and sisters, whose schooling had been completed, was even more strikingly different in the two groups. Moreover, the higher the mean educational level from the eighth through the twelfth grade, the greater was the contrast. For instance, 19 per cent of the older siblings in the student group left school at the end of the eighth grade, but 52 per cent of the withdrawees' brothers and sisters dropped out at this level; 45 per cent of the in-school group's brothers and sisters completed high school, but only 2 per cent of the brothers and sisters of the out-of-school group did so.

Certain other familial factors are important in the withdrawal process. In the first place, if an adolescent's father is a farm

[6] $X^2 = 25.0712$, 4 degrees of freedom, $P < 0.01$.
[7] $X^2 = 4.3507$, 2 degrees of freedom, $P > 0.01$.

tenant, the chances are about three to one that he will not be in school. Approximately one-fourth (26 per cent) of the withdrawees in class IV come from farm tenant families, but only 9 per cent of the in-school group. All these farm families live from one to twelve miles from the high school. There is no bus, and neither the state, the county, nor the district provides mileage for those who drive private cars. On a tenant farm where normally one-half of the crops go to the landlord, the family is hard pressed to supply a car and meet the cost of upkeep. Then, too, there is the constant need for the girl's help in the farm home and the boy's in the fields. Moreover, the hired girl's role, as a supplement to the farm wife's labor in the home, is well developed among farm owners, part-owners, and prosperous tenants. The source of this help is most generally the poor farm family where a teen-aged girl with her demands for clothes and feminine finery, on however meager a scale, is a burden. By taking a job with a neighbor, the girl can earn her room and board and a few dollars a week. Likewise, the tenant's son is looked to as a source of labor in the fields. Few landlords have any sympathy for a tenant who does not get the crops planted on time if he has a son in school who is big enough to run a tractor, plow, harrow, and drill. During the summer months the boy cultivates the corn; mows, rakes, loads, and bales hay. In the late summer he helps to harvest the small grains and prepare for the big harvest—soybeans and corn. Since corn pickers are found on only about 15 per cent of the farms, there is a great demand for corn huskers from late October until Christmas or later. By that time the stock has to be brought into the barn or feed lot; this necessitates daily feeding, watering, and an occasional barn cleaning. The feeding cycle is broken by corn shelling, feed grinding, and a periodic trip to town with a truck of corn or livestock.

Skilled workers in the Mill, the Foundry, the Factory, and the mines work regularly, most live in town, and their children are twice as likely to be in as out of school. The children of class IV—machine operators, laborers, proprietors, sales and service workers—are just as likely to quit as to continue school. In these occupational groups there is no association between residence in town or in the country and a child's continuation in or withdrawal from school. Farm tenants and skilled workers in class IV are the only groups that reveal a significant relationship between occupation and residence and a youngster's school status.

In Elmtown proper, area of residence, broken homes, rented homes, family income, gainful occupation of the mother, and township relief are associated significantly with a class IV adolescent's leaving school. These relationships indicate that families with children in the out-of-school group tend to be comparatively worse off than those whose children are in school. They are indicative also of the relatively poorer start in life the out-of-school class IV child receives from his family when it is compared on a series of important items with families in the same class whose children are in high school.

Tentatively, we believe that the significantly poorer family heritage, as measured by the items mentioned in the preceding paragraph, among the out-of-school class IV youth gives rise to their poorer adjustment to the demands of the school in comparison with those of this class in school. Moreover, we are convinced that this pattern has been handed down in many cases from the grandparents to the parents, and on to the adolescents' generation. We shall go one step further and say the adolescents may be expected to transmit it to their children through the subtle processes of social learning in the family and the community, *not* through the germ plasm. Spatial limitations forbid more than the briefest outline of a single case, that of the Crater family, to illustrate this generalization. However, we have an abundance of similar materials in our files.

Mrs. Crater's father was born in Scotland in 1869. He was taken by his father into the Scottish coal mines at the age of nine. When he was eleven his parents brought him to Elmtown, where he worked in the coal mines until he was disabled in an accident. When he was 18 he married Libbie Scanlon, a seventeen-year-old English-born girl who worked as a housemaid. She had a fourth-grade education. Eight months after marriage the first of nine children was born.

Mrs. Crater, the mother of two class IV withdrawees, was the sixth child in this family. She "went through" the seventh grade and then started to make beds in the old Hogate House. In due time she became acquainted with "Pa" (Mr. Crater) when he delivered groceries to the hotel kitchen. She married him a few months later, and Lonnie, the first of seven children, was born on her eighteenth birthday, seven months after marriage. In her own words:

> I've been living with Pa for almost 20 years, but sometimes I don't know why I do it. I haven't slept with him for almost seven years. When the youngest boy was a baby, I told him if he didn't stay away from young girls he couldn't come near me. He said he wouldn't give them up; so I started sleeping on the couch in the front room, and he sleeps in the back room.

Mrs. Crater summarized a decade of family history that told part of the story, but not all:

> Pa was out of work [1932] and he couldn't find any. We had six children and they had to eat; so I started sewing. I made handkerchiefs at first, then I started making scarves. I sent Pa and the children out to sell them. I sent the oldest boy out first, then the girl that's married and lives in Texas; she and her brother, the boy that's in the Army now, they sold for a time. Later the second girl, Freda, the one that works [nights as a waitress] at the Five Stars, started selling. She got Tom to selling after a while. After the oldest girl got married and the boy went in the Army, I quit. A couple of years ago Pa got his job with the candy company [driving a truck]; so I said, "That's enough." Now Tom's started to work, only the little boys are home, and things are much easier.

In response to a question about a niece in the withdrawee group Mrs. Crater related:

> This girl Alice Ann you asked about is my oldest brother's first child. He had an unfortunate experience when he was young. He was going with a girl over near Blue River. Mother just couldn't see her. The first thing we knew he started running around with this Helen Evans [from a well-known class V family]. It wasn't very long until he had Helen in trouble. He married Helen as a matter of decency, but he never cared for her much though. Then another little girl came along, and about three years ago a little boy was coming, and he disappeared.
>
> After he left, Helen started working down at the Factory; Ralph Fraser was working there too; they got acquainted and started going around together, and after a while they married. Alice Ann

took Ralph Fraser's name and her little brother took his name too. The second girl was taken by another family here in town to raise. She's never been adopted, the family just takes care of her. My mother buys all of Alice Ann's clothes and tries to help Helen all she can.

"Pa" Crater's father and mother completed somewhere between three and seven years in the elementary school, married when they were in their late teens, and had six children. The boys finished the eighth grade, and the girls started high school, but only the youngest one finished. "Pa" began to work as a delivery boy for Kraus' Grocery after he finished the eighth grade; after his marriage he became a clerk and continued in this capacity until the intrusion of chain stores into Elmtown in the late 1920's, combined with the depression, forced his employer into bankruptcy.

When unemployment hit the family, Mrs. Crater tried to salvage its dignity, continue payments on their home, and make a living. The children were compelled to hawk her handiwork on the streets from the time school was dismissed in the afternoon until after dark and all day Saturday. The oldest boy after a time found part-time work in a grocery, and his sister (the second child) began to wash dishes in a small restaurant when she was 13 years of age. Each left school when the elementary grades were completed. The boy ran away and joined the Army when he was 16; the girl moved from the dish sink when she was 14 to a waitress' job, which she followed around town until she became pregnant at 17 and married.

Freda, age 17, and Tom, who was 15, left school as soon as they were able to find work that would enable them to escape from peddling their mother's pan holders, handkerchiefs, wash cloths, scarves. Freda, when asked late one night, as she stood behind the counter in the Five Stars, why she quit school, answered bitterly:

How would *you* like to ring door bells and have some little rich snot say, "We don't want any of your *Maw's* stuff" and slam the door. I got so I couldn't face the kids any longer. It wasn't Maw's fault, but Jesus! How I hated that job! She beat Tom and me when we didn't want to sell. In the winter I got so cold my feet pained me for hours after I got in bed. Tom and me talked of running away a lot. Once we pretty near did, but Grandma talked us out of it.

Tom told almost the same story as Freda:

> I was always tired. I pulled the wagon, and Freda sold. We pulled the wagon all over town most every night. If we didn't sell good, Maw raised hell and Dad beat us. We had some awful fights. When Freda quit, I wouldn't go out alone and Maw stopped. I got a paper route for a year. Last summer I had a chance to get this job, so I stayed out when school started. [Tom as a baker's assistant worked from 11 at night until 7 o'clock in the morning.] I didn't want to make Maw work so I could go to school. I didn't care much for school, especially high school.

Tom and Freda lived at home and paid their mother five dollars a week for their room, laundry, and part of their meals. Mrs. Crater worked half days cleaning for people and on week ends cooked at the Five Stars. "Pa" Crater worked on his candy route but gave little money to his family. Mrs. Crater stated, "Pa keeps his money. That's why I have to work."

Although this is only a segment of a single family, it illustrates the way irregular family patterns so prevalent in the out-of-school group are passed on from one generation to another. Unfortunate family background within the context of the class system is undoubtedly the most potent factor in any explanation of the reasons underlying withdrawals from school in Elmtown, and perhaps elsewhere for that matter.

## The dynamics of withdrawal

When an adolescent leaves school, he may think his is an individual decision, and each can give his personal reason. The reason given may be real to the person who frames it, and we believe that it is, but this does not mean that it is sociologically adequate.

The adolescents' own reasons for leaving school may be grouped under three main headings: (1) *economic need;* (2) *peer isolation and discrimination;* and (3) *mistreatment by teachers.*

*Economic need* is a more or less standard explanation with boys, but isolation and mistreatment often enter their conversations. For instance, Robert Campbell (class V), the eleventh child in a family of 12, withdrew when he was 16 years old, as had his older brothers and sisters. The following excerpts taken from an interview a few minutes after he walked out of the high school the morning he quit illuminate this facet of the withdrawal process. After we settled ourselves in the back booth of Sutton's Soda Fountain I commented, "So you're going to quit school."

"I've quit. I've decided not to go any more."

"Didn't you like high school?" I asked.

"Well, I don't know. I wouldn't say yes and I wouldn't say no. It was all right, I guess. I was 16 on Saturday, and I wanted to quit. I'm going to get a job. I understand they're paying twenty dollars a week at the Factory, and they'll take you when you're 16. Down at the Mill, they won't take you until you're 18. Frank Burton quit the other day, and he was down there a few days; when they found out he was only 16, they made him quit, so he's back in school. But Frank won't stay in school the rest of the year. He told me he's going to stay until he can find another job. Just as soon as I'm 17, I'm going to join the Navy Air Corps [pronounced Korpse]."

He stopped, and I asked, "Why didn't you finish out the year?"

"Well, there's no sense to it. If I finished out the year, I wouldn't finish high school anyway."

Another long pause. "How does May [younger sister] feel about it? Does she want to go on?"

"No, I think May will finish this year, but she won't go after she's 16. She'll be 16 this December. Neither one of us wanted to come this year."

To prompt him I asked, "Why didn't you?"

"Well, money and other things."

Another pause. "What do you mean, money and other things?"

"You see, Dad's on pension [father, age 67, on old age assistance]; he's too old to work. My sister Josie, she's the one that works at the Mill, bought my books this year, and an aunt in the country bought May's books. Otherwise, we couldn't have come [this year]."

A pause. "Have you had a job?"

"I've set pins at the bowling alley all winter. I was just an extra down there. I worked after school sometimes to about midnight. The regular boys go to work at one o'clock in the afternoon and work until midnight or one o'clock. Us extra fellows didn't have to work after supper unless we wanted to, but I used to work most of the time. They pay you 5 cents a line, and what you earn depends on how many there are. The most I ever made was $9.85, but I worked every afternoon after school until one o'clock that week and all day Saturday and Saturday night. I usually made about $3.75 to $4.00. Of course, some weeks I only made $1.50 or $2.00. It just depends on how many lines you set up."

A long pause! I then asked, "Did you have a good time in school?"

"I can't say I did. I was going out for football last fall and then I didn't. The folks didn't want me to. They were afraid I'd get hurt. I didn't go to any games all last year, and I didn't see any basketball games this year. I went to one dance, the Freshman Mixer. I didn't have a date. When I get a job, I'll have money, and I can have dates."

"Whom are you going to date?"

"There's a girl that lives down on Eastern Avenue close to the canal. I want to date her. I don't know her name. I just know her and I like her."

After a long pause, I asked, "If you could start over again and have things the way you wanted them, what would you do?"

"I'd like to live uptown, I'd like to have money, and I'd like to have clothes and dates. I'd like to go out for basketball and football, and I'd like to be in things. There are fellows like that in school."

Another pause followed by, "How did you get along with them?"

"They treated me all right. They'd speak to me when they saw me, but I was different from them and they were different from me."

Here we see economic need, and a sense of isolation, but no hard feelings toward the teachers and the social system.

The isolation of children from low class families by their peers from the higher classes may occur as early as the second, third, or fourth grade. To illustrate, Washington School is located between the 400 residential area and the West End; consequently, it draws its pupils from all segments of the social structure. One afternoon shortly after the third grade was dismissed, we saw a little boy throwing rocks at six other little boys and girls, and they in turn were throwing rocks at him.

As we walked closer, we saw that the lone boy was Charlie Limburg, the ninth child in a class V family that lived in a tent house south of the canal. The other children came from families in classes I, II, and III. The group was chanting repeatedly in unison, "I smell a Limburg, I smell a Limburg," to the tune of "Johnnie Is a Sissy."

On another occasion we saw a group of fifth-grade girls torment another fifth-grade girl whose father ran a hog farm. To feed hogs was not unusual, but "Greasy" Dill, the father, fed his hogs mainly on scraps he gathered daily from various restaurants and alleys. The girls had driven Mamie into a corner of Central School yard next to a high wire fence. There they were singing a song someone had composed about the Dill family. We caught but two lines of the doggerel in the excitement of Mamie's crying and the noise of the playground, but they told the story. "Mamie Dill lives on a hill; Mamie Dill lives on swill."

Girls complain approximately three and one-half times as often as boys about the way they are treated by the other girls while they are in school. To illustrate, a prosperous farm tenant's daughter (class IV) who was at home helping her parents stated the issue, as far as she was concerned, as follows:

> I want to tell you something about that school [the high school]. All the kids in it are broken up into little groups. Those gangs start in the seventh and eighth grade, and they carry them on into high school. If you're in a gang you're all right, and if you aren't you're left out of things. When I started to high school, I was lost. I did not know anyone but Harry Swenson. We graduated from the Dickerson School together. I tried to get in with some of the girls, but I never did. They made me feel like I wasn't wanted. About the fourth week, I heard Anne Hogate [class III] call me "that hick." I wanted to quit after that, but Mom made me go on for a few weeks. Pop said if I didn't want to go I didn't have to; so I quit.

This girl might have completed high school if she had not been isolated from the girls with whom she wanted to clique.

Another class IV girl combined the position of her family, peer isolation, and teacher discrimination in her statement:

> Back in the depression, Dad lost out on the farm, and he had a chance to drive the truck for the Baker Oil Company, so we

moved to town. Us kids went on up through the grades, and when we came to the eighth grade we really saw things happen. The kids were all right in a way, but they looked down on us. At least, there was a gang around here that looked down on us because Dad drove the oil truck. [Nine class II and 2 class III girls were named here.] They thought they were somebody. They had a club called the G.W.G. I don't know much about it because, you see, we didn't belong.

Now, I'll tell you the dirtiest thing that was ever pulled. It wasn't pulled on me, but they pulled it on my sister Josephine, in the eighth grade. Josephine was really smart. She worked on the books and made the second best grades in the class. Mary Curry [class II] was the highest. She was the valedictorian. Now Josephine should have been salutatorian, but some people didn't think we were as good as the other people. Besides, Dad wasn't on the School Board; if your dad's on the School Board, you have an "in" and a lot of the teachers give you better grades. But do you know what happened? They made Judy Wingate—that's Doc-tor Wingate's daughter—salutatorian. That really burned me up. It hurt Josephine and she's never been the same since.

That Country Club crowd really thinks they are somebody. They think they're way up. Now my dad's drove the Baker Oil Truck for ten years. We're as good as anybody, but a lot of people try to treat us like we weren't. I don't take anything off anybody. I've got spunk, and if they don't like me they can go to the devil. Some of the girls who thought they were somebody used to snub me when I waited tables in high school. Mom wouldn't let me quit until I was 16, but you can bet your rights the day I was 16 I walked out of that high school. They can't treat me that way and get away with it.

Attitudes of parents, often reflected in the child, help condi-tion a youngster's behavior in the school situation, as the follow-ing incidents indicate. In February we were in Central School talking to the school nurse when the sixth-grade teacher, Miss Cook, came in and voiced her feelings about William Campbell, a nephew of Bob Campbell discussed above. She began,

That little William Campbell makes me sick. We had a Valentine party yesterday afternoon and I invited him to come, like I invited all the rest of the class, and he said, "Miss Cook, I don't like parties and I'm not coming." I said, "Well, why don't you want to come?"

And he said, "I just don't like parties and I don't have to come and I'm not going to come."

When we had our Christmas party, that little devil was the same way. I talked to him and tried to get him to come. I said, "Is it that you do not have any money you do not want to come to the party?" He said, "No," and I said, "If you do not have any money, I will see that you get a present." He said, "You don't need to be thinkin' I don't have no money." Then he reached in his pocket and pulled out 65 cents. I asked him just now, "Did you ask your parents about coming to the party?" He said, "Yes, I said something at supper, and Dad said I didn't have to go to parties. He never went to parties, and if he didn't have to go to parties I don't have to go to parties. So I'm not going to any parties." He was defiant! There is no use to turn him in because it wouldn't do any good. The whole Campbell outfit is that way.

Miss Cook was "an Elmtown girl" who had lived and taught all her life in the community. She knew the Campbell family, as did the nurse, who was also an Elmtown girl, and, what is important here, she reflected the school's expectancy of the "Campbell outfit."

Each morning about ten o'clock the elementary school principal made a routine check of the absence slips which the different teachers turned in to the combination school nurse and truant officer. On this particular morning, he thumbed through the slips on Miss Gay's desk, sorted four out of the pile, read them, turned to her and said, "I think you ought to go down to the Svensons' [class V] and stir them up a bit. This type of thing should not be allowed to go on."

"I'll go down, but I don't know as it'll do much good."

He looked at two or three more slips and said, "Did you see these yesterday?"

"I saw one, but the other family wasn't home. I will try to get around there this afternoon."

The principal threw the slips on the desk, uttered a disgusted "humph" and left the room. Miss Gay turned to me,

He just doesn't know this town like I do. I know a lot of people say I am too easy on these kids that skip school and on their parents, but if they had been doing this work for fifteen years they would know a truant officer's life isn't an easy one. Take these

Svensons he was talking about. There are ten kids in the family. I have been going to that place and trying to make them keep their children in school since 1927. I feel so sorry for that poor mother. She looks like she is worn out and she tries to do what she can, but she doesn't have much to do it with. She was just a kid when she was married [age 15] and she had a kid that year and they have been having one at least every two years.

I have prodded those people and I have talked to them, I have threatened them, I have bawled out the kids, I have tried to help the mother, but there's not much I can do. She will cooperate, but I can't get any cooperation from the old man. He is a drunk and a gambler, and he doesn't care about education. That's one of those Norwegian families where the father has never learned American ways and just doesn't care. He used to be a good cabinetmaker, but he has let liquor get him. I have been down to the house, and that poor mother will be so tired she can hardly drag herself around, and I will feel so sorry for her. She does not have any clothes and practically no clothes for those kids, and they haven't any furniture in the house. In the front room, there isn't even a rug on the floor, and there's only one chair to sit in, and that's an old broken-down hard one. When you face things like that, you can't really expect the children to come to school and be enthusiastic. I have wasted more shoe leather, gas, and breath on that family than I want to think about, but it doesn't seem to have done any good.

There are a lot of families like that. I go to see them, I try to do for them, I get their kids glasses, I get bedclothes for them. When they haven't clothes, I even see they get clothes and still they don't seem to care.

When I get to thinking about it, I don't blame these kids for not coming to school. Over here [elementary school] it's not so bad, but when these kids get into high, especially the girls, it's mighty hard on them. Some girls have better clothes than others, they have more money, their hair is fixed nice, they can go to beauty parlors, and these poor girls just can't do it. These kids get snooted around, and you can't blame them for feeling the way they do. I used to feel the same way myself. My mother died and left me an orphan. Dad was a good provider, but we didn't have a lot of things many of the wealthy families around had. There's a lot to be said on the side of these poor families, but you can't get the wealthy people to see it that way.

Miss Cook was talking yesterday about little William Campbell not wanting to come to her Valentine party. If I were William

Campbell, I don't think I would come to a Valentine party either, because I've heard these kids talk out on the playground. I have heard them say he stinks. You can't expect a kid to come to a Valentine party when his playfellows say things like that about him.

So I don't know. I guess I will keep doing the job, and that's about all anyone can expect of me. But it makes me so darned mad when these people who don't know these poor families even exist, let alone the way they have to live, sit around and criticize. I do the best I can and all I have to say is, why in the devil don't they do a little bit themselves?

A few weeks before this occurrence, the principal walked into Miss Gay's office and told her he had just received word that Jesse Jessup (class V), who had run away, had been found. Miss Gay asked, "Where was he this time?"

He replied, "I don't know, but I was told over the phone by one of the deputies he had been found out in the country."

I turned to Miss Gay and asked, "Is that one of the Jessup children who live south of the canal?"

"Yes, this is the fourth one. I suppose I might as well go tell the mother, poor soul, they have found Jesse. Would you like to go along?" We put on our coats, hats, and gloves, and walked into the winter air. We climbed into Miss Gay's car, drove through town, up the old road to the canal bridge, then down the frozen mud road that led into the Jessup yard. An abandoned, partially dismantled automobile with the hood, radiator, and two wheels off blocked the entrance. Another car, a 1929 model "A" Ford with an icicle extending from the radiator to the ground, was parked beside the wreckage. Two or three broken, half-buried stoves lay along the path to the house. A clothes line with some frozen clothes on it flapped in the January wind blowing in from the river. A pile of broken boxes salvaged from the town dump leaned against the porch. The porch steps were made of railroad ties and pieces of driftwood. There were several gaping holes a foot or more in diameter in the floor; one especially big one had been covered by a Polarine Oil sign. We walked to the house, up the steps, threaded our way between the holes in the floor, and knocked on the door. After the sound of scurrying feet had subsided, we noticed several children peeking at us through the curtainless window. We next heard the clump-clump-clump of leather heels on bare boards, then the door was thrown open by Mrs. Jessup; she stood in the open doorway for a moment before she recognized Miss Gay; she then said, "Hullo."

Miss Gay greeted her and went on, "I came down to see if you had found Jesse."

"Yah. We found him today. He was out in the country with some friends of ourn." Miss Gay introduced me and stepped across the threshold, saying, "May we come in?" Mrs. Jessup did not say whether we could or not, but Miss Gay pushed in, and I followed. She asked cheerfully, "Was Jesse all right?"

"Yes, he just went out to see some friends in the country and forgot to tell us where he'd gone."

"Is he here? Can we see him?"

"No, he's gone to Indianapolis. He wanted to go there. We thought he might go up there and stay with some friends. He's got a little brother up there."

"Is that the one who is staying with a colored family?"

"Yes, but Jesse's not goin' to stay with them. He's goin' to stay with some friends of ourn next door."

"Why didn't he want to come back to school?"

"Jesse was afeared the kids would laugh at him."

Miss Gay in a deprecating tone, "Oh, I don't think they would."

"Well, he thought they would. He said they laughed at him all the time."

The next morning the fifth-grade teacher came into Miss Gay's office and asked, "Have you heard anything about Jesse?"

"Yes, he was out in the country with some friends of the Jessups. They have decided to send him to Indianapolis to school."

"Then he won't be back?"

"I guess that's the way it is."

"Good riddance! He wasn't getting anything out of his school work. Besides, he was a trouble maker. I'm glad he's gone." With that, she stalked out of the office.

A few minutes later, the principal came in and asked, "Did you see anything about the Jessup boy?"

"Yes, I was down there last night."

"Did you find out why he ran away?"

"Yes, his mother said he didn't want to go to school because the kids laughed at him. The parents are going to send him away to school. Probably that would be better than to have him come back here."

"Yes, I imagine it is better for him to go away."

When the principal had left, I asked, "How old is Jesse?" Miss Gay replied,

He is 12, and he was in the fifth grade. He ran off last year several times; once he got up by the Henry Nelsons' and wandered into the yard as it was getting dark. Mrs. Nelson took him in and called me. She told me he came into the yard crying with a tall tale that his mother had just died, and his father had gone away, and he was trying to find his father. She felt so sorry for him she took him into the house and fed and warmed him. I got in the car, drove out there and brought him back to town. I went down to Jessup's and found his mother in the house. I said to her, "Where's Jesse?" She said, "I went to the show today and I let Jesse stay home because he said he felt sick. When I came back he was gone. I don't know where he is. I guess he's gone to the show." I told her he had wandered off and was found in the country, and I had him out in the car. She said, "Bring him in." I brought him in and that was all there was to it. This time he left on Saturday and they did not find him until Wednesday afternoon. The family did not start to worry about him until some time Tuesday. With a background like that, the poor kid doesn't have much chance.

I asked, "Where was he when they found him?"

Night before last he slept with Fred Tolliver's hogs. Fred found him in the barn about ten o'clock yesterday morning drinking milk out of a tin can and eating wheat. I guess he milked one of the cows.

Elementary teachers who had taught adolescents in the study were asked to tell us anything they could remember about a particular child's work habits, interests, adjustment to the other children, family background, and their judgment about the child's character. Three types of facts came out of these interviews. First, these teachers remembered the children from the upper and lower ends of the prestige structure more vividly than they did those from the middle ranges. Second, they had lost contact with almost every withdrawee. Third, they recalled unpleasant episodes about seven times as often as they did pleasant ones. These interviews commonly developed along these lines:

"Do you remember Henry Todd?" [Class V.]

"Yes, that boy has quit school though. He gave me no end of trouble in the sixth grade. He fought on the playground, he cheated and lied. I remember he used to steal lunches."

"Was Frank Stone, Jr., in your class?" [Class I.]

"Yes. He was a leader. He was so much like his father, always courteous and dignified."

Or, "Was Mary Meyers in any of your classes?" [Class IV.]

"The name is familiar, but I don't seem to be able to place the child."

Miss Franklin was being interviewed relative to what she remembered about former pupils. When we came to Harriet Gates' name (class V) she remarked:

> I have had three of the Gates children through the years. Each one was a problem. I have visited the home on a few occasions, and I am not so sure but what the father isn't brutal to the mother. She seemed so scared and negative all the time. The father is one of these big husky fellows who swaggers around, talks loud, and pays little attention to his children. [The father finished the seventh and held education above the eighth grade in contempt. He had been a nightwatchman for a barge company for 11 years.]
>
> When this little Harriet was in the sixth grade she developed some very bad moral habits; then in the seventh I noticed she was very dishonest.

Miss Franklin stopped, her face flushed, and I quietly asked, "What are these habits?"

Miss Franklin hesitated a few moments, then said,

> When she was in the sixth grade, she started to have intimate relations with those two Garrett boys who lived across the street. This is not gossip either, because a neighbor woman of theirs I know very well caught them in the chicken house with her. She told her mother about it, and the mother worked with her. I do not know whether she has stopped that or not, but I know it went on while she was here [in Central School]. I tried to talk to the girl,

but it did not seem to do any good. Then she took to cheating and stealing things. When she was in my class, she had her spelling words and arithmetic problems written down for a test.

She never played with the other girls. I have had her break down and cry in my class a number of times. She played truant whenever we had parties. She came to school the day we had our Easter party with her hair straight, dressed in an old black dress her mother had made out of one of hers. While the children were playing games, I noticed she was missing. I started looking for her and found her in the girls' toilet standing in the corner crying. I tried to talk to her, but she only cried worse. I put my arm around her and started to take her back and she bit me on the arm. I just let her go.

About a month ago her little brother Bob ran away. He slept two or three nights in Bates' cowshed. The Bates' live up the street from them near the coal yard. After the Gates' found out where Bobby was, they made him come home. We could not get anything out of him here at school. Joe Brennan [class IV] wanted to take Bob home with him and have him asleep there. Bob told Joe his father whipped him with a horsewhip. When I heard this, I was boiling. If I had gone up there I would have told them something, but then they would have resented my interference. They sent a letter here and asked Miss Likert [sixth-grade teacher] not to let Bobby out of her sight. They asked her to deliver him to his brother Harold [in the seventh grade]. It was very humiliating for little Bobby, but she did what they asked.

Just yesterday he spit in a little boy's face, and Miss Likert made him stand up before the class and apologize. He blurted out, "I— I'm sorry"; then he started to cry, and cried all through the period. Miss Likert came to me and said, "What do you do when a child cries?" I said, "Let him cry."

Harriet Gates summarized her reaction to school in terms of the peer group rather than of the teachers, courses, grades, or extracurricular activities:

The kids all run around with each other in bunches. They are snobbish; unless you are just so, you are ignored. Sometimes they speak to you and sometimes they don't. I hated the kids.

Mrs. Barber, neighbor of the Gates' (class IV) and the mother of a freshman boy, raised the question of Harriet's morals during an interview by asking about Harriet's operation for appendicitis the winter before. Questioned about her reason for asking, she replied:

> They live near here, and a number of women have discussed the question. We wondered if it was really appendicitis! All of us have told our boys to stay away from Harriet because she's free and easy. I think it's terrible! That child ought to get out of this community, and the sooner the better. Some mothers have been so suspicious they have told their boys if they go over there to play not to use the toilet because they are likely to pick up something.

Interviews with Harriet's peers both in and out of school indicated that the girls, outside of a clique of low-ranking class IV's and class V's, isolated her because of her reputation. That she was a sex attraction for the boys, and a nuisance from the viewpoint of the school and the neighborhood mothers, was clear. Harriet's statement that the girls snubbed her was true, and it no doubt motivated her withdrawal from school, but it was only one of several pertinent factors which impinged upon her. In the first place her family's class position channelized her contacts in the school to other low-class youngsters. In the second, she had poor clothes, and from Miss Franklin's statement we may infer that she keenly felt this, at least on the occasion of the Easter party when she sought refuge in the girls' room. Her isolation from most of the girls appeared to follow the chicken house episode, but there were conflicting stories on this point.

Mrs. Gates censured the girls primarily and the teachers "over there" (Central School) secondarily for Harriet's withdrawal. She believed that Harriet should have gone "at least until she was 16," but, "She hated it over there. I hadda hard time get'n' her through as it wuz."

Teachers and parents often blame clique and peer group relations for a boy's or girl's withdrawal. Unquestionably clique connections do play an important part in a youngster's decision to leave school, and they may determine within limits when he does, but this oft-repeated accusation must be interpreted carefully, *for the child who is susceptible to withdrawal from school generally associates with boys or girls who are also exposed to the same class and social pressures which motivate him to leave school.* Therefore, any conclusion which assumes that membership in a clique causes a child to withdraw from school is un-warranted. It would be as sensible to say that cliques keep children in school; however, we never heard anyone make this claim. The factors which keep children in school bring them together in cliques whose members have similar views, hopes, tastes, and chances in school. Likewise, the boy or girl who is vulnerable to the withdrawal process is also likely to be associated with a clique whose members are similar to him in status and in opportunity in life. Thus, the commonly observed fact that, when some members of a clique start to drop out of school, the others soon follow is a symptom of underlying factors which condition the process. For example, in the latter part of the sixth grade Harriet Gates became a member of a clique com-posed of Freda Crater and Alice Ann Griner, and 2 class V girls. These girls stayed together throughout the seventh grade. One class V girl did not enter the eighth grade; she remained home to help her mother with the housework and to care for a new baby, the eleventh in fourteen years, while her mother worked part-time as a cleaning woman for four higher ranking families. The other class V girl and Harriet continued as friends in the eighth grade, but Freda and Alice Ann withdrew. Freda ex-plained this break in these terms, "Harriet got a bad 'rep,' and we stayed away from her." Harriet and her friend left school at the end of the eighth grade and took jobs as housemaids. Freda Crater left high school in the fourth week of her freshman year, and her cousin, Alice Ann, dropped out in February, 1941, the week she was 16, to take a job in the ten-cent store. We believe that the basic factor which conditioned these withdrawals was the culture complex associated with the families of these girls. Their clique ties as well as their withdrawal were adjust-ments they made to the pressures and demands which bore upon them as maturing members of families who occupied low-rank-ing positions in the social structure. That they possessed family cultures which resulted in their being placed in these positions by other members of the community was evident in all the data we accumulated about them.

Severe punishment for misbehavior is often followed by with-drawal. If the delinquent comes from a family with some in-fluence, discipline is tempered in accordance with the effects the family influence may have on the teacher, the principal, and the Superintendent. Under these circumstances, a class IV or class V pupil is punished more severely than a youngster from the higher classes. Then, too, as we demonstrated in Chapter 8, the high school teachers expect more misbehavior from the lower than from the higher classes. Twenty-nine boys in the withdrawee group—20 from class V, and nine from class IV—related that they had been beaten prior to their withdrawal from school. The boys' stories tallied with chance accounts we picked up from teachers as well as incidents we encountered in process. The elementary school principal, discharged in 1939, administered most of these beatings, but beatings were still used in 1941–1942, as the following episode indicates. Late one afternoon the Superintendent walked into the high school principal's office and said to us in a strained voice:

> "There was some vandalism over at Central School last night. Two Flaherty kids [class V] and a boy named Reitz cut eight spokes out of Tommie Huddleston's bicycle [class I] with a pair of pliers. Tommie's mother called me just as I was sitting down to dinner. This morning neither of the Flaherty kids was in school. The principal got word from some little kids that the Flahertys were hanging around school last night. We called the sheriff's office, and a deputy went down to their place and brought them in. We took them up to the prosecuting attorney, but he was not in, so we handled it ourselves."
>
> I asked, "Did they confess?"
>
> "Yes, by third degree methods and a few other things. Those . . . those boys—if they don't straighten out—will have to be put away. Do you know where they live?"
>
> "Yes."
>
> "Say, do you want to go out there with me? I would like to talk to their father."

We walked out of the high school, climbed into the Superintendent's car, and I directed him to the Flaherty home. As we crossed the canal, he remarked, "I have never been down here before. I did not know this area existed."

The Flaherty home was a two-room shack built on filled ground between the river and the town dump. The floor was level with the ground, the walls were covered with tar paper, and the shack was roofed with various pieces of corrugated tin, flattened five-gallon cans, and sheet iron signs. The yard was littered with broken boxes, a sledge hammer minus most of the handle, some rusted bed springs, parts of a washing machine, and an old, partially dismantled automobile. Mr. Flaherty was in front of the door breaking old lettuce crates into kindling as we drove into the yard. The Superintendent stopped the engine, climbed out of the car, pulled his hat down, squared his shoulders, walked up to Mr. Flaherty, and with a stern show of authority said in a loud voice, "I am the Superintendent of Schools, and I came down here to report your boys cut the spokes out of a bicycle last night. Unless they pay for it, we will have to send them away."

Mr. Flaherty looked at us for several seconds without speaking. Then in a hollow voice asked, "Why don't you have the police chase them home?"

"It is not my place to chase them home."

Flaherty became belligerent, raised his voice, and shouted, "Hell, I never know where they are. They never come home here until late at night."

"I don't care about that. Those boys are going to pay for the damage they have done, or we are going to send them away."

Flaherty countered with, "How-dja know they done it?"

The Superintendent replied, "We saw them do it." (This is in sharp contrast to his earlier statement.)

"Did the boys own up to it?" asked Flaherty.

"Yes, they did."

"How much will it cost?"

"We don't know. That is to be found out tonight, but I want you to know they are going to have to pay for the damage, or we are going to turn them over to the prosecuting attorney."

The next day neither boy was in school. The principal called the sheriff's office and asked for the deputy who had found the boys the day before. He visited the Flaherty home immediately and learned, from a sixteen-year-old girl—in the out-of-school group—who was living with the Flahertys, that the two boys had been given a dollar that morning and sent to school. About noon, an elementary school teacher and a deputy found the boys playing in a gravel pit near the river. They brought them back to school; the principal was called, and the deputy left. The boys denied that their father had given them money to pay for the damage. After a half hour of argument, questioning, and threats, the principal lost his temper and hit the older boy with a leather belt he kept in his office. The teacher interrupted with, "We cannot do that here," that is, in the principal's office.

The men marched the two boys out of the office, down the hall, and across the gymnasium floor. Fifty-odd students in the high school band were seated on the bleachers which formed the ceiling of the band room, facing the group as they walked across the floor. The principal said to the teacher as they passed the band, "The usual serenade." The teacher grinned and nodded. The two boys were taken into the band room, and the band repeated a march until the end of the period, when they were dismissed to go to other classes.

The next day, the band teacher said to us with a grin, "[the principal] beat the hell out of the Flaherty kids for cutting up Tommie Huddleston's bicycle. I would really have liked to have seen that."

The boys played truant the next two days, Thursday and Friday. Saturday the older one, age 14, asked a local man, who had an older brother working for him, for a job picking corn on his farm in the next county. The farmer told the boy he could work Saturday and Sunday, but he would have to come back to town Sunday night. The boy promised he would do this, and the farmer took him to the farm. When he was ready to come back, the boy could not be found.

Monday morning the farmer called the truant officer and told her the story. He was reported to have said among other things, "That boy ought to be in school, and I don't want him down there." The conversation was reported to the principal, who checked with the Superintendent. He was told, "We have no responsibility in the matter. As long as the boy is out of the district, we have nothing to worry about. It is up to the farmer to get the boy off his farm if he wants him off."

The farmer changed his mind after the school authorities did nothing, and the boy continued to work. However, the younger boy, age 12, was made to continue in school for the rest of the year.

Real and alleged illnesses forced the withdrawal of 16 adolescents. Tuberculosis, rheumatic fever, heart trouble, and fainting were the reasons given. There was probably more illness than this, but no others used sickness as an excuse to justify withdrawal from school, even though it might have been the immediate motivating reason.

Four adolescents claimed "heart trouble" to justify their withdrawal. Later we learned that the families of these youngsters were on township relief when the children were said to have weak hearts; they were also on relief when the young people started to work shortly after they left school. What we did not find out until we worked with the relief office was that the supervisor of the poor would not give relief to a family if there were children 14 years of age or older in it, unless the children left school and took a job. The relationship between township relief and withdrawal from school cannot be ignored, especially in class V where 53 per cent of the families were on township relief rolls for at least three months some time between January 1, 1937, and June 30, 1942.

## Conclusions

The out-of-school adolescents are products, in large measure, of the impact of the Elmtown social system on them as constituent members of this system. Cleavages, frictions, and clashes between classes, institutions, families, and individuals are intertwined in devious ways which reach into many phases of community life. The policies of the Board of Education are conditioned in a number of ways by class interests, particularly with respect to their ties with property ownership and taxation. The effects of Board policy are reflected in (1) the administration of the schools, specifically with the way the compulsory attendance law is administered; in (2) the sensitivity of the school officials to the wishes of the upper classes; and in (3) the invidious way discipline is carried out in the case of children from very low-ranking families, such as the Flahertys. These things are reflected further in the large number of withdrawals in the two lower classes.   Administrative policy in the local relief offices is an additional factor.

The family culture, however, is the most powerful factor, and a very complex one itself, which conditions a child's continuation in or withdrawal from school.   That a very close connection exists between the position a family occupies in the class structure and whether an adolescent is in or out of school is demonstrated by the fact that all class I and class II adolescents, and 9 out of 10 in class III were in school, but almost 9 out of 10 in class V had withdrawn.   The relationship between a youngster's family's class position and his connection with the high school is not so clear in class IV.   The point made was that in this stratum the withdrawees had a significantly poorer family background than those in school.   It was inferred that poor family background was the basic factor which gave rise to these youngsters' withdrawal from school at an earlier age than their class peers in school.

The class V adolescent's family background and prestige position are such that he is made to feel unwanted in the classroom, on the playground, or in the clubs and extracurricular activities that are an integral part of the school situation.   This same isolating process operates in the churches and youth groups.   Within the confines of the adolescent world, intangible barriers are erected against the class V boy or girl by boys and girls who belong to the acceptable segments of the social structure which channelize the social relations of the class V youngster to his class equals.   His family has been isolated in the same manner by both necessity and choice, and he accepts this pattern, for there is nothing else he can do until he becomes old enough to leave it.   By that time he has been stamped with his family and class characteristics, and he finds escape from his low class position well-nigh impossible.

The class V adolescent's family experiences provide him with the only picture he has of the society which surrounds him, for he has been isolated from counter-influences by his family's isolation from the higher classes and the values and practices common to each of them.   The class V family's world is centered in the struggle for the necessities of life, and in a search for pleasure to break the monotony of work, unemployment, and insecurity. Family life all too often is punctuated with quarrels followed by fights and physical violence.

The class V child learns very early that he must have money to do the things he wants to do. And in the class V family money is a very scarce commodity which has to be earned by doing some kind of work. Therefore, an essential conditioning factor in his childhood is the desire to grow up and get a job; this means for all practical purposes withdrawal from school. What the class V adolescent does not realize is that the social system limits his opportunities to do the things he desires, and that by withdrawing from school his chances are restricted still further to the things he knows. The negative orientation of class V children toward education and positively toward work and pleasure was expressed succinctly by an aged janitress in her advice to a freshman girl who was working her way through school: "Why work so hard tryin' to learn sumpthin', and spend all that money? Go to work and have a good time!"

# 14

## TOIL AND TROUBLE

### Job channels and levels

ELMTOWN'S ECONOMIC SYSTEM from our viewpoint is differentiated into what we shall call job channels and job levels. There are six principal job channels in the system—agriculture, business, professions, factories, service trades, and, for a low class girl without special training, domestic service. Each channel is organized internally into several different levels. There are four main levels in the farm channel: large owner who hires a manager, owner-operator, tenant-operator, and hired laborer; at least four in the ordinary retail business, owner or manager, office worker, clerical worker, and common laborer; the professions have numerous specialized subdivisions such as lawyer, doctor, teacher, engineer, nurse, with positions and levels in each specialized channel based on independent practice or salaried employment. The two large factories have an elaborate hierarchy with several divisions and levels: owners, executive managers, professional specialists; engineers and accountants; technicians, clerks, craftsmen, line workers, and laborers. The service trades are not so elaborately organized as the factories or such businesses as a bank, department, or chain store; but one encounters the inevitable division between owner and employee, and, within the employee category, supervisor, skilled or semi-skilled and unskilled, the experienced and the inexperienced. Domestic service is not highly differentiated, but there are good employers and bad ones, exacting housewives and those who allow a girl to do about as she pleases as long as the work is done "after a fashion."

Prestige, earnings, freedom on the job, pleasantness of the job, amount of physical energy expended, whether one dresses in a suit with white shirt and tie or in a blue shirt and overalls; whether one deals with people, paper, and ideas, or works with his hands; whether one works in an air-conditioned office with walnut-paneled walls or outdoors; whether one punches a clock or comes and goes as he wills; whether one enters through the office door or the plant gate, the front or the back door; all these factors and many others are connected with the job channel in which one earns his living; more particularly with the level on which he functions in the channel.

By the educational, vocational, and ethical standards prevailing in the three higher classes, adolescents in the out-of-school series entered the work world prematurely. The three higher classes were the ones who offered or withheld jobs, hired and fired, and within the limits of the local labor market set wages. The two lower classes were the ones who worked at these jobs.

What job channels do the withdrawees enter, and at what levels? What tools do they possess with which they can compete for jobs? Are the jobs they get related to class position? How do they adjust to the demands of the job? What conceptions do they have of themselves as competitors? And, perhaps more important, what do employers think of them as employees? What do they think about their future? Before we attempt to answer these questions, we shall sketch the outlines of the Elmtown labor market as it existed from 1937 through May, 1942.

THE EXPANDING LABOR MARKET. The Elmtown labor market contracted sharply in the spring of 1937 and remained static for about 18 months; throughout the latter half of 1938 and on into 1939, it expanded slightly. After the outbreak of war in Europe in August, 1939, the mines and mills hired a few more employees, but not many; farmers hired about the usual number of casuals to harvest their crops that fall, and things moved on an even keel for the next 6 months. Early in the summer of 1940, the news came that a huge war plant which would employ several thousand men was to be built about 25 or 30 miles away. Almost overnight the demand for construction workers at one to two dollars or more an hour drained off the unemployed, enticed many men out of the Mill, stores, service stations, garages, and off the farms. This vast project was underway in the summer of 1941, and it went into production early in the fall.

Although these developments did not draw young people out of high school before our field work ended, they had an indirect effect on the out-of-school group through the job opportunities they opened to adolescents. As men, and later women, were hired out of the community, local employers turned to younger workers for replacements. Then, too, as families earned more money, they bought more food, spent more on recreation, went to the bowling alley oftener, and so on, all of which produced a cumulative effect on employment. The 34 [1] boys and girls who left high school between September, 1941, and June, 1942, were very confident of their ability to find and hold a job, a confidence produced by the expansion of the labor market in the face of war. This self-confidence in one's ability to get a job was in marked contrast to the experiences reported by youths who quit school from 1938 through the spring of 1940. They too had left school under the illusion that they could find a job, only to discover that work was scarce, jobs temporary, and the pay low; but they found jobs eventually. The expanding labor market of 1940–1942 merely provided more immediate job opportunities; it did not change the structure of job channels, nor had it, at that time, altered customary requirements connected with different jobs.

JOBS AND THE SOCIAL STRUCTURE. The family, economic, and prestige systems are so intertwined in Elmtown that one cannot be discussed without some consideration of the others. The family enters the job picture in three different but related ways. First, its position in the prestige structure is connected very closely with what its members do in the economic system. Second, where its members work, if they work, is related to the prestige attached to a place of business. Third, whom an employer will hire is determined quite often by family connections. In short, the rights, privileges, obligations, and penalties inherent in the class system are carried over into economic relationships. Class I and class II families tend to place their younger members in positions which enable them to maintain the control over economic processes gained by an earlier generation. The concentration of economic and social power in these strata not only

[1] This was 5 higher than the average that prevailed for drop-outs during any school year from 1937 through May, 1941.

enables families to provide good jobs for their members, but it also places limits on the channels in which they operate and on the levels at which they function. By way of contrast, class V families do not possess either economic or ancillary legal and political power derived from high prestige; in addition, they are *stigmatized* by a complex of low values which acts as a barrier to their being hired for many jobs they can do, simply because the family has a notorious reputation. In these cases the stigma the family carries is transferred to the children. Although the vast majority of families in classes III and IV are not able to place their children at will in the economic structure, neither do employers refuse to hire them because of family reputation. Nevertheless, a family's position in the prestige structure is recognized locally as an important factor in the determination of who gets what job, no matter where the family is in the structure or where the job is in the economic system.

About 95 per cent of the out-of-school group belongs to families who have made less successful adjustments to the demands of society as the average Elmtown family has.[2] Therefore, their families are not in a position to place them in jobs deemed desirable from the viewpoint of the higher classes. Indeed, the families of most class V adolescents are a positive hindrance to the child's efforts to find work. For example, the Supervisor of the Poor was emphatic in his assertion, "If a family has a relief reputation, it's pretty hard in this town to get any place. I always tell these young people to get out of town—go somewhere else where their family is not known and they'll have a chance. They don't have any here." He punctuated this remark by the citation of some 20 cases in which he had tried unsuccessfully to talk employers into hiring youngsters whose

[2] We have not hypothesized an "average Elmtown family." This statement is based upon the fact that 59 per cent of the withdrawees belong to class V, 37 per cent to class IV, and 4 per cent to class III. In the preceding chapter evidence was presented which indicated that the out-of-school class IV's came from families who are "more unfortunate" than those of the class IV's in school. Since only 4 per cent of the withdrawees are from class III; since the class IV's out of school seem to be below the average for the bulk of the class IV families; and since the class V families are conspicuous for their low positions, we believe that the above generalization is sound.

families were on relief, in some cases after he had put pressure on the families to have the children leave school and get a job to help support the family.

Such factors as family, class position, education, and employers' ideas that withdrawal from school is *prima facie* evidence of dumbness operate as interrelated parts of the complex. They severely limit the out-of-school adolescent's access to jobs he might fill if he were judged on his merits rather than on his family's reputation. Unfortunately, the young worker does not understand the hazards which surround his efforts to adjust to a world that judges him more by what his family is than by what he might himself become, simply because possible employers assume that he will be like his parents: "Water cannot run uphill."

A child's escape from family domination is symbolized particularly in classes IV and V by his ability to "pay his own way." This is especially true when a large number of children combined with a meager family income creates, in the child, an acutely felt need to earn money early in life. The lower class child hears money questions discussed from his earliest years—the lack of money, how hard it is to earn, the need of a job if the family is to live. Gradually, he realizes that money is the key to his existence. The desires his culture instills in him can be achieved only by getting money—food, candy, toys, amusement; to have these things he must have money! Since his parents cannot furnish it, he feels that he must go out and earn the money to buy the things his culture makes him want—or to steal them, but that is another story. His idea of the way to acquire money is also a product of his experiences in the class system. In the lower classes, money is earned usually by the expenditure of time and physical energy on a job in the employ of someone else.

To be "big" enough to earn money is an important element in the lower class child's world of values. To him, "bigness" is connected with having a job, having a job with earning money, and earning money with personal freedom. The child, however, does not realize that this assumed freedom is purchased at the expense of the freedom he seeks. This is indeed a vicious circle, and he cannot escape from it as long as he must purchase what he considers freedom by enduring restrictions imposed by the job. The implications of the system under which he lives lie beyond his comprehension. He is interested in its outward manifestations, and they attract him toward the work world as irresistibly as an open flame does the moth. The lower class youth, like the moth, becomes a victim of his own flight into reality, where he finds that the freedom he seeks develops into the collar of the job.

Although the vast majority of the out-of-school adolescents state that they left school to earn their own way,[3] they continue to live at home and to accept the domestic facilities provided by their families as a matter of right. Their mothers continue to do their laundry, cook their food, supply furniture, bed clothing. Practically all the girls living at home help with the housework, and some do most of it. But the boys report that they do little work around home; indeed, most of them do none, particularly the town dwellers. Yet they pay only a few dollars a week to their parents for room and board. All buy their own clothes and provide for their amusement and pleasure, but it is clear they do not "pay their way," for they continue to be partially dependent on their family. This partial dependence continues almost invariably until they marry or until they leave home; and, in class V, couples often live with one of the parents until they can find "something."

Childhood dependency is justified by the value system of each class; moreover, the length of this dependent period varies with the different classes. In class I, it may last well into the late twenties or early thirties, when adult children and in-laws gradually take over the management of family property or possibly the practice of a profession, such as law or medicine. In class II, it lasts at least through the high school years; but in most families it continues through the college years and, in some cases, through the years a son or son-in-law is learning a business or a profession and establishing himself in it. Class III dependency tends to stop in the late teens or early twenties in

[3] Four out of 5 girls in class IV and 6 out of 7 in class V give this as their reason for leaving school. The ratio among the boys is even higher, almost 9 out of 10 in class V and slightly less than 7 out of 8 in class IV.

the majority of cases. In class IV, it is largely over by the middle and late teens, and in class V in the early teens.

## Work history

The work history of these adolescents covers more than six years, from 1936 to the summer of 1942. Nineteen hundred and thirty-six was a prosperous year for farmers, workers, tradesmen, and industry in comparison with earlier depression years, but it was a poor year by the standards of 1942. Nevertheless, there was a demand for unskilled cheap labor on the local market. Boys could and did find part-time jobs delivering papers, clerking in stores after school or on Saturday, delivering milk, and working on farms; these jobs paid them from a few cents an hour to a few dollars a week. A girl could earn from 25 to 50 cents taking care of children for three to six hours in the evenings; others found jobs doing housework after school or on Saturdays.

Forty-one per cent of the class IV boys and 59 per cent of those in class V report that they did *not* work regularly on a part-time job before they left school. The percentages for the girls are similar, 43 of the class IV's and 61 of the class V's. The higher percentage without regular part-time work experience among the class V's is conditioned by their earlier age and lower grade in school at the time of withdrawal as well as by the generally poorer work habits found in this class. It is a paradox that the class with the least opportunity and training for a job is the one in which the adolescents are prone to leave school earliest to go to work.

Certain part-time jobs go to class IV boys, in large part, whereas others go to class V boys. Of 7 boys who report that they worked in stores, 6 were class IV's and 1 was a class V. On the other hand, of the 19 boys who held jobs in the bowling alley or the roller rink, 7 were class IV's and 12 class V's. Both classes work at odd jobs, but a disproportionate number is class V. The same is true of farm work, except that here the situation is reversed: 13 class IV boys were part-time farm hands, but only 7 class V's. Among the girls, the same pattern is observed, except for the difference in sex roles. Three times as many class IV's cared for children as class V's (18 in contrast to 6), but the class IV's were the store clerks, 7 to 1. The number employed as housemaids is slightly in favor of the class V's (16 against 13). These figures indicate that the culture provides rather sharply different roles in these two classes for such a job as clerking in a store; for other jobs the differentiation is not so sharp. However, on the whole, a class V boy is more likely to start his work career in a more disagreeable job than a class IV youngster, and on tasks which did not bring him into contact with the public.

Part-time jobs open to low class adolescents in their early teens are menial in nature, demand little knowledge or skill, pay only a few cents an hour, and for the most part are seasonal or occasional; paper routes are the exception. Employers who have periodic need for a boy or girl hire youngsters by the hour, the day, or the job. Only the poorer jobs are available to the low-ranking class IV's and class V's who later leave school; the better jobs are given to the higher ranking class IV's and class III's in high school and in the upper elementary grades. For instance, an implement dealer hires from 4 to 6 boys in the afternoons and on Saturdays to clean and to help repair used farm machines taken in on trades. The boys who clean the dirt, grease, and grime off the used machines are class V's who are not allowed to take the machines apart and put in the new parts. This repair work is done by the dealer's high-school-aged son and two of the son's class III pals. He justifies this procedure in these terms, "I can't trust the clean-up crew to do the repair work." This illustrates the higher classes' conception of the role the class V boy is expected to play in the economy. Other businesses hire class V boys because no one else will do the required work. An example of this type of business is the junk yard, where 4 or 5 boys tear down machines for scrap, then sort, pile, and load it.

THE FULL-TIME JOB. The only jobs available to fourteen-, fifteen-, and sixteen-year-old boys and girls, whose educational level ranges from the sixth to the eleventh grade, and whose families are known for their low "social level," are mean, dirty, undesirable, and generally seasonal or temporary. Almost one-half of the part-time workers continue at the job they held when they left school. Their decision to leave school is often precipitated by the opportunity to work full time instead of part time on this job. This is not to imply that they would have finished elementary or high school if they had not had this job; on the contrary, there were too many influences which contributed to their decision to leave school.

The girls start their full-time work history in one of three or four kinds of jobs—housemaids, waitresses, service workers, or petty clerks. The boys have a much wider individual range. Employers are reluctant to pay more than 20 cents an hour when they can hire adults for 30 cents or less for the same type of work. The prevailing pay for adolescent workers in 1938 and 1939 was nearer 10 to 12 cents an hour than 20. One boy reports that he started his work career shoveling shelled corn out of farm trucks at the elevator for 10 cents an hour; another loaded bottles in racks and cases at the soda pop factory for 12 cents an hour. Until the summer of 1940, the prevailing wage for boys on the farm was $1.50 a day for a ten- to eleven-hour day; lunch was included. Housemaids generally received from $4 to $7 a week, but one fourteen-year-old who left school in the summer of 1939 reports that she worked from 9:30 in the morning to 3:30 in the afternoon for $1 a week with lunch included. This girl belonged to one of the lowest ranking families in Elmtown—one so low that all the raters agree that it was "on the bottom." The woman this girl worked for was the wife of the junk yard owner, whose family was noted for its exploitation of adolescents from the lower ranking families.

The withdrawees' job skills are limited to what they have learned from contact with parents, relatives, friends, and through observation and personal experience, largely within the community; no withdrawee has any technical training for any type of job; furthermore, few have plans to acquire it in the future. The girls know something about housework, as it is done in the lower classes, the care of children, and waiting on tables or washing dishes. The boys have some acquaintance with working on farms, washing cars, loading and unloading grain, repairing cars, driving trucks, doing janitor work, clerking in stores, and odd jobs, but their lack of training, job skills, and experience combined with their youth and family backgrounds severely limit their job opportunities. These factors, along with need, force them to take whatever jobs they can find. Many of those who do not have a job when they quit school know about a job they think they can get. Often they are disappointed because they are not old enough, do not have the experience it requires, or because someone else has already taken the job. Disappointment is often followed by a period of unemployment or a part-time job, with a shift to some other type of work when it can be found. Menial tasks, long hours, low pay, and little consideration from the employer produce discontent and frustration, which motivate the young worker to seek another job, only to realize after a few days or weeks that the new job is like the old one. This desire for a more congenial job, better pay, shorter hours, and a better employer gives rise to a drift from job to job.

We believe that the adolescent's search for a good job is his way of adjusting to the demands of the work world. While it is in process, he is maladjusted on the job, but he does not realize this; so he projects his frustration on his employer, the job, his family, his associates, and society in general. This process is symbolized in folk belief as the revolt of youth, but youth revolts only as long as it is adjusting to the adult society. After it has accepted its functions and roles, the controls society imposes upon it are viewed as comfortable, protective, and beneficent.

Adolescents in the out-of-school group are in the midst of this adjustment process. They have left school in an effort to adjust to the demands, as they conceived them, that society makes upon them. In their search for a self-sufficient role, they seek and find a job. But the first job, like the school, constrains them, and they are unwilling or unable to adjust satisfactorily to its requirements. Subjectively, it does not satisfy their real or imagined personal needs. Perhaps it does not give them the ego satisfaction they expected or the freedom from the restraints imposed by their family and by the demands of a pecuniary culture. Once a work career has been launched, few adolescents consider a return to school as a solution to their problem, even if this were possible. For the frustrated youthful male worker, the one solution is to find a better job. For the vast majority of girls, the proper solution is marriage. These apparently personal solutions are not at all personal. On the contrary, the general and class cultures provide them for each sex: the boy has to continue working if he is to realize goals his culture sets for him, and the girl has to marry or be considered "queer."

What the job pays soon develops into a major problem, especially for the boy. Once he has a full-time job, he considers himself a man; but if the job does not pay him enough to buy the things he believes essential to man's estate, he blames the job. In his eyes the job has to pay enough for him to meet the standards set by his class and clique. Above all, it has to pay enough for him to have clothes, a car, and enough left over to take girls to places of public amusement three or four nights a week, as well as some spare change to buy tobacco and drinks, and to finance a little gambling on the side. If his parents ask for a contribution toward room and board—and about 6 out of 7 boys indicate this is required—what the job paid is of still greater importance.

Once the gap between needs and pay is realized, the adolescent begins to re-evaluate the job, its future, and his relation to it. If the $10 to $12 a week he receives for work in a service station, grocery, bakery, or on a truck does not fit into his dream of marriage, a home of his own, and a place in the community, he begins to look around for a job which pays more. Perhaps he hears in the pool hall, the skating rink, or the tavern that "the Mill is putting men on." He knows you have to be 18, or claim to be, before you can "get on at the Mill," but the Mill pays beginners $18 a week. That dream of $18 for 40 hours' work often gives a boy courage to ask for a raise. When this happens, more often than not, the employer answers with an emphatic "No." Shortly after this the Mill has another applicant, and, if there is a vacancy, a new employee. The boy's old job is taken by a new aspirant who is likely to repeat the process. The new mill hand knows that he will have to start on the night shift, a situation he does not like, but as soon as there is an opening on the day shift he will have a chance to work days. Then some other "green kid" can take his place on the night shift.

The typical young worker passes through a two-phase cycle in his adjustment to the work world. The first normally lasts from a year to a year and a half after he leaves school. The average boy holds five jobs in this phase—one reports 13; the average girl reports 4 different jobs—one reports 11. Most of these jobs are seasonal: farm work, the vegetable gardens, house cleaning, loading trucks at the elevators, working in stores during the Christmas rush. This phase of the work cycle is a period of adjustment to the demands of the job, of accumulation of some experience, and of learning how to get and keep a job. The requisite of experience is a hurdle the new recruit to the labor force has to meet on almost any permanent job, even though the job actually requires little or no skill or previous training, for practically all employers ask applicants where they have worked, what they have done, how old they are. It seems to be a ritual one must go through; in most cases it enables the young worker to say where he has worked and what he has done, no matter whether there is any connection between experience and alleged requirements.

Once the experience and age requirements are met, a youth generally enters the second phase of his work career. This phase is marked by better performance on the job, higher pay, and a steady job by local standards. The work may not be different from what was done before, but the worker becomes a steady instead of an extra. However, in many cases there is a real change in jobs. Regularity of the job is really more important than the higher pay, since greater responsibility and dignity is attached to being a regular at the bottling works than a pin boy at the bowling alley, or to being a clerk in the five-and-ten than a nursemaid. Farm boys usually go through a similar cycle: farm work for a year or two, then a shift into better-paid town jobs connected in some way with the work they have learned on the farm, perhaps truck driving, automobile or machinery repair; then into the Mill; only a few remain on the farm as laborers. Farm girls, on the other hand, tend to work as maids for farm owners' wives or prosperous tenants until they marry; less than half a dozen shift to work in town after they start to work in the country.

The longer a boy works as a farm laborer, as a "swamper" on a truck, as a casual laborer around town, at the bowling alley, or in the garages, and the longer a girl works as a housemaid or a janitress, the less opportunity each has to leave this type of work and cross over into sales, clerical, or factory work. Furthermore, if the work record was not satisfactory on these jobs, the factories—under the conditions which prevailed from 1938 through the summer of 1940—would not hire the youngster. The workers in this group, where job turnover was high, merely went from job to job. Only a few were able to change from casual to permanent employment, and still fewer moved into the sales and clerical fields.

During the second phase of their work history the differences between the work patterns of class IV and class V become clear. In the first period, adolescents from the two classes follow about the same kinds of jobs, except store work, and drift from one to another with almost the same regularity. But, once the experience hurdle has been passed, workers in the two classes start down slightly different roads. Regular employees in the more desirable jobs tend to come from class IV families; only 37 per cent of the gainfully employed withdrawees are class IV's, but class IV's hold 68 per cent of the regular jobs. Job turnover among the class IV's in the second phase of the work cycle drops, among the boys, to 46 per cent and, among the girls, to 31 per cent of that among the class V's. The higher turnover rate among the class V's is conditioned by the seasonable nature of the jobs available, and their poorer performance record on the job.

Because the class V workers possess a very rudimentary understanding of economic processes, the social system, and their place in it, they continue to be dissatisfied with the work or the employer, unhappy about the poor pay and the disagreeable nature of the work, but helpless to do anything about the situation. Their one hope is for a better job. They have little hesitation about quitting one job, without notice, to look for another one. If they obtain a new job, they start on it immediately. In the meantime, the old employer does not know what has become of his worker. He may be told by another employee that so-and-so is working for such-and-such. A few days later, the errant worker may come back for the remainder of his pay. Sometimes, if he does not like the new job, he drifts back to the old one, as though nothing has happened.

Employers are aware of this tendency, and they become indignant and vocal about it; but they know that they have no recourse except to fire the youngster. If they do this they are faced with breaking in another on the job, and the process is likely to be repeated. From the employers' viewpoint, such behavior is characteristic of "that class." This explanation overlooks the fact that these people are paid so poorly that they cannot subsist on the wages they receive. The employer rationalizes his position by saying that "these people are not interested in getting ahead," and he cites their unstable job performance to justify his argument. We believe that such statements are the employers' means of showing their resentment.

Class V boys, if they are fortunate, manage to find work in marginal retail stores, service stations, garages, trucking businesses, or the Mill. In May, 1942, the majority (72 per cent) were employed as farm laborers, general laborers, and janitors or pin boys at the bowling alley. These boys tend to be a year younger and less experienced than the 28 per cent in the more desirable jobs open to class V, but there are not enough of these jobs available in the local labor market to absorb the others or even a large part. Thus, unless the war radically altered the situation, the vast majority of the class V's will continue into adult life as laborers, menials, and poorly paid casuals in the same way their fathers did in the previous generation.

The class V girls' work history is similar to the boys' except that they look forward to marriage, even though more often than not they do not openly admit the wish. In about 8 cases out of 10, first jobs are connected with housework and care of young children. Very few start to work in sales, clerical, or service jobs such as waitress. Like the boys, they go through a period of adjustment during which they drift from job to job. As they grow older, gain some experience, and acquire a sense of responsibility on the job, the turnover rate falls, and the better workers move into the more desirable jobs open to young girls with little training or education.

The class V girl has two avenues open to her when she reaches her sixteenth birthday. She may continue in domestic service of one kind or another—housemaid, laundress, janitress—

or she may try to get on at the Factory. The Factory is a haven of refuge to the girl who works as a domestic at $3 to $7 a week for six or six and one-half days a week, from 7 to 10 hours a day. At the Factory she can earn from $9 to $15 a week for 40 hours, depending upon how dexterous she is on the job. The Factory has a reputation for poor wages, a driving production policy, and little consideration for the worker. The Mill, on the other hand, enjoys a high reputation. A girl feels that she is lucky if she can get on the payroll in the box factory, which was the part of the Mill where women are chiefly employed, but she has to be 18 before she can work there. This age barrier keeps all but a few girls in the study out of the Mill. The class IV girl is four times more likely to work as a waitress than as a line employee in the Factory. The class V girl over 16 is thus attracted to the factory and taken away from domestic service.

## Occupational pursuits in May, 1942

An occupational census taken in May, 1942, revealed that the occupational pursuits of the class IV males and females in the

### TABLE XVIII

OCCUPATIONAL PURSUITS FOR MALES BY CLASS, MAY, 1942

|  | Class | |
| --- | --- | --- |
| *Occupational Pursuit* | *IV* | *V* |
| Farm hand | 14 | 21 |
| General laborer | 8 | 33 |
| Factory worker | 17 | 10 |
| Truck driver | 7 | 13 |
| Garage mechanic | 6 } * | 3 } * |
| Service station | 5 | 2 |
| Janitorial and service | 1 } * | 5 } * |
| Bowling alley | 2 | 7 |
| Store clerks | 9 | 2 |
| Armed forces | 7 | 3 |
| Unemployed | 3 } * | 7 } * |
| State institution | 1 | 3 |
| Total | 80 | 109 |

$X^2 = 33.0891.$    $P < 0.01.$    $C = 0.39.$    $\bar{C} = 0.49.$

* Cells combined for $X^2$ analysis.

out-of-school group differ significantly from those followed by the
class V's. The class IV boys are attracted to the factories, stores,
garages, service stations, and the armed forces. They avoid
general labor jobs, janitor work, the bowling alley, and the skating rink. The class V boys on the contrary are concentrated
disproportionately in the latter types of jobs. Both classes are
represented in almost equal proportions in the farm labor field.
The complete figures for the males in each class by occupational
pursuits are given in Table XVIII. The war may have completely disorganized the more or less orderly progression from
job to job within the relatively narrow confines of low skill and
low class, but we have no way of knowing its effect.

The occupational pursuits of the girls follow a pattern similar
to that of the boys in so far as class is involved. The class V
girls tend to be housewives, factory workers, and domestics in
disproportionate numbers. The class IV girls, on the other hand,
are more likely to be employed as clerks, saleswomen, and waitresses. Although there are no jobs that one could label clearly
as belonging to either the class IV's or the class V's, there is
enough differentiation between jobs along class lines to make
the observed differences statistically significant at the 1 per
cent level.

### TABLE XIX

OCCUPATIONAL PURSUITS OF GIRLS BY CLASS, MAY, 1942

|  | Class | |
| --- | :---: | :---: |
| Occupational Pursuit | IV | V |
| Housewife (not employed) | 10 | 25 |
| At parents' home (unemployed) | 3 | 8 |
| Housework (gainfully employed) | 8 | 24 |
| Factory work (gainfully employed) | 6 | 16 |
| Clerical sales (gainfully employed) | 9 | 3 |
| Service work (gainfully employed) | 4 | 15 |
| Waitress (gainfully employed) | 9 | 4 |
| Total | 49 | 95 |

$X^2 = 19.8707.$     $P < 0.01.$     $C = 0.34.$     $\bar{C} = 0.44.$

The mean weekly earnings of the class IV boys is $2.42, and
of the girls $2.59, higher than those of class V workers. The

usual sex differential also appears, as the following tabulation indicates.

| Class | Mean Weekly Earnings, May, 1942 | |
|---|---|---|
| | Males | Females |
| IV | $17.60 | $11.83 |
| V | 15.15 | 9.24 |

These earning figures supplement those on occupational pursuits in that they show that the class IV boys and girls tend to be found in more desirable and better-paying jobs than those in class V. It would be interesting to know if this differential between the classes continued under the impact of the stringent labor shortages of the war years.

### Performance on the job

With few exceptions, mutual dissatisfaction exists between the school withdrawee and his employer. The young worker has not learned to work consistently; neither has he acquired the simple skills required on most jobs. Complaints about low pay, the menial nature of the job, and employer discrimination are common—many examples were cited of someone who, the boy or girl claims, is no better than he, does less work, but receives higher pay. It is not unusual for the person cited to tell the same story about the other boy or girl. The employer usually expects better work than he receives and greater consistency on the job than the adolescent has learned is necessary to hold the job. Poor job performance makes the employer dissatisfied; but, when he speaks to the boy or girl about uneven work or lack of regularity, the adolescent often resents the rebuke. Many times he stalls more, thus creating further discontent in the employer.

A large part of this difficulty arises from the fact that the adolescent does not understand that he has an obligation to his employer. The employer, on his part, often pays the youngster an inordinately low wage and expects him to do as much work as a mature person for one-half to three-fourths the pay the older person would receive, justifying his policy on the ground that the worker is "only a kid." This patronizing attitude is resented by the adolescent who feels that he is an adult and should be treated as such, certainly in the way of pay.

That the job is a means to an end—pleasure—is a potent contributory factor to the poor adjustment these youngsters make. The pleasures the job will enable them to purchase in their off hours are more important to many than what they do during working hours. From the stories they tell it is apparent that thoughts about these pleasures, flitting through their dreams while they work, often hinder the efficient execution of their duties. But memories of past pleasures and dreams of those to come form a pleasant fantasy world which helps the time pass when one is forced to spend long hours alone cleaning house, cultivating corn, polishing cars, washing milk bottles, or one of the half hundred other monotonous, always menial, and often hard jobs these youngsters work at from 8 to 12 hours a day, six days a week. Abundant interview evidence forces the inference that night life, which is directly traceable to the adolescent's off-the-job pleasures, is the most common factor interfering with job performance. Many stories are told by employers about "troubles" they have experienced with help who have fallen asleep on the job as a result of night life, or who have feigned illness to get time off to enjoy it with their peers. Because of spatial limits only two such tales will be sketched here.

One matron related that she left her maid, a class V girl, in the basement one Monday morning to do the laundry. She returned three hours later to find the washing machine running with the first batch of clothes still in it, and the girl fast asleep on a pile of dirty clothes. This woman awakened the girl, gave her "a dressing down," and the girl quit in anger. The girl later said that the matron had called her a "drunken bitch." "Who does she think she is? They have drinks all the time." Questioning revealed that the girl and her boy friend had been to a dance in Diamond City until 1 A.M. the night before; then they had gone to a roadside tavern where "we had some wine." On the way back to Elmtown they had parked by the Three Pines for "a little while." The girl had reached home "about four o'clock." "God, but I was tired."

The manager of a chain grocery employed a seventeen-year-old class IV boy in October, 1941, ostensibly to help in the

Christmas rush, with the idea that he would be kept as a permanent employee to replace an older youth subject to military service. This boy had left school the previous summer to drive a farm tractor after he had successfully completed his sophomore year. He had not liked farm work; so he found a job in a service station in September. But he had not liked to work in the rain and grease, neither had he "taken to" the janitorial work connected with this job. The store was "just what I wanted." The manager was highly satisfied with the boy's cheerful disposition, promptness, treatment of customers, and his eagerness to learn the business. He did not like the boy's listlessness on Saturdays and Mondays or his eagerness to leave Saturday night before the produce was taken out of the window, the window washed, the floor swept, and the shelves faced. These things did not irritate the manager too much since "a person has to learn to do these things on this job." All went well until New Year's Eve. On December 30, the boy began to complain of a "sore throat," a "headache," "dizziness," and a "pain in my back." The manager assumed that he was developing influenza and sympathized with him. The next morning the boy came to work with a cloth saturated with bacon grease and black pepper wrapped around his throat. He talked in a hoarse whisper, walked slowly, never smiled, and as the manager said, "looked awful." As the day wore on, he complained openly of how bad he felt. About three o'clock, he went to the manager and said, "I guess I can't make it. Can I go home? I hate like hell to leave you like this with inventory and all tonight, but I feel like I got a fever and I got spots before my eyes." The manager told him to go home, go to bed, and forget the inventory; the rest of them would make out all right.

About five-thirty an older man, who was a regular customer, came in to trade. He started talking to the manager, whom he knew quite well, and innocently asked, "Has young Swain quit?"

"No. Why?"

"I thought he had. I saw him a few minutes ago in Brock's Tavern buying a bottle."

The manager said nothing more to the customer about Swain's illness, but, as he said later, "I thought, 'Ah, ha, so that's it!'"

After dinner the manager called the boy's home on the tele-

phone and asked about his health. Mrs. Swain told him her son
was in bed with a high temperature and she had called the doctor, but he had not arrived. This satisfied the manager; so he
went back to work with the impression that the customer must
have been wrong. The store crew worked until 3:45 A.M. on
the inventory. Then the manager, and two other employees,
walked uptown to the Blue Triangle to have something to eat
before going home to bed. He later related to us:

> I walked in the Blue Triangle and who should I see but Jack
> Swain sitting at a table with three other fellows. All of them were
> drunk. I was so God-damned mad I could have choked that little
> bastard, but I walked by them and sat down at the counter. The
> next morning about ten o'clock I went down there, and his old
> man came to the door and said Jack was sick in bed. I saw red
> again, but all I said was, "When he sobers up, tell him he can have
> his check." The old man didn't say anything to that. Four or five
> days later the kid's sister came in and meekly asked for Jack's
> check. I haven't seen any of the outfit since.

Jack's version of this incident tallied with the store manager's
in most details. He said "the gang" had planned a New Year's
party for several weeks, and he had "made a date," arranged
to get the family car, and take another couple. Jack and his
friend and two other couples had gone to a roadhouse about
twenty miles away, where they had danced, eaten, and drunk
the old year out and the New Year in. They took the girls
home around three o'clock, and, like the manager and the two
clerks, went to the Blue Triangle for a cup of coffee. Jack did
not know that the manager had seen him in the restaurant; he
believed that "some rat had squealed." He justified his behavior
on the grounds that "the gang had planned the party for weeks.
I didn't know about the inventory. I wuzn't gonna let 'em
down."

## The vocational horizon

The jobs in which these young men and women were engaged
in May, 1942, promised little in the way of a future, from the
viewpoint of either pay or promotion. The unskilled and semi-
skilled jobs they held were not directed toward training them
to become skilled workers; moreover, the employers had no plans

or programs for on-the-job training because almost everyone except the Factory and the Mill had few employees. The little a boy learns is picked up on the job, either from other employees or through his own ingenuity. Employers are chiefly interested in seeing the job done each day in a satisfactory way; they have little interest in the welfare of their workers. The workers, on their part, desire more money and a better job, almost without exception, but only a small segment have plans to prepare themselves for a brighter future through specific vocational training.

About 14 per cent of the boys and 12 per cent of the girls have vague ideas about going somewhere to school. Closer questioning revealed that they have practically no accurate information regarding prior preparation, costs of courses of training, the abilities needed, the length of time required to finish a course, and where one could work after the training is finished. Their ideas about future training have been gleaned from the many advertisements of proprietary trade schools, located mainly in Chicago and St. Louis, in the back pages of pulp magazines. These advertisements tell how to become a Diesel engineer, an air-conditioning engineer, a fireman, a steam engineer, a barber, a cook. The girls are attracted to "beauty school," nursing, secretarial, dress design, and "actress school" training. The glowing claims these schools make for themselves are believed implicitly by many youngsters. As one class V maid said about a self-styled "dramatics school," which indirectly promised its students "a Hollywood career," "It was right there in the ad. If I go there, I can be an actress, and Oh, boy!" As she said this, she placed the palms of her hands on the back of her neck, ran her fingers through her stringy, dun-colored hair, and aped a slow, glamorous smile she had seen in motion pictures. Such dreams are seldom implemented by definite plans, even to the extent of writing to the schools for literature.

A few boys and girls, however, say that they have written to different schools, but "they want money right away, and I don't have any." One class IV boy wrote to an "air-conditioning school" whose advertisement he had read. A salesman called upon him a few days later and sold him the idea of "coming to school." He told the boy he had to pay one-half of the course fee, which was $300, to show his "good intentions"; the boy, however, had only $61. The salesman took this "on account," and the boy signed the contract to pay the $150, plus the other $150 when he "came to school." The boy did not ask for a receipt for his $61, and the fact that he had paid $61 was not written into the contract. A few days later he received a bill for $150. This was followed by a series of threatening letters and several visits from a collection agency. The boy refused to pay this bill, but the loss of his $61 made him bitter about schools, education, and advertisements in general; he remarked, "It's all a racket." [4] This experience circulated from youngster to youngster in his circle of acquaintances, and 9 or 10 different versions were told by adolescents and adults to illustrate the point that a poor boy has no chance to gain an education. This story may have acted as a deterrent to other young people who were motivated toward some type of vocational training; but it is very doubtful that any of them would have gone away to school if this incident had not happened.

The 17 boys and 10 girls in class IV and the 9 boys and 7 girls in class V who indicate that they would like to go away to learn a trade are making little or no preparation to do so. Even though these young people verbalize a desire to go on to school, the memories of their earlier experience act as emotional blocks to further effort. Moreover, their families see little value in additional education, particularly since it will cost money directly rather than indirectly through taxation. These factors, combined with the immediate demands of the present job, obligations to the clique and dates, and the search for happiness through pleasure, rather effectively preclude the probability of further formal vocational training.

### Ideas of "good" jobs

An open-ended question designed to give some idea of what each adolescent thought he would like to do if he had the opportunity was included in the schedule. The boys named 53 different occupations, but their choices were limited largely to vocations about which they knew something from personal ex-

---

[4] The boy had never thought of going to an attorney with his problem.

perience.  We thought one boy's desire to be an archeologist very unusual until he told us that he had watched anthropologists from Home State University excavate an Indian mound on the farm where his father is a tenant.  Another boy wants to be a river pilot; "You don't have to work like the men do."  This boy helps load grain barges, and to him a pilot's life is an escape from hard labor.  One chap who delivers packages for a drug store on his bicycle dreams of becoming a pharmacist.  Certain hard, disagreeable occupations which carry low prestige are never named, such as garbage collector, tiler, janitor, night watchman, particularly if the boy or some member of his family works in them.  Others that are well known, such as farming, have little appeal.  Farming is particularly distasteful to the class V boys, probably because many have worked at one time or another as farm hands.

On the whole, the boys are both modest and realistic in their occupational desires.  The dream of a business or a professional career, so prevalent among the high school boys,[5] is not found here.  Their experiences in the work world have destroyed any illusions they may have held earlier about becoming "millionaires," "big shots," or "wealthy."  Five per cent of the boys in both classes think they would like to get into business or a profession.  One wants to own a skating rink, another a service station, a third wants to be a "horse doctor."  These boys do not have plans to realize these dreams; so they are very likely to remain but a youthful hope.  White collar clerical jobs are eschewed—only 5 name such jobs as working in a bank and selling insurance.  Public service is also beyond their desires—6 mention being a policeman, fireman, or deputy sheriff.

The skilled crafts have the greatest appeal for boys in both classes.  Thirty-six per cent of the class IV's and 28 per cent of the class V's say that they want to become barbers, machinists, carpenters, plumbers, tinners, molders, miners, printers, mechanics, draftsmen, butchers, truck drivers, linotypists, bricklayers, electricians, welders, and papermakers.  An additional 19 per cent of the class IV's and 27 per cent of the class V's indicate that they would like to have skilled jobs in the Mill, the Fac-

[5] For a discussion of this point see Chapter 11, pp. 282–287.

tory, or the mines. One-fourth of the class IV's and one-third of the class V's do not know what they would like to do. The latter group represents, in the main, the drifters; they have no ideas about what the future might hold, nor are they overly anxious about it.

From the answers these young men gave to the question about their vocational choices, we concluded that they have adjusted their hopes, in most cases, to the reality of the work world. They have learned that they have little chance to become white collar workers, professionals, or owners of businesses. Moreover, they have developed what we shall refer to as the "employee state of mind." None of them is in business for himself, few hope to be, or appear to desire it. This response is normal for them, since their parents are almost all employees or farm tenants who have never been able to acquire a business or a farm. It appears that both parents and children have come to accept the dependent attitude the employee and tenant hold toward employer and landlord.[6] When these youngsters leave school, they go to a prospective employer and ask for a job; this process is repeated whenever they leave one job and look for another. Therefore, it is natural for them to conceive of themselves as employees rather than as employers. For a goodly number a job in the Mill spells security and measures what they hope to gain from the economic system.

If we assume that their answers to the question about desired vocations are sincere, the vast majority of these boys are content to be employees. The change they desire to make is from unskilled to skilled labor. This is revealed by the fact that almost one-half of the class IV's and over one-half of the class V's name a craft as their choice of avocation. By setting these crafts as their occupational goals, they place upon themselves limits which will operate in connection with their limited educa-

---

[6] It might be well to qualify this generalization by limiting it to the unorganized employee. Organized employees in the Mill and the mines who were backed by a powerful trade union had a different viewpoint. The reader should also remember that these families recently had experienced ten years of more or less continuous depression, years when these young people matured, and most were thankful for what little they had, "be it ever so humble."

tion, employee status, and family background to keep them, within the limits of probable expectancy, in their present strata in the social structure. We believe that a few in class V, who become skilled artisans, will move into the next higher class in their lifetime. If this move is supplemented by a successful marriage, approved moral actions, and an effort to adjust to the expectancy of the higher classes, they may eventually be accepted as class IV's.

The girls' vocational desires reflect the three general feminine roles existent in American culture—the business-professional careerist, the mother, and the glamorous siren. Possibly as a consequence of the fewer possible vocational opportunities that are open to women, they list only 18 different occupations in comparison with the boys' 53. The girls reveal far more fantasy in their desires than do the boys; they also indicate a much higher percentage of white collar jobs within the business-professional groups, 39 in class IV and 29 in class V. These girls express desires to become teachers, librarians, nurses, dietitians, secretaries, office workers, beauticians, "a department store buyer," and a designer. The glamour role is associated very strongly with class V, for 17 girls (18 per cent) said that they would like to be actresses, dancers, torch singers, ballet dancers, riders in a circus, fancy ice skaters. Four class IV girls, 8 per cent, indicate a preference for this role. The mother role is encountered with almost equal frequency in the two classes— 18 per cent of the class IV's and 17 per cent of the class V's report that they would be wives and mothers if they had a free choice. The Mill and the Factory appeal to both classes, but the frequency is three times as high in class V as in class IV; 6 per cent of the class IV's state that they would like to work in the box factory, but 18 per cent of the class V's think this would be "ideal." Twenty-eight per cent in class IV and 20 per cent in class V have not decided on anything.

Although slightly more than 47 per cent want to play business, professional, or glamorous roles, only an occasional girl is found who has any idea of the requirements a woman has to have to become a dietitian or a ballet dancer. The girl who wants to be a ballet dancer saw this role played by a motion picture actress. Another one dreams of becoming a screen siren "like Joan Crawford." She claims that she went to all her pictures and "read everything about Joan" in the screen magazines. And to clinch her argument on the similarity between herself and Miss Crawford, she said, "And she usta work in a restaurant too." The glamour role appeals most frequently among class V's to housemaids who dream of a miraculous Cinderella-like transformation from a despised domestic drudge into a famous actress, singer, or dancer. One fifteen-year-old nursemaid said that she often transforms herself into Claudette Colbert as she works around the house. She saw Miss Colbert play this part in "a pitchur." The girl tried to model her coiffure as well as her make-up after Colbert's. The most pathetic case of escape we encountered was a cross-eyed seventeen-year-old class V girl who came from one of the lowest ranking families in Elmtown. This girl was known for her "B.O.," poor clothes, dirty skin, and her habit of singing while she worked. She had been fired from at least three jobs because she sang "all the time." She said, "I am always practicing the latest thing," in order to realize her hope to become a torch singer in a night club. Few, if any, of these girls will ever realize their dreams. Inevitably they are drifting toward marriage, and the dream of a business-professional career or one as an entertainer is likely to recede into the background as they mature.

The employer's evaluation of the job places more effective limits on the job horizon than the employee's conception of himself, since the employer has the power to hire, promote, or fire an employee. Speaking broadly, Elmtown employers place a low value on the out-of-school adolescent as an employee. His age, educational level, lack of training, poor performance on the job until he learns he has to produce or be fired, and the drift from job to job give the employer adequate justification to pay him low wages, work him long hours, and limit his work opportunities to relatively unskilled jobs.

The heads of the Factory, the Mill, and a group of coal mines were interviewed to discover their conceptions of these young people as employees; the work they do; opportunity for promotion through the job hierarchy; and the requirements in the way of general educational and vocational training for different jobs in their plants. These men believe that no boy or girl without a high school education has a chance to work into the office or the positions which require technical training.  Moreover, they are very skeptical about their chances to work into supervisory positions on the foreman level.  The manager of the largest coal-mining company stated, "A shovel costs a half-million dollars. When I put a man in that control house, I want to be sure he is intelligent enough to know what he is doing.  One mistake could cost us $50,000."  The superintendent of the Factory was emphatic:

> I have a class in the plant that's barely smart enough to do the mechanical work.  Some of them are so darn dumb Jake [the line foreman] has to work with them for weeks before they get the knack of the thing.  After they learn what's wanted, they make good workers.  I often think they are better workers than the educated ones.
>
> I cannot take them in here [the office].  They are too dumb. We do not use them in the foundry or the shipping department either.

The superintendent at the Mill is convinced that "the relief class is no good.  These people have been this way for generations.  The kids will be the same way; and if you think you can do anything for them, you are crazy."  He refuses to hire persons who are identified as class V's except as extras and only in unskilled jobs in the yard.  They are kept out of the forming and mixing rooms or wherever skill, knowledge, and responsibility are required.

The president of the First National Bank considers adolescents in the out-of-school group "too dumb" to do office work.  He told, with evident delight, a story on the small loans broker which illustrated his argument that the withdrawees are "dumb"; it also disparages the despised "little man's banker," and, in the judgment of the banker, the broker "got what he deserved." When help became scarce in the spring of 1942, the small loans broker hired as his secretary a class IV girl who had completed three years in the secretarial division of the high school commercial course before she left school to take this job at $65 a month.  Shortly after she started to work for the loan company, a poor tenant farmer came to the broker and asked for a $50 loan. The broker called in his new secretary and dictated the list of implements and livestock to be included in the chattel mortgage. Among the items were ten ewes and a buck. When the girl brought the mortgage back to the broker, this item appeared as "10 yous and $1.00." The banker did not seem to realize that the girl lacked a knowledge of agricultural terms; moreover, she merely reflected the common slang usages in the society. To the banker this revealed "the dumbness of these girls."

The withdrawees have little comprehension of the way they are viewed by their employers. They are aware that they are not wanted in certain jobs, but few have enough insight either into themselves or into the economic system to realize why. When they work alongside a high school graduate or an older worker, they are discriminated against in pay and promotion opportunities. They often rationalize the situation in personal terms, such as "the boss doesn't like me, see," or "I won't suck around him the way John does; so I get the dirty jobs."

By way of conclusion, the fact must not be overlooked that other employees, particularly if they are high school graduates, look down upon the "kid that quit school." The high school graduates believe, more often than not, that they are entitled to more pay and a better job than the person with less education. They are supported in this attitude by the mores which equate education with ability until the person proves otherwise by performance on the job. In Elmtown, a high school diploma has come to be regarded as an index of a young person's capacity to enter white collar jobs. The association between education, job levels, and prestige in the social structure is so high that the person with more education moves into the high-ranking job and the person with little education into the low-ranking job. Furthermore, and this is the crucial fact from the viewpoint of the person's relation to the social structure, each tends to remain in the job channel in which he starts as a young worker. This is especially true if he has less than a high school education; then he starts as an unskilled menial and has few opportunities in later years to change to skilled labor, business, or the professions. Therefore, his chances to be promoted up through the several levels of the job channel in which he functions are severely limited. As the years pass, his position in the economic system becomes fixed, and another generation has become stable in the class structure. These young people come from families near the bottom or on the bottom. They start where their parents are, and they are likely to remain about where they started. As a young class V mother of two babies put it, "Mother said, 'Toil and trouble is our lot.' She had her share, and it looks like I got mine comin'." Her husband had been arrested that morning for driving a car he did not own across a state line. This pressure of everyday events is likely to keep these young people where they are in the social structure for the rest of their lives.

# 15

## LEISURE HOUR ACTIVITIES

ELMTOWN ADULTS RECOGNIZE that boys and girls in their middle teens may play one of two major roles in the community, that of pupil or young adult. High school students play the pupil role; the withdrawees that of the young adult. The boundary between them is determined entirely by their connection with the school system. Those playing the pupil role are accorded the status of older children. Consequently, adults do not consider them responsible for their actions. Parents, school authorities, and leaders of voluntary associations designed especially for adolescents are thought to be the ones responsible for what these adolescents do from hour to hour, day to day. The withdrawee, since he has left school and has entered the work world, is looked upon as an adult by the same institutional leaders who define his age peers in school as dependent children. The withdrawee, accepting the role provided by the society, conceives of himself as an adult, but not in the same way as adults do. They think in terms of his responsibility for his actions; he thinks in terms of what he wants to do, usually without regard for consequences. Thus, the out-of-school adolescents play distinctly different roles from the high school students in formal organizations and informal leisure time activities. The facts that the withdrawee assumes the status of young adult and the community accords it to him results in his assumption of adult roles from one to five years earlier in life than boys and girls of the same age who finish high school.

### Formal organizations

Ties with formal organizations normally are severed when an adolescent makes the transition from the pupil to the young adult role. Once the school connection is broken, school authorities have no interest in the withdrawee or contact with him, since he usually avoids the school. The withdrawee also breaks his connections with Scout and church groups when he leaves school or shortly thereafter. This became apparent when we studied the connections withdrawees had with organized groups. In the spring of 1942, only 4 (1 per cent of the group) belonged to adolescent associations: 2 class IV girls and 1 boy from class IV were active in church groups, and 1 class III boy belonged to the 4-H Club. The class V's were isolated completely from organized social groups. Moreover, only 9 per cent of the boys and 11 per cent of the girls claimed membership in these organizations while they were in school; these memberships were concentrated in classes III and IV, with only 3 from class V.

Membership lists were obtained for all known voluntary associations to which young people in the post-high school age group belonged in order to determine to what extent the withdrawees were being assimilated into them. We found that 12 boys and 2 girls were active members in a ping pong club, a bowling league, and two softball teams. These clubs, sponsored by the Mill and business houses, were composed mainly of the sponsors' employees. Thus, exactly 5 per cent of the withdrawee group were members of some voluntary association. The other 95 per cent did not have any ties with organized groups.

The question may be raised: Do adult leaders in Elmtown realize that this condition exists? On the whole, they do, but they are not concerned. The leaders of student associations are interested in keeping their groups alive. The easiest way to do this is to cater to the young people in the three upper classes and to allow the two lower classes to go their way. Three ministers show some interest in the question, but each admits that he can do nothing to better the situation. We pointed out in Chapter 10 how the Methodist minister had tried to interest all young people in the church in youth activities, only to run into active opposition from some high school students and their parents who refused to associate with "the lower element." The attitudes of the two adolescent groups toward one another were the basic reason for the lack of contact between them. On the one hand, the in-school adolescents look down upon those who quit school;

on the other, the out-of-school adolescents look upon church and Scout groups as "kid stuff."

The church is the one institution outside the economic sphere with which these young people claim contact in large numbers (70 per cent of the class V's and 85 per cent of the class IV's said that they belonged to a local church), but actual participation in religious affairs is a far cry from what they report it to be.[1] Elmtown's ministers have never heard of three-fifths of the class V's who claim to be church members. Of the 40 per cent who are known by different ministers, 18 per cent are believed to have left the church, 20 per cent are thought to be church members but they do not attend church or young people's meetings; thus, only 8 of the 204 withdrawees in class V, or 2 per cent, are active in some measure in religious affairs. Within class IV, 35 per cent are not known by the ministers, 9 per cent are believed to have left the church, 23 per cent are known but do not attend church or young people's meetings; 33 per cent come to church. Most of this group belongs to either the Catholic or the Lutheran churches.[2]

A reader may raise the question: Are these young people godless? They may be; we do not know. To answer this question we should have to design another research problem and work on it specifically. We did accumulate enough evidence to lead us to conclude that in the main they do not feel comfortable in church with people dressed better than they are, people who drive newer and larger cars, live in better houses, and treat them as inferiors. To a large segment of these young people, the church, the preacher, and the outwardly pious members of church boards represent the acme of hypocrisy. A class IV boy who worked as a common laborer for a contractor epitomized this attitude when he told how his employer, a member of the Board of a prominent Protestant church, ordered the cement-mixer crew to use seven shovels of sand to one of cement in a sidewalk he was building for a fellow churchman. The boy knew this was not the proper mixture for a sidewalk; he also knew who made a profit from this practice. In his scheme of

[1] See Table XXIII of the Appendix.

[2] Exact figures by sex and class are presented in Table XXIV of the Appendix.

values, ushering in the church on Sunday, carrying the collection plate, and uttering a fervid *Amen* did not compensate for the extra sand in the concrete. It may be argued that this was merely a rationalization on the boy's part to justify his position on religious questions. And it may be, but so far as the boy was concerned it was an adequate reason. Moreover, it was a typical lower class symbolization of upper class behavior.

### Cliques and clique relations

The withdrawee's leisure hours revolve around two axes—*the clique* and *the date.* Off the job, and in his daydreams on it, he is caught in a network of social and biological forces which attract and repel him from one axis to the other. The clique satisfies his desires for intimate associates of his own age, sex, and position in the social structure with whom he can share experiences. It does not satisfy his deep-seated biological drives to associate with persons of the opposite sex and to select one or a few for further, more intimate experience.

The withdrawee spends practically all his leisure time away from home in the company of his clique mates or a date. A lone boy or girl is seldom seen on the streets in the evening, or in hangouts and places of recreation. Girls almost never go to public places alone, even the class V's, unless they have arranged to meet a girl or boy friend there. A boy may start out alone with the idea that he will meet an acquaintance in one of the hangouts, or possibly pick up a date. He does not wander around town alone with the intention of staying alone. To have fun one has to share the experience with a pal.

We intended originally to enumerate the withdrawees' clique relations in the same thoroughgoing way we did those of the student group, but this proved impossible. The withdrawees were so widely scattered geographically, occupationally, and in their social contacts that there was little opportunity to observe interpersonal relations with the frequency necessary to catch the entire group in our data net. Therefore, we limited our study to those we could observe repeatedly in their relations with other adolescents and adults. In this way, reasonably complete clique relationships were traced for 105 boys and 83 girls. These young people are mainly unmarried town-dwellers who spend many

evening hours in one public place or another. The farm youth
are so widely scattered over the communal area, and they come
to town so infrequently that they are under-represented in this
clique picture. The young married group which has withdrawn
from the clique pattern so characteristic of the unmarried is also
under-represented. The 105 boys and 83 girls we discuss here
were observed over an eight-month period to see with whom
they associate intimately and repeatedly. Observations were
supplemented by informal interviews, and in 37 cases (21 boys
and 16 girls) itemized lists of clique connections were worked
out with the adolescents. The distribution of cases by class in
this sample is:

| Class | Boys | Girls |
|-------|------|-------|
| III   | 4    | 2     |
| IV    | 43   | 28    |
| V     | 58   | 53    |
| Total | 105  | 83    |

The number of cases in the two lower classes is large enough to
give us an adequate basis for a few generalizations. There are
too few cases in class III to do this; but it should be remembered only 7 boys and 5 girls in class III had left school.

This sample includes 41 boys' and 28 girls' cliques that range
in size from a minimum of 2 to a maximum of 6 persons. The
boys' cliques average 3.2 members and the girls' 2.8. The typical out-of-school clique has 3 members supplemented at times
by a fourth. Unusual is the clique of 5 or 6 adolescents so typical of the student group. The small clique is an adjustment to
the conditions associated with the jobs these adolescents hold.
In the first place, jobs are widely scattered; and second, working
hours are not regular, particularly in the late afternoon and early
evening. For example, in a girls' clique, one girl may work in
a restaurant, another as a maid in a home, a third in the factory.
The factory girl normally finishes work at five o'clock; the maid
may finish by seven in the evening, but she has no set hour to
leave, since custom decrees that she work until the dinner dishes
are washed and the kitchen cleaned. Unless the family is extremely punctual at meals, the time the maid finishes varies an

hour or more from one evening to another. When the waitress is able to leave is contingent upon the amount of trade, when her last customer arrives, and possibly other conditions. Boys are subject to the same type of uncertainty; therefore, every added person complicates the problem of getting together. If clique mates cannot get together often during their leisure hours, the clique soon splits, and the members gravitate toward persons with similar work and free hours.

Most clique ties in class IV are broken soon after an adolescent leaves school, and within a year to eighteen months an entire new set of clique ties is built. This generalization is particularly true of the girls. It applies also to the boys, but, since more class IV boys than girls have left school, a boy is not separated so definitely from his former friends as a girl is. A very different set of conditions prevails in class V; here the great majority have left school by the end of the eighth grade, and the boy or girl in high school is unusual. In spite of these differences, withdrawees in both classes indicate that they belonged to cliques while in school which were two to three times larger than those to which they belong after they leave school. During the first few months after leaving school, the withdrawees tend to maintain clique relations with their friends in school, but as the months pass they become isolated from the school group as well as from most of their old friends who have left school. In class V the best friend of school days continues, in many cases, as a clique mate, along with another pal or two. But in class IV the new clique tends to be made up of boys or girls who have been drawn together by the circumstances of their jobs.

The development of the dating pattern produces another reorientation in personal and clique interests. Instead of the adolescent finding more or less complete satisfaction within the clique and its action pattern, as he did before, his interests begin to be focused outside the clique on persons of the opposite sex. As the young person dates more and more, and usually fewer and fewer, persons until a steady dating relation is established, he increasingly loses interest in the clique. As the dating relation becomes more regular the boy and girl spend more of their leisure time together, and each has less left to give to the old clique group. If the clique is a threesome, the two who are left often function as a clique for a time; a third party may be added from a clique which has been dissolved by the growth of another dating relationship. Gradually one or another member begins to date and the clique dissolves. In many cases, clique ties are severed completely, but more frequently they pass from a dynamic set of emotional and psychic bonds, which appear to be all-important to the persons subject to them, to a latent phase in which the former pals remain friends. They meet occasionally, discuss the old days when they did everything together, and wonder why it is no longer the same. They often exchange confidences, ask one another for advice, discuss a personal problem, and tell about their plans for the future—usually plans which involve a person of the opposite sex. Former clique mates may go out together occasionally for "old times' sake" rather than for any actively felt current need. When this phase of a clique relationship is reached, the clique as a clique is dead. Neither person feels constrained to abide by the codes once believed to be "the most important thing in the world."

"Disappointment in love" normally brings a person back into a clique for a time. While these emotional disturbances last, the boy or girl seeks solace in the clique—if it still exists. If it does not, new ties may be joined with a clique the person never belonged to before. Again, if the boy or girl has been a "fringer" on a clique some time previously and his old clique has dissolved or does not allow him in it, he may make strenuous efforts to work into a new clique. This rekindling of enthusiasm for the clique generally does not last more than a few weeks, at most a month or two. As soon as a new dating pattern is established, the person loses interest in the clique and turns his attentions to his new love.

CLIQUE AND CLASS. Analysis of the clique ties of the 105 boys and 83 girls, when the class positions of the participants were known, revealed a very significant association between class position and clique relationships. The clique ties of the 43 class IV boys are distributed as follows: 67 per cent with other class IV's, 30 per cent with class V's, and 3 per cent with class II's and III's. The picture is similar in class V: 73 per cent of the 58 boys' clique connections are with other class V boys, 26 per cent with class IV boys, and 1 per cent with class III's. The girls trace the same pattern in both classes. Seventy-one per cent of the 28 class IV girls' clique ties are with other class IV's, 3 per cent with class III's, and 26 per cent with class V's. Seventy-nine per cent of the 53 class V girls' clique relations are with other class V girls, and 21 per cent with class IV girls. There are no clique ties between class V girls and the three higher classes. These figures make it very plain, first, that the withdrawees' clique ties follow a pattern congruent with the high school group, except that they are on a lower level of the prestige structure. Second, the withdrawee has little opportunity to associate on an intimate, give-and-take level with persons more than one class removed from himself.

CLIQUE RELATIONS AND SCHOOL STATUS. Clique ties between high school pupils and withdrawees are concentrated, in both sexes, in the two lower classes. Seventy-seven per cent of the in-school boys' clique relations with out-of-school boys are in classes IV and V; 86 per cent of the student girls' ties are in these classes. Two class II boys in school have some connections with 1 class III boy and 2 class IV boys in the withdrawee group. There are no connections among the class II's with out-of-school girls.[3] Eighty-four per cent of these intergroup clique ties are between freshmen and sophomores, 13 per cent between juniors, and 3 per cent between seniors. Moreover, they are strongest between students and withdrawees who left school after June, 1941. This means that the gulf between the two groups widens as they grow older. This is understandable, since the older withdrawees have been away from school longer and a considerable number have married and started families of their own.

## Spending leisure

Some of Elmtown's most conspicuous landmarks are set aside for recreation and pleasure. These include two city parks, an adjacent state park, the Country Club, four gun clubs, two fishing clubs, a race track, the Mill's athletic field, the Boy Scout Camp. In addition, there are the bowling alley, two roller-

---

[3] Clique connections between the two groups are significantly different from class to class. For the boys, $X^2 = 87.7385$; 3 degrees of freedom; $P < 0.01$. For the girls, $X^2 = 27.9129$; 2 degrees of freedom; $P < 0.01$.

skating rinks, the pool hall, three motion picture houses, twenty-four bars, about twenty hamburger and soft drink parlors, the high school extracurricular program, the Carnegie Library, several private social clubs, the weekly meeting of the service clubs, periodic church bazaars and carnivals, two or three itinerant carnivals each year, more than a half-dozen dance places, Polish Paula's brothel, and over a dozen gambling spots. All contribute something to the community's efforts to relax and have a good time. The reader may say, "But most of these are commercialized." This is true—too true! Businessmen have long since learned that people are willing to pay for pleasure. Furthermore, there is hardly a voluntary association in Elmtown that does not at some time or other in the course of the year subordinate all activities, for at least a few hours, to pleasure. And on the most pleasurable occasions the primary object is fund raising to defray some of the association's expenses. The annual church bazaar, where games of chance are played, is a most pleasurable occasion for all except "blue noses"; even to them it is justified by the need for funds. On such occasions staid churchgoers have fun in the church basement, buying chances on hand-crocheted bedspreads and tickets to determine the most popular girl in the church. Sober businessmen may pay a profusely lipsticked pretty girl fifty cents to kiss them on the lips, cheek, even their bald heads. Pleasure at a price is the dominant popular motif in Elmtown's use of leisure hours among young and old.

The typical withdrawee's conception of the value of money is to use it to satisfy his search for pleasure; he has to have money to go places and to do things. The girl has to have dresses, hats, stockings, shoes, coats, purses, handkerchiefs, jewelry, perfume, cosmetics, and the "right" hair-do. In her search for glamour, she spends most of her meager earnings on herself. The boy, like the girl, has to have two sets of clothes, one for work and one for dress. In addition, a boy has to have an automobile of his own, or his status as an adult, in his own and his peers' eyes, is not secure.

As soon as the boy finds a job, he begins to figure out ways and means to buy an automobile; a new one is the ideal, but an old one is the reality. His low wages limit his ability to pay for one; so he looks around for a roadster or coupé that is for sale cheap—coaches or sedans are all right, but they are his second choice. Fords, Plymouths, and Chevrolets are the most popular makes. Cheapness in a car means age; age spells low efficiency and many repairs; but these factors mean little to these boys. To have a car is the all-important thing.[4] Cars are bought with the lowest possible down payment, the remainder of the purchase price being paid weekly or monthly; some cars are purchased for as little as $10 in a junk yard or from a neighbor. These jalopies were worn and rusted wrecks that have to be towed home in some cases. Once there, the boy and his pals set out to overhaul them. This is not too difficult, as the neighborhoods where these boys live are sprinkled with more ancient wrecks, and one old car is stripped to repair another. If the necessary part cannot be found around home, a trip can always be made to a junk yard where it can be bought cheap, or stolen. Quite desirable cars in fair repair can be bought for $50 and a "de luxe job" for $150.

By the time a boy pays for his clothes, his automobile, repairs, gas, and oil and gives his mother from $3 to $5 a week for room and board, he does not have much left out of his weekly earnings for pleasure. Nevertheless, this is how he uses it; moreover, it is more than he had before he left school.

The search for something exciting or novel is a major part of a clique's activity. Many hours are squandered in restless, random movement from one public place to another. Early in the evening, a boy may leave home in his car and pick up a pal. They may drive around town for a few minutes, park in front of a hangout, get out and go in. There they may meet a third friend, have a coke or a beer, play the pin ball machine for a few minutes. Suddenly one of them suggests, "Let's go over to Diamond City and see what's going on." The others respond, "Yeh, that's a thought." They get in the car and drive to Dia-

---

[4] Of the boys who have been out of school a year or more, 83 per cent in class IV and 65 per cent in class V own an automobile. The class IV boys' cars average 7 years in age, and those of the class V's slightly over 9 years; some of these cars are Model T's, none is under 2 years of age. Six of the 7 class III boys own cars that average 4 years in age. Two have cars less than a year old.

mond City, go to Mike's Tavern and have a beer, then start for
the Gay Paree to see if they can "find a babe or two." Possibly
they will see some girls on the way, drive by them slowly,
whistle, and circle the block, but the girls are not interested.
They go on, but "nothing may be doing" at the Gay Paree.
After a drink, one of the party suggests, "I wonder what's new
at Angel's Point." This starts them for Angel's Point, about nine
miles away. On the way they pass Piccolo Pete's, and the new
"three-way" girl "Pete just brought down from Chicago" is discussed. "Boney tried her last week. He says she's the best in
the county." The second observes, "Let's go back and look her
over." The driver retorts, "None of that stuff for me; I'm broke.
I was out to Paula's the other night." The first boy ruefully
remarks, "No cat houses for me; there's plenty on the streets for
free." The driver rejoins, "Yeh, but you have to scratch for that
stuff. When I want my ashes hauled, I want it now." The car
pulls into Angel's Point, drives down the main street, and out
to the skating rink. The boys park, go in and watch the skaters
for a few minutes, and decide, "No likely meat here; let's go."
They drive back to Elmtown on the river road and note that the
highway signs they used as targets last week have been replaced
with new ones. "Jeez, but they changed them quick this time."
"Yeh, we gotta be careful; the state cops are patrolling this
road." They park in front of the Blue Triangle upon their return
to town and go in for coffee. There they meet three or four
other cliques, exchange greetings, talk about where they have
been; then the group breaks up as each one starts home about
ten-thirty or eleven o'clock.

This aimless activity goes on night after night as one clique
or another seeks excitement and girls. When some girls willing
to go for a ride are found the group usually heads into the
country. They ride for a while, stop for something to eat and
drink, then ride some more. If the weather permits, they park
along a country road where they pet with varying degrees of
intensity.

Although Elmtown is the center of activity, cliques, couples,
and groups of couples regularly range over an area fifty miles
in diameter. Periodically some take a trip to Chicago, Indianapolis, Peoria, and not infrequently as far as St. Louis. Public

transportation is never used on these forays, for it is too rigid, costs too much, and takes too much time. A clique of boys can drive to a neighboring town, pick up some girls, go to a dance, drink, and pet, and no local person will see them. They can return before morning and be back to work the next day, jaded but satisfied. Some activity which involves the clique, a couple or two, is the thing that appeals to these young people. Quiet, solitary pleasure, such as reading a book or a magazine, occupies little of their time or interest.

The typical boy, and many of the girls, habitually go to one of the public places scattered along Freedom and Canal Streets in the search for companionship and excitement. There they meet their pals, talk, play, drink, loaf, and perhaps make a date. These hangouts include the pool hall, hamburger stands, taverns, and combination soda fountains, stores, and gambling halls. A person may loaf in any of them as long as he desires, if he spends a little money. A young man may drift uptown and with a reasonable degree of certainty know that by going to one of two or three hangouts he will find friends of either sex with whom he can spend the evening. He also knows that, if he goes to certain other places, he is sure to run into enemies. An evening may start, end, or be passed in these hangouts with his clique mates.

Each hangout is rated by the young people on the basis of its appointments, location, cleanliness, what the management tolerates, and, above all, who frequents it. The eight hangouts frequented regularly fall into three broad groups which we have categorized as: (1) "respectable"—the "best people" go there (such as Glotz's restaurant, or Cherry's); (2) "respectable, but"— the "best people" do not go there for one reason or another (the Blue Triangle illustrates this group); and (3) "disreputable joints" (such as Scrugg's Tavern) which "decent people" avoid. The respectable establishments are headquarters largely for high school students and young adults from classes I through III. Many class IV's in the high school and withdrawee groups patronize the second type. Low-ranking class IV's and class V's congregate in the "disreputable joints."

Where a young person goes to loaf, visit, and eat helps to rate him in the circles where he is known. For roughly 3 out of 4 class IV and 9 out of 10 class V adolescents the hangout used most frequently is as diagnostic of class position as clique ties. Class IV boys avoid the respectable places; 63 per cent go to the "respectable, but" spots, and 32 per cent to the "disreputable" ones. In class V the distribution is practically reversed; 67 per cent are habitués of the "disreputable" places, 33 per cent of the "respectable, but" group, and none frequent the "respectable" ones. The class IV girls eschew the "respectable" places, but they are not attracted to the "disreputable" ones in the same proportion as the boys of this class. About 19 per cent of the class IV girls go to the "disreputable" hangouts and 81 per cent to the "respectable, but" ones. The class V girls divide their patronage unequally between the "disreputable" and the "respectable, but" places; 36 per cent go to the former and 64 per cent to the latter ones. This pattern is an aspect of the sex game that many class IV boys and class V girls play with one another. The girls go to the hangouts where they meet the boys, if the boys do not go to the lower ranking hangouts in search of the girls. In many cases, the class V girls seek the class IV boys in the "respectable, but" hangouts to avoid trouble between boys of these two classes.

Saturday night is the most popular time for all kinds of pleasure. During the course of any Saturday night, some 80 to 85 per cent of the unmarried withdrawees may be found in one of three places: the motion picture theaters, the roller rinks, or the dance halls and taverns. Most of the remainder go uptown, for a ride, or to a hangout for something to eat and drink. Dancing is the most popular recreation on Saturday night. It claims about one-half of the young people; the remainder are split about equally between the shows and the roller skating rinks.

The motion picture theaters consistently attract a significantly higher percentage of patrons than any other form of recreation. Ninety-three per cent of the boys and 92 per cent of the girls go to the movies once a month or oftener, 79 per cent of the boys and 84 per cent of the girls attend one or more shows a week, and 35 per cent of the girls and 26 per cent of the boys go to two or three a week. The percentages attending the movies are not significantly different in the two classes, but the theater they patronize is associated very definitely with class position.

About 65 per cent of the class V's go to the Bright Star, 35 per cent to the Silver Bell, and 10 per cent to the Elmtown. Among the class IV's, 15 per cent regularly attend the Bright Star, 75 per cent the Silver Bell, and 10 per cent the Elmtown. This tendency to go to public places patronized predominantly by the members of a person's class appears to be a tie which binds the class together. Simultaneously, it differentiates it from other classes integrated around other focal points in the community's social system.

Roller skating is participated in two or three times a week by a number of enthusiasts of both sexes and classes. Eighty-three per cent of the class V girls and 68 per cent of the class IV girls skate once a month or oftener. The comparable figures for the boys are: class IV, 47 per cent, class V, 72 per cent. Some four out of five skaters go to the Elmtown commercial rink, except on Sunday when it is closed; then they go to out-of-town rinks.

Saturday night attracts from two to three times as many skaters as any other time. The action pattern of the skaters before and after the skating phase of the evening, however, is little different from that which occurs among the dancers or movie-goers. The skaters drift into the rink in couples or cliques; now and then a boy or girl comes alone. Couples skate together, cliques skate in groups of two, three, or four. Sooner or later boys who come without dates begin to pay court to particular girls. When a waltz or fox trot is played, a boy might ask a girl to skate with him. Another dating technique: Two or three boys follow two or three girls, skate around them or in between, cut them off from the milling mass, and work them into a corner. After the necessary preliminaries, the two cliques might pair off as couples. Again they might stay as a single group with couples as the internal organizational unit. After the skating stops about midnight, the boys take the girls home; there is a preliminary stop at a tavern or a café followed by another delay along the way where the really interesting part of the evening is focused on sex play.

Of the approximately 25 possible dance "spots"—halls, taverns, and "clubs"—within a radius of 20 miles from Elmtown, 13 are frequented more or less regularly by the withdrawees. They avoid the rather exclusive night clubs, such as the Five Stars, and flock to cheap taverns like Scrugg's, where one can dance to a juke box, buy beer for a nickel, and raw, cut whiskey for 15 cents a glass.  Outside Elmtown these combination liquor, eating, and dance spots are open nightly until twelve o'clock or later, and until three or four on Saturday night.  On a typical Saturday night, about one-half of the dancers can be seen in Morrow's Dance Hall and in taverns; the rest are at "The Bucket of Blood" or other places outside Elmtown.

The dancers follow two patterns in the course of an evening. Younger boys and girls leave home alone or with a pal, go to a hangout, where they pick up the rest of the clique or join another.  Girls often loiter in the hangout for an hour or more, talking, coyly flirting with the boys, or dancing with each other. The boys often go directly to the hangout, but more generally they wander into their favorite tavern for a drink or two, then on to the hangout to look the girls over.  About nine o'clock the non-dating boys head for Morrow's Dance Hall, located over a store on the lower end of Freedom Street, or for "The Bucket" on the edge of town.  At Morrow's they walk upstairs, push their hats or caps on the back of their heads, shove their hands deep into their pockets, and rock back on their heels as they look the crowd over with an eye to their prospects for an evening of pleasure and, if it is a total success, a date and a period of petting.  After some minutes of looking and discussion, they usually pay the admission fee of 75 cents, and the doorman pins a small ribbon on the lapel of their coat or windbreaker to signify that they have paid.  Girls without dates drift in, but they seldom stop at the door to survey the situation.  They are welcomed by the management as free customers.  The girls' first stop is the rest room, where they make last-minute adjustments in their make-up and clothing.  Upon their return to the dance floor, they walk to one side of the entrance where the girls sit or stand in groups until the boys come to ask them to dance. The boys cluster on the opposite side near the men's rest room. Dating couples normally stand or sit on the opposite side of the hall well away from the stags.  When the music, provided by a five- or six-piece local orchestra, starts, the boys approach the girls and ask for dances.  As the evening grows old, the clique pattern tends to disappear as a boy attempts to make a date with some girl for the rest of the evening. Youths with dates start the evening as a couple; those who make a date at the dance end it that way.

In the course of the evening almost every couple or clique leaves the dance hall to get refreshments at a nearby tavern or at a soft drink place across the street. If a boy and girl have not made a personal date, they often arrange a group date with another clique; then they pair off within the group for refreshments, a ride, and a petting party after the dance. This group dating tends to be preliminary to the more mature couple date where the boy and girl go to the dance together, dance most of the evening with one another, and never outside a limited circle of friends.

Competition between boys, and sometimes girls, for particular dates frequently leads to conflict between young men in different cliques. The girl normally enjoys these affairs, often stimulating the rivalry until it precipitates a quarrel, which almost invariably includes the entire membership in each clique, who stand by their friends. The manager tries to keep these quarrels under control; he generally succeeds, but once or twice a month a fight starts in the hall.

Fighting in the hall is not permitted by the mores, and the code is seldom violated except by a half-intoxicated person. When this happens, the management stops the music, turns on all the lights, separates the antagonists as soon as possible, and rushes them outside. Most of these conflicts, however, smolder until one boy "invites" the other one "outside." If a bully tries this on a little fellow, the little fellow's friends attack the bully. When the two boys are more or less evenly matched, they and their friends troop into the alley behind the dance hall; here the affair is usually settled with a few well-aimed blows. The loser and his friends leave the dance and go to a tavern to drink and to plot revenge. The winner goes back to claim the girl, often to find that she and her friends became frightened by the fight and left. These alley fights sometimes involve two cliques in a free-for-all. Such a melee does not happen more than two or three times a year, commonly only when some boy draws a knife, tries to gouge his opponent or knee him, or when his friends enter the fight without adequate justification. These "gang fights" are often the fruition of a long feud between rival cliques.

In the sample of 105 boys and 83 girls whom we followed closely, 86 per cent of the boys and 88 per cent of the girls in class IV and 83 per cent of the boys and 87 per cent of the girls in class V attend Saturday night dances rather regularly. Although there is no appreciable difference between these overall percentages for either sex or class, the class IV group patronize Morrow's Dance Hall 37 per cent more frequently than the class V group; furthermore, 28 per cent more class IV's than class V's go there. The class V's usually spend the evening in taverns, two spaghetti-and-meat-ball "night clubs" a few miles out of town where a quart pitcher of "dago red" can be bought for a "half-buck," or in "The Bucket."

In respectable circles "The Bucket" is known as a place to avoid. It is patronized principally by class V's; not more than 20 per cent of its patrons come from class IV. It is reputed to be a hangout for Poles, Italians ("Eye-talians"), "bush apes," "brush monkeys," "yellow hammers," and "reliefers." The four-piece orchestra—piano, drums, saxophone, and trombone—sits on a platform at the back end of the hall; a bar extends along one side. A covered porch runs across the front end of the long, low, one-story building; a gravel-covered parking area approximately an acre in extent surrounds it. The men's and women's rest rooms are located about fifty yards behind the building on the edge of an open field. Most patrons come in cars and park them in a circle around the hall. The boys pay 50 cents to dance, when they enter the door that leads off the front porch, and the girls, as is customary here, enter free. When a boy pays his "half-buck," the doorman pins a small, colored ribbon on his shirt, jacket, or suit coat lapel. Boys with ribbons are allowed to come and go with girls or alone. In mild weather, from 10 to 20 young men congregate on and around the front porch, talking, loitering, arguing, and quite often passing remarks at girls who come unescorted. Sometimes remarks are passed about girls with a date, but this does not happen often, since it usually leads to trouble.

Most boys wear "dress pants," white shirts, and ties, with jackets or suit coats; very few, however, wear hats. Standard headgear is a visored, cloth cap adorned with a dozen or more metal buttons, miniature toys, and animal tails. Such a cap marks a boy's low class in Elmtown, but those who wear them consider them the height of fashion. The higher class boys either go bareheaded or wear hats.

"The Bucket's" habitués usually have had a few drinks before they arrive; but, if they have not, beer, wine, and whiskey are available at the bar. Many boys, to save money, carry bottles in their cars or in hip pockets. The owner does not allow anyone to drink from a flask in the hall, but he makes no effort to stop it outside. Raiding cars for liquor is a favorite activity of the younger boys who come to the dance without dates. Liquor thieves watch cars to see where the driver puts his bottle, and they raid the car after the owner has left. Roadsters and touring cars are systematically searched by turning the seat over, looking under it, behind the instrument panel, in the back seat, and so on. Closed cars are checked to see if they are locked. It is not unusual for a clique to use a short piece of pipe to force a lock, if a bottle is known to be locked in the car. Sometimes older boys trap the raiders by taking their dates inside and leaving a watcher outside. On these occasions, when the signal is given that raiders are active, boys in the plan rush out and "beat up" the thieves. This invariably results in a first-class fight which the raiders generally lose. Raiding cars for liquor in this fashion begins in the lower classes before boys finish elementary school and continues until they get cars of their own and date girls.

At least one quarrel occurs at "The Bucket" almost every Saturday night over liquor or girls, often both. Some appear to develop out of class rivalry. We witnessed one that arose over the contemptuous violation of common decency by a drunken class IV boy, and his reaction to a class V youth who tried to correct his behavior. This boy, accompanied by two pals, had driven to "The Bucket"—as they said later—"to see what was going on—maybe pick up an easy mark or two." They had drunk several beers before their arrival and had "taken on" four or five shots of whiskey at the bar while they were dancing with pick-ups. Eventually the boy who started the trouble needed to visit the toilet. Instead of going to the men's room, he walked to the edge of the porch and started to urinate. Several couples were sitting in cars, and 10 or 12 young men were standing on the porch. One boy in a car honked his horn; a class V boy told the delinquent to clear out; there were "ladies present." He retorted angrily, "Ladies, Humph! Don't make me laugh!" The class V boy "swung a haymaker" that missed. The class IV boy's two pals jumped to the rescue, and a vicious fight ensued. Car lights were turned on, boys piled out of cars and the hall to get into the fray. Sides were taken by boys who recognized the difference between themselves and others. When it was over, the guilty boy, one of his pals, and several others were marked by blackened eyes, cut hands, bruised faces, and torn clothing. After the crowd had quieted down, and word had passed through it about the cause of the fight, the consensus of those present was that this was an insult of the worst order. Within a half hour practically every class IV had left without anyone coming into the open and saying this was a class fight. There was widespread gossip about the incident in the two lower classes for several days, then the matter was forgotten. The next Saturday night, however, only a handful of class IV young people went to "The Bucket's" dance.

The withdrawees' interests in reading and art are satisfied by *The Bugle* and the magazines they purchase in their hangouts. The headlines of *The Bugle* are scanned quickly, a few front-page articles read hurriedly, but an article about some local person in trouble ordinarily is read carefully. The boys read the sports page and the funnies; the girls read about fashions, motion picture stars, and the funnies. Approximately one-third of the class IV girls and one-fifth of the class V's claim to read serial novels in *The Bugle*. The boys avidly read salacious comic books sold by disreputable hangouts. These stores also commonly sell "sport," "screen," and "art" magazines so full of suggestive pictures and sex stories that they have been barred from the mails. On the racks of these stores, titles, such as *How to Attain Perpetual Potency, The Forty-Three Positions, The Young Man's Guide, The Maiden's Fulfillment, Love's Dream Manifest, What Every Woman Hopes, Get Your Man and Hold Him,* are prominently displayed along with legitimate screen, comic books, and popular magazines. The Public Library is not a hangout for any withdrawee. Between September, 1941, and the end of June, 1942, only 1 boy and 4 girls in class IV borrowed books. Obviously, reading is not a popular pastime.

### Delinquent behavior

The proprietors of taverns, dance halls, skating rinks, bowling alleys, pool halls, and theaters treat the withdrawees as adults. Some establishments, such as Paula's, which do not allow high school students to participate openly in what they offer to the public, draw no line against the out-of-school adolescents. The latter go where they will and act as personal and class tastes dictate. From the viewpoint of the proprietors of pleasure spots, they are adults, and, just as important, these youngsters conceive of themselves in the same way; thus, their recreational behavior is nearer to that of the age group from 18 to 25 than it is to the age group 14 to 17 in high school.

Freed in large part from restrictions imposed by childhood and the lack of money, the vast majority are willing to try everything to demonstrate to themselves and to their associates that they are mature personalities. Thus, their recreational patterns cover the gamut of things available in the local culture. "Whoopee" is the order of the night; the fleshpots beckon, and these youths, reveling in their new-found freedom and prosperity, respond as often as money and circumstances permit. To be sure, there are variations in individual tastes, and limits imposed by conscience. This is the general picture—a good time tonight and a headache tomorrow, but "I will do the same thing again; it was worth it."

Practically all boys (91 per cent) smoke, irrespective of age or class. The fourteen-year-old class V boy is just as likely to smoke as a seventeen-year-old. When a girl quits school, she generally knows how to smoke or soon learns. Smoking is a symbol of manhood to the boys and of independence to the girls. However, restrictions on women smoking so prevalent a generation ago still hold some force, for only 73 per cent of the girls smoke. The out-of-school girl who smokes does so on the job, in the clique, on dates, and at home unless her parents object strenuously, but few do, so far as we were able to determine.

Use of alcoholic beverages is general in both sexes and classes among about two-thirds of the withdrawees. Few efforts are made either by law enforcement agencies or tavern keepers to keep liquor from them. Drinking is a pattern of lower class life which these youngsters acquire early from their parents, older brothers and sisters, clique mates, and others in the community. When a boy is able to walk into a tavern, order a "shot" of whiskey, toss it off, shake a little, belch, and say, "Gimme another," he has demonstrated to himself and to his associates that he is, indeed, a man among men. Drinking at the bar is unusual among the girls; they may be seen more often sitting at a table to one side or in the rear of the tavern in the company of other girls or a date.[5] The modal group drinks at a few taverns and night spots, and the deviants tend to drink in a number of different places. About three-fourths of the class V's do their regular drinking in four taverns which cater to class V, and about the same portion of the class IV's in three other taverns.

About 90 per cent of the boys and 15 per cent of the girls gamble from time to time. Bets on poker, crap, and pool games are most popular with the boys; slot machines, punch boards, and numbers are secondary. Gambling is distinctly a clique activity. Every "disreputable" and several "respectable, but" hangouts tolerate gambling in either the back room or the back booth. Thus, it is a simple matter for a few friends to start a poker game; as one or two drop out, some new arrivals join. In this way, the game may go on for hours, and a dozen or more boys may be in and out of it in the course of the evening. The stakes are kept to a 10- or 15-cent limit, with now and then a splurge to 25 cents. Stud, blackjack, and draw are the favorites. Playing the slot machines is simple and easy, but not too popular except in a crowd or with a date, as it uses too much money in too short a time. Betting on horse races, football, and basketball games is not popular. This form of gambling is available through a bookmaker on Canal Street, but his patrons are almost all adults.

---

[5] A slight differential is found between each class and sex. The percentage known to drink by class and sex is: class IV boys, 68; class V boys, 74; class IV girls, 51; and class V girls, 57. These figures are derived from the practices of the 105 boys and 83 girls we observed most frequently. They may be biased because this is the most active segment of the unmarried portion of the withdrawees.

Betting, to be interesting, has to be on something visible, here and now. Also, it has to appear to be a sure thing. Merely to gamble for the sake of gambling, such as betting on a horse race when the race is hundreds of miles away, is no fun. But, if a boy says he saw a white cow in Nelson's pasture, and another boy says it is a bull, this is a fit subject for a perfect bet. Tempers might wax as the point is argued, until one boy reaches the ultimate, "I'll betcha a buck it was a white cow. Put up or shut up!" The other boy has either to "put up or shut up"; if he puts up, a third party holds the stakes while the group goes off to check on the sex of the disputed animal. The loser loses face with himself and with his pals until he figures out a way to win a later bet. These boys bet on anything from how far they can spit to the number of bottles of beer a boy can drink in ten minutes.

The nightly search for excitement by speeding, shooting firearms along the river roads, drinking, picking up girls, gambling, with now and again a fight, brings many of these young people face-to-face with the law. Pleasure-bent youths violate the mores, if not the law, almost every night, but they are not overly interested in the consequences of their acts. Actually they seldom think about this aspect of their behavior until they find themselves in trouble. This does not occur often, for they seldom commit offenses serious enough to bring them to the attention of the police or the sheriff. When they do, the differences which adults attach to the roles played by the withdrawees in comparison with the high school students become clear. The police, and adults in general, assume that parents, often the school, are to blame when a student is apprehended for violation of law. However, when a withdrawee of the same age commits an offense of the same nature officials hold him responsible. The deliberate protection-of-the-pupil policy which fails to place responsibility on the student who violates the law, in contrast to the application of adult judgments to the withdrawee, before he has developed a sense of personal responsibility for his behavior, results in a very much higher incidence of official delinquency in the out-of-school series than in the in-school one.

The crude delinquency rates, based on convictions in local courts, are very significantly different in the two groups. The combined rate for the high school boys in classes III through V was 9 per 1,000; whereas the rate, also for these three classes, in the withdrawee group is 165 per 1,000. No rates are available for the high school girls; only one, a class IV member, was charged with an offense, and the charge was later dropped without further action. The withdrawee girls have a rate of 104 per 1,000. These rates were calculated from total convictions in the two series irrespective of the year in which they occurred.

In almost every one of these cases the delinquent behavior is a concomitant of clique activity or sex play. Nineteen boys were convicted of theft; 17 collaborated with their clique mates. Three cliques stole gas from tractors, farm storage tanks, and automobiles on the street; two stole automobiles. Two boys were caught stealing corn from cribs on farms. Tragedy stalked another clique which broke into a bulk oil plant. One boy was inside an oil house when, it was conjectured, he lighted a match and naphtha fumes caught fire. He was burned to death, and his three pals were apprehended. One of two solitary operators worked as a farm hand. In the course of his work, he stole eggs and sold them in town; eventually, he was caught. The other boy stole a gun from a hardware store; he was caught with it later. Some two-thirds of the sex offenses arose from a girl's complaint that she had become pregnant and the male she accused had refused to marry her. The others developed out of such things as a boy exposing himself outside a schoolhouse window or peeping in windows.

A total of 29 boys and 14 girls were convicted of 47 offenses, but only 7 boys were sentenced to state institutions. These sentences resulted from the robbery of the oil plant and two cases of car theft that involved driving a stolen car across a state line.

Elmtown's law enforcement officers prefer to place boys and girls on probation unless the offense is too serious or "raw"; then the offender is normally fined and given a term in the county jail. The prosecuting attorney, in collaboration with the district judge, follows a very enlightened program in the administration of justice in this group. They are more interested in seeing that the young person is given a chance to adjust to the demands made upon him by the community rather than in ruthless punishment in accordance with the letter of the law.

Nevertheless, the delinquency pattern so prevalent among class V parents was taking shape among the children of this class in the withdrawee group. Fifteen per cent had been arrested, tried, and convicted in the city, justice, county, or district courts at least once; 3 boys out of 18 and 1 girl out of 12 had been convicted twice. Delinquency among the class IV's was less than one-half as high as among the class V's; 7 per cent against 15 per cent. The sharp contrast that appeared between the sexes among the adult class IV's [6] also was found in the young people; 10 per cent of the class IV boys had been convicted of an offense, but only 4 per cent of the girls. Stealing was the most frequent offense among the boys, 65 per cent, and sex for the girls, 50 per cent. The girl sex offenders were all in class V, as were also 6 of the 7 male sex offenders. The 2 class IV girl delinquents had been convicted of public intoxication.

There is far more delinquency in both the high school and the withdrawee group than the official records indicate. Siphoning of gasoline out of cars parked on dark streets is a regular practice of many boys. Others steal gasoline from farmers whenever they need it, or the opportunity presents itself. Petty shoplifting from drug stores, the ten-cent store, and service stations is common. Stealing from employers is general among housemaids; linens, jewelry, and underclothes are taken occasionally, food most frequently.

In conclusion, we shall point out that the withdrawee is trying desperately to mature and to take his or her place in adult society. He is doing it as an individual, largely without the help or guidance of adults, even within his own family. His approach to the problem is along the road of withdrawal from all types of institutional guidance, such as that which the school or the church might have given him. Then, too, we infer from his remarks that he is motivated by a fierce personal pride, a belief in individual liberty, and his own ability to adjust to the demands society makes on him. "I will make out" may be said to be his motto, but his community is not giving him any positive direc-

[6] See pp. 110, 119.

tion.  His only intimate associations are with his clique mates and dating partners.  As a group, the withdrawees resent advice from parents, employers, and adults in general.  Consequently, they go their way, acting as they have seen their brothers, sisters, and friends act in their homes, on the job, and in places of recreation.  That they behave in significantly different ways from the high school students is to be expected.

# 16

---

## SEX AND MARRIAGE

THE MATURATION OF SEXUAL CAPACITIES several years before society allows young people to marry presents adolescents with a serious dilemma. They must repress their sexual desires or violate the mores. This perennial problem has been solved, in a way, in our culture by the development of a clandestine complex that enables individuals to release sex tensions secretly and simultaneously to maintain their "good name" and dignity publicly, but not without compromising the mores and creating serious personal and social problems. As a result, an adolescent who breaks the sex taboos does not talk about his "vices" even to his closest friends, for as long as the mores are adhered to outwardly no public embarrassment is experienced by youngsters who profess one thing and do another. It is only when accident or ill fortune brings secret violations of the sex mores into the open, and persons other than the participants in the experience learn what has happened, that delinquents are compromised by their conduct and condemned severely by the community.[1]

---

[1] The strong taboos attached to the discussion of clandestine sexual behavior in all classes precluded the systematic accumulation of data in this area of behavior on all the withdrawees. Consequently, the materials presented here were gathered by indirect interviews, visits, open-ended questions, and in the case of 11 boys and 6 girls extensive sex histories. Altogether, we collected sex materials from 44 boys and 17 girls who belonged to classes IV and V. In view of this situation the reader must remember that the materials on which the following discussion is based apply strictly to a portion of the withdrawees, and only in a general way to classes IV and V. We might go further and infer that they are probably representative of the lower ranking class IV and class V adolescents rather than of all.

Interview materials indicated that young people in classes IV and V in the withdrawee group acquired the principle of secrecy associated with the clandestine complex when they were taught, as little boys and girls, that they should not talk about the genitals or anything connected with sex in polite society. It was also evident that by the time most of them were seven or eight years of age, they had a good working knowledge of the "facts of life." These facts were learned, in the main, either in secret conferences between children of both sexes, usually within the neighborhood, or, as quite often happened, from an older brother or sister who had been enlightened by some older youngster, who in turn passed the information on to his younger brothers or sisters. The children also learned to be careful about revealing this knowledge to adults, because if they did they were scolded, at the very least, for being dirty, filthy, nasty, and, at the very most, they were severely beaten and, in some cases, they had their mouths washed out with laundry soap.

Because custom decrees that each sex pass such information on to its own members only, most sex lore is learned from the association of younger boys with older boys, and younger girls with older girls. Boys appear to be far more prone to discuss sex questions in their cliques than girls. However, we were led to believe that girls in class IV and particularly in class V discuss sex more frequently and openly than girls in the higher classes. From our association with the class II and class III girls in high school we concluded that there is a sharp difference in the amount of sex discussion between each of these classes, and a still sharper break with class IV. We are of the opinion that from the viewpoint of the higher ranking girls this is an important difference between themselves and lower class girls. Lower class girls, especially class V girls, are believed by the class II and class III girls to be "filthy-minded," "dirty," "full of sex." This judgment has some basis in fact, for the class V girls are closer to the problem than the higher ranking girls. Their homes are small, and privacy is almost non-existent; families are large, and both boys and girls often sleep in the same room (in class V, it is not unusual for parents to sleep in the same room with their children). Then, too, promiscuity is more easily detected in class V because it generally occurs in the neighborhood, not in an automobile, a hotel, apartment, or out of town. Therefore, girls in the two lower classes come into direct contact with the clandestine sex game and how it is played at an earlier age than the girls in classes II and III, and they are more prone to talk about it. Finally, the available evidence inclines us to the view that the social barriers erected by girls in classes II and III against some class IV and practically all class V adolescent girls are, in part, a response to talk about sex, and, in part, recognition of the differences they feel exist between their sex roles and the sex roles of the low-ranking girl.

Knowledge of the ways sex tensions can be released is acquired in this lower class group on which we are reporting here some four to seven years before it eventuates in normal heterosexual relations. Sex experience among the boys most commonly begins in the clique when an older boy introduces a younger boy to the new "sport" when the younger boy is 10, 11, or 12 years of age. Thirty-seven of the 44 boys admit that they have masturbated at one time or another, but they are rather ashamed of the practice. But, even so, many tales are told of masturbation down by the river, in the woods, a shed, a barn, or some other secluded place, often with a friend, but many times alone. In some instances, younger boys who have been told about the practice by an older chap decide to try it in solitude. During these early adolescent years a considerable proportion of these boys develop a behavior pattern which brings them into contact with farm animals on a scale that has only recently been emphasized.[2] Young farm boys have relations with animals more frequently than the town boys, but town boys often visit friends in the country and in the course of their play a visit to the barn is not unusual. Twenty-six boys admit that they have had intercourse with animals at one time or another—calves most frequently, but mares, sows, and ewes are included. Masturbation, however, is more general than animal contacts, and more prevalent among the town than the farm boys. It was common in the group of 44 boy withdrawees with whom we discussed the subject from

---

[2] Our data on this point accord closely with the findings of Kinsey and his associates; see Alfred C. Kinsey, *et al.*, *Sexual Behavior in the Human Male*, W. B. Saunders Co., Philadelphia, 1948, pp. 667–678.

about 12 years of age until contacts were made with girls, most generally beginning when the boys were 14 years of age.[3] These boys showed more evidence of guilt over their confessions of masturbation than they did over their sex relations with girls. This is a class factor which we shall discuss in a later paragraph.

Eight of the 17 girls in the withdrawee group who volunteered sex data, by circumlocution and indirection, indicated they had masturbated at one time or another. Only three admitted they did so at the time of the interview. Three had tried homosexual practices with other girls at about 12 years of age, and 9 had "seen what it was like" with boys when they were 12 or 13. These girls believed "a lot of others" did the same thing.[4]

A considerable proportion of the adolescents in the withdrawee group, in their efforts to release sex tensions, particularly through normal heterosexual contacts, play an intricate game of outward conformance to the publicly professed sex mores while they violate them in secret. This game has elaborate rules that are transmitted informally and in the main from boy to boy, girl to girl, but some are communicated across sex lines. Specific rules vary from class IV to class V, and in each sex; in effect, though, they are similar in that they have one objective— the release of sex tensions privately while the ideal of chastity is upheld publicly. In this game some adults aid and abet the adolescents, while others work against them and attempt to maintain the mores; one sex plots against the other, not infrequently males outwit males and females hoodwink females; adolescents defy adults, and children their parents. The churches try to uphold the mores; the taverns and public dance halls aid in their circumvention. Although the police are charged with the maintenance of the mores, they regularly compromise between their strict enforcement and their open violation. For example, one night while looking for a stolen car, a policeman saw a car parked under an overhanging elm on the edge of town, drove up beside it, and threw the spotlight on it. As the policeman opened the door, he saw a class IV withdrawee couple he recognized in a sex embrace, closed the door, and left. He

---

[3] *Ibid.*, pp. 497–516, 547–562.

[4] These figures are isolated. They come from a small low class group; therefore, no generalizations should be drawn from them.

justified his action by the remark, "There is no use to run the parkers out of town. If we chase them off the streets, they will go into the country. As long as they mind their own business, we leave them alone."

Although the sex mores are violated consistently by a considerable proportion of the withdrawees, knowledge of this violation is seldom community-wide. When such facts become common knowledge they are discussed in the form of gossip, and the unfortunate adolescents involved are viewed as unusual miscreants. This situation is a result of the way those who violate the mores work with one another to protect their clandestine behavior from the searching eyes of the public. This process is illustrated in the following incident. Gene Henry, a class IV withdrawee, told how he liked to go out to Paula's "to drink beer and look around." One night when Gene was in Paula's with two class IV friends, also in the withdrawee group, he walked upstairs "to look around" and met a class IV father of a high school girl, and a next-door neighbor, coming out of a room. This man looked at him in surprise, and Gene returned the startled stare; neither said a word. Gene said to us, "I was really scared; I was afraid he would tell my old man, but he never did." Gene said he always "felt funny" whenever he saw this neighbor, but neither one ever mentioned this meeting to the other.

The strongest moral judgments in the culture are applied to the violation of the sex mores. Perhaps the clandestine complex has developed as a reaction to the severity of these judgments. By following the commonly understood but seldom voiced rules, which bind the participants in a situation that involves the violation of the sex mores into a conspiracy of silence, persons who violate the mores protect one another from the prying eyes and censorious judgments of those members of society who would condemn them. By acting in this way they protect the clandestine culture complex and their own "good names." If the violation of taboos becomes known, a person must deny the accusations or he will suffer for his conduct; denial will not absolve him from suspicion, but it helps members of society in their efforts to rationalize away violations of the mores. The clandestine mores even in class V decree that if a person violates the professed mores he should not be shameless about it.

Close personal association between the sexes according to the mores has but one legitimate end: marriage. The folkways, however, recognize that a young couple may go together without any serious thoughts of marriage. A girl is not supposed to be a "lady" if she admits enjoying the physical thrills connected with petting, but a number of girls readily say they go with boys to have a good time, to be taken places, and to participate in petting parties. Boys are freer in their admissions about why they "play" a certain girl than girls are in their motives with respect to a boy. This does not mean the girl's intentions are more honorable than the boy's. The role they play in this game simply requires that they be more discreet about discussing their emotional reactions. Girls learn from older girls and from the boys that they are expected to be submissive to physical advances after the boy has made the proper overtures by bestowing material favors such as a show, a ride, food, candy, perhaps some small gift. Both boys and girls know that there has to be an exchange of favors or the game is not being played to the mutual satisfaction of the players. "To have a woman" is a male prerogative most women and girls in the two lower classes accept as inevitable, even though they condemn the practice.

Although open promiscuous behavior is not tolerated in lower class girls by lower class adults or adolescent boys, the lower class girls play the sex game avidly. But girls, according to the verbal usages of classes IV and V, do not "sow wild oats"; they have to "have some fun before settling down," "enjoy life," "have a few romances," "look for the right man." No condemnation is attached to a girl who goes with several different boys or young men "before she settles down" and marries. The one thing she has to avoid is becoming known as "free and easy with the boys," "common property," "a little chippy," or "a home wrecker." If it becomes known generally among the girls and older women that a girl is "loose," she is gossiped about, ridiculed, perhaps ostracized. When this happens, the outcast seeks feminine companionship with other girls in the same predicament.

A class IV or class V girl in the withdrawee group may be talked about, but so long as she is discreet enough about her love life not to be openly promiscuous, people soon forget about her flirtations. In a few months, at most a year or two, her friends and relatives may notice that she has started "keeping company" with some young man. In due course, she marries the boy, settles down, and raises a family. This process may be illustrated by the story of a class IV girl we shall call Mary.

Mary quit high school in her sophomore year after being ostracized by the high school girls for dating young men in their twenties from other towns. She got a job in a local store and began to date a class IV boy who also worked there. Mary and the boy petted heavily and, in her own words, she "held him off for weeks." Then one Saturday night, she and the boy went to the dance at Morrow's. After the dance, Mary said, "I feel like a drink tonight." They went to a tavern and Mary ordered a double Bourbon. The boy ordered the same, and each drank three double whiskies in about a half hour. They then drove to the Buggy Wash and parked. Mary said later, "I made up my mind at the dance Oscar [the boy] could have it; I had to get drunk to go through with it though. Oh, it was wonderful. That night I thought, 'I don't care if I have a baby.'" Mary and Oscar maintained this liaison for several months, quarreled, and drifted apart. Within three months, Mary had "an affair" with a class III high school graduate who clerked in a store next door. She later quarreled with this boy, but before she "settled down" and married a twenty-one-year-old class IV mill worker in the spring of 1942, when she was 18, she had had "affairs" with four other young men, all store clerks or mill workers. After her first experience Mary said she refused to date boys from other towns, and she had "at least four dates" before she became intimate with a boy. Apparently her lovers played the game according to the rule: only a kid and a fool tells on a girl—for no one ever mentioned that Mary "knew what it was all about" or "had been around."

Boys are not expected to adhere as closely to the mores as girls. "Boys sow wild oats" is a common expression of this tolerance. By the time he is 14 a boy usually knows that a woman can be "had" for money, favors, a good time. Lower class boys generally look upon girls as possessing the same passions as themselves. They do not consider them unapproachable ladies whose wish is law. The girls like to be "treated as a lady," but they interpret this as not being manhandled. A lower class boy who treats a girl as a lady is not respected by the girls; and he is ridiculed by the boys. One class V boy was a joke among his friends because he was "afraid to touch a girl." He was popular for a while with each girl he dated, but lost out with everyone. He was, as one class V girl put it, "not interesting enough."

A withdrawee boy who had not "laid a girl" by the time he was old enough to leave school claimed that he had to protect himself from being called "a sissy," or "a pansy," by his clique mates. A boy who is known or believed to be a virgin is not respected by his peers. A boy is condemned severely, however, if he does not have enough knowledge of contraceptives and prophylactics to keep from getting "in trouble." "Trouble" involves two things, "knocking a girl up" (impregnation) or "getting a load" or a "dose" (venereal disease). Easy access to cheap contraceptives —and every boy knows something about them—proves an efficacious barrier against "trouble" most of the time if a boy is careful.

The class IV and class V boys place a high value on "making a girl." Thus, a boy achieves status in his own eyes when he "makes a girl" the first time he takes her out. If a girl is known as "an easy mark" and a boy does not seduce her with relative ease, he believes that there is something wrong with either himself or his "technique." This egocentric pride in their sex prowess motivates many boys deliberately to "fool with" girls they know they can have in the course of an evening.

Withdrawee boys on the prowl like to boast that they get "what they can, where they can, as soon as they can, and as cheap as they can." This means pick-ups, not prostitutes; pickups are made on the street, in a hangout, a tavern, the skating rink, the dance hall, or theater. Automobile trips to neighboring towns in search of a pick-up occur almost every night, but week ends are preferred. On these expeditions two or three boys go to taverns, restaurants, and hangouts similar to the ones they patronize in Elmtown in search of girls they hope to take on a petting party with the admitted purpose of seducing them. Particular cliques go to the same places on every trip. They may drive to two or three different ones on the same night if the "hunting" is not good. When they find girls who will go with them, the party starts out to have a good time. On these occasions, a few beers, or some more potent drink, are in order, perhaps a show, followed by a ride, some more drinks, and then the party gets down to the serious business of the evening. Generally, the boy follows the accepted aggressive male role, but every now and then the girl may be the aggressor. When this happens, it is not unusual for the boy to take the defensive. Sometimes the couples switch partners half way through the evening in response to verbal or physical cues which indicate that a change would produce more fun for the parties involved. In this relationship the girl has to look out for herself, since she is separated from her family and there is no neighborhood control or supervision. The evening is counted a complete success when the participants make sex contacts, but here it is each couple for itself.

Elmtown girls who accept invitations to go riding with boys from other towns lose status, particularly in their own class and associational group. Boys tend to condemn these girls even more severely than do other girls, since it is assumed that once a girl starts going with boys from other towns she is promiscuous.

One clique of class V boys take great pride in its members' ability to seduce girls. The high school students refer to them as "clippers" and "wolves," and all the high school girls except one clique of class IV and class V girls who are known as "easy marks" avoid them. They call themselves the Five F's—"find 'em, feed 'em, feel 'em, f—— 'em, forget 'em." This clique is held in high esteem by younger boys in the withdrawee group because of their real and alleged sex conquests. They whistle at girls from the poorer sections of town, try to pick up girls on the street, and drive from town to town in search of adventure. These boys usually have a group of low class housemaids, waitresses, and factory hands around them at the dances, in the taverns, and at the roller rink. Although they talk loudly of their activities, one member of the clique admitted that about half of their talk is "front," but he stoutly maintained the boys "get their ashes hauled" almost every Saturday night.

A significantly larger number of class V boys than of class IV report that they have visited Paula's or one of the brothels in and around Angel's Point. The figures by class are: 21 out of 27 class V's said that they have visited prostitutes, in contrast to 8 class IV's out of 17. The withdrawee boys in both classes prefer pick-ups, and relations with girls with shady reputations, because they are cheaper and less stigma is attached to the contact. Several low class Elmtown women are known to be "common property" among the young men. Two in particular are known to cater primarily to boys between 14 and 20 years of age. One was a nineteen-year-old divorcee who lived in an apartment about a block from a dance hall. She regularly attended the dances on Saturday night and selected her customers from the stag line. A number of stories had reached us about her promiscuity before we saw her one night dancing with a boy, when another boy on the sidelines held up two dollars in front of his chest, whistled, and pointed toward the money. The girl grinned and nodded her head affirmatively. In a few minutes she left the pavilion with this boy; she came back alone in about a half hour. This act was repeated five times in the course of the evening.

The second woman was a class V who was married to a laborer. The couple lived over a vacant store located on the edge of the business section. Their apartment was entered from an alley, so it was easy for the neighbors to observe anyone who went in or out. About eight o'clock one Saturday night a middle-aged woman who lived near this woman's apartment telephoned us and said, "Myra is entertaining tonight. If you want to see the show, come over and watch it." Although this woman abhorred what she saw from the outside of Myra's apartment, she did not think it was "any of her business." Upon her invitation, we observed Myra's doorway from eight-thirty in the evening until long after midnight. Periodically, a teen-aged boy would wander out of Sutton's Soda Fountain and turn down the alley. Some looked furtively about to see that they were not followed and walked on; then another look up and down the alley before they walked upstairs. Each boy came out in from 10 to 15 minutes, and walked down the alley in the opposite direction from which he entered. In the course of the evening, 11 boys in the withdrawee group visited Myra. Eight were class V's; the others were class IV's.

Discreet interviewing revealed that the nights Myra "entertained" she went to the store shortly after dinner and sat in the back booth until some of her patrons came in, when she "passed the word" and left. From then on, the boys visited her singly. As soon as one returned to the store, another would slip out, and so went the evening. So far as we were able to learn the boys who hung out at Sutton's were about the only ones with whom Myra did business. She charged from fifty cents to a dollar, depending on the age of the boy and how much he was willing to pay.

### Dates and dating

The dating patterns of the out-of-school boys and girls are very different from those of the high school students.[5] In the first place 94 per cent of the unmarried withdrawee girls said that they were dating in April, 1942, in contrast to 81 per cent of the high school girls. Among the boys the respective figures were 70 per cent and 87 per cent. The contrast was greater in the percentage who reported steady dating. In the high school group 18 per cent reported steady dating, but in the withdrawee group 53 per cent of the girls and 21 per cent of the boys were "going steady." This differential between the two groups is traceable to the tendency of the lower class withdrawee girl to marry in her middle teens, whereas the girls in high school, who are in the main members of higher ranking class groups than the withdrawee girls, postpone marriage until the late teens and early twenties. The wide differential between the boys and the girls in the withdrawee group who "date steady" is traceable to the widespread custom of girls marrying two to four years younger than boys. Another aspect of this trait appears in the significantly higher percentages of class V than of class IV girls and boys who "go steady"; 59 per cent of the class V girls go steady in contrast to 37 per cent of the class IV's. For the boys, the figures are: class V's, 26 per cent; class IV's, 15 per cent.

The dates of the withdrawees were tabulated by class, when the class position of both participants was known, to see how

---

[5] The dating patterns of the student group were discussed in Chapter 9, pp. 227–237

they are distributed in the prestige structure. Seventy-one per cent of the boys' dates are with class equals, 9 per cent cross a class line, and 21 per cent are with girls whose class position is unknown; 91 per cent of the boys' dates with girls of unknown class position involve class V boys who date girls in other communities. This tendency to date out of town is related to the scarcity of available class V girls in Elmtown. The pattern of the girls' dates by class is not significantly different from the boys': 76 per cent are with class equals; 9 per cent cross one class line; and 15 per cent are with boys of unknown class position. Slightly fewer boys and girls cross class lines in their steady dates (7 per cent) than in all dates. It is improbable that the minority (17 per cent of the girls and 19 per cent of the boys) going steady with persons of unknown position cross class lines to any greater extent than those on whom we have data. If we assume that this is so, then from 85 to 90 per cent of the withdrawees date class equals, either casually or regularly.

The boys primarily date girls in the withdrawee group or out of town; but some 23 per cent date high school girls. Dating relationships between high school girls and withdrawee boys are strongly associated with the class position of the boy. There were 6 unmarried class III withdrawee boys, 5 of whom dated high school girls; of the 63 unmarried boys in class IV, 26 dated high school girls. In class V, 4 of the 82 single boys dated high school girls. These figures make it very clear that there is little dating contact between the class V boy and high school girls. The class III boy, however, has no difficulty dating high school girls. Moreover, 79 per cent of the high school girls they date are class III's and 21 per cent are class IV's. The class IV boys date equals 67 per cent of the time, one class lower 26 per cent, and one class above 7 per cent.

This pattern results from a boy's tendency to date down if he crosses a class line, and for a girl to date up under the same conditions. Girls in all classes are reluctant to date down, but especially so in class III, where the girls believe that they are better than the class IV boys. The dating down of the class IV boys is a reflection of the male's tendency to cross class lines when he is "on the prowl," but to stay within his class or above himself, if possible, when his intentions are aimed toward matrimony.

Differences in the boys' and girls' in-school and out-of-school dating patterns are produced by the oversupply of girls in this age group in high school and an undersupply in the out-of-school group. The surplus of class IV girls in school (111 to 72 boys) is balanced by a surplus of class IV boys out of school. In April, 1942, there were 63 unmarried class IV male withdrawees, and 26 dated high school girls. This left an excess of 37 class IV boys, but there were 36 unmarried class IV girls. Thus, the sex ratio of the unmarried class IV's was balanced, when the high school girls dated by withdrawee boys were added to the datable out-of-school group. If we add the class V girls dated by class IV boys, the supply of girls available to the class IV boys was well in excess of their numbers.

The unmarried class V boys' dating potentials were restricted almost exclusively to unmarried class V girls or girls from other towns. The 82 unmarried class V boys faced this situation: 4 dated class V high school girls; this left 78 unattached. But there were only 52 unmarried class V girl withdrawees, 3 of whom dated high school boys almost exclusively. The 49 unattached class V girls were shared by the 78 class V boys, plus the class IV boys who dated them from time to time. In addition, the withdrawee boys in class V had to compete with older class IV and class V youths who dated girls from one to seven years younger than themselves. Folklore holds that girls mature faster than boys; that women age faster than men. In conformance with these beliefs, boys prefer to date girls younger than themselves, and the girls reciprocate by going with boys older than themselves.[6] This dating pattern compels the class V boys to forego dates, compete with older youths, date girls in their early teens in elementary school (this is frowned upon by parents to such an extent that it does not occur on an extensive scale), or go to other towns in search of dates. The sex ratio is clearly so unbalanced in class V that these boys have rather limited opportunities to date girls of their own age. This may

[6] The age of dating partners before marriage is reflected in the differential ages of husbands and wives in the parental group. The fathers of the study group in classes II through IV were 3.4 years older (mean figure) than the mothers; in class V, the differential was 4.5 years.

have been one reason why class V boys prowl in their cliques and visit prostitutes and semi-prostitutes far oftener than the class IV boys.

### Getting married

"Going steady" is interpreted as courtship in classes IV and V. Moreover, these classes presuppose that it will lead to early marriage, and why not, since both young people play adult roles in society?

The dating folkways allow an adolescent to date a number of different persons of the opposite sex over a longer or shorter period without becoming "serious" about any one of them. This is an accepted preparatory phase to "falling in love" and thinking about marriage. Prevalent folk beliefs also hold that a person "falls in love head over heels when Miss or Mr. Right comes along"; then he is "swept off his feet." In accordance with these beliefs, low class parents expect a couple to marry a short time after they start going steady, a belief that is substantiated by experience. Consequently, if they have any grounds for not desiring a son or daughter to marry the person being courted, they begin their objections immediately and keep them up until they succeed in "breaking up the affair" or the young couple is married.

Love had worked its charms on the 26 per cent of the withdrawees who had married before June 30, 1942, 31 boys and 59 girls, in ways that were far removed from romantic traditions.[7] These couples generally drifted into marriage, often against the desires of one or both partners, and in the face of parental objections. Most parents objected to these marriages because of the family history of the other party or personal traits associated with the boy or girl. Practically every one of these families had "skeletons in the closet" about which many other families knew; this fact was presented to the child in its worst light to bolster the parents' stand. Personal traits of the other party—stealing, drunkenness, laziness, dishonesty in a boy; promiscuity, slovenli-

---

[7] The average age of the married girls on June 30, 1942, was 17.1 years; the unmarried girls averaged 15.4 years of age. The figures for the boys were 18.0 years for the married and 16.8 years for the unmarried group.

ness, deceit in a girl—were used by parents to justify to a child the parents' objections to the other person.

The usual effect of these parental objections is an intensification of the romance, but away from home. Life has taught these boys and girls to make their own decisions and suffer or enjoy the consequences; if they have to defy their parents, they do. The decision to go with a certain person in the face of pressure is a part of the independent action pattern which characterizes lower class adolescents. The vast majority of the couples continue to keep company, and most of them marry in the face of parental warnings, admonitions, and threats, some because they want to, others because they have to.

When a boy asks a girl to marry him and the girl agrees, the couple normally keep it secret if their parents object to their courtship; if the parents do not object, the couple sometimes tell their families and friends, but not usually, as the courtship pattern decrees this to be a private matter. None of the engagements in the married group, so far as we have been able to determine, has been announced publicly by parties, showers, or a "piece" in *The Bugle.*

After a couple become "engaged," they go out together three, four, and five nights a week. If the boy has a car, they usually go for a ride and park in one of a half-dozen popular petting spots—the Buggy Wash, the Three Pines, near the Boy Scout Camp, in the park, near the graveyard. Heavy petting followed by sexual relations often occurs in the parked car, except in the very coldest weather. Some couples use contraceptives, but most trust to nature. In the natural course of events, a very high percentage of the girls become pregnant.

Once the decision to marry has been made, the couple may go to the courthouse to obtain a license, walk over to the county judge's office, and be married immediately, or they may "run away." Those who wish to be married locally often go to a justice of the peace if the judge is not in. Lutherans normally want to be married by the minister or priest; so they go to the rectory and ask to be married. If the clergyman is satisfied, the ceremony is performed immediately. Other Protestant clergymen marry couples with few or no questions relative to their religious beliefs or moral status, but few Protestant couples other

than Lutherans go to a minister. Young Catholics generally are
married by the parish priest after they have satisfied church law
and custom to his satisfaction.

Marriages performed in Elmtown are publicized in *The Bugle*
under courthouse news, since the license is obtained there and
the county judge performs the largest share of these marriages.
An elopement is normally not announced in *The Bugle*. In these
cases the couple upon their return to town usually tell their
families and friends, but not when they are embarrassed by their
new status or afraid of the reception such an announcement will
receive at home or from their friends. These quiet, more or less
secret marriages are not followed by a honeymoon or a wedding
trip. The couple often go to a neighboring city for a week end
or an overnight trip, but more often than not both parties simply
go to work the next day or the next week. The wedding day is
taken off from work, but seldom more than two or three additional ones.

The young couple are generally "shivareed" or "belled in" by
their friends and relatives as soon as the marriage is made known.
This party is held at night at the home of the couple. A spirit
of reckless jubilance rules on these occasions. Rice and old shoes
are thrown if the couple have not had a wedding and, since few
do, these symbols of good luck accompany almost every shivaree.
Tin cans may be piled in front of the door of the couple's home,
or the place where they are staying, before their friends move
in with songs and yells. Boisterous behavior prevails from the
beginning to the end of the evening; the groom may be tossed
in a blanket, ridden on the shoulders of his friends, and objects
placed in the couple's bed. When this is done, the girls giggle
and the boys guffaw. The sole purpose of this type of prank
seems to be the embarrassment of the young couple. The serving of food is obligatory on the couple, but the boys in the crowd
usually bring liquor to enliven the party. We believe that
shivaree behavior is a survival in the lower classes of folk practices that were common in the area three or four generations
ago.

If we believed all the "true" tales that circulated about who
was intimate with whom, every marriage would have been a
"have to." As a check upon purported loose sexual behavior

before marriage, the 90 marriages were checked as closely as circumstances permitted to determine the extent of forced marriages. The assumption we made in this phase of the research was that the indirect evidence gained from the married segment of the withdrawee group would throw light upon the behavior of the unmarried portion. In 49 cases (55 per cent of the group) in which the couple were married locally, there was little question about the validity of the gossip—a baby was born within eight months after marriage. In a second group, 12 per cent, which was rumored to have been "shot-gun affairs"—a baby was born from eight to nine months after marriage. A third group, 16 per cent, was under suspicion, because the couple had left the state to be married and then kept the marriage secret for several months. *The Bugle* coyly printed an item about some of these marriages when the facts became known, usually at the time the couple's child was born; such an item often read: "A cute baby girl was born to Mr. and Mrs. —— —— last Wednesday. Mrs. —— will be remembered as Mary ——. The parents report they were married in [name of state] last February." Whenever such an announcement appeared, people "put two and two together and it didn't make nine." There were 14 of these out-of-state marriages, and 11 couples had children when the field work ended. The evidence was clear enough in some 20 per cent of the marriages for us to assume that the young couple married before the inception of pregnancy, but they were not all free from gossip.

Some bizarre marriages (as well as personal tragedies) were encountered. We acted as witnesses to two "shot-gun" marriages. One involved a class IV boy and a class V girl, both withdrawees, who were married by the Lutheran minister when the girl was four months pregnant. This couple walked into the parsonage, asked to be married, and the ceremony was performed within five minutes without a wedding ring, the couple joining hands in substitution, at the request of the minister. The other was performed under even less happy circumstances.

Late one chilly, wet winter afternoon, a class V country girl arrived in the prosecuting attorney's office, mildly hysterical and grim in her determination to see justice done. Her ankle-high men's shoes were soaked from walking over seven miles of country roads, and her legs were covered with mud and coal dust. That morning she had told her mother she was pregnant, and a family quarrel ensued among the girl, mother, and grandmother. When the father came home for lunch, he was told of the girl's condition. Another quarrel developed, this time between the father and the girl, with the grandmother and the mother doing what they could to keep the father from "horsewhipping" the girl. In his rage, the father told her to marry the boy before sunset. "When I come home, if you aren't married, I'll kill you both." The girl also reported that the father took his shot gun and a box of shells out to his truck and drove off to work. The girl's mother said, "You better go marry him; you know your father." The girl requested the prosecuting attorney to find the boy and make him marry her "right now." The attorney sent a sheriff's deputy and had the boy brought to the courthouse. The prospective groom drove a truck, which he parked in front of the courthouse while he came in with the deputy. The girl sat silent and wooden-faced in the attorney's office as the boy was brought in and confronted with her statement. He admitted he had been "with her a few times." The attorney asked, "Do you know what this means?"

"Sure, I'll marry her, but I won't live with her. The kid isn't mine."

"When do you intend to marry Martha?"

"Now's as good a time as any. I gotta deliver that load yet tonight; so let's get goin'."

The attorney turned to Martha and asked, "Do you want to get married now?"

"Yeh, the sooner the better; the old man means business."

At this, the little party walked out of the prosecutor's office and down the broad marble stairs to the county clerk's office where the groom-to-be bought a marriage license. The party solemnly went into the judge's office, where the judge read the marriage service. After he had pronounced them man and wife, he signed the marriage certificate. The young couple stood quietly looking at one another while this took place. The judge arose and carefully rolled the marriage certificate into a scroll. As he flipped a rubber band around its center, he said, "Young lady, you are a married woman now."

The girl grinned, and the boy said, "Is that all?"

The judge said, "I guess so."

To the prosecutor, "Can I go now? I wanna get that load off before dark." As he was told that he could leave, the boy turned, put his grimy cap on, and bolted for the door. In a few seconds the truck started and pulled away from the curb.

The girl said, in a voice with a slight tremble in it, "Thanks, I better get started home." She then turned, walked out the back door, across the courthouse yard, and down the back street toward the bridge over Indian River.

No one spoke until the girl was out of sight, then someone remarked with a sardonic grin, "Now, that's a military wedding."

The prosecuting attorney shook his head sadly and said, "That's no way to start out in life. It's things like that that make me wonder. But what can I do?" He turned to us, "You simply cannot explain things like that to people, but they happen! There's a problem for *you* to solve!"

### Class position and marriage

Who is available to whom as a marriage partner is one of the most critical factors in the organization and continuance of the class system. If young men and women select their marital partners without regard to class lines, we may assume that the class system does not have the vitality we saw in it. On the other hand, if both marital partners belong to the same class in a significant proportion of cases, we may conclude that class is a real factor in the selection of marriage mates. For these reasons, we were interested in determining the class position of each person married to the 90 adolescents in the withdrawee group. This proved to be relatively easy, because 72 of the 90 married into families we had placed in the social structure. To complete the data on the class position of all marital partners, 18 additional families were rated by the method used on the families to which the adolescents belonged. Of the 72 marriages that involved a family in the study group, 40 were within the withdrawee group itself, 27 were with a brother or sister of a withdrawee, and 5 were with a brother or a sister of a high school pupil. A little reflection on these figures will indicate: first, that the great majority (74 per cent) married within families represented in the withdrawee group; and, second, that the families of the high school students were largely beyond the reach of the withdrawee group as potential marriage partners.

Whom these boys and girls married is very strongly associated with class position, as Table XX shows. It is evident that in

### TABLE XX

CLASS POSITION OF EACH OF THE MARITAL PARTNERS

| | Class of Boy or Girl | | |
|---|---|---|---|
| Class of Spouse | III | IV | V |
| III | 1 | 1 | 1 |
| IV | 2 | 18 * | 3 * |
| V | 1 | 3 * | 60 * |
| | — | — | — |
| Total | 4 | 22 | 64 |

$$X^2 = 55.0474. \quad P < 0.01.$$

* These cells only were included in the $X^2$.

classes IV and V equals marry equals in the normal course of events, and marriages across class lines are very unusual. The concentration of intraclass marriages in class V, where in 60 out of 64 cases the marital partners were both class V's, makes the fact strikingly clear that the class V boy or girl has little choice of marital partners outside his own class. Class V's are separated socially from the other classes more effectively than they are from one another under the conditions which prevail in Elmtown. The values placed on their reputations and standing in the community by families in the higher classes impel these classes to avoid a marriage with a class V if at all possible. The case discussed below in which a class III boy married a class V girl is an unusual incident in which the rule of avoidance in marital relations between the higher classes and a class V person was breached.

The number of marriages that involve class III persons is too small to be indicative of whom other class III youngsters will marry. These three marriages were "shot-gun affairs" that developed while the young people were high school students. Each had been "scandalous" from the viewpoint of the class III parents; they all felt that they had been "terribly humiliated" by their children. One class III mother whose daughter had got in trouble with a class IV high school athlete told a close friend, "My motherhood has been disgraced. I will never be able to hold my head up again in this town." The 1 class III boy who married a class V girl was considered to be a "hot shot" by the high school pupils before his "accident" with this fifteen-year-old. A class II girl, commenting on the "affair," characterized the boy as "a good kid with a car and too much to spend." She then commented, "It was unfortunate he got caught with a girl in *that* class. If he hadn't been that kind, it wouldn't have happened though." Later in the conversation, she snapped, "The books are closed on him now."

A local official reported to us that this boy's father had tried to "buy off" the girl's family after it was established that she was pregnant. The girl's father reputedly refused to accept any payment and threatened to take the case to court unless the boy married his daughter. The official said he "inquired among the high school kids to try to find out if the girl had been promiscuous. No one seemed to think she had. The —— kid had been with several girls apparently, so the case did not look too good from his side. Personally I think the —— kid seduced an innocent little gal and got caught. I finally told the ——s they better let the kids marry." In response to this advice the young couple married in the face of a storm of gossip.

### Home conditions

The conditions under which practically all these marriages take place preclude the preparation of a home of any kind for the young couple before marriage. In addition, all these young people, except the 3 class III adolescents, come from poor families who have a difficult time meeting the demands of everyday life. They live in the poorer residential areas and follow poorly paid work.

In the case of secret marriages each partner normally goes to the parental home and pretends that the marriage has not occurred. This pretense lasts for varying lengths of time that range from a few days to several weeks. After the marriage becomes known the young couple either move in with one of the parents (this is the tendency in class V) or make an effort to locate a small apartment or house that they can afford to rent. In June, 1942, 21 couples were living with one of the parental families, 15 of these were class V, 6 were class IV, and 1 class III. The remaining couples who had established homes of their own had rented either small furnished apartments (almost all were in lofts over stores in the poorer sections of the business district), or small one-, two-, or three-room cottages in the same low class residential areas where the young couple had matured. These apartments and small houses could be rented at that time for $10 to $15 a month, if unfurnished, and from $20 to $25 furnished. As soon as a place was rented the young couple established their household with a minimum cash expenditure. Each partner moved clothing and personal possessions from the parental home. At this time the couple also generally received gifts of dishes, bedding, linen, and some kitchen utensils and furniture from their families. These items were most often old and well worn, yet serviceable. They were gratefully received in most cases, as were gifts from relatives and friends. Shopping expeditions to the ten-cent and second-hand stores rounded out the essentials needed to set up housekeeping.

We shall conclude by observing that these young couples start their married life about where their parents did a generation earlier. They also start with about the same cultural characteristics, and we think the chances are very strong that they will be in about the same circumstances during their adult years. This generalization is based on our knowledge of these young people and our knowledge of the way the Elmtown class system operates. We shall cite only a few facts to bolster it, before we leave these adolescents to time and circumstance. In December, 1942, 88 per cent of the couples had one or more children; 47 per cent had two, and 17 per cent three. All the husbands held unskilled or semi-skilled, low-paid jobs. Thirty-nine per cent of the wives in class V and 18 per cent in class IV were gainfully employed outside the home. Economically, most of these young families had been or were in dire straits; 37 per cent of the class V's and 13 per cent of the class IV's had received township relief; 64 per cent of the class V's and 41 per cent of the class IV's had applied to the local small loans broker for loans. He had denied loans to 78 per cent of the class IV applicants and to 95 per cent of the class V's. Seven cases of family neglect, and four of desertion had appeared in the courts, all in class V.

Sex delinquency was apparent in the relations of husbands and wives in eighteen cases, and four instances of wife beating were known. Tales of violent quarrels and fights that circulated around the neighborhood where these unhappy families lived were a source of delight to the neighborhood women; those who heard them told their friends, and they in turn handed them on to their friends. The one given here is typical. It was told to a woman being interviewed by a neighbor woman in our presence.

"Mercy [class V] is having trouble with her husband again. Last Friday night they came home dead drunk. They started arguing in the hall and woke Mrs. Duncan up [landlady who ran the apartment house located on the second floor of a business building]. Mercy said he had been chasing that little Soper hussy [one of Pearl's daughters]. He told her she was drunk and crazy. They started to curse and get vulgar. Mrs. Duncan heard something crash against the wall. Bang! Bang! They were yelling and throwing the furniture around. They made so much commotion the whole house was awake. Pretty soon they were in the hall yelling and fighting. He threw her down the stairs and left. The neighbors came out to see what was the matter. They were horrified. Mrs. Duncan told Mercy she had to move. I hear she's gone back home."

"She would!" rejoined the woman being interviewed.

# RECAPITULATION

HEREIN THE RESEARCH PROBLEM is restated, the salient points of the study are emphasized, a tentative theoretical statement is made to explain the wide differences in behavior we found in a single, long-established small community, and, finally, we give our judgment of what may be done about it and why.

# 17

---

# SUMMARY AND CONCLUSIONS

### The problem restated

THE STUDY ON WHICH WE HAVE REPORTED in preceding chapters was designed to test the hypothesis that *the social behavior of adolescents is related functionally to the position their families occupy in the social structure of the community.* The data used to test this hypothesis were assembled in a Middle Western community of some 10,000 inhabitants between June, 1941, and December, 1942. The group studied consisted of 369 boys and 366 girls between the ages of 13 and 19 inclusive, who resided in the community during the school year, 1941–1942, and who completed the elementary grades between 1938 and 1941. A complete cross section of this "high school generation" was attempted, adolescent by adolescent, family by family.

Empirical test of the hypothesis required: (1) accumulation of extensive information of many kinds from varied sources on the community's social structure; (2) placement of the adolescents' families in the social structure; (3) observation of the behavior of the adolescents; and (4) analysis of the data on the adolescents' behavior to see if they verified or nullified the hypothesis.

The Elmtown social structure was found to be stratified into five classes. A procedure was developed which enabled us to place each adolescent's family in its appropriate class. The procedures used in this phase of the study were described in Chapter 2. The nature of the Elmtown class system was outlined in Chapter 4, and the characteristics associated with each class were analyzed in Chapter 5. There it was shown that each of the five classes differed from the others by the possession of a complex of traits that we called the class culture.

Once it was established that the social structure was stratified into classes, and the families were placed in their appropriate class positions, we were able to turn to the analysis of the crucial question on which the research hinged: Is there a functional relationship between an adolescent's social behavior and the class to which his family belongs? In our efforts to solve this problem objectively we relied upon statistical procedures, supplemented by descriptive qualitative materials set in their social context, to give us the answer.

$X^2$ was selected as the statistical tool to test the significance of the relationship between class position and the behavior of the adolescents for two reasons: first, this technique enables the investigator to apply mathematical procedures to categories that are not strictly quantitative in all their aspects; and, second, it weights every case proportionately to every other one. In our use of $X^2$, the 1 per cent level of probability was adopted as the criterion of significance. This means, for those unacquainted with statistical language, that the specific distribution of a behavior trait, when measured against class, might be attributed to the chances of sampling 1 time out of 100. But in our data, since practically every $X^2$ calculated for the different behavioral configurations was much larger than that required by the $X^2$ test at the 1 per cent level, the probability was much less than 1 in 100 that the behavior of these adolescents was attributable to chance factors. Therefore, we were able to proceed with confidence to assume a functional, rather than a chance, relationship between the behavior of the adolescents and the class their families occupied in the social structure.

After we had determined that there was a significant connection between class position and a behavioral trait we measured this relationship, in most instances, by the use of the coefficient of contingency. The coefficient of contingency states the degree of association between variates in a positive figure that varies from 0 to 1, but it never reaches 1 for reasons we shall not discuss here. Thus, it has to be corrected to allow for understatement of the degree of association.[1] The nearer the coefficient

---

[1] The coefficient of contingency was corrected in accordance with the formula and table given in Thomas C. McCormick, *Elementary Social Statistics*, McGraw-Hill Book Co., New York, 1941, pp. 206–207.

of contingency came to 1, after it had been corrected, the closer the relationship between class and the item or trait measured.

The $X^2$ test revealed that the behavior of the adolescents is related significantly to class in every major phase of social be-havior—the school, the church, the job, recreation, the clique, dating, and sex. Although the degree of association between class and behavior varied from one activity to another, and was in no instance perfect, the coefficients of contingency obtained were highly significant. That is, *there is a functional relation-ship between the class position of an adolescent's family and his social behavior in the community.* Therefore, we can conclude with confidence that adolescents who have been reared in fam-ilies that possess different class cultures may be expected to follow different behavior patterns in their responses to situations they encounter in their participation in the community's social life. Furthermore, this study, if it has done nothing else, has demonstrated clearly that, for a complete cross section of a rela-tively homogeneous age and sex group in one community in contemporary America, the home an adolescent comes from con-ditions in a very definite manner the way he behaves in his relations with the school, the church, the job, recreation, his peers, and his family.

## Family background and behavior

We believe that one of the important things this study high-lights is the diversity of behavior exhibited by adolescents in the different classes in their day-to-day activities. We might have assumed that in a community the size of Elmtown with a stable, white, native-born population there would be more uniformity in the behavior of this age group than we found. Common-sense judgments might have inclined us to think that in such a nar-rowly restricted age group social behavior would fall into a more or less common pattern in each sex group. That it did not was a surprise. In view of this fact, we shall attempt to explain ten-tatively how we think the functional relationship between class position and behavior develops.

To begin with, we must recognize that the child receives the vast majority of his experiences during the pre-school years in his parental home and in the immediate neighborhood around his home. During these years essential aspects of the class culture which characterize the family are transferred through the subtle processes of informal learning from the parents to the child. What the child learns in the home is carried out of it to the neighborhood, and the child is not aware of the connection between home influence and what he does. In this way, family background goes along with the child wherever he goes, and what he has learned in the home acts as a powerful influence on his behavior in non-family social situations.

The class aspect of this learning process is intensified in Elmtown by the fact that families in a given neighborhood belong, with few exceptions, either to the same or an adjacent class; inevitably, they possess the same or similar class cultures. Consequently, the neighborhood children, with whom a child is prone to play, tend to have the same or similar traits and attitudes. As a result, children in the same class, living in the same neighborhood, learn similar definitions of acceptable and unacceptable behavior relative to the family, the job, property, money, the school, the government, men, women, sex, recreation. It is thus perfectly normal for families in the same or an adjacent class, concentrated in a particular residential area (the 400 area for classes I and II, and "down by the canal" or "below the canal" for class V) to provide their children with significantly different learning situations from those of families in other classes who live in other residential areas. Moreover, children in a given neighborhood who belong to the same or adjacent classes, and who are associated intimately in their play groups, also tend to develop similar conceptions of themselves, of other children, of adults, and of society.

The behavior patterns and conceptions of right and wrong, of self, of others, and of society learned by the child in the home and the neighborhood are carried into the school, the church, and other areas of community life. In these situations the child encounters children from other neighborhoods who have other behavior patterns and other definitions of behavior. In these non-family, non-neighborhood situations the attitudes and behavior patterns associated with certain classes are more acceptable than others. In the school situation, for example, the behavior patterns of classes I, II, and III are generally acceptable, whereas those of class V are tabooed. This means that children from the three higher classes are not only socially acceptable to the school and to one another, but also that the things they have learned at home and in the neighborhood are not abhorred. On the contrary, the little class V boy or girl is not acceptable socially, nor are the things he has learned "across the tracks" approved in the classroom or on the playground. Thus, from his earliest years in school the class II youngster knows what is "right"; he also knows he is "right." On the other hand, the class V youngster is "wrong" socially, and he is soon taught that he is "wrong." Furthermore, he is never allowed to forget that he is "wrong."

Children reared in class I, II, and III homes are taught to be "polite," to have "good manners," to be "refined," and to use "judicious" speech. They are taught also that personal aggression is extremely dangerous from the viewpoint of social acceptance. By precept and example, they learn that one's aims are to be achieved by stratagem and subterfuge rather than by combativeness. They are taught not to play with hoodlums, to watch their manners, to select carefully their friends, hobbies, and recreational pursuits. There is continual pressure from parents to study, to avoid the lower classes, to go to Sunday School regularly. The parents generally know the parents of the children with whom their children associate. If these friendships do not meet with their approval they ordinarily bring pressures to bear on the child to drop the friends and activities which do not conform with parental expectation. They are not always successful, but the pressure is active. On the whole, though, children in these three classes are guided by their parents along lines approved by the class cultures with remarkable success.

By way of contrast, the class V child reared "below" or "near" the canal learns very soon that his family is stigmatized in many ways—area of residence, kind of residence, occupation, reputation, number of children—and that he is held in contempt by boys and girls in the higher classes. He learns to resent his family,[2]

---

[2] Resentment toward the family by class V youngsters was pronounced in the interviews and the Bavelas Test statements.

but he must rely upon it for food, clothes, and shelter. However, he has almost unlimited freedom to do as he desires, for his father is generally away from home, at work, or in search of pleasure, many times in jail, and his mother is busy trying to eke out a bare existence for her many children by means of a job outside the home. Since there is little or no room in the severely overcrowded small house where he may play, he plays along the river and the canal, in and near the coal chutes, and along the railroad tracks. His parents admonish him to be a "good" boy (a "little lady" in the case of a girl), but there is little effective control over his play. From the age of 5 or 6 he is faced with the responsibility of looking out for himself in the neighborhood, in school, and around the community. By the time adolescence is reached he has assumed full control of himself and his activities. He earns his own money, makes his own choices, and believes that he is acting as a "free agent." Actually he does what he and his fellows have learned they must do if they are to play the roles appropriate for their age and class statuses. In his thoughts and actions, he is bolstered by his clique mates (and it is not coincidence that almost all are class V's, and the rest are class IV's) as well as by older youths and adults in the social circles in which he moves. He insists upon absolute freedom in the spending of his money. If one tells him he is foolish to spend his money for old cars, flashy clothes, liquor, gambling, and sex one will be told forcibly—we experimented on this point with a few class V's we knew well—"No one can tell me how I am going to spend my money. Did you earn it?" This insistence upon freedom to do what he desires brings him into conflict with the law with significantly greater frequency than the other classes. This situation, however, is accepted by the class V youngster as something he must expect for he has seen it happen with parents, relatives, and friends.

Our points are: first, children's behavior patterns are established primarily by their early experiences in the family and secondarily in the neighborhood; and, second, similar experiences in family and neighborhood mold children into similar social types because their learning in both areas tends to be strongly associated with class. The great majority of these adolescents have had most of their childhood experiences in the intimate, limited area of family and neighborhood. In this world of close, interpersonal relationships they have learned how their families are regarded in the larger non-family area of society. In the neighborhood they also come in contact with persons, both children and adults, from other classes and neighborhoods. It is here that they first become aware that there are people socially different from themselves.

Thus, we infer that the family and neighborhood sub-cultures not only set the stage upon which the child acts, but they also provide him with ways of acting and definitions of action. In addition, they make him realize that he will be rewarded for some kinds of behavior and punished for others. They provide him with roles, teach him how to play them, and accord him different status positions as he plays such roles as child in the family, pupil in the school, and little boy on the street. As he participates in successive social situations, he learns to act in certain ways, to regard himself as a valued member of the group or as an unwanted person. Unconsciously, he is being molded into a personality that is simultaneously a creature of his experiences and a creator of new situations in which he will act as a molder of conduct.

The child, as actor in the social process, *manipulates* what he has learned from his associates in previous situations as he strives to adjust to new situations which make demands upon him moment by moment, hour by hour, day by day, week by week, and so on through the years. By the time he reaches adolescence his personality is formed. Also he has developed conceptions of (1) himself; (2) the social structure; (3) his place in it along with appropriate roles and statuses; (4) forms of behavior, approved and disapproved; and (5) means of doing what he desires even though it involves the violation of law and the mores.

Conceived of in this way adolescent behavior is a complex response to a series of definitions the child has learned in the family, the play group, and the school which have varying degrees of relevancy in recurrent and new social situations to which he has to adjust. Situations which children face daily are defined in a general way by the communal, the class, and the family cultures, but they are defined explicitly by the clique in which a child plays. Within the clique, definitions are placed on a situation which influence the child's behavior in that situation. The adjustments he makes to these definitions appear to be determined by the meaning each has for him, in relation to the others, as it applies in the situation of the moment. The effective definition that he follows appears to be more closely related to the definitions other children place upon the situation, at least what he thinks the others think, than it is to definitions his parents, teachers, ministers, police, and other adults place upon it. Therefore, the specific behavior traits exhibited by adolescents tend to be along lines approved by their clique mates, who also tend to be members of the same class.

The definition the child thinks his associates place upon the behavior demanded of him cannot be ignored, nor should it be separated from the complex, for the social situation the child participates in is a shared experience, and the definition placed upon it is shared generally by the participants. Moreover, the form it takes is often a response to what the group has learned previously in similar situations. Thus, past learning is redefined, when necessary, to fit the present. This process results in the constant projection of past learning into the present, the adolescent's present behavior being an adjustment to past learning interpreted in terms of the demands of the moment.

If this theoretical position is sound, the effects of differential learning in the home and the neighborhood during the childhood years are the basic conditioning factors which give rise to the highly significant differences in social behavior observed among the adolescents in the different classes. We shall conclude with the general proposition that, if an adolescent has been trained in the home and the neighborhood to act, let us say, like a class I person, and his clique associations are with class I boys or girls, that adolescent will reveal a class I behavior pattern in his non-family social activities. We believe that this generalization will apply to each class and to each area of social behavior. In view of it, we may expect adolescents reared in a given class to exhibit the behavior characteristics peculiar to that class. However, if these persons are presented with a different set of conditions in later years which come to have value for them in their efforts to adjust to new conditions, we may expect that there will be significant changes in their behavior. This implies that social mobility may be expected when a new set of definitions is learned in response to a new set of social conditions. This is a problem we have not touched in this study, but it is of great importance theoretically to sociologists and psychologists. It is also of interest from a practical viewpoint, because of its supposed prevalence in American society.

### Class and community institutions

The reader may think of the same question an educator in a Middle Western teachers' college asked after reading parts of the manuscript: "Don't you think you are shirking your responsibility, as a citizen, when you see such striking differences in opportunities open to children in the different classes and you do nothing more than present your results?" In a discussion which followed the posing of this question, we pointed out to our friend that this study was designed to find facts for or against the hypothesis, not to change the community. Our friend assented to this point, but then he went on and made some observations to the effect that American democratic ideals are being undermined by the class system. He said with considerable emphasis, "The public schools should face the facts and try to solve the problems you have brought to light." Unquestionably he is right in his conviction that the ideals embodied in the democratic creed [3] of official American society are being compromised by the operation of the class system in the schools. We go one step further and include the churches, the lodges, the economic system, recreation, and leisure time organizations. All these institutions give lip service to the American creed, then ignore it as they follow the principles of the class system in their daily operation. Our friend ended the discussion with the admonition, "Tell us what to do to overcome the inequalities you have shown to exist."

We should like to be optimistic enough to think that we had the knowledge necessary to carry out this man's advice, but out of honesty to the facts we must leave him, and possibly many readers, unsatisfied. This is too big a problem for any one

[3] The best single statement of the American creed and its implications is found in Gunnar Myrdal, *An American Dilemma*, Harper and Brothers, New York, 1944, 2 vols., especially pp. 3–25, 667–688.

person even to grasp, let alone try to solve. Instead of attempting to tell readers how to bring about equality of opportunity between persons, we shall approach the problem from the viewpoint of the resistance that must be overcome in Elmtown, or any town, before we can hope to see the effects of the class system appreciably mitigated. We lived close enough to the Elmtown social system to know that, before substantial changes can be wrought in local institutions from the schools to the Boy Scouts, persons who would like to change them must have a thorough understanding of all aspects of American society, not merely of its ideals and the divergence from them.

If we assume that it is desirable to change American society so that the ideals embodied in the American creed supplant the ideals of the class system, we must begin our program of planned action by recognizing two basic organizing principles in American society. The first is that *the American class system is extralegal.* The second follows from the first: *society has other dimensions than those recognized in law.* The class system is one of these non-legal dimensions.

The first principle means that a program of change cannot appeal to the state for support through the passage of new laws or the enforcement of present ones. The structure of the American political and juridical systems is derived from the denial of classes and all varieties of inequality, at least on the publicly professed level. The law for the most part conceives of individuals as possessors of equal rights, obligations, and duties to one another and to the state. The second principle, by recognizing that the state is one dimension of society and class another, opens the way to a more realistic approach to an understanding of the relationships which prevail between the state as one aspect of society and class as another than that made available when the existence of class is denied. If we start with the assumption that both the state and class dimensions are part of society, it will be possible to see that one supplements the other in many ways, and that they also work at cross purposes.

The class system as an *extralegal* dimension of society is not subject to legal pressures, except indirectly and occasionally. The law, however, as a formal dimension of society is subject to the pressures of the class system in many ways, the most obvious one being that it is made and administered by persons who occupy selected positions in the class system. In this connection, it should be realized that legislators who draft laws and public officials who execute laws, of necessity, function in dual capacities in society. On the one hand, they have a formal, legally defined relationship to the office they fill in the state structure. On the other, they are members of society and a part of the class system. Therefore, in the making and administration of law, they are caught in the dilemma of legal obligations to their office and moral obligations to their class. However, the reader should not make the mistake of assuming that, because the law does not recognize the existence of classes, members of society caught in the dilemma of class interests versus public interests do not exercise privileges associated with their positions in the class system to manipulate the law.

It is our contention that, where values associated with the class system run counter to legal requirements, there has to be a compromise between the two, and it is not unusual for the law to be tempered to fit the mores of the class system. As a consequence, persons who desire to see the American creed applied realistically in the schools and other local institutions must realize that effective controls are often the product of a long-standing compromise between vested class interests, legal requirements, and social ideals, and that the values of the class system are more important in the eyes of people who control these institutions than the ideals of the framers of the Declaration of Independence, or law makers in Washington, Indianapolis, Columbus, Lansing, or the other forty-five state capitals.

Persons interested in the application of the American creed to everyday life in the Elmtowns scattered over the United States must understand certain other facts about American society. Among them is the ideological relationship that links success or failure in the economic sphere with social position. The competitive process in some mystical way is supposed to sift, weigh, sort, and classify persons into categories according to their "worth." An implicit part of this thought structure is the idea that each individual through the operation of the competitive process will find his "natural place" in society. In this culture success is measured, in large part, by the acquisition of material things—land, factories, businesses, professional practices, houses, commodities, stocks and bonds—all calculated in terms of *the* common denominator whose value has meaning for every Elm-towner above the age of infancy, namely, dollars. The many persons with few dollars occupy the low-prestige positions in the social structure, and the few persons with many dollars occupy the high-prestige positions. To be sure, other cultural factors enter the picture, but in this acquisitive, success-dominated ideology the primary criterion of "social worth" is measured in terms of dollars.

Another facet of this complex is the idea that wealth accumulated by the person in his own lifetime is good, but it is not so desirable, in terms of social position, as wealth accumulated by an ancestor two or more generations ago. Other beliefs in the pattern include the ideas that accumulators of dollars have "brains," "what it takes," "ability." This elusive "something" that is attributed to a "money maker" is ascribed to his children even though they may not add materially to the wealth he accumulated. Thus, in the second generation, certainly the third, if wealth is maintained, wealth making and retaining is believed popularly to be an inherited "quality," a quality inherited through the germ plasm, of course.

Most persons who have been successful in the competitive arena believe firmly that they have a sacred obligation to see that the social system is maintained into the indefinite future in the same condition it was in in the 1920's. Thus, reverence for the past, the status quo, and private property are central values in the ideological structure of those who possess the requisites which give them high social prestige—wealth, family, and power. Their fiercest desire is to continue to possess them; to add to them; and to pass them on to their descendants. They are in a word conservatives; they have something precious to conserve.

Persons who have been successful in our competitive system, or whose ancestors were, have implicit faith in American society. It has been good to them, and they want to see it perpetuated. Thus, persons who question or criticize it are viewed as "enemies," "traitors to the country which gave them birth," "traitors to the land" which enables them "to enjoy the highest standard of living in human history." These "enemy ingrates" must be denied any voice in questions of community leadership and excluded from exercising any control over institutions. Many persons in the higher classes would even deny these questioners and critics the opportunity of making a living in the society.

The competitive explanation of the success of the few and the failure of the many assumes that the competitive process is free from all hindrances and that a person's success is attributable directly to hard work and ability, with the greater emphasis being placed on ability. Since it is assumed by the ideology under discussion that the American system sifts and sorts men according to their "social worth," the failure of the lower classes to rise to "the top of the heap" is taken as irrefutable evidence of their "lack of ability." It is believed by the successful that "the ruck of humanity," "the common man," "the masses" have less "ability" than they have. Because of their "ability" they are the "responsible leaders," and the "failures" who occupy the low-ranking positions are "irresponsible followers."

Persons who accept this ideology as "eternal truth," and the vast majority of Elmtowners appear to do so, do not need to think about the society in which they live, its manner of operation, or its objectives. These things have been worked out already for them by God if they believe in the omniscience and omnipotence of Deity, by the laws of nature if they are scientifically inclined, or by the Founding Fathers if they are ordinary, honest, patriotically oriented, loyal citizens. The control of community institutions by the upper classes is "natural" in this system of thought, for the people in these classes have "ability." And what is more natural than that persons with "ability" should occupy institutional offices?

This question will have to be answered to the satisfaction of people in control of the social system before they will listen to idealists and allow them to implement their ideas with a program of action. Furthermore, idealists will have to convince the "simple citizen" that the basic tenets of the American system not only *can* but also *should* be improved. This will be no mean feat in itself, for the average American in the Midlands believes in the American system and what it stands for as interpreted for him by his daily and weekly papers, his radio, and the motion pictures.

This ideology fails to consider the fact that the social system does not provide all competitors with equal opportunities. Neither does it recognize that the class system is maintained in part by the control of institutional offices by the upper classes. This control is achieved either by placement of persons who belong to the higher classes in key offices, or by allowing only upwardly mobile persons who have the "right attitudes" to have access to them.

A third fact ignored by this ideology is that upper class control tends to result in the manipulation of institutional functions in the interests of individuals and families who have wealth, prestige, and power. When such manipulation occurs, it is justified always, however, as being in the interest of "all the people," so that the popular ideology which identifies class welfare with public welfare is maintained in the thoughts of the "common man." This explanation not only seems to be accepted by the vast majority of people, but, more important, it is also apparently thought to be the only explanation. The acceptance of this view by the rank and file of Elmtowners will seriously hinder the development of any effective program designed to reorient the schools, the Boy Scouts and Girl Scouts, the churches, and other institutions in the interests of all adolescents. It also guarantees the continuation, into the indefinite future, of the class system and its inequalities.

One further brute fact that men and women of good will and ideals should face is that the ideology sketched in preceding paragraphs has survived the attacks of innumerable visionaries, idealists, reformers, and, in our own national history, a Revolution and a Civil War. It has been under attack periodically in the United States for nearly two centuries, but its utility as the keystone of practical everyday American social philosophy is unimpaired. The current product is a class system which provides persons in the higher reaches of the social structure greater opportunities to gain and enjoy the benefits of our culture than it does persons on the lower levels. Finally, we must voice the conclusion that this class system is far more vital as a social force in our society than the American creed.

If men and women of ideals who hope to make the American dream a reality in the lives of America's boys and girls think that Elmtowners have failed in some measure to make this dream a fact, they should realize that the society and its culture should be indicted rather than the Elmtown Board of Education, the teachers, preachers, youth leaders, parents, or adolescents. These people act as intelligently as they know how to; they act as good Americans trying to respond to the needs of real life situations in terms of the definitions they have learned in the culture. It is the culture which makes men face toward the facts of the class system and away from the ideals of the American creed. Those aspects of the culture which foster and perpetuate the class system over against the ideals of official America, embodied in the Declaration of Independence and the Constitution, will have to be changed, if there has to be change, before Americans will face in practice the ideals they profess in theory. But this is going to be a most difficult task.

Truly, as our educator friend observed, there is a "job to be done."

Will it be? Can it be? This is the challenge American society faces in the second half of the twentieth century.

# APPENDIX

## TABLE I

PLACE OF BIRTH OF FATHER, MOTHER, AND ADOLESCENTS

| | Father | | Mother | | Adolescent | |
|---|---|---|---|---|---|---|
| Place of Birth | Number | Per Cent | Number | Per Cent | Number | Per Cent |
| Elmtown | 202 | 27.5 | 208 | 28.3 | 442 | 60.1 |
| Elm community (outside Elmtown) | 233 | 31.7 | 260 | 35.3 | 153 | 20.8 |
| Home State | 65 | 8.8 | 51 | 6.9 | 47 | 6.4 |
| Midwest | 102 | 13.9 | 92 | 12.5 | 65 | 8.9 |
| Rest of U. S. | 61 | 8.3 | 74 | 10.1 | 28 | 3.8 |
| Europe and Canada | 72 | 9.8 | 50 | 6.9 | | 0.0 |
| Total | 735 | 100.0 | 735 | 100.0 | 735 | 100.0 |

## TABLE II

NATIONAL ORIGIN GROUPS BY CLASS

| National Origin Group | Prestige Class | | | |
|---|---|---|---|---|
| | I and II | III | IV | V |
| American | 27 | 66 | 141 | 134 |
| Norwegian | 4 | 46 | 68 | 35 |
| Irish | 2 | 30 | 50 | 20 |
| German | 2 } * | 16 } * | 40 } * | 21 } * |
| Polish | 0 } | 0 } | 13 } | 20 } |
| Total | 35 | 158 | 312 | 230 |

$X^2 = 43.9513.$    $P < 0.01.$    $C = 0.24.$    $\bar{C} = 0.29.$

* These cells were combined in the $X^2$ analysis.

## TABLE III

SELECTED CHARACTERISTICS OF THE THIRTY-ONE RATERS

| Rater | Class | Age | Sex | Place of Residence | National Origin * | Occupational Group |
|---|---|---|---|---|---|---|
| 1 | III | 40–49 | F | Town | A | Small professional |
| 2 | III | 50–59 | F | Town | A | Small professional |
| 3 | I | 30–39 | M | Town | A | Large professional |
| 4 | II | 40–49 | M | Town | G | Large professional |
| 5 | II | 30–39 | M | Town | A | Large professional |
| 6 | IV | 50–59 | M | Town | N | Service worker |
| 7 | V | 50–59 | M & F † | Town | N | Factory laborer |
| 8 | V | 40–49 | F | Country | I | Housemaid |
| 9 | IV | 40–49 | F | Town | I | Service worker |
| 10 | I | 50–59 | M | Country | A | Farm owner |
| 11 | II | 40–49 | M & F | Country | A | Farm owner |
| 12 | III | 40–49 | F | Town | I | Small professional |
| 13 | IV | 30–39 | F | Town | N | Clerical |
| 14 | IV | 40–49 | F | Country | N | Farm wife (tenant) |
| 15 | III | 50–59 | F | Town | A | Small proprietor |
| 16 | III | 40–49 | M & F | Country | N | Farm owner |
| 17 | IV | 50–59 | M & F | Town | P | Laborer |
| 18 | V | 60–69 | F | Town | P | Chronically unemployed |
| 19 | II | 50–59 | M | Country | I | Land owner |
| 20 | III | 40–49 | M | Town | A | Small proprietor |
| 21 | IV | 40–49 | M | Town | N | Machine operator, factory |
| 22 | IV | 50–59 | M & F | Town | I | Machine operator, factory |
| 23 | V | 50–59 | M | Country | A | Farm laborer |
| 24 | II | 30–39 | F | Town | A | Housewife |
| 25 | IV | 40–49 | M & F | Country | N | Farm tenant |
| 26 | V | 50–59 | M | Town | A | Laborer |
| 27 | III | 40–49 | F | Town | I | Housewife |
| 28 | IV | 50–59 | M | Town | I | Service worker |
| 29 | V | 50–59 | F | Country | A | Housemaid |
| 30 | II | 50–59 | M | Town | A | Large proprietor |
| 31 | V | 60–69 | M | Country | I | Mine laborer |

* The national origin group of the raters were: A—American; G—German; I—Irish; N—Norwegian; P—Polish.

† The symbol M & F indicates a husband and wife combination.

## TABLE IV

### Socio-Economic Group of Father by Class

| Socio-Economic Group | I and II * | III | IV | V |
|---|---|---|---|---|
| | | *Class* | | |
| Professional workers and proprietors | 21 | 41 | 23 | 8 |
| Farm owners | 9 | 26 | 2 | 0 |
| Clerical and saleswork | 5 | 28 | 14 | 2 |
| Craftsmen and machine operators | 0 | 39 | 98 | 48 |
| Farm tenants | 0 | 20 | 54 | 9 |
| Service workers and laborers | 0 | 4 | 121 | 163 |
| Total | 35 | 158 | 312 | 230 |

$X^2 = 308.1409.$    $P < 0.01.$    $C = 0.55.$    $\overline{C} = 0.68.$

* Classes I and II are not included in the $X^2$ analysis.

## TABLE V

### Economic Status of Mother by Class

| Class | Gainfully Occupied | Not Gainfully Occupied |
|---|---|---|
| I and II | 2 | 33 |
| III | 25 | 133 |
| IV | 93 | 219 |
| V | 128 | 102 |
| Total | 248 | 487 |

$X^2 = 86.5378.$    $P < 0.01.$    $C = 0.32.$    $\overline{C} = 0.44.$

## TABLE VI

### Church Affiliation by Class

| Church Affiliation | I and II | III | IV | V |
|---|---|---|---|---|
| | | *Class* | | |
| Federated | 20 | 26 | 16 | 1 |
| Methodist | 5 | 31 | 45 | 12 |
| Lutheran | 3 | 45 | 80 | 32 |
| Catholic | 3 | 35 | 57 | 48 |
| Baptist; others * | 3 | 12 | 72 | 71 |
| No affiliation | 1 | 9 | 42 | 66 |
| Total | 35 | 158 | 312 | 230 |

$X^2 = 229.9916.$    $P < 0.01.$    $C = 0.49.$    $\overline{C} = 0.58.$

* Free Methodist; Pentecostal; Church of God; Church of Christ Scientist; Protestant Episcopal.

## TABLE VII

CHURCH ACTIVITY, BY SEX AND CLASS AS REPORTED BY THE MINISTERS OF ELMTOWN'S CHURCHES

### FATHERS' CHURCH ACTIVITY

| | Class | | | |
|---|---|---|---|---|
| Level of Church Activity | I and II | III | IV | V |
| Minister does not know | 0 | 13 | 75 | 102 |
| Does not attend church | 13 | 56 | 138 | 123 |
| Attends church rarely | 3 | 19 | 51 | 4 |
| Attends church irregularly | 5 | 37 | 34 | 1 |
| A church worker | 14 | 33 | 14 | 0 |
| Total | 35 | 158 | 312 | 230 |

$X^2 = 195.0372.$     $P < 0.01.$     $C = 0.49.$     $\bar{C} = 0.55.$

### MOTHERS' CHURCH ACTIVITY

| | Class | | | |
|---|---|---|---|---|
| Level of Church Activity | I and II | III | IV | V |
| Minister does not know | 0 | 9 | 58 | 93 |
| Does not attend church | 3 | 33 | 103 | 114 |
| Attends church rarely | 3 | 14 | 35 | 12 |
| Attends church irregularly | 6 | 31 | 61 | 5 |
| A church worker | 23 | 71 | 55 | 6 |
| Total | 35 | 158 | 312 | 230 |

$X^2 = 240.5162.$     $P < 0.01.$     $C = 0.50.$     $\bar{C} = 0.66.$

## TABLE VIII

EDUCATIONAL LEVEL ATTAINED BY EACH PARENT BY CLASS

### FATHERS

| Education Completed | Class | | | |
|---|---|---|---|---|
| | I and II | III | IV | V |
| 1–4 years of college | 17 | 11 | 4 | 0 |
| High school | 11 | 26 | 17 | 1 |
| 9–11 grades | 2 | 26 | 32 | 6 |
| 8th grade | 5 | 74 | 158 | 67 |
| 5–7 grades | 0 | 13 | 61 | 80 |
| Less than 5th grade | 0 | 8 | 40 | 76 |
| Total | 35 | 158 | 312 | 230 |

$X^2 = 379.0945.$    $P < 0.01.$    $C = 0.58.$    $\bar{C} = 0.66.$

### MOTHERS

| Education Completed | Class | | | |
|---|---|---|---|---|
| | I and II | III | IV | V |
| 1–4 years of college | 18 | 63 | 10 | 0 |
| High school | 10 | 33 | 28 | 4 |
| 9–11 grades | 5 | 55 | 39 | 2 |
| 8th grade | 2 | 5 | 174 | 70 |
| 5–7 grades | 0 | 1 | 42 | 99 |
| Less than 5th grade | 0 | 1 | 19 | 55 |
| Total | 35 | 158 | 312 | 230 |

$X^2 = 583.7303.$    $P < 0.01.$    $C = 0.67.$    $\bar{C} = 0.76.$

## TABLE IX

ECOLOGICAL AREA OF RESIDENCE AND CLASS FOR FAMILIES RESIDING
IN ELMTOWN

| Ecological Area * | I and II † | III | IV | V |
|---|---|---|---|---|
| | | *Class* | | |
| The 400 | 15 | 26 ⎫ | 3 ⎫ | 0 ⎫ |
| Old residential | 13 | 57 ⎬ ‡ | 26 ⎬ ‡ | 0 ⎬ ‡ |
| The West End | 0 | 2 ⎭ | 12 ⎭ | 4 ⎭ |
| Down by the Mill | 0 | 6 | 46 | 21 |
| The Mill Addition | 0 | 7 | 54 | 21 |
| Down by the canal | 0 | 7 | 58 | 75 |
| North of the tracks | 0 ⎫ ‡ | 3 ⎫ ‡ | 21 ⎫ ‡ | 22 ⎫ ‡ |
| Below the canal | 0 ⎭ | 0 ⎭ | 5 ⎭ | 48 ⎭ |
| Total | 28 | 108 | 225 | 191 |

$X^2 = 283.0657.$    $P < 0.01.$    $C = 0.59.$    $\bar{C} = 0.73.$

* Ecological areas are arranged in order of prestige value.
† Cases in classes I and II are not included in the $X^2$ analysis.
‡ These cells were combined in the $X^2$ analysis.

## TABLE X

ENROLLMENT IN HIGH SCHOOL COURSES BY CLASS (BOTH SEXES)

| Course | I and II | III | IV | V |
|---|---|---|---|---|
| | | *Class* | | |
| College preparatory | 23 | 40 | 16 | 2 |
| General | 11 | 75 | 107 | 14 |
| Commercial | 1 | 31 | 60 | 10 |
| Total | 35 | 146 | 183 | 26 |

$X^2 = 69.3889.$    $P < 0.01.$    $C = 0.39.$    $\bar{C} = 0.49.$

## TABLE XI

NUMBER OF OBSERVED CLIQUE RELATIONS BY SEX AND CLASS

### BOYS

| Class | Number of Clique Relations | Number of Boys |
|---|---|---|
| I and II | 69 | 21 |
| III | 235 | 73 |
| IV | 194 | 72 |
| V | 16 | 8 |
| Total | 514 | 174 |

$$X^2 = 1.8601. \quad P > 0.01.$$

### GIRLS

| Class | Number of Clique Relations | Number of Girls |
|---|---|---|
| I and II | 70 | 14 |
| III | 269 | 73 |
| IV | 355 | 111 |
| V | 50 | 18 |
| Total | 744 | 216 |

$$X^2 = 2.9807. \quad P > 0.01.$$

## TABLE XII

CLIQUE RELATIONS WITHIN AND BETWEEN SCHOOL CLASSES BY SEX

### BOYS

| Class in School | Freshman | Sophomore | Junior | Senior |
|---|---|---|---|---|
| Freshman | 119 | 16 | 4 | 2 |
| Sophomore | 16 | 90 | 19 | 4 |
| Junior | 4 | 19 | 65 | 21 |
| Senior | 2 | 4 | 21 | 36 |
| Total | 141 | 129 | 109 | 63 |

$X^2 = 484.4478.$  $P < 0.01.$  $C = 0.72.$  $\bar{C} = 0.86.$

### GIRLS

| Class in School | Freshman | Sophomore | Junior | Senior |
|---|---|---|---|---|
| Freshman | 145 | 19 | 8 | 3 |
| Sophomore | 19 | 147 | 33 | 9 |
| Junior | 8 | 33 | 109 | 15 |
| Senior | 3 | 9 | 15 | 84 |
| Total | 175 | 208 | 165 | 111 |

$X^2 = 867.0136.$  $P < 0.01.$  $C = 0.75.$  $\bar{C} = 0.90.$

## TABLE XIII

NUMBER OF PERSONS STUDENTS DATED CLASSIFIED BY IN-SCHOOL GROUP
OR OUT-OF-SCHOOL GROUP FOR EACH CLASS AND SEX

### BOYS

| Class | In School | Out of School |
|-------|-----------|---------------|
| I and II | 34 | 2 |
| III | 82 | 5 |
| IV | 50 | 19 |
| V | 6 | 4 |
| Total | 172 | 30 |

$X^2 = 21.9431.$    $P < 0.01.$    $C = 0.31.$    $\bar{C} = 0.42.$

### GIRLS

| Class | In School | Out of School |
|-------|-----------|---------------|
| I and II | 35 | 2 |
| III | 74 | 19 |
| IV | 61 | 94 |
| V | 4 | 19 |
| Total | 174 | 134 |

$X^2 = 74.8336.$    $P < 0.01.$    $C = 0.44.$    $\bar{C} = 0.60.$

TABLE XIV

NUMBER OF DATES STUDENTS HAD WITH PERSONS IN OR OUT OF SCHOOL
BY SEX AND CLASS

*BOYS*

| Class | In School | Out of School |
|---|---|---|
| I and II | 56 | 5 |
| III | 135 | 10 |
| IV | 74 | 52 |
| V | 8 | 7 |
| Total | 273 | 74 |

$X^2 = 59.8781.$    $P < 0.01.$    $C = 0.38.$    $\bar{C} = 0.52.$

*GIRLS*

| Class | In School | Out of School |
|---|---|---|
| I and II | 70 | 3 |
| III | 134 | 40 |
| IV | 83 | 220 |
| V | 8 | 62 |
| Total | 295 | 325 |

$X^2 = 214.9271.$    $P < 0.01.$    $C = 0.53.$    $\bar{C} = 0.73.$

## TABLE XV

Number of Dates Reported by High School Students by Class of Dater and Dated during April, 1942

### BOYS

| Class of Girl Dated | Class of Boy | | | |
| | I and II | III | IV | V |
|---|---|---|---|---|
| II | 30 } * | 22 } * | 4 } * | 0 } * |
| III | 21 | 80 | 15 | 1 |
| IV | 9 | 39 | 68 | 4 |
| V | 0 } * | 0 } * | 5 } * | 7 } * |
| Class unknown | 1 | 4 | 34 | 3 |
| Total | 61 | 145 | 126 | 15 |

$X^2 = 152.9252.$   $P < 0.01.$   $C = 0.55.$   $\bar{C} = 0.70.$

### GIRLS

| Class of Boy Dated | Class of Girl | | | |
| | I and II | III | IV | V |
|---|---|---|---|---|
| I and II | 33 } * | 29 } * | 8 } * | 0 } * |
| III | 23 | 83 | 24 | 1 |
| IV | 5 | 42 | 176 | 15 |
| V | 0 } * | 3 } * | 16 } * | 37 } * |
| Class unknown | 1 | 17 | 79 | 17 |
| Total | 62 | 174 | 303 | 70 |

$X^2 = 333.9769.$   $P < 0.01.$   $C = 0.59.$   $\bar{C} = 0.75.$

* These cells were combined in the $X^2$ analysis.

## TABLE XVI

CLAIMED RELIGIOUS AFFILIATION BY DENOMINATION AND CLASS

| | | Class | | | |
|---|---|---|---|---|---|
| Denomination | I and II | III | IV | V | Total |
| Federated | 20 | 26 | 13 | 0 | 59 |
| Methodist | 5 | 31 | 35 | 2 | 73 |
| Catholic | 3 | 30 | 28 | 7 | 68 |
| Lutheran | 3 | 41 | 44 | 5 | 93 |
| Baptist; others * | 3 | 11 | 40 | 8 | 62 |
| None | 1 | 7 | 23 | 4 | 35 |
| Total | 35 | 146 | 183 | 26 | 390 |

$$X^2 = 88.2262. \quad P < 0.01. \quad C = 0.43. \quad \bar{C} = 0.49.$$

* The denominations included, followed by the number of claimed affiliations, were: Free Methodist, 5; Church of Christ Scientist, 3; Pilgrim Holiness, 5; Gospel Tabernacle, 6.

## TABLE XVII

MINISTERS' JUDGMENT OF THE STUDENTS BY CLASS

| | | Class | | |
|---|---|---|---|---|
| Ministers' Judgment | I and II | III | IV | V |
| Child unknown to all ministers | 2 | 23 | 53 | 11 |
| Child has left church | 7 | 39 | 51 | 10 |
| A good Christian child | 9 | 47 | 39 | 1 |
| A church leader | 12 | 23 | 16 | 1 |
| An unreliable person | 5 | 14 | 24 | 3 |
| Total | 35 | 146 | 183 | 26 |

$$X^2 = 43.8287. \quad P < 0.01. \quad C = 0.32. \quad \bar{C} = 0.37.$$

## TABLE XVIII

TYPE OF PART-TIME WORK PERFORMED BY GAINFULLY OCCUPIED HIGH
SCHOOL STUDENTS BY CLASS (III–V)

| Type of Work | Class | | |
| --- | --- | --- | --- |
| | III | IV | V |
| Clerk in store (M & F) * | 48 | 45 | 2 |
| Paper routes, odd jobs (M) | 3 | 12 | 3 |
| Care of children (F) | 21 | 30 | 2 |
| Housework (F) | 2 | 11 | 6 |
| Mechanical and farm (M) | 9 | 13 | 3 |
| Total | 83 | 111 | 16 |

$X^2 = 32.5349.$    $P < 0.01.$    $C = 0.37.$    $\bar{C} = 0.46.$

* The symbols M and F refer to male and female respectively.

## TABLE XIX

VOCATIONAL AIM BY CLASS

| Vocational Aim | Class | | | |
| --- | --- | --- | --- | --- |
| | I and II | III | IV | V |
| Professional or businessman | 27 | 57 | 72 | 16 |
| Clerical worker | 2 | 32 | 64 | 25 |
| Craftsman | 1 | 19 | 54 | 32 |
| Farmer | 4 | 16 | 20 | 6 |
| Miscellaneous | 0 ⎤ | 13 ⎤ | 40 ⎤ | 57 ⎤ |
| Undecided | 1 ⎦ * | 21 ⎦ * | 62 ⎦ * | 94 ⎦ * |
| Total | 35 | 158 | 312 | 230 |

$X^2 = 176.4789.$    $P < 0.01.$    $C = 0.44.$    $\bar{C} = 0.51.$

* These cells were combined in the $X^2$ analysis.

## TABLE XX

FREQUENCY OF ATTENDANCE AT MOTION PICTURES BY SEX AND CLASS

### BOYS

| Attendance Level | I and II | III | IV | V |
|---|---|---|---|---|
| | | Class | | |
| Does not attend | 0⎫ | 6⎫ | 0⎫ | 1⎫ |
| Less than once a week | 3⎭ * | 17⎭ * | 24⎭ * | 5⎭ * |
| Once a week | 3 | 22 | 41 | 2 |
| 2–3 times a week | 15 | 28 | 7 | 0 |
| Total | 21 | 73 | 72 | 8 |

$X^2 = 44.7979.$    $P < 0.01.$    $C = 0.45.$    $\bar{C} = 0.54.$

### GIRLS

| Attendance Level | I and II | III | IV | V |
|---|---|---|---|---|
| | | Class | | |
| Does not attend | 0⎫ | 10⎫ | 8⎫ | 1⎫ |
| Less than once a week | 3⎭ | 14⎭ * | 13⎭ * | 9⎭ * |
| Once a week | 3 | 20 | 71 | 7 |
| 2–3 times a week | 8 | 29 | 19 | 1 |
| Total | 14 | 73 | 111 | 18 |

$X^2 = 40.8183.$    $P < 0.01.$    $C = 0.40.$    $\bar{C} = 0.48.$

* These cells were combined in the $X^2$ analysis.

## TABLE XXI

PARTICIPATION IN NON-HIGH SCHOOL DANCES BY SEX, CLASS, AND TYPE
OF DANCE

*BOYS*

| Type of Dance | I and II | III | IV | V |
|---|---|---|---|---|
| None | 4 | 39 | 27 | 1 |
| Private | 11 | 12 | 4 | 0 |
| Semi-private | 4 | 15 | 17 | 1 |
| Public | 2 | 7 | 24 | 6 |
| Total | 21 | 73 | 72 | 8 |

*Class* header spans columns I and II, III, IV, V.

$X^2 = 52.4803.$     $P < 0.01.$     $C = 0.48.$     $\overline{C} = 0.57.$

*GIRLS*

| Type of Dance | I and II | III | IV | V |
|---|---|---|---|---|
| None | 1 | 29 | 40 | 4 |
| Private | 11 | 18 | 8 | 0 |
| Semi-private | 2 | 19 | 14 | 3 |
| Public | 0 | 7 | 49 | 11 |
| Total | 14 | 73 | 111 | 18 |

$X^2 = 78.4201.$     $P < 0.01.$     $C = 0.52.$     $\overline{C} = 0.62.$

## TABLE XXII

AGE AT TIME OF WITHDRAWAL FROM SCHOOL BY SEX AND CLASS

BOYS

| Age at Time of Withdrawal | Class | | |
|---|---|---|---|
| | III | IV * | V * |
| 13 | 0 | 6 | 10 |
| 14 | 1 | 14 | 27 |
| 15 | 0 | 32 | 40 |
| 16 | 2 | 15 | 21 |
| 17 | 3 | 10 | 7 |
| 18 | 1 | 3 | 4 |
| Total | 7 | 80 | 109 |

$$X^2 = 2.7930. \quad P > 0.01.$$

GIRLS

| Age at Time of Withdrawal | Class | | |
|---|---|---|---|
| | III | IV * | V * |
| 12 | 0 | 0 | 2 |
| 13 | 0 | 4 | 9 |
| 14 | 0 | 16 | 24 |
| 15 | 0 | 11 | 40 |
| 16 | 3 | 11 | 12 |
| 17 | 1 | 6 | 6 |
| 18 | 1 | 1 | 2 |
| Total | 5 | 49 | 95 |

$$X^2 = 6.6780. \quad P > 0.01.$$

* Classes IV and V only were included in the $X^2$ analysis.

## TABLE XXIII

CLAIMED RELIGIOUS AFFILIATION OF OUT-OF-SCHOOL ADOLESCENTS BY CLASS

| Claimed Affiliation | III | Class IV * | V * |
|---|---|---|---|
| None | 1 | 19 | 62 |
| Lutheran | 4 | 36 | 27 |
| Catholic | 5 | 29 | 41 |
| Baptist | 1 | 18 | 38 |
| Gospel Tabernacle | 0 | 12 | 13 |
| Methodist | 1 | 10 | 10 |
| Federated | 0 | 3 ⎫ † | 1 ⎫ † |
| Free Methodist | 0 | 1 ⎭ | 12 ⎭ |
| Total | 12 | 128 | 204 |

$$X^2 = 21.8654. \quad P < 0.01. \quad C = 0.26. \quad \overline{C} = 0.34.$$

* Classes IV and V only were included in the $X^2$ analysis.
† These cells were combined in the $X^2$ analysis.

### TABLE XXIV

MINISTERS' JUDGMENT OF BOY OR GIRL BY CLASS

#### BOYS

| | | Class | |
|---|---|---|---|
| Ministers' Judgment | III | IV * | V * |
| Minister does not know | 3 | 32 | 76 |
| Child has left church | 0 | 9 | 15 |
| Comes to church | 2 | 20 | 2 |
| Known, but does not attend church or young people's meetings | 2 | 19 | 16 |
| Total | 7 | 80 | 109 |

$X^2 = 30.6828.$     $P < 0.01.$     $C = 0.37.$     $\overline{C} = 0.49.$

#### GIRLS

| | | Class | |
|---|---|---|---|
| Ministers' Judgment | III | IV * | V * |
| Minister does not know | 1 | 13 | 44 |
| Child has left church | 0 | 3 | 21 |
| Comes to church | 2 | 23 | 6 |
| Known, but does not attend church or young people's meetings | 1 | 10 | 24 |
| Total | 4 | 49 | 95 |

$X^2 = 34.9630.$     $P < 0.01.$     $C = 0.44.$     $\overline{C} = 0.57.$

* Classes IV and V only were included in the $X^2$ analysis.

# INDEX

Adolescence, 4–8; defined, 6

Adolescent behavior, defined, 7

Adolescents: in the economic system, 158–159, 267–287, 360–388; and social institutions, 152–156; social roles and status, 148–152, 159; *see also* Schools, Cliques, Dating, Recreation, Employment, Marriage, Out-of-school adolescents

Bavelas, A., 245

Burgess, E. W., 3

Chapin, F. S., 26

Class: characteristics of, 77–82, 83–120; -consciousness, 68–77, 155; defined operationally, 25–40

Class factor: and attendance at plays and parties, 198–199; and attendance at sports events, 195–196; and attitudes on school privileges, 175–178, 180–192; and attitudes on school system, 142–147; and behavior, 442–445; and books borrowed from library, 308–310; and bowling and skating, 310–312; and Boy Scout membership, 290–293; and Camp Fire Girl membership, 293–294; and children's dependence on family, 365–366; and church affiliation, 248–250, 459, 460, 468, 473; and church folkways, 259–260; and cliques, 208, 211–214, 392–394, 463; and composition of student council, 200–201; and conflict

with church taboos, 263–265; conflicts, 404–407; and dances, 196–197, 305–306, 471; and dating, 230–232, 424–427, 467; and dating outside of student group, 227–229, 465, 466; delinquency, 408–412; desire for money, 364–365; and discipline in school, 185–192; and educational motivation, 175–178; and employment, 272, 281–282, 372–374, 374–376, 379–381; and family background, 67, 163–167, 441–445—class II, 91, class III, 98, class IV, 105–106, class V, 113–114; and family characteristics, 83–120—class I, 84–90, class II, 90–95, class III, 95–102, class IV, 102–110, class V, 110–120; and family church participation, 460—class I, 88, class II, 94, class III, 98, class IV, 107–108, class V, 117–118; and family education, 461—class I, 88, class II, 93–94, class III, 99–100, class IV, 107–108, class V, 117–118; and family income—class I, 85–86, class II, 91–92, class III, 96, class IV, 103–104, class V, 112; family prestige—class I, 84, class II, 90, class III, 95, class IV, 102–103, class V, 110; and family recreation and leisure—class I, 86–88, class II, 94–95, class III, 100–102, class IV, 109–110, class V, 118–119; and family residence, 462—class II, 91, class III, 97–98, class IV, 105–106, class V, 114–115;